The Music Industry Handbook

The Music Industry Handbook provides a clear introduction to the music industry and how it works, unpacking the complex structures within the industry and mapping it as it exists today. Paul Rutter introduces readers to key industry sectors in an easy-to-digest format, then goes on to explore the essential elements of these sectors and how they work in practice.

The Music Industry Handbook opens with a foreword by Feargal Sharkey, and has specialist contributions from Pete Astor, Marius Carboni and Stu Lambert. It boasts interviews and profiles with major figures in the industry such as Colin Lester, Simon May and Mike Smith, offering insightful background knowledge into working in the music business. The book has a practical focus, yet it also discusses relevant theoretical perspectives and chronology, and thus avoids being simply an 'exposé'. In a fast-evolving market, the author offers advice on keeping up-to-date with future developments, and guides those wishing to enter the industry on the myriad of occupational roles available.

The Music Industry Handbook provides valuable business strategies and 'start up' tools for those who wish to set up independent music ventures, and offers clear explanations of numerous issues including legal trading, ownership and IP music law, copyright, exploitation and protective measures, gatekeeping and hidden music income streams. Throughout the book there are suggestions for further reading and valuable source links that guide the reader towards key music industry and media texts, as well as a comprehensive glossary of industry-related terms.

The Music Industry Handbook will be invaluable to both new and veteran music makers, promoters, musicians and managers, and students who want to build confident futures within the music industry.

Paul Rutter is a musician, international songwriter/composer, music producer, writer and principle lecturer in music. He has over 30 years' experience in the music industry and has ongoing research interests in evolutionary global music industries.

Media Practice

Edited by James Curran, Goldsmiths College, University of London

The *Media Practice* handbooks are comprehensive resource books for students of media and journalism, and for anyone planning a career as a media professional. Each handbook combines a clear introduction to understanding how the media works, with practical information about the structure, processes and skills involved in working in today's media industries, providing not only a guide on 'how to do it' but also a critical reflection on contemporary media practice.

The Newspapers Handbook
4th edition
Richard Keeble

The Radio Handbook
3rd edition
Carole Fleming

The Advertising Handbook
3rd edition
Helen Powell, Jonathan Hardy, Sarah Hawkin and Iain MacRury

The Television Handbook
3rd edition
Jonathan Bignell and Jeremy Orlebar

The Photography Handbook
2nd edition
Terence Wright

The Magazines Handbook
2nd edition
Jenny McKay

The Public Relations Handbook
3rd edition
Alison Theaker

The Cyberspace Handbook
Jason Whittaker

The Fashion Handbook
Tim Jackson and David Shaw

The New Media Handbook
Andrew Dewdney and Peter Ride

The Alternative Media Handbook
Kate Coyer, Tony Dowmunt and Alan Fountain

The Documentary Handbook
Peter Lee-Wright

'This interesting Handbook discusses many important issues relevant to today's industry and tackles challenging subjects such as the latest income streams for creators, in an easy to understand way, providing a very useful resource for any young individual aiming for a career in music.'

Guy Fletcher, *Chairman of PRS*

'Marius Carboni's chapter on the classical music business makes compelling reading, with key trends in marketing, social networking and the digital revolution observed from the perspective of a real specialist in the field.'

Professor Timothy Blinko, *University of Hertfordshire, UK*

'Paul Rutter has captured the real essence of working in the modern day music business with accuracy and honesty!'

Colin Lester, *International Music Manager, Twenty First Artists*

'An invaluable introduction to all students seeking an insight into today's rapidly-changing popular music industry.'

Dr Colin Riley, *Composer and Senior Lecturer, Brunel University, UK*

'In his chapter, Marius Carboni helpfully elucidates the complexities of the classical music industry in terms which are not daunting for the layman and offers insider insights to the artistic ambitions and business goals of the multi-national record companies.'

Hugh Canning, *Chief Classical Music Critic, The Sunday Times*

'Dr Carboni provides a fascinating survey of what goes on behind the scenes to harness new strategies and technology in maintaining and broadening the audience for classical music.'

Geoffrey Norris, *Music Critic, The Daily Telegraph*

'Stu Lambert on music synchronisation and non-music brands, provides fascinating insight and comment on this highly creative field of music making and exploitation in respect of these contemporary emerging markets.'

Simon May, *International Music Composer*

The Music Industry Handbook

Paul Rutter

Routledge
Taylor & Francis Group

LONDON AND NEW YORK

First published 2011
by Routledge
2 Park Square, Milton Park, Abingdon, Oxon OX14 4RN

Simultaneously published in the USA and Canada
by Routledge
711 Third Avenue, New York, NY 10017

Routledge is an imprint of the Taylor & Francis Group, an informa business

British Library Cataloguing in Publication Data
A catalogue record for this book is available from the British Library

Library of Congress Cataloging in Publication Data
Rutter, Paul, 1960–
   The music industry handbook / Paul Rutter.
   p. cm. — (Media practice)
   Includes index.
   1. Music trade. 2. Music trade—Vocational guidance. I. Title.
   ML3790.R87 2011
   780.23—dc22   2010046772

ISBN: 978–0–415–58680–1 (hbk)
ISBN: 978–0–415–58681–8 (pbk)
ISBN: 978–0–203–81685–1 (ebk)

Typeset in Helvetica and Avant Garde
by Florence Production Ltd, Stoodleigh, Devon

Printed and bound in Great Britain by
TJ International Ltd, Padstow, Cornwall

Contents

Figures

Tables

Contributors

Pete Astor is a lecturer in Theoretical and Practical Studies in the music faculty at the University of Westminster, UK. He has enjoyed twenty-five years as a critically acclaimed musician, composer, record producer, writer and consultant. A one-time *NME* journalist and leader of The Loft – one of the first ever acts on Alan McGee's epochal Creation Records – he was a stalwart of British rock in the 80s and 90s, regularly topping the indie charts with The Loft and his next band The Weather Prophets. A subsequent solo career made him a star in Europe, while later work with more electronically orientated ensembles the Wisdom of Harry and Ellis Island Sound saw him making records for Matador, Warp and Heavenly EMI. He has combined this with artists and repertoire (A&R) work for Beggars Banquet and 4AD music and lecturing in music.

Marius Carboni is a marketing and public relations consultant in the classical music field. He set up his own business in 1995 after working as Head of Press and Promotion at EMI and, prior to that, at Decca Classics. He has worked for an array of music organisations, including BBC Radio 3, the BBC Proms, Decca International and Warner Classics, various music festivals and a range of artists. Marius also lectures on the music business at the University of Hertfordshire, UK, where he has just completed his PhD, researching changes in the classical music industry since 1989. He is a Fellow of the Royal Society of Arts, member of both the Incorporated Society of Musicians and the Musicians Union, and a Director of University Recordings Limited.

Stu Lambert is a senior lecturer in Commercial Music at the University of Westminster, UK, specialising in the live music industry and international music. He got there by working in bands, doing a degree in communications, writing for music industry magazines, working in bands further and running a small record label. He has an MA in Music Business Management and is a Taiko drummer.

Colin Lester formed Wildstar Records in 2001 in partnership with Capital Radio and was responsible for artists such as Connor Reeves, Lutricia McNeal and Craig David, who signed to the label in 2002. As Wildlife Entertainment, in partnership with Ian McAndrew, Colin Lester signed and managed the careers of artists such as Arctic Monkeys, Travis and Brand New Heavies and has overseen global sales in excess of 25 million records. Colin Lester was awarded the highly prestigious 'Roll Of Honour' award by the Music Managers Forum (MMF) in 2005 and received a Gold Badge of Merit Award from The British Academy of Songwriters and Composers (BASCA) in 2007 for his work with songwriters. In 2008 Colin was made a Visiting Fellow of Southampton Solent University, where he currently lectures on the music industry. In 2010 Colin Lester was appointed CEO of Twenty First Artists, which is part of the Universal Music Group and has represented artists such as Elton John, Jamiroquai, James Blunt and Lily Allen among many others.

Simon May is a UK composer and Visiting Professor in Education who graduated from Cambridge University, UK, and started his professional musical career by co-writing the stage musical *Smike*, which was later televised by the BBC. Simon has composed popular music in synchronisation for television, film and broadcast since 1973 and created numerous TV themes and film compositions, including the iconic theme tune to *Eastenders*.

Lynne McDowell is Industry Relations Manager and Communications Executive of the British Phonograph Industry in London. Prior to her role with the BPI, Lynne worked as a Political Adviser in the European Parliament.

Fran Nevrkla is Chairman and Chief Executive Officer of Phonographic Performance Limited (PPL) and Video Performance Limited (VPL) in the UK. Born and educated in the former Czechoslovakia, he studied music at the Conservatoire and The Academy of Music and Fine Arts in Prague and subsequently at the Royal College of Music in London. A classical violinist, he performed, recorded and toured the world with several major British orchestras, including the English Chamber Orchestra, London Symphony Orchestra and the Royal Philharmonic. In 1976 Fran joined Warner Music UK in Distribution Operations and was responsible for Business Affairs from 1981. Fran also studied for an external Law Degree course at London University (Red Lion Square) in the 1980s. He became Director of Commercial and Business Affairs in 1985 and subsequently a Board Director of Warner Music UK and many of its subsidiaries. Fran has served two terms as Chairman of the British Phonographic Industry (BPI) Rights Committee (1986–1988 and 1997–1999), and has been a Board Director of PPL and VPL since 1985. He has been actively involved in many industry-type negotiations, Copyright Tribunal Referrals, MMC and OFT Inquiries, as well as political lobbying in the UK and Brussels. Additionally, he is a Fellow of the

Radio Academy, a Fellow of the Royal Society of Arts, Manufactures and Commerce and a Trustee of the British Association for Performing Arts Medicine (BAPAM). He left Warner in September 2000 after twenty-three years in order to become Chairman and Chief Executive Officer of PPL and VPL.

Dave Robinson has been editor of *Pro Sound News Europe* (*PSNE*), the leading news-based monthly title for the entire European audio industry, for ten years. Before that he was deputy editor on *Future Music* magazine. Dave's professional research interests lie in the health of the live sound industry sector, via commissioned research regularly undertaken by his publication *PSNE*. He comments monthly on the issues facing the sector. He plays piano, keyboards and drums and is an avid Tangerine Dream fan.

Paul Rutter is a musician, international songwriter/composer, music producer, writer and principle lecturer in music. He has over thirty years' experience in the music industry and has ongoing research interests in the evolution of global music industries.

Feargal Sharkey found fame as lead singer in The Undertones and later as a solo artist – enjoying some twelve years of world tours and international hit albums and transferring later to the business side of the industry, holding posts as A&R manager, record label managing director, Member of the UK Radio Authority and Chair of the Live Music Forum. In February 2008, Feargal was appointed Chief Executive of British Music Rights. Later, Feargal's role was expanded significantly with the creation of UK Music. Feargal is currently CEO of UK Music, representing the collective interests of the UK's commercial music industry, from artists, musicians, songwriters and composers, to major and independent record labels, managers, music publishers, studio producers and collecting societies. In his role at UK Music, Feargal has been tasked with tackling the issue of digital piracy and has also campaigned on music copyright issues. Feargal is also involved in new scheme initiatives, such as opening a national network of rehearsal spaces, funded in part by the UK government.

Mike Smith is Managing Director of Columbia Records UK, part of Sony Music, where he looks after a number of acts including Kings of Leon, Bob Dylan, Bruce Springsteen and Foo Fighters. Mike started his career in the music industry as an A&R scout at MCA Publishing in 1988, where he signed Blur alongside numerous other acts, before moving to EMI Publishing in 1992. Mike was instrumental in signing The Scissor Sisters and Arctic Monkeys – and also while at EMI, Mike worked with Robbie Williams, PJ Harvey and The Verve.

Acknowledgements

Special thanks to those who provided knowledge, information and patience in the production of *The Music Industry Handbook*.

Aileen Storry, Routledge/T&F
Carole Smith, Concert Promoters Association
Charlotte Rutter, MSM
Clare Goldie, PPL
Colin Lester, CLM/Twenty First Artists
Dave Robinson, *Pro Sound News Europe*
Doreen Rutter, MSM
Emily Laughton, Routledge/T&F
Emma Pike, Sony Music
Feargal Sharkey, UK Music
Fran Nervkla, PPL
Ged Doherty, Columbia/Sony Music
James Curran, Goldsmiths, University of London
Janine Rutter, MSM
Jeff Nosbaum, Florence Production
Jo Dipple, UK Music
Joe Rutter, MSM
Lynne McDowell, BPI
Marius Carboni, University of Hertfordshire
Mike Smith, Columbia/Sony Music
Nicola Slade, UK Music
Pete Astor, University of Westminster
Rosie White, Florence Production
Sarah Coward, UK Music
Simon May, music, television and film composer
Stu Lambert, University of Westminster
Sybil Bell, UK Music
Vickey Ellis-Jones, Columbia/Sony

Foreword

Feargal Sharkey

The UK is defined by its music and the innovation and creativity of its artists. Given the history of UK popular music and the global success the UK music industry has enjoyed to date, the UK can be proud in saying 'we're pretty good at it!'

Today, however, the industry faces new challenges; the internet has had a profound impact on the global music industry. And although the internet is a truly extraordinary achievement, it has transformed society, communication, entertainment and business. The web is alive with the sound of music. We can now experience and buy music online via iTunes, Amazon, 7digital, Bleep, Play, HMV, Tesco, Spotify, We7, MySpace Music, Sky Songs, Napster, eMusic and a host of others. Social networks revolve around music. You can even enjoy music bundled into the price of a mobile handset. And yet there is still corporate ambition to establish an even greater range of services. All artists, labels and producers of music can now look forward to new innovative services that will cater for every taste and pocket and that allow audiences to consume safely and legitimately the music they want, by a method of their choosing. But, vitally, these services must reward the UK's phenomenal creative talent, and all those who invest in it. And this only comes with the co-operation and the tacit adaptation of creative companies, tech companies, internet service providers (ISPs) and, most importantly, music fans.

Today we face an unprecedented scale of unlawful and unlicensed downloading. According to some ISPs, such usage over peer-to-peer (P2P) networks can consume over 70 per cent of their network's capacity. For those making and investing in music, film, TV, books, sports and games, sustaining a viable business is, as with all business, difficult at times. But when your products are being taken, for free, without your knowledge or consent, and on this scale, the consequences for artists, producers and all labels are counterproductive. Government in the UK has sought to address such challenges with its Digital Economy Bill – revolutionising the UK's telecommunications backbone while paving the way for a world-beating digital economy. But these measures must be taken globally – the UK cannot achieve this purely on its own; the digital market will only reach its potential if our creative industries, internet providers, technology companies and consumers move forward together. We are all part of the solution. Today, reconnecting audiences with the value of creativity is crucial – to engage with fans and to help, support and encourage them towards legal services. Legal global services are the only way to secure a solid foundation from which we can build a successful, vibrant online industry. For our artists, performers, investors, shareholders, lovers and users of music everywhere, that can only be a very good thing. For me, the burning issue – and this is as equally relevant to newspapers, games, TV, film makers, authors and software manufacturers as it is to music – is how creative individuals can commercially reconcile their activities both online and offline. Both are vital. Most artists need to sell CDs and downloads, they need to play live, their music needs to be distributed to a huge variety of digital stores, they need a web presence, they need to be played on radio and they need to be marketed to 'traditional' media. Although global media culture may fully embrace the principle of universal broadband, record labels and artists cannot continue to innovate and invest in the shadow of an illegal peer-to-peer ecosystem. To tackle this issue, worldwide co-operation of all internet service providers is required. Creativity is not confined to an online vacuum. Most songwriters, composers, artists and musicians do not make distinctions as to where their creative labours will be heard and enjoyed. They don't care if it's on download or vinyl, via terrestrial radio or online streaming. They simply create. (Although most like to get paid and have a keen interest in how their music is presented.) Copyright allows this. It encourages creativity and offers the creator freedom of choice. (Want to sign to a music company? Strike a sponsorship deal with a brand? Give your music away for free?) Copyright gives you the option. It also offers the creator a degree of moral rights as to how the creator's work is used. Giving the individual creator the right to decide how their work is used is paramount. Many artists will encourage fans to post clips to social network sites or give away the odd track in exchange for an email address (and let's face it, 'unsigned' artists have always given their work away for 'free', usually in the form of a demo). However, a line will probably be drawn when it comes to an unlicensed Russian website selling their work, or if it's appropriated by a political group whose views they fundamentally disagree with. This is a 'horses for courses' scenario. But, for me, the creator should always retain the opportunity to decide.

I was Chair of the Live Music Forum, a government advisory body, and have spent many years debating, with three different Secretaries of State, how interpretations of some of the measures contained in the Licensing Act are having a very detrimental effect on live music, and particularly small-scale live music. Creating fair licensing systems for grassroots performers in pubs, clubs and small venues to allow artists to grow is crucial also to the future of music, whether in the UK or internationally, as the stranglehold of unfair licensing simply discourages music making. Small-scale venues should be valued for the pioneering work they do in giving new artists a platform; live music is vital to our local communities and to my industry. It provides a focal point of local community interest and is sometimes the only outlet for a jobbing musician. It is the bedrock upon which rests the future of the incredible success story that is the British music industry.

One final thought, in getting hung up on side issues, we potentially miss the elephant in the room: quality. The potential of digital distribution is great, but fundamentally our business is still focused on the pursuit of great music, great songs, great live performance, great entertainment and great art. Whether online or offline, this is what draws a crowd. If we lose sight of that, we lose everything.

CHAPTER 1

Introduction

Paul Rutter

WORKING IN THE MUSIC INDUSTRY

This book was devised for those who are considering a career in the music or entertainment industry; they may wish to gain understanding concerning the greater complexities of the music industry, or simply explore a small section of it. This introduction discusses the broad principles of working in this entertainment sector and will discuss common working principles, coupled with the relevant and important global attributes required to embark on a career in the music industry.

From the outset, it should be pointed out that the vast majority of jobs available in connection with music are executed in a freelance manner; specifically, the persons carrying out the tasks are largely self-employed individuals providing services *to* music. Many of these freelance roles have evolved as a result of starting out on a small-scale basis and subsequently building reputation and usefulness through a particular service offered to the music industry, thus increasing industry status and income as a result. Alternatively, there are those who may have resigned from a full-time music industry post but stayed within their specialism or service, using the knowledge and contacts they have earned working as a 'freelancer'. If a musician signs a recording or publishing agreement and collects an advance or wage from a manager or music company – they would still fit in the freelance business trading model. Setting up as a 'freelancer' legally, and what this may entail, is covered later in this book; the 'freelance' model should be carefully observed as this requires a certain degree of entrepreneurship. Occupations in the music industry of a full-time nature, whereby a regular monthly salary is provided on a long-term or permanent contract, have become less common as a whole. Full-time employment is far more likely when working for larger music companies that inhabit capital cities and larger office spaces; hence there are many more job applications sent into these companies than there are available posts. With electronic communication, there are roles that would permit working outside capital cities, but many roles in the music industry are dependent on its workers being connected directly with it physically – so in the UK, London is still the largest hub of music industry activity. Finding full-time jobs in connection with the music industry is difficult, but there are alternatives; for instance, working for a music administrator in a music publishing company or a music society would afford more regular work patterns and therefore facilitate a full-time post.

Regular working hours and salaries should not be confused with job security in the music industry; volatile, shifting markets, new media trends and fickle audiences can render certain job roles defunct in a very short space of time, and this is why many music companies only operate using freelancers. Sometimes smaller music companies struggle ever to make a profit, become financially self-sufficient, or enjoy any form of longevity in connection with the industry. Yet there are music companies that manage and own long-term copyrights and catalogues of music that would appear to sell *ad infinitum*, providing lasting job security for those involved. Companies such as this, with solid 'music earning' foundations, are far more likely to be the providers of full-time occupations for those interested in pursuing such routes. There are a far greater number of independent and smaller music companies in existence than larger ones, so this would naturally dictate that there is more competition and demand in persons applying for the 'full-time' and allegedly 'secure' posts in the music industry. However, the ratio between numbers of applicants as against the number of jobs available should not discourage individuals from trying to enter a competitive industry where they really feel they have something to offer. There are many other industries that hold glamorous reputations that are also difficult to enter; entering the music industry will require persistence, but it is not impossible and there are alternative routes. It is often said that luck plays a huge part in getting a job in the music industry, but if luck occurs one should be prepared for it in order to capitalise on the situation and secure any opportunity. Being in the 'right place at the right time' is arguably associated with luck, but researching where the right place is – and when the best time is to be there – can only happen with increased awareness gained through detective work. Many professionals in the industry believe that one should be fully prepared for luck when it presents itself; finding out exactly what is required in certain music job roles is crucially important, alongside being proactive and professional. Knowing how the whole industry functions and is structured will assist greatly and may save much time in *not* pursuing routes that are clearly unsuitable. Researching all music industry job roles will help to identify the true attributes required before entering a lengthy pursuit, in vain. A comprehensive list of music and media entertainment industry jobs in the UK can be identified using music industry yearbooks, such as *Music Week Directory*, or online job description searches. Many individuals place great expectation on what the music industry has to offer, but managing this expectation and being aware of the realities and actualities are crucially important when venturing into it to save time and unnecessary financial investment.

AN IRREGULAR OCCUPATION

It should be established at the outset that roles carried out in the music industry and their connected freelance occupations do not fall within regular daytime hours; the message from music industry employers and moguls is clear: if you want a job, go and get a job; working in the music industry is not a job – it's a 'lifestyle'.

Looking at the roots of music creation – how, when and where music is made and performed – it can be seen that this practice does not usually fall into 'regular daytime hours'. Known as a 'night owl' occupation, most songwriters, musicians and producers create and record music late into the evenings, working either in home or commercial studios. Couple this with the fact that most live music is performed in the evening and there follows an industry support network wrapped around these times and occurrences; therefore, it will follow that the hours worked will be irregular, to a greater degree. Administration of music presents a more regular pattern of daytime working (e.g. working in a music law firm), when most verbal business communication has to take place. Yet electronic communication has opened up these boundaries to permit more flexible working patterns across a range of music businesses and enterprises. Persons wishing to enter the music industry should expect the unexpected and the irregular, being prepared to work whatever hours might be needed – to get the job done. Often, getting the job done may take much longer than expected, especially when working 'on tour' – and that does not always mean getting paid for the extra hours worked. In many areas of the music industry there are sometimes few guarantees of remuneration, success or longevity. Some music companies offer a chance to experience the music industry through 'work placement' opportunities – usually this is unpaid work but can open doors and create valuable associations. With such job insecurity, irregularity and a distinct lack of stability, why do so many young people wish to be employed in connection with music? The answer is difficult to fathom, but there are those who wish to make their hobby their lifetime occupation. After around thirteen years of traditional education subjects (that is, from the ages of five to eighteen), young individuals with an interest in music and the arts often want diversification in their career path, away from traditional jobs. Music is a magnet that fascinates and draws people to it, and for many the music industry promises a lifestyle outside of the norm. The industry attraction begins with the end product much of the time; the CD or the download – or just being associated with music, successful artists and performances. The boundaries of these music occupations are vast; from music creators and performers, through to exploitation structures that bring music to audience, held together in unison with peripheral support industries that service these structures, such as concert audience security and catering.

Can a security official working 'stage front' at the UK's Glastonbury Festival be classified as a music industry employee? Some may argue not, but service industries such as these can be so closely connected to the music industry that they provide an invaluable insight into concert logistics on a grand scale. This scenario highlights seemingly hidden roles that are needed in and around music; these essential support industries can yield unexpected employment opportunities. When seeking occupations, roles and responsibilities, it is worthwhile exploring the breadth of requirements to service music, just as the artist or performer is also a servant to their audience. It is easier to understand the industry when segmented into separate core areas, from the live music industry sector and recorded music sectors, managing and publishing music through to promotion and public relations. Through this model, it is possible to research what the industry has to offer in its key sectors, clarifying where the different job roles exist, the connections that exist between them and the responsibilities that individuals face.

As the music industry is increasingly reliant on a growing range of digital technologies and the margins of the sector are ever expanding, how far to step outside of the core area of music is for the individual to decide when considering employment opportunities. The music industry resides in the wider entertainment industry, which has even greater boundaries; for many, working in the entertainment industry and retaining strong connections with music, is preferable to working in an industry not connected with music at all. In forging an industry career, it is helpful if some misconceptions can be addressed at the outset, in consideration of which I offer the following summaries:

- The vast majority of music and entertainment industry roles exist and operate within a self-employed, freelance structure.
- Competition for full- or part-time industry employment is usually high, regardless of any financial incentive – this includes simple unpaid support roles or work experience opportunities.
- It is important to understand the way in which industry roles fit together, how peripheral services to the music industry manifest themselves and exist – in order to trace appropriate employment opportunities.
- Being proactive and developing good communication skills are essential attributes.
- Few music industry posts are actually advertised in regional or national press, so researching the work and output of music companies with one's employment aims and objectives in mind is paramount.
- Tenacity, perseverance and 'networking' skills will be useful – for those who are not easily discouraged by a highly competitive industry where rejection is commonplace.
- The music 'venturist' will adopt an entrepreneurial approach, choosing not to wait for employment opportunities but forging their own independent pathway.

- For many, music may form income in part, but not in whole – where the idea of full-time occupation in music may not be realised. Being a part-time music industry freelancer can be a rewarding experience.
- Registering with music industry publication email job alerts and recruitment agencies that specialise in entertainment media recruitment in the UK, such as *Music Week* or Handle Recruitment, will demonstrate what skills the industry is looking for.

LEARNING MORE ABOUT THE MUSIC INDUSTRY

There are a growing number of books available on the music industry, but this number is relatively tiny in comparison to, say, the amount of books written on advertising. Many of these publications are derived from the US industry; understandably, this is due to historical reasons and the more developed business model in North America, where the music industry grew up after the turn of the nineteenth century. There are a smaller number of publications that have come out of the UK. The focus of these publications varies and most do not deconstruct the whole industry, but focus on author specialisms, such as music law, music promotion or solely the recorded music sector. Monetising music through live performance is the first incarnation of the music industry, yet this profitable arena is usually overlooked in preference of the recorded music industry sector. This book aims to segment the music industry, acknowledging concepts and roles connected to music that are often overlooked. The relevance of many of these industry segments serves as an introduction to new areas for further investigation beyond pure roles and responsibilities, such as the cultural value of the industry to a worldwide consumer audience. The music industry is considered a 'moving target', due to shifting economies in recorded music sales as a direct result of new media technologies and the consumer response. This forced changes in how the industry perceived itself throughout the early 2000s. Despite changes that are centred on the value of recorded music, there are core constructs, however, that remain unchanged. Making and discovering exciting new music, recording and playing it to a live audience, remain key driving forces that lie at the roots of an industry that attracts a far greater infrastructure of personnel that want to make a living from it.

MUSIC INDUSTRY EDUCATION

Music industry education is a relatively new concept, even in the developed music industry in North America and the UK. Although courses have existed globally for many years teaching music performance, the origins of this concern classical music. Musicians have been taught how to play instruments for centuries, yet little was taught on how they may make a living from those skills – in the classical domain it would be hoped that good players would secure employment in an orchestra perhaps. Subsequent emerging music courses in jazz and popular music have highlighted a need for increased knowledge concerning the industry that surrounds music, so commercial music industry study modules were integrated into these courses. In the UK the growth of music production courses at the end of the 1990s, known as 'music technology' programmes, also gave rise to the need for more music industry knowledge. As a result, the mid-2000s saw universities developing whole commercial music courses with a mix of either performance or music production and music industry modules of study. Musicians and producer-musicians are now drawn to a wide range of full- and part-time courses that offer post-16 students the opportunity to learn about the commercial music industry. At higher education level, there are courses that are designed to allow students to specialise purely in the study of the music industry. In the UK, searching for these courses is relatively simple; at higher education level, searching the Universities & Colleges Admissions Service (UCAS) website reveals a wide range of music courses that will include music industry study modules. For post-16-year-olds in further education, searching local colleges will reveal music courses usually with some music industry coverage included; vocational music qualifications such as Business and Technology Education Council (BTEC) programmes often include music industry subjects as compulsory study modules. Through these programmes there is an increased awareness of industry constructs, encouraging young people to seek out further opportunities in these spheres. In respect of increased competition for posts in the music industry, courses such as these can enlighten potential job applicants, assisting in their understanding of appropriate career pathways. Many questions surround whether music industry education and qualifications are a prerequisite when trying to secure work within the industry; but put in the employers' situation, the question to ask would be who is the most fitting applicant for the post. This not only involves education, but skill-set, experience and personality. Given that before the 2000s there was little music industry education at all, the existing opportunities today to forge worthwhile pathways in music supersede the singular experiential learning model of the past, that is, solely by asking those in industry how it worked.

COMPARTMENTALISING THE MUSIC INDUSTRY

In order to clarify what this industry consists of and to conclude this introduction, it would be worthwhile considering the compartmentalisation of the music industry and its key sectors. The following diagram (Figure 1.1) provides a simplified overview of what appears to be a complex arrangement of structures and activities. This book will discuss these 'compartments' and examine many of the key roles that interconnect in demonstration of the music industry infrastructure.

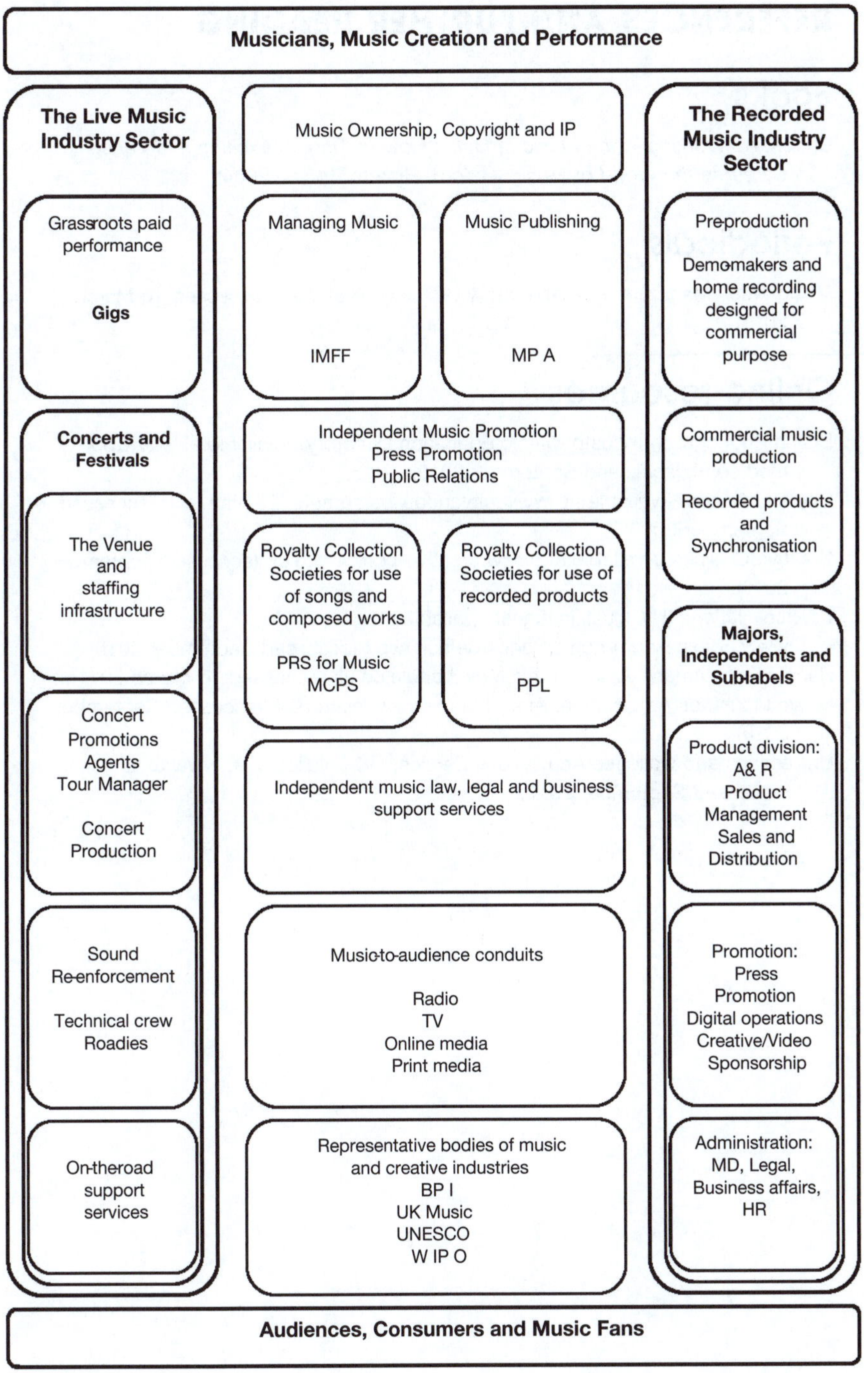

Musicians, Music Creation and Performance		

The Live Music Industry Sector		The Recorded Music Industry Sector
	Music Ownership, Copyright and IP	
Grassroots paid performance **Gigs**	Managing Music IMFF	Music Publishing MP A	Preproduction Demomakers and home recording designed for commercial purpose
Concerts and Festivals	Independent Music Promotion Press Promotion Public Relations	Commercial music production Recorded products and Synchronisation
The Venue and staffing infrastructure	Royalty Collection Societies for use of songs and composed works PRS for Music MCPS	Royalty Collection Societies for use of recorded products PPL	**Majors, Independents and Sublabels**
Concert Promotions Agents Tour Manager Concert Production	Independent music law, legal and business support services	Product division: A& R Product Management Sales and Distribution
Sound Re-enforcement Technical crew Roadies	Music-to-audience conduits Radio TV Online media Print media	Promotion: Press Promotion Digital operations Creative/Video Sponsorship
On-the-road support services	Representative bodies of music and creative industries BP I UK Music UNESCO W IP O	Administration: MD, Legal, Business affairs, HR

Audiences, Consumers and Music Fans		

FIGURE 1.1
Compartmentalisation of the music industry

REFERENCES AND FURTHER READING

Books

Britten, A., *Working in the Music Industry: How to Find an Exciting and Varied Career in the World of Music* (Oxford: How to Books, 2004).

Periodicals

Music Week Magazine. Available at: www.musicweek.com (accessed 10 March 2011).

Online resources

British Phonograph Industry Music Education Directory. Available at: www.bpi-med.co.uk (accessed September 2010).

City and Guilds. Available at: www.cityandguilds.com/46727.html?s=2 (accessed September 2010).

Creative Choices. Available at: www.creative-choices.co.uk (accessed September 2010).

Edexcel National UK Qualifications. Available at: www.edexcel.com/quals/Pages/default.aspx (accessed September 2010).

Handle Recruitment. Available at: www.handle.co.uk (accessed 10 March 2011).

Music Industries Association. Available at: www.mia.org.uk (accessed September 2010).

Universities and Colleges Admissions Service, UK. Available at: www.ucas.ac.uk (accessed September 2010).

CHAPTER 2

Music into industry

Paul Rutter

INTRODUCTION

This chapter discusses music creation and explores further reasons for doing so in the first place. Historically, the relationship between music creation and the music industry can be as fruitful and rewarding as it can be disappointing; in extreme cases it can end in a courtroom disaster. The idea of creating music for 'purpose' falls at the feet of music industry and signifies the beginning of the 'music into industry' process. Where music into industry begins, the 'expectation' of those who are creating music also begins. Creating music for pleasure outside of the music industry is commonplace, but when payment exchanges hands for music, whether live or recorded, the business ethic therefore must ensue as music is 'monetised'. At this stage we could define music providers as those who may include artists, bands, musicians, performers, music creators and songwriters in any genre. The scale of payment will vary for music services – many music providers would wish to be paid and reach professional status, but in reality they must be prepared to provide much free music before reaching that pinnacle. The way in which music providers earn their money is often mixed with other occupations, as the music pursuit may be a part-time activity with the aim of becoming a 'professional'. The definition of the 'creative music professional' (in the guise of musician, producer, composer or performer) has always been a difficult status to maintain permanently for the vast majority practising in these fields. A relatively small minority maintain professional status for a lifetime music career with sole reliance on this form of income. The difficulties that face professional creative music providers are many: consumer trends, lack of new musical ideas and inspiration, the inability to maintain performance of a required standard and a lack of external financial investment in the music concept, to name but a few. Given these ongoing and ever present difficulties, coupled with the way in which the music industry operates, the music 'creative' should not perhaps feel too defeated if they do not reach the demanding professional goals that they may have set for themselves. However, setting career sights high with challenging goals and having a strong 'music-work' ethic and enduring commitment are obviously commendable attributes that are not to be discouraged.

COMPETITIVE MUSIC AND 'SHREDDING'

Many professional musicians practice for hours on end from a young age in order to reach the goals they set themselves, yet the lack of guarantees in music outweigh the opportunities in many cases. Although the music industry is a competitive place, compare music with sport; if you can run faster than all the other athletes, you will win the race. In music, if you are the best musician in the populous (vocalist, guitarist, drummer or other instrument), this may actually carry little weight in the music industry, and there are few prizes to be won. Defining the words 'best musician' creates the first problem; 'best' in the eyes of whom? Guitar 'shredding' talents may demonstrate amazing dexterity – but not everybody will be impressed; conversely, on the positive side – a certain 'demographic' *will* be very interested, and it is that target that the guitar shredder must focus and concentrate on, if considering a career in the music industry. There is a commonly existing fear in the minds of many 'creatives' that if their music is not accepted by industry, there is little requirement for their music at all. This, however, is not the case – just because an industry investor does not invest in a particular music venture does not mean that the music has no audience or purpose. There may well exist companies or persons that recognise strengths in the concept and have the foresight to invest.

THE 'WORLDWIDE MUSIC SPHERE'

With so many creative music projects undertaken every day on a global level, questioning how much room there is for all the music that is produced in the world starts an interesting argument. There has always been enough room for as much music as collective populations can produce; with the advent of digital technologies, there are not only more opportunities to purpose music commercially, but infinite advantages for those who want to make their music venture a worldwide, public-sphere commodity. There is evidently worldwide accommodation for all styles, genres and productions that any creative can produce, in new digital spheres of exploitation. The small independent can simply bring their music before a potential worldwide audience in electronic format, for little investment. This can create audience and potential financial return if managed and promoted in the correct way. However, it would be incorrect to assume that opportunity exists for all music creative projects to gain sponsorship and attract greater investment from large music companies. Large commercial investment can lead to exploitation in mainstream media, including other public spheres such as TV, radio, national press and concert tours. Greater financial backing in a music project from specialist companies – for example, music production and major music companies, music publishers, managers, agents, concert promoters and others – are usually what many young music creators aspire to engage with. In this regard, the sheer number of creative projects will vastly outweigh the number of companies that can invest in the music venture and that have the financial means to do so. The ratio of commercial limitation versus the worldwide music sphere should not discourage those wishing to pursue the music investor; the music venture offered may possess a unique or 'fit for purpose' quality that the music investor seeks. Without music, the music investor will not even have a business, so it is worth considering the ideals that surround the notions of music industry in respect of managing expectations in the music venture.

Contained within artistic fields there are those who purely want to express themselves personally and musically without any commercial objective; sometimes this music may prove attractive to investors, but more usually, it may not. Should artists consider the commercial ethics of the music industry while engaged in their creative music-making processes? It has been proven many times that it is more important for the music creator to enjoy the art of music-making; this is usually the single most important catalyst for interesting product and is far more likely to attract a certain audience. Therefore, it naturally follows that where an audience is drawn to a music creator or provider (especially a large audience), the music industry and investors will be following very close behind.

CREATING MUSIC: PURPOSE OR PLEASURE?

Why create music in the first place? There has always been a need for the creative individual to express themselves through artistic means, using whatever tools are available. In the case of the musician or musical explorer, the tools of the trade would be musical instruments or, in more recent times, computer software and hardware. From the primitive drum or acoustic guitar, to the digital sample-based technologies on offer, those that feel the need to express an audio comment may do so, both privately and publicly. This is where the music industry beckons; what may start out as idle musical pleasure may take on a much more commoditised state – from a teenager's bedroom to the concert stage. The tsunami of media incentives that drive young music creators and artists is large enough to draw thousands of enthused creative individuals towards the bright lights, big stages and music industry exploitation routes. The term exploitation can be simply defined as 'utilisation – especially for profit', and the common predatory beliefs and associations with this word are certainly there to be argued; yet utilisation of music and its associated talent lies at the core of the music industry. A question presides over whether a hobbyist creator wants their music output to be exploited and utilised; if they share or upload the music, ownership and copyright law applies by default – effectively drawing the music into commercial online territories. Often the encouragement of others may urge the music creator and performer to promote, expanding the original innocent intention. Close relatives, friends, colleagues and peers are often the catalyst for many music creators to venture into commercial territories, urging them to seek wider appeal and commercial success. Much of the inspiration for new music makers arises as a result of observing existing successful music artists and, by comparative means, the sound of the 'successful' is assessed, then emulated via an approximation.

CYCLES OF MUSICAL INFLUENCE

Historically, the inspiration for many music careers has been based largely on those that have already been successful; for instance, The Beatles and the works of John Lennon provided strongly influential musical reasons for turbulent rock outfit Oasis to create music in the first instance as Noel Gallagher has commented:

> It's beyond an obsession. It's an ideal for living. I don't even know how to justify it to myself. With every song that I write, I compare it to The Beatles.
> (Noel Gallagher, in Glassman, 2001)

Gallagher's confession fosters a new stylised musical individuality in its own right. In the perpetual cycle of musical influence, many future bands may look retrospectively to bands such as Oasis as fuel for their personal creative ambitions. Investigating the confessed musical roots of The Beatles, their cited inspirational predecessors were American rock 'n' roll artists such as Chuck Berry, and they recorded material from his catalogue such as 'Roll Over Beethoven'. Cycles of influence and the passing of the 'musical baton' will continue through many styles, genres and musical subcultures influencing artists to create music. It is common for aspiring artists to research the works of other professional acts and their musical commodities, believe that they could do better and so forge ahead with their commercial approach. The main issue to consider, however, is that the 'famous' widely known musical act already has a huge head start in being backed by a large music industry infrastructure. Careers such as these may have taken many years to forge. For the aspiring creative, the famous and iconic can serve as inspiration. As some musicians feel competitive about their art, some may see this as a 'throwing down of the gauntlet'; a scenario that invokes motivation and aspiration, especially in young musicians. In the 'cycle of musical influence', all musicians are influenced by other musicians; it would be difficult to find a musician and creator who is not influenced by anybody, as musicianship often dictates a long learning process in replication of what others have already mapped and achieved. Musical mimicry of genre, artists, styles and matched approaches to music creation will perpetuate; there are also those who offer musical innovation, new approaches, experimentation, new attitudes and ways in which to present music to audience and consumer. A host of reasons motivates the hobbyist to become a professional; ambition, financial incentives, dreams, goals, lifestyle, musical pleasure, musical process and music status are all driving factors that aid the transition.

MUSIC AS COMMODITY: COMMERCIAL CONNECTIONS

Music creation and performance forms the bedrock of the music industry; without it, there would simply not be a music industry, which is fed on creativity from those that care to perform musical works, or commit ideas to a recorded format. Arguably, the music industries have succeeded in promoting musical creativity and bringing it before an audience and, historically, large-scale music business investment has always been behind mass audience awareness of musical products. Traditional models of large-scale musical exploitation exist in the public psyche; for example, a small-scale local band is signed by a major record label and propelled to worldwide stardom, with generous support from its cultivated fan base. But the public are increasingly aware that this is now 'old school' thinking, and many of the myths that surround the industry are complex, unseen and require more explanation. To simplify, any recording company, large or small, is a business and must be regarded as such at all times. For the creative artist to employ a business mindset, this is often opposed to the aims of creativity – often musicians believe their primary concentration should be applied to the 'creative' and less so to the 'business' essentials. Ideally, many music providers today would like to work directly with their customers – their fans and audience; yet to cultivate success on a large scale is hugely complex and would require an equally complicated music industry infrastructure to manage success. Major 'star-making' operations such as these command significant investment, and the costs will ultimately be passed on to the artist, as companies naturally seek their belated financial returns. Modern technology now provides new alternatives in the electronic distribution of music and is providing an infrastructure that is cheaper to run and maintain. As these new electronic internet structures and alternatives develop further, an awareness of business practices in music is essential, in order to safeguard the monetary returns from creative elements in music. To survive, any business, regardless of its specialism, must be financially solvent, leading to questions of 'music-art-viability' versus 'business solvency and financial progression' for the investing music company. Therefore, it is imperative that creative ideas supplied by musicians, songwriters, bands and music producers create a strong impression in the eyes of the music industry investor and its consumer audience.

THE DEMO-MAKER

The demonstration recording, or 'demo', has been in existence since the recording industry began. The demo can be used as a 'musical venture business proposal' and should provide a comprehensive and accurate representation of the musical package on offer. The nature and format of the demo and expectancy of it by music entrepreneurs and investors have changed in recent years. In the past, for example, on presentation of songs to music publishers, it was often thought that a good recording of simple voice and piano would suffice in 'selling' the song to the publisher and recipient. If the song really audibly suggested that it was a viable business proposition to a publisher in its most basic raw demonstrated form, the song suggested 'self-sale' and therefore 'must be good'. However, this model has become increasingly outdated and the new notion of the demo is that it must be technically well produced and competently executed. Demos may be uploaded to an online music hosting service, which potential music consumers may use as a barometer before attending gigs by the artist, so greater thought and effort in demo-making is now required and expected by both casual consumer and industry alike. A larger skill-set is required for demo-making by the musician: competent musical playing and ability; technical sound engineering skills to capture the playing; production, mixing and mastering skills to prepare the music; good design and visual presentation skills, to offer product to a potential music company. Communicating the visual aspect of the artist is all-important in the package, so additional competencies in computer generated artwork, text and photography are hugely beneficial. Essential considerations for the demo-maker are as follows:

- Creativity: Provide initial new ideas and conceptualisation.
- Musicianship: Convey ideas musically using instruments or technology.
- Musicality: Ability to manipulate a range of sounds and voices.
- Composition and authoring: The inclusion of music and optional lyrics.
- Arranging: The ability to disseminate musical parts and assemble them in an order appropriate to the musical work.
- Equipment: Providing mediums and equipment to record and capture the musical work.
- Sound engineering (basic to advanced): Capture audio with sufficient technical knowledge to understand the sonic properties in making the recording.
- Sound production: Ability to prepare the music for public consumption.
- Finalisation and mastering: Final preparation of the stereo mix aiming towards a 'radio broadcast standard' sound.
- Art, photography, graphics and text: Knowledge of credible presentation in the visual aesthetic of the product.

- Finance: The financial means to see the music project through from start to finish (and further if required).

- Visuals: Investors may expect strong personal image attributes in association with the recorded work, in order to promote the product in providing additional appeal to the intended market demographic.

In reality, a solo music creator may only possess a few of the skills above, yet there are those who 'go it alone' with competence and can facilitate a good demo package – given enough time to learn the essential skills and organise the resources. The points raised above may also vary slightly, depending on the music project. It can also be seen that the attributes required above may not be wholly present in any one individual – often collaboration or 'contracting out' services will return a better result. It is probable that many solo demo-makers will have a weakness in one of these areas, which will affect the musical outcome and, ultimately, the approach to industry. Whatever the final outcome is – the overall music product must be 'good', both audio-wise and visually. Furthermore, one could argue that to get noticed by a music industry investor or smaller music company, the product should be 'exceptional'. The notion of 'standing out' and being exceptional raises questions for the demo-maker; it is worthwhile investigating the theories of A&R expectations of music companies and how they define 'exceptional'.

RE-INVENTING THE WHEEL

It has been argued that there is no such thing as good or bad music, only subjectivity. Purposing any music for financial incentive will divert the music firmly in the direction of the music industry, yet there are those music creatives who would turn away favourable 'incentivised' music industry offers, in preference for protected anonymity and 'home music maker' status.

Who really sets the required standard for modern music exploitation and primes consumers and audiences for consumption? It could be argued that the recording industry has shaped this phenomenon over the last one hundred years. Recorded music as commodity began when the first recorded music products became available for sale: phonograph and cylinder recordings released in the late 1800s – at this point the recorded music product became a 'must have' for the few Victorians who could afford it. It would be worth noting at this stage the infancy of recorded music, it has only been ensconced in society for around one hundred years. Recorded music is a relatively young invention compared with its 'big brother' – live performance – which has been in existence as long as music has. Yet the business of creative music making undergoes constant daily reinvention, and just quite where it will go next is always uncertain, as there are no rules. New technologies have played the greatest part in the evolution of recorded music, regardless of the constant changes inherent in musical creation and innovation by the exponents of music. The technologies associated with recorded music have recently had a significant impact on the music industry and its income in a worldwide piracy and file-sharing revolution, cultivating an inherent threat to any company that survives purely from recorded works.

PRODUCING RECORDINGS IN THE HOME AND THE 'PORTASTUDIO'

It would be worth considering the recent history of home music production in order to realise the benefits of current music production, as well as how the revolution in home production has had an impact on new music industry structures and production practices.

Engineering and producing music at home has become much more commonplace since the early 1980s. Before this period, virtually all recordings were made in commercial recording studios using tape-based analogue equipment. A revolutionary home recording tool – the Tascam 144, known as the 'PortaStudio' – was first introduced in 1979, allowing cheap analogue four-track recording to cassette tape. The notion of unlimited home studio time became a reality and the demo-maker was born. Separate recorded music tracks could be 'bounced' to increase multi-track capability. Initially marketed as a device for musicians and composers to experiment with music recording, the trend in home recording continued to explode throughout the 1980s and onwards. The 'lo-fidelity' of the PortaStudio's audio and sonic quality was a hindering factor in the early devices, but they provided creative musicians with a tool for unbridled creation and experimentation. The PortaStudio's palette proved invaluable for creators, even if used in a pre-production phase before taking music ideas into a paid, commercial studio environment. A variety of larger tape machine multi-track recorders were available for the novice in the 1980s, but few had the funds or premises in which to equip a large studio, so many opted for the PortaStudio experimental route (at the retail sum of around £450). All musical parts would be played in real time by the musician to tape with no digital or computer technology available at the time to further assist the home music creator. Recording artist Bruce Springsteen used a PortaStudio to record his album *Nebraska* and Marilyn Manson used a similar device to record his album *The Family Jams*; both artists and their recording companies found the lo-fi appeal of these machines appropriate to the recording project.

Mixing down from multi-track audio to stereo master from these devices was usually made to quarter-inch tape, running at 15 or 30 inches per second for better quality, or, where budgets were limited, mastering and mixing down was transferred to cassette tape. The finished 'master' tape would then be duplicated, usually to cassette tape; the 'demo' was then made ready for submission to music companies. It should be noted that sonic degradation would occur through the duplication process in the analogue form. Sonic degradation or 'colouration' has become a feature in some modern recordings today, sought after for its differing qualities, adding character to certain types of music making. Others would argue against analogue colouration, which may manifest itself as increased low frequency (bass) and subdued high frequencies (treble). Many producers would actually prefer the original sound of the multi-track or master tape in favour of the finished mix down.

THE RISE OF THE DEMO-MAKER

As home multi-track recording continued to advance, the demo became arguably easier, quicker and cheaper to make; hence, demo submissions to record companies naturally increased in number. Computer technologies in the 1980s saw the birth of music hardware and software recording mediums, Musical Instrument Digital Interface (MIDI) sequencers and the arrival of digital recording devices for the home recordist. Around the mid-1980s many larger recording companies would estimate figures of around forty or more cassette tapes being received every day; such a large number of submissions made it impossible for a limited A&R team to listen to them all. Historically, there were many 'home demo production' submissions to

FIGURE 2.1
The rise of the demo-maker, courtesy the author

music companies that were poor in presentation and audio quality, with low production values. The significance of the rise in demo submissions to music companies from the 1980s onwards also highlights the ratio of actual opportunities available, set against ever increasing approaches to the record companies. Although the latter comment may seem negative to the submitter, it should be realised that a music company may have a full roster of acts and not actually be looking for any new acts at certain times of the fiscal investment calendar. A&R policy contradictions may appear; some music companies would claim that 'the door is always open' as they are always seeking new talent that will succeed commercially, while others purely commit funds to their established roster. The majority look to discover music through known conduits, managers and contacts and would now prefer to 'discover' via online searches.

ELECTRONIC MUSIC PACKAGES

It transpires that those wishing to bring their recorded music before a large audience must look seriously at the necessary skills required to facilitate a professional music package. To ensure quality control through the creation of the music, the performance and the packaging, there are literally millions of professional product examples already in existence that can be observed. These products have been tried and tested and are worthy of investigation. Music creators should research at least some of these forms in order to establish exactly what may be required in a music product that is 'fit for purpose'. New music creators should consider the importance of the following key stages inherent in music preparation, design and packaging, with the music consumer in mind:

- the song
- the recorded performance
- sonic audio qualities
- visual presentation.

The song

The song must work first and foremost, as this is usually the main component that will reside in the mind of the audience, long after the performance has taken place. The song will urge audiences to revisit the online domain of the performer. The song may be defined as a main melody that can be sung, whistled or hummed; it may carry a series of recurring musical 'hooks', so called due to the way in which infectious melodies 'hook' a listener. The song may also be an instrumental venture with a complex movement or a single instrument. Meaningful lyrics may be carried in the song evoking nostalgic empathy and a series of complex emotions in its listener. The only method of gauging how successful a song is and if the song is really working is if an audience is drawn to it – repeatedly. Radio will play a song repeatedly if it feels its listenership will stay 'tuned', web visitors will revisit music artist sites many times where good songs may be found. The song is a subjective entity and often takes on a life of its own; most never reach a mass audience, some do but 'burn out' very quickly and other songs appear to go on forever in daily life due to their appropriateness and purpose (e.g. 'Happy Birthday'). As the typical pop music song usually only lasts three and a half minutes, it is worth considering the repetition factor – the more a song gets played, the more income it generates for its creator.

The recorded performance

The recorded performance often needs to be unique, as a distinctive vocal performance, for example, may demonstrate innovation and individuality. These qualities are essential in such a large world music market for those that wish to earn recognition. If the performance is not unique, but is at least 'good', with a professional delivery and sound, the music may still appeal to audiences – perhaps within a set genre, subculture or fan base. Recorded performances often must translate to the stage, so live performance and the consideration of visual application and perhaps choreography should be further considerations in the production of music.

The recording studio provides a very different environment for artists to capture performance, one that may take some getting used to, but the only way that studio performance will improve is by repeated exposure to that environment. When the 'record button is in' many performers may feel nervous about their musical delivery; in other performers, adrenaline may fuel a spirited performance.

Sonic audio qualities

To guarantee the correct audio qualities in a recording, a combination of audio engineering skills and music production skills are required. Good engineering will ensure that the technical side of audio recording is taken care of: correct microphones are chosen for instrument recording; the correct levels are set for recording; and the optimum performance is captured by the artist. Intervention and overseeing by the music producer will assist in this and should encourage good relations in the studio environment. Programming skills, audio editing, mixing and mastering should be taken into account to ensure that the finished audio product can be readied for exploitation and promotion. The craft of music production may take years to hone; starting from the 'ground up' would be advisable, perhaps attending additional courses in support of learning both good audio engineering and music production. Many courses now exist that will deliver a structured programme to further the knowledge and skills required to deliver music to a high standard. At the time of writing, greater knowledge on the craft of music production can be sought from books, periodical magazines and online resources such as:

- *Sound on Sound Magazine*
- *Future Music Magazine*
- *Mix Magazine*
- *Music Tech Magazine*
- *Pro Sound News Europe*
- *Electronic Musician Magazine*
- *EQ Magazine*
- *Recording Magazine*
- *365 Pro Audio Magazine*
- *Audio Media Magazine*
- *RecordingMag.com*
- *Tape Op Magazine.*

Visual presentation

The visual presentation in any music project has always been an essential item; from electronic images that are uploaded to domains and social media sites, to CD covers and 12″ vinyl record sleeve covers. Professional photography and design in the images that will be perpetuated are an important feature in the music project, as this should say something to the intended purchasing demographic. The way in which the visual aspect communicates with its audience should create enhancement for the music; on many occasions the appropriateness of the imagery will spell out the inherent music genre. Subliminally, these images communicate with and to their intended demographic; if audiences feel comfortable with the images that are promoted, they are more likely to be drawn to the product. Strategies and marketing theory can be applied to get the best out of the product (see Chapter 11, 'Music venture strategies'). It is important not to mislead the consumer; doing 'what it says on the tin', requires being direct in any associated imagery in an effort to steer the right listeners to the product. Falling short of the 'professional presentation mark' will simply make it harder to interest the demographic and investing companies. Looking 'interesting' has always been a good way to entice customers, and this aspect should never be overlooked. It is worth investing time to create the right effect; a visual catalyst is important alongside the musical offering.

EXTERNAL STUDIOS

If the greater music industry sets the bench mark for the standards that should be reached in music production, then this pre cursor surely sets the standards by which demonstration recordings should be made. Where individuals do not possess their own equipment and knowledge to produce music to a high standard, a local recording studio may prove a good starting point. Many small, local recording studio businesses have acquired the knowledge to produce at a competent level; however, the following points would be worth considering before booking time in a local studio:

- Visit the studio premises first, before committing to book studio time.
- Check the hourly rate and subsequent discount day rate available.
- Listen to examples of recordings made at the studio.
- Try to obtain knowledge concerning the experiences of others who have recorded at the studio.
- Ascertain what is included in the price; is equipment seen present in the studio? What instruments are included in the rate – or are there additional hire fees?
- Is the engineer fee included in the hourly rate?
- Is a mastering service or facility available for finalisation of the music production?
- Check duplication costs concerning copies of the final recording if applicable.
- Is your style of music catered for at the studio? Some studios and engineers/producers are capable of better results in some genres rather than others.

Producing music in a local studio can prove to be a hugely rewarding experience, and much can be learned from the process of working with those that record music on a daily basis; it is helpful to learn as much as possible from the processes and personnel encountered. Enhancing 'music maker' knowledge and status leads to greater confidence in engineering and producing one's own recordings in the future, so working in a variety of studios will enhance executive producer capabilities and decision-making processes.

COMMERCIAL MUSIC PURPOSING – WHAT DRIVES COMMERCIAL MUSIC?

Historically, the recorded tangible music format and its existence in consumer society has characterised the national commercial music industry. However, the 'individual environment' has played a crucial part in this shaping; consumers will only purchase music where they see it enhancing their 'personal' space. Music commodities permit individuals to define themselves through music possession and collection. Large companies that exploit and promote into these lifestyle spaces (such as Universal Music Group) have examined trends in consumer spending on music, coupled with the genres that music inhabits. The credibility of music has always been the defining factor in mass marketing for obvious reasons; why would a music company invest in something that will not sell? A cyclic situation arises whereby music must be 'good' to sell in the first place and 'good enough to sell' means having a demographic and consumer base to sell to. It requires significant investment to nurture, produce and record, then market a major music artist, and there is no guarantee to the investing company that the music will sell whatsoever. The requirement for commercial creators is to make music that is 'good enough to sell' – this in itself will influence the style of music creation and steers the musical intention. It could be argued that if commercial exploitation was disassociated from music, we would see a very different musical landscape, a musical landscape that would be free from commercial encumbrances and a freedom for music makers and producers to create music – *l'art pour l'art* (from the French 'art for art's sake'). There are some artists that do just this. Yet the modern commercial popular music landscape as a model has itself been a source of influence for countless young performers and music creators, driving ambition forward. The promise of fan adulation, stardom, financial reward and lifestyle provided by the commercial music industry still inspires greatly. For some music creators, the actual process of music making may only be a means to an end, a passport to new attractive lifestyles and an alternative to perceived 'ordinary' domestic lifestyles.

The 'blue-sky' beliefs held by some music creators coupled with the ivory tower status of the music industry, cultivates a 'moth-to-the-flame' attraction for many who seek a new, exciting and attractive existence. Because the music business is often seen as the answer to an 'indifferent' lifestyle, many thousands of young music creators and venturists flock to an industry that is largely oversubscribed. Artist contract opportunities offered by major music companies are few due to the limitation of investment funds. Investment is and always will be prioritised for those commercial music projects that are best suited to meeting the criteria of market trends and the consumer focus of the investing label. The music company must simply believe that the act is good enough to provide a return on the large-scale investment (in time and money) when a signing occurs. The costly infrastructure required to break and maintain the career of the music artist is outlined in further sections of this book.

BRINGING MUSIC TO THE AUDIENCE AND CONSUMER RELATIONS

Looking further at the way in which music eventually makes its way to audience (from home creation to a commercial environment), it is possible to identify both supportive and prohibitive mechanisms for the commercial music provider. The principles of A&R feature heavily as a significant force in commercial music exploitation pathways. The importance of A&R theory should not be overlooked, as this concept remains embedded in and around notions of musical acceptance, even if self-managed and promoted. The independent artist would benefit from understanding key principles of A&R, as these can inform self-applied quality control methods – tools that will assist the future success of any music provider.

A&R THEORY

The importance of the 'worldwide music sphere' and the quantity of music it possesses has a bearing on our earlier consideration – is there room enough for all music creators and producers to have careers within today's commercial music industry? We can deduce that there is certainly not enough room for *all* music providers to sign with large music companies. Comparing this with other business investment scenarios, creative inventors (making any new type of innovative product for consumers) find that not all their deserved inventions will be discovered and progressed with commercial support. In music, as the sheer amount of musicians and music producers far outweigh the contractual opportunities, this would leave many producers and musicians without a deal. This is where musical talent becomes a 'buyer's market' for the recording industry; it can clearly be argued that in statistical terms, the recording industry can have its 'pick of the crop'. Considering the huge amounts of music (both physical products and electronic music files) that music companies get sent, 'good' submissions are simply not good enough. Due to the sheer weight of musical competition, for A&R, the 'good' music as deciding factor changes to artists who are 'exceptional'. An act or artist that really stands out from the competition will increase its odds of commercial exploitation opportunity with any music company. Usually an exceptional artist has already secured interest from personal management, who can assist in the journey. 'Exceptional' talent can be defined in many ways, with subjectivity playing a large part in A&R psyche, coupled with market and genre trends, consumer popularity, investment available and sustainability in the act.

Steve Proud, in A&R for Atlantic Records UK, supports the argument for the 'exceptional': 'I am always looking for something unique and special' (in Beattie, 2007:25).

To be concise, there is no 'magic formula' for success, but there are certainly recurrent attributes that are found in many acts that have secured music company investment and have then gone on to have illustrious careers:

- Sound distinctiveness: Usually the vocal sound is unique and does not sound like any other known successful act.
- Audio difference: The musical project is 'different' from other acts and offers a clear measure of audio individuality.
- Similarity: In contradiction of the above, the musical act is similar to other successful acts in its genre and will appeal to an established market.

- Song appeal: Interactions inherent in the 'song' between music, melody or words captures the affections of the listener who 'empathises' with the song.
- Commerciality: The music is perceived to have commercial appeal to a mass audience and can translate well through mainstream media such as radio and TV.
- Image: The musical act is aesthetically pleasing to look at – especially within a certain consumer demographic.

There are many additional contradictions within the above – with human subjectivity once again playing its part in finding new music projects that will appeal to a mass audience. Some music companies endeavour to be unique and individual in their contribution to the world of music, but it must be considered that any company wishing to shape the music landscape must rely on consumer purchase to recoup investment. It could therefore be argued that there are serious limitations in the pursuit of being unique, and financial risks will always be associated with this strategy. Yet currently the major recording industries have survived these risks and rule the airwaves in terms of public-sphere music exploitation, access to commercial exploitation routes and the funds to bring music to a wider audience. It follows that an act that wishes to be considered for major exploitation must follow the rules set out by the music industry or face a route of independence. However, an independent route should not be seen as a negative move; in musical terms, such a route may prove more artistically and personally satisfying than signing to a larger music investor. The evident success of many independent labels in the past should not be overlooked either (e.g. The Beggars Group and others). The financial implications of major or independent contractual signing and new music company models can generate endless discussion, but where creating music and getting it heard by a national audience is concerned, the capital major music model cannot be overlooked.

THE DISCOVERY SERVICE

If the odds of earning a recording contract with major music investors are very slim, should music creators and producers really create music with such commercial endeavours in mind? Is it worth contacting large music companies if project approaches are largely frivolous? The first step for music venturists would be to assess the potential for success in the project in accordance with the music market, its trends and demands. Every day new music can be heard on radio supplied by large music company infrastructure, and that music has originated from those who had the original impetus to realise the global fruits of their musical labours. Ultimately, new music must be discovered by the labels somewhere, somehow, and the A&R department must provide the 'discovery' service to the record company (the varying duties of A&R personnel are discussed later in this book alongside the departmental structure). There are common contradictions associated with the practice of A&R and the way in which new music is discovered and subsequently 'signed' and exploited. The practice of A&R varies between music companies, but each company would want to be the first to discover any new talent worthy of worldwide dominance. Listed are some common negative themes and common myths concerning getting music heard by the larger music companies:

- Music companies receive 'bin bags' full of demonstration recordings.
- Music companies do not listen to unsolicited demonstration recordings.
- Most music companies do not have the time or manpower to sift through the huge number of physical recordings or music files received.
- Most demonstration recordings remain unheard and end up 'in the bin'.
- MP3s sent to recording companies are deleted without being listened to.

It must be noted at this stage that major music companies and investors rarely request approaches from 'would be' music producers or artists. Music companies do not advertise for 'artists wanted' as in usual job vacancies; they simply do not have to, due to the 'moth-to-the-flame' effect of the industry. Yet there is an unending obligation for the company to 'discover'. For the major label, a lack of discovery would mean dwindling financial returns and a reliance on back catalogue record releases.

If major music companies cannot cope with the sheer amount of music project approaches, how does the A&R department have enough time to 'discover'? Does a question mark preside over the efficiency of the A&R model to 'discover', and are unique musical projects being overlooked? Is there a better way to discover? There are further questions associated with the probability of the new artist being discovered and the efficiency of the A&R model.

A&R FILTERING AND NATURAL SELECTION

A common misconception has existed in the music industry for many years – that is, if a demonstration music project is sent to a music company unsolicited, it simply cannot be good enough for signing and exploitation. The music is deemed unsuitable for further investigation, simply due to its anonymous approach (though music submitters would argue, how can any music company assess commercial potential in unheard, unseen music submissions?). It could therefore be argued that the 'unsolicited' equals the 'unworthy' and therefore provides a default filtering mechanism for companies who cannot deploy enough A&R resource to assess all incoming material accurately. Conversely, there are music companies who will employ staff to sift through the material received (electronic MP3 or otherwise), and the

A&R junior staff will look out for appropriate material and forward it to the A&R manager for the next stage in the filtering process. It should be highlighted at this point that many artists are actually represented by personal managers and publishers, so A&R personnel get to hear pre-evaluated material supplied by these contacts. There may be many more stages in this process, including board meetings and discussions, before an artist nears a contractual arrangement with a major. Often these recordings will be listened to by junior A&R personnel, a talent scout or a work experience student working in the department. The smaller music label's A&R duties are usually carried out by the label owners themselves, but these companies generally receive fewer music submissions, due to the lack of notoriety of the label.

Where a music project sender or demo-maker has no contacts or alternative routes into the recording industry, they may pursue their own direct route by sending in unsolicited material in the hope that they will get noticed and listened to. Due to time constraints surrounding the discovery process, it has been suggested that some A&R departments adopt common policies as follows:

- A&R personnel will only listen to the first twenty seconds of a song on average. If it 'grabs them', they will listen further to other songs on the demo.
- A&R do not want to hear a whole album at first – just one to three songs are sufficient initially.
- A&R will get in contact with you if they feel your project has potential, so no need to pursue them.
- A&R are too busy to speak to unknown, unsolicited music 'hawkers'.

A&R policies will vary between companies, these being dependent on what particular labels are looking for at any given time and the investment funds available. Individual A&R personnel may have their own particular way of working and, as personnel change, so will individual and joint A&R policies. Presently there are four major music companies in the UK, each with their own unique A&R structures: Universal Music Group (UMG), Sony Music Entertainment UK, EMI Music and Warner Music Group (WMG). It should be noted that A&R provides a landscape that is constantly shifting, with personnel quickly in and out of its departments and the industry. Listed advice on actual A&R policy for those wishing to submit material is often available via individual music company websites. Also, there are many other music companies who operate on a large scale, such as Live Nation, which concentrates on the music industry from a live perspective first and would look at how many tickets an artist can sell rather than how many recorded products could be sold. The shift in brand identity from 'record company' to 'music company' in recent years demonstrates the new diversification of music industry; this involves a move away from just purely recording and distributing music, therefore expanding the music business model for new artists.

ESTABLISHING OPPORTUNITY AND A&R RETICENCE

It may seem awkward for a creative music 'sender' to question the investment motives of a record company before approaching with new music, but it would appear to make sense to do so. Establishing if the music company is actually looking for new talent before submission or targeting material to specific personnel would be advisable.

Factors that prevent labels signing new artists are many and complex, but for the A&R manager, taking the plunge will mean 'sticking one's neck out' – whereby A&R recommends an act for signing. In this regard it would follow that the act simply must succeed; if it does not, such a large investment decision would be hugely negative, not only for the act, but also for the careers of the personnel who recommended the signing in the first place. Many thousands of pounds may be invested in a new act in order to bring it to public attention; this perceived level of risk alone can create A&R reticence towards new music offerings. As in any product or invention, serious investment is required by industry to stir national public interest, raising the product profile through advertising and multimedia. The music industry survives in this way on a daily basis, and as the music industry model morphs, large music companies seek new ways of making money from music and its music creators and performers. The principles of A&R have not really changed since this mechanism was conceived, but technology has made the A&R job easier in part, providing an anonymous 'electronic window'. A&R personnel can now scour music websites and ascertain the level of wider public interest that artists can generate. Establishing whether or not there is a 'buzz factor' will fuel any urgency to make the next potential signing.

BEYOND A&R

For many commercial music creators and artists, it could be argued that A&R theories have influenced the way in which their projects have been devised and taken shape. A&R is situated in a 'gatekeeping' role between the music project and possible wider exploitation in the public sphere. There are, however, further considerations, regardless of how viable A&R perceives the project to be; beyond A&R, mainstream media and audience perception are factors governing success in the long term. Planning an extensive campaign to break a new artist is difficult to say the least, given the constant changes that occur in market trends and consumption. Many new artists take positive steps by engaging fans and audiences first, through live performance and using online media before going into the A&R selection process.

BUZZ FACTORING

Audiences that engage commercially with artists build the fan construct; this commitment by consumers (and followers) establishes value in the music project. This basic concept is welcomed by music companies and identifies with the common modes of exploitation expected by the music company. Where an act or artist can cultivate greater audiences, 'viral marketing' can result: wider general conversation about the act through personal communication, email or blogging online through the electronic fan base. The terminology given to this phenomenon in the music industry is known as 'buzz'; when an act creates a 'buzz' it increases its chance of being taken seriously quite considerably. A&R representative Amy Daniels highlights the way in which a 'compact' music industry responds to buzz; 'The music industry is so well connected it's impossible for record labels to not hear about bands that are creating a buzz' (Beattie, 2007:31).

Buzz is difficult to falsify by an artist, as much of the A&R role is to be engaged with the 'grapevine' of discussion on acts that are making a significant impact in a crowded marketplace. The realisation of buzz is demonstrated when an act plays live to audience, there are significant numbers in attendance and there is a healthy public response. If this has happened without commercial support, the job of the music company is made easier, supplying immediate belief that an act has good market potential. The music company now has a head start, using the fan base as a good starting point in the market. Social media plays a huge role in this phenomenon, as buzz now manifests itself in many other ways, for example, a significant amount of hits on a MySpace page or on YouTube. Buzz can exist purely between record companies, whereby the A&R staff across several companies and departments will clamour to sign the music project all at once. Often, when an act is close to 'signing', all other record companies are aware of the same act; it is not unusual for an act to have several offers from more than one music company at the same time. It would be worth considering the converse, whereby it is more common for many acts to have little or no record company interest at all, having made their approaches using various methods of submission and attempts at buzz factoring. Trying to get a busy A&R person to attend key gigs or events will prove difficult without a buzz factor in existence; this signifies that new acts must be aware of the phenomenon and consider exactly how they will cultivate buzz.

ALIENATION FOR THE CREATIVE MASSES

It is often regarded by many music creators that A&R alienation (as a result of rejection) produces many negative feelings – that perhaps their music serves little purpose in the commercial marketplace and personal aspirations are therefore destroyed. Many creatives recover from setbacks quickly to pursue their goals further, ignoring the advice of A&R in continuation of their art. Of course, A&R

theories alone cannot provide deciding factors on whether artists should have music careers; there would be far less music made available for sale had this been the case. What many artists crave is to have access to mainstream media mechanisms in order to exploit and promote their music before a mass audience, yet these mechanisms are dominated by the major labels.

It should be noted that smaller music companies that are licensed to, or owned by, a major will receive many demos and often have similar A&R policies to that of the major to which they are connected. As labels get smaller, so do their overheads and staffing infrastructure, so the head of A&R at a small independent label is generally the label owner. Often as smaller labels do not demonstrate the same high profile appeal of a major, they may be overlooked by artists. Yet some smaller labels may welcome music submissions, as they do not get sent nearly as many as the majors. The artist then has the benefit of the label owner (as chief decision maker) listening to the material, rather than an A&R scout in a larger label further down the chain of command. The smaller label may also have music distribution agreements with a larger network and have the ability to release in many worldwide territories. It has been proven that seemingly small independent music companies can provide a way forward for certain artists, which can leader to greater things as time progresses.

MEDIA ACCEPTANCE FOR THE CREATIVE MASSES ON A GLOBAL SCALE

Modern technology has provided many new alternative routes for modern day creators and performers in music; there are now infinite new modes of worldwide musical dissemination. The growth of the internet and the advancement of broadband, fast information streaming and enhanced graphic presentation, afford a virtual free platform for those that want to showcase music to a potential worldwide audience. Internet hosts YouTube and MySpace have revolutionised this area in music and have become brand and market leaders in the 'free music access' online domain. Music artists may now upload their music, graphics and biographies to these platforms for the world to see, via the home computer medium. Uploading visuals to YouTube increases 'visibility'; it is now commonplace for any artist that is serious about their presence to have online materials associated with MySpace or Facebook, in an effort to cultivate a 'buzz' factor. This does not guarantee major music company interest, but it certainly puts the artist in a stronger position as a commercial entity. Building a healthy fan base will build a career in music – and the tools are now available to do this. There are continuing shifts in which different sites are the most popular to users at any given time, and it is worthwhile researching these before uploading music content and ventures. Some popular online 'stages' and platforms for uploading music in order to cultivate fan bases are as follows:

- YouTube
- Facebook
- MySpace
- Twitter
- Flixster
- Linkedin
- Bebo
- Orkut
- Flickr
- Soundcloud

In July 2010 Facebook was surveyed as the most popular site, with over 24.2 million users in the UK (bbc.co.uk, 2010). New social media has provided a fresh set of encouraging tools for the commercial music demo-maker, in allowing the creation of new strategies to gain wider recognition for their music on a worldwide basis. Using these electronic tools to attract real audiences to music in an independent and entrepreneurial way can demonstrate potential commercial value in a music project. Creating genuine buzz demonstrates that the music has integrity with its fan base; these online tools have probably provided the best way to cultivate interest in new music to date. 'Counters' that exist on these sites will give an indication of the amount of visits and hits the site has had, so the notion of the 'counter' has become an important tool for A&R. Before electronic social media arrived, A&R signing models relied on untested acts in regard to their mass appeal; a music company had to agree internally that the music act was indeed good enough to constitute a worthy risk of investment. The odds of success were, and still are, in this 'chance' style investment, small. Music companies increasingly look towards electronic methods of fan approval for new music, before an investment risk is taken. Many music companies invest more time and funding into market research, exploring markets and consumer trends first before investing in certain genres. For instance, if a heavy metal band is exceptional in its delivery of its music, a large company may not invest in this act if market research proves the metal genre itself is shrinking. If the metal band could still cultivate a large audience it could still survive by relying on income streams from live performance and utilising independent or specialist release conduits. Where an act can draw a healthy audience, it will always attract healthy business interest. Electronic social and music media have provided the largest 'consolation prize' for music creators and artists who could not attract the investment of a major music company. Exponents of commercial creative projects, whoever they are and regardless of the quality of their projects, can now have an electronic voice.

Music submitters can learn from the music marketplace; the commercial requirements for music products are demonstrated by the range of models already in the world marketplace. Although a demo-maker or artist may strive to be musically different, there are music models in existence that set the standards for tomorrow's new music. Learning from the pre-existing form will make the job of the music submitter easier: research all similar released music forms in the field; know the competition; listen to and learn from 'broadcast standard' audio productions; observe the visual presentations and sense of brand that accompany the product (in both electronic and tangible forms). Through comparison, it may be possible to assess how close a music submission can resemble the competition. One must aim to be in this arena, or at least very close to it, to attract serious music company interest.

STANDARDS IN MUSIC DEMO PRODUCTION

Rarely, a music trend may surface that will break the 'good music demo production' rule; for instance, raw low budget music productions that surfaced in the punk era made an impact, but as punk's consumer base grew, punk production became increasingly sophisticated and less independent in its nature. Many successful early punk records were in fact produced to a high standard by professionals, even though punk music product purported to be unprocessed and raw in message. This rawness was a key strategic marketing objective for EMI in releasing the Sex Pistols album, *Never Mind the Bollocks*, produced by Chris Thomas in 1977. Thomas had worked previously with The Beatles and Pink Floyd among others, and his well-engineered punk productions paved the way for healthy public broadcast and consumption. It is worth noting that music companies today would wish to see a well produced music package and something that they can see a market for directly. In this regard, it is imperative that the music production is the best that it can be. Essentially, where the skills base of the individual music producer may fall short, it would be worthwhile enlisting the services of others to facilitate the very best demo production, in order to impress potential investors.

APPROACHING MUSIC COMPANIES

An awareness of business etiquette is likely to help a music submission in this regard; go about business in the correct manner and once again chances are increased. Be professional in the 'approach' and it is less likely that you will upset those that you wish to invest in your music product. Business etiquette and professionalism are skills that need to be learned, forged and applied in the product pitch to the music company.

Whatever the style of music being produced and whoever is actually being approached with a musical pitch or submission, the notion of 'targeting' should be carefully considered. This method would dictate that there is a direct relationship between the style of music being pitched and the target label output, or roster of acts residing with the music company. Many music companies, whether large or small, would generally have a 'brand' identity forged through the music they release;

for example, Tamla Motown (a current subsidiary of Universal Music) is a strong music brand in the US, internationally known for its past soul genre output, and Roadrunner Records is famed for its rock and metal releases. Comparatively, it would be reasonable to assume that a rock genre label such as Roadrunner would not wish to receive soul music submissions, just as a soul genre label would not wish to receive metal music. Where there is a lack of research into the music company act roster on the part of the music submitter, there may be much time wasted approaching the wrong label with the wrong style of music.

As any business model would suggest, a marketing strategy must exist for finding customers; theories such as the marketing mix four Ps – Product, Price, Place and Promotion – could be investigated and applied (see Chapter 11). In this regard the record company would assume the role of customer and the music 'submitter' would become the company that is selling.

REFERENCES AND FURTHER READING

Books

Barrow, T. and Newby, J., *Inside the Music Business* (London: Routledge, 1995), pp. 196–204.

Beattie, W., *The Rock and Roll Times Guide to the Music Industry* (Oxford: Spring Hill, 2007), pp. 1–42.

Blake, A., *The Music Business* (London: Batsford, 1992).

Davis, S. and Laing, D., *The Guerrilla Guide to the Music Business* (New York: Continuum, 2006), pp. 144–206.

Massey, H., *Behind the Glass – Top Record Producers Tell How They Craft the Hits* (Berkeley: Miller Freeman, 2000).

Robinson, D.C., Buck, E. and Cuthbert, M., *Music at the Margins: Popular Music and Global Cultural Diversity* (Communication and Human Values series) (London: Sage, 1991).

Periodicals

365 Pro Audio Magazine. Available at: www.365proaudio.com (accessed 4 September 2010).

Audio Media Magazine. Available at: www.audiomedia.com (accessed 4 September 2010).

Electronic Musician Magazine. Available at: http://emusician.com (accessed 4 September 2010).

EQ Magazine. Available at: www.eqmag.com (accessed 4 September 2010).

Future Music Magazine. Available at: www.futuremusic.co.uk (accessed 4 September 2010).

Home Recording Mag.com. Available at: www.recordingmag.com (accessed 12 March 2011).

Mix Magazine. Available at: http://mixonline.com (accessed 4 September 2010).

Music Tech Magazine. Available at: www.musictechmag.co.uk (accessed 4 September 2010).

Pro Sound News Europe. Available at: www.prosoundnewseurope.com (accessed 4 September 2010).

Recording Magazine. Available at: www.recordingmag.com (accessed 4 September 2010).

Sound On Sound Magazine. Available at: www.soundonsound.com (accessed 4 September 2010).

Tape Op Magazine. Available at: www.tapeop.com (accessed 4 September 2010).

Online resources

'The Beatles: The Influences and Music', at City Portal Liverpool. Available at: www.liverpoolcityportal.co.uk/beatles/beatles_influences.html (accessed 10 January 2011).

Demo-making and home recording. Available at www.tascam.com (accessed 12 January 2011).

Glassman, J., 'The Beatles Musical Footprints', BBC News online (30 November 2001). Available at: http://news.bbc.co.uk/1/hi/entertainment/1452393.stm (accessed 10 January 2011).

Keller, D., 'Bruce Springsteen's "Nebraska" – A PortaStudio Two SM57's, and Inspiration', Tascam News (25 July 2007). Available at: www.tascam.com/news/display/226 (accessed 10 January 2011).

TASCAM US-144mkII, at Tascam. Available at: http://zmtest-a.com/product/us-144mkii (accessed 10 January 2011).

'The Ups and Downs of Social Networks', BBC News online (22 July 2010). Available at: www.bbc.co.uk/news/technology-10719042 (accessed 10 March 2011).

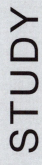

GATEKEEPING IN THE MUSIC INDUSTRY

Pete Astor

What is gatekeeping?

'What do you want?' The night is dark and it's raining heavily. The four keen young faces look into an older, wizened one, hoping for entry. The old man asks the group what business they have; they reply that their business is their own. There is a pause; the gatekeeper opens the heavy door, saying 'Alright young sirs, I meant no offence'. They have been let in, into the town and a raucous pub for the night, continuing their journey.

This scene from Peter Jackson's film of Tolkien's *Lord of the Rings* articulates a typical idea of what a gatekeeper does. The fantasy element of the story and the act of a simple entry or refusal also fits well with the idea in the general imagination of how a gatekeeper might function in the music industry; he is there to guard entry to a desired place, and once he has decided to let you in, your journey can continue, facilitated by entry into the area and the powers that come with it that the gatekeeper has unlocked.

C@SE STUDY

The concept of gatekeeping as applied to roles in the music industry has its roots in sociological studies of news media of the 1940s and 1950s and is used to describe the whole range of individuals that are between an artist and a potential public. According to Shuker, it can be said to cover the people in power who make 'the initial decision about who to record and promote, and filtering material at each step of the process involving the recording and marketing of a song' (2005:118). These include record company employees, radio programmers and DJs, journalists, promoters, as well as people – professional or not – circulating information online. Negus, in *Producing Pop: Culture and Conflict in the Popular Music Industry* (1992), argued that the idea, developed from Bourdieu, of 'cultural intermediaries' is a better fit than 'gatekeeper' within the – as Shuker terms them – 'anarchic practices' of the music industry, where roles and power structures are not rigidly defined but are part of a shifting set of taste cultures influencing what creative work gets the most attention. On a basic level, as Shoemaker states in her study of the term, 'the gatekeeping process involves every aspect of message selection, handling and control, whether the message is communicated through mass media or interpersonal channels' (1991:1). This primary definition of the concept is also true for the way the music industry is changing, where creative products are now disseminated in a far wider and more layered way; since the advent of the internet and DIY culture in general, the more clearly defined roles of the gatekeeper as part of 'the industry', either letting product through or not, have also changed. Nonetheless, more straightforward processes of gatekeeping still operate within certain areas, depending on artist, genre and cultural ideology. Arguably, its role and function has changed most in the more artist-driven, DIY-derived, and more self-consciously 'authentic' areas of popular music, while still taking place in a more straightforward way in the 'pop' arenas.

In order to best understand how the concept functions across a range of music industry practices, the term needs to be placed within its historical context and its use and development traced, including examples of how gatekeeping has operated in some distinct areas of industry practice. Gatekeepers still, on some level, exist in the manner portrayed by Tolkien in *The Lord of the Rings*, but their appearances and functions have evolved with the changes in the industry; therefore, continuing debates about the validity of the term itself need to be addressed.

The idea of the gatekeeper was first used by sociologist Kurt Lewin in 1947 in 'Frontiers in Group Dynamics II. Channels of Group Life; Social Planning and Action Research' when looking at habits of food consumption, where he used the term to describe the various agents that controlled the flow of food down a series of different channels on its journey to the family dinner table (1947:145). In a chapter from *Field Theory and Social Science*, published in 1951, where ideas in the earlier paper were revisited, Lewin states, in relation to his ideas about gatekeepers, that: 'This situation holds not only for food but also for the travelling of a news item through certain communication channels in a group, for movement of goods, and the social locomotion of individuals in many organisations' (1951:187). Previously David Manning White had put ideas of gatekeeping into research practice when he looked at the actions of a newspaper wire editor, whom he named 'Mr Gates'. In the study, the reasons for the inclusion and exclusion of news was evaluated and the editor's decisions were deemed to be based very much on subjective personal opinions (Shoemaker, 1991:10).

Following various studies through the 1950s and 1960s, where the initial models were expanded on and developed, ideas about gatekeeping were applied to the music industry by Paul Hirsh in the early 1970s. Here, in 'Processing Fads and Fashions: An Organization-Set Analysis of Cultural Industries Systems', Hirsh highlights some of the differing roles of gatekeepers more specific to the cultural industries:

> For book publishers, record companies, and, to a lesser extent, movie studios, then, the crucial target audience for the promotional campaigns consists of autonomous gatekeepers, or 'surrogate consumers' such as disc jockeys, film critics, and book reviewers, employed by mass media organisations to serve as fashion experts and opinion leaders for their respective constituencies.
>
> (1972:649)

This usefully highlights some of the complexities of the roles of different levels of power and influence in the music industry. However, he still maintains the idea of a unidirectional flow of artistic product, as proposed by Lewin and White, where the gatekeeper controls access as though he or she were in charge of operating a simple 'on' or 'off' function, based on the idea of a 'filter flow' system. This is where some more recent commentators, such as McQuail, have seen shortcomings in the use of the term:

> Despite its appeal and plausibility, the gatekeeping concept has a number of weaknesses and has been continuously revised since its first applications. Weak points are its implication of there being one (initial) gate area and one main set of selection criteria, its simple view of the 'supply' of news, and its tendency to individualise decision-making.
>
> (2005:309)

C@SE STUDY

This is particularly relevant in relation to the changing structures of production and dissemination in the music industry, where a set of major changes has been gathering pace over the last few years, particularly with the increasing use of the internet as a conduit for consumers to access popular music product. McQuail states that, where there was once a relatively limited set of channels through which musicians could sell and promote their work (record companies, major or independent, or self releasing), the internet now provides a more direct link to a potential audience, its increasing ubiquity governing the far wider distribution of cultural products:

> The arrival and growth of the Internet does widen the possibility of access to global information and cultural resources. Access is now also possible without reliance on the various gatekeepers that always restrict and control the flow of content in more traditional media. These gatekeepers operate at both the sending and receiving ends of distribution channels.
>
> (McQuail, 2005:261)

On some levels the hierarchies that were previously in place have been broken down and opened up by the internet. However, as McQuail also points out, this does not mean that – whatever some proselytisers about the potential freedoms of the World Wide Web would have us believe – access is now entirely open and uncontrolled: social and interactive structures still develop and exist, meaning that for an artist to break through, they must still pass through different gates, although – and this is a key point – those gates and their keepers will now be less clearly defined and identifiable: 'The traditional publications functions of gatekeeping, editorial intervention and validation of authorship will be found in some types of Internet publication, but not in others' (McQuail, 2005:139).

However, the basic idea of gatekeepers can still be useful in various areas of today's music industry. In terms of artistic production, the idea has a far stronger presence in what might usefully be called the 'pop' arena. The idea of 'pop' in genre terms is, of course, notoriously difficult to pin down, but for our purposes, the term will be used to describe the area of popular music that is aimed at a broadly mainstream, chart-orientated market. This area is now more audience-specific than it was. For our purposes here we also need to recognise the changes that have taken place in the workings of the industry in recent years; the way the industry functioned until relatively recently accommodated the model of

C@SE STUDY

unidirectional flow far more comfortably. Forty or fifty years ago, artists, in order to make records, had to a be signed to a record company. The possibility of a self-released product was practically impossible. The costs of manufacture, production and recording were well beyond the financial reach of any but the very rich, or those who might have been vain, brave or foolhardy enough to finance their own release. The major record companies and distributors also functioned within a fixed and standardised infrastructure, so in mainstream popular music there was no workable outlet for a record to be released and promoted outside of existing frameworks. The Beatles had to pass through an audition process in order to secure their record contract with EMI. Indeed, their earlier audition for Decca did not yield a record contract and subsequent success. In fact, A&R man Mike Smith had enjoyed The Beatles work on the audition tape very much, but it was his superior, Dick Rowe, who turned them down, acting in a clearly recognisable gatekeeping role. He, from his range of subjective and conditioned opinions and informal expertise, deemed the group unsuitable for a record contract; the gate remained closed for The Beatles in 1962 at Decca records (Davis, 1985:202). This model of gatekeeping is also still strongly in evidence in the music industry today, not only in the more mainstream 'pop' world but also in an almost cartoonish manner in the proliferation of talent shows such as *X Factor*. Here, the simple model of acceptance or rejection is comfortably still in place, just as it once had been in the roles of the record personnel and artist managers in the popular music industry.

In the mid-1970s with the advent of punk there was the beginning of a change in some of the traditionally fixed roles of artists and gatekeepers in the industry. Broadly speaking, popular music had always functioned in the unidirectional model adopted by Hirsch. In this, A&R people acted as gatekeepers representing the record companies who – if the artist were to be signed to a contract – would provide the necessary promotional, manufacturing and marketing costs in order to facilitate a possible career. With elements of the punk sensibility, actually rooted in hippie ideals of self-sufficiency and alternative means of production, the idea of DIY came to the fore. Simon Reynolds outlines its progenitors:

> Do it yourself/release it yourself, for Desperate Bicycles, spelled the overthrow of the establishment music industry because it was the people seizing the means of record production, making their own entertainment, and selling it to other creative and autonomous likeminds.

(2005:97)

Thus, 'The Medium Was Tedium' in 1977 gave a signal to artists like Daniel Miller to form Mute Records in order to release his first (and only) record, 'Warm Leatherette' under the name The Normal. Mute Records, his label, went on to sign and develop million selling artists such as Depeche Mode, Moby and Goldfrapp. In each case the company's methods bypassed many traditional music business practices, such as regular A&R meetings or standard contractual practice between many of the artists and the label. Mute is just one example of a host of labels, since the punk era, that were artist-driven and eschewed much standard industry practice.

This meant that the previously clearly defined flow of creative product through gatekeepers in established roles changed. Gatekeepers were still in place, but their role was less one-dimensional; no longer did 'cultural items merely arrive at a "gate" where they are either admitted or excluded' (Negus, 1992:45). This stands in useful opposition to the model proposed by Lewin, White and Hirsch *et al.*: the relationship between those wanting to be let in and those potentially letting them in, is too redolent of an industry model where, having impressed 'the man', the aspiring artist will then gain access to all they need to achieve fame and success. For most creative people working within the music industry, this relationship is far less rigidly defined. This means, for Negus, that, 'recording industry personnel are therefore more than gatekeepers . . . in contributing to the words, sounds and images of pop . . . record company personnel can be conceptualised as "cultural intermediaries"' (1992:46) – indeed, it is all those 'occupations involving presentation and representation and workers involved in providing symbolic goods and services'. This is arguably a far better fit with the very wide range functions and roles of those in the music industry now, where cultural intermediaries have 'jobs and careers [that] have not yet acquired the rigidity of the older bureaucratic professions' (Bourdieu, 1984:151).

In the workings of those involved in the cultural industries, the 'artist' now is very rarely only that; working, hoping and waiting to be 'let in' by industry gatekeepers. If we take the example of someone running a small record company, releasing, say, the niche product of the 7″ single, this person will often also fulfil some of a range of other roles in the industry. Some of these functions may also yield finance, providing funds for less immediately profitable elements of their creative enterprises. The roles they fulfil might include: posting online content; playing in other musical projects; writing for print publications; promoting concerts; teaching music-related subjects; recording and producing music (for themselves

C@SE STUDY

and others); working in music retail; doing product artwork or taking photographs.

Obviously this is an informal list, but this kind of qualitative approach can provide a way forward to a broader definition of the gatekeeping idea and better articulate how things might function now, with 'players' of all stamps acting as cultural intermediaries across the wide diversity of creative work in the music industry.

REFERENCES AND FURTHER READING

Bourdieu, P., *Distinction: A Social Critique of the Judgement of Taste* (London: Routledge & Keegan Paul, 1984).

Davis, H., *The Beatles* (London: Jonathan Cape, 1985).

Hirsch, P.M., 'Processing Fads and Fashions: An Organization-Set Analysis of Cultural Industries Systems', *The American Journal of Sociology*, 77, 4 (1972), pp. 639–659.

Lewin, K., *Field Theory in Social Science: Selected Theoretical Papers* (New York: Harper, 1951).

Lewin, K., 'Frontiers in Group Dynamics II. Channels of Group Life; Social Planning and Action Research', *Human Relations*, 1 (1947), pp. 143–153.

McQuail, D., *Mass Communication Theory*: Fifth Edition (London: Sage, 2005).

Negus, K., *Producing Pop: Culture and Conflict in the Popular Music Industry* (London: Edward Arnold, 1992).

Reynolds, S., *Rip It Up and Start Again: Post Punk 1978–1984* (London: Faber and Faber, 2005).

Shoemaker, P.J., *Communication Concepts 3: Gatekeeping* (Newbury Park, CA: Sage, 1991).

Shuker, R., *Popular Music: The Key Concepts*: Second Edition (Abingdon: Routledge, 2005), pp. 117–118.

White, D.M., 'The Gatekeeper: A Case Study in the Selection of News', *Journalism Quarterly*, 27 (1950), pp. 383–396.

C@SE STUDY

CHAPTER 3

The live music industry sector

Paul Rutter

INTRODUCTION

This section looks at roles associated with the staging and performance of music in a live context, taking into consideration both small and large venues. Roles associated with touring shows are largely of a freelance nature; more permanent forms of employment may fall within the venue itself, its maintenance and management structure. This section begins by highlighting the 'venue' and discusses the personnel associated with it. Those considering entering the live music industry sector should carefully consider the infrastructure that supports the staging of live music events, from key personnel involved in the 'hands on' execution and delivery of the event itself – to the peripheral roles that exist in support of the staging of live music events, from large concerts and festivals to smaller town venues. When attending an event as audience member, it is possible to observe personnel or crew taking on a variety of roles, many of which will go unnoticed, as audience usually concentrates purely on the performance of the artist. The venue is a good place to start when researching jobs in this sector, as most towns and cities have at least one or two venues with a staffing infrastructure to execute music events. Taking time to observe how music venues and events are staffed will reveal valuable information and provide possible inspiration in choosing a job role in this sector to investigate further.

THE VENUE: STAFFING INFRASTRUCTURE

Larger venues have an in-house management structure that will work with concert promoters and tour managers in respect of the incoming act or performers. A touring show is a large, moving independent animal with its own infrastructure and inhabitants, from the performers to the supporting road crew. The touring show is brought to the venue, or in the case of an outdoor festival, the venue may be one or more fields, with a brand name or theme associated, as in Glastonbury Festival held each summer in the UK. The responsibility of the venue manager is to decide which acts are to be staged within the venue; in Glastonbury's case, this would be Michael Eavis and his team. Profitable high profile acts that draw large audiences and are well promoted are an attractive prospect for the venue manager. The venue manager will negotiate the venue terms, commissions or fees for the hire of the venue and often handles ticket sales. The venue manager will also negotiate with the concert promoter of the artist and ensure the tour manager of the artist works with the venue and conforms to its rules. Most venues operate a curfew and are only allowed live music performance between certain times; if they exceed this they may lose their licence to entertain, or be fined by their local governing body or council. The local council grants the venue with a licence to entertain and its conditions must be upheld. To ensure artists conform to their playing times (and meet local council licensing contractual obligations), venues operate a fining system to ensure artistes do not play later than they should. Consequently, venue management will monitor arrival, set up and performance times of each show executed. Individual venues have their own set of house rules that would need to be observed by the visiting show and tour manager.

Promotion of forthcoming events staged at the venue is an essential, ongoing requirement, so shows must be advertised using media and online conduits. An advertisement known as a 'ladder-ad' is paid for by the venue and appears as a block calendar advertisement in the press; this cost will be written into the hiring agreement, and ultimately the concert promoter will pay for this. The venue management must ensure that there is an appropriately skilled workforce in place to cope with incoming events of varying sizes. The venue manager will employ additional occasional staff to guide audiences and monitor crowd safety. Depending on the size of the venue and its budget, permanent full-time roles in the venue may include:

- venue manager
- assistant manager
- operations manager
- box office and venue ticketing
- venue finance and accounts managers
- venue promotions and marketing
- advertising and design
- technical and maintenance personnel
- administration team.

There may be many other additional personnel employed on a permanent basis associated with larger venues that host a wider range of events alongside music, such as conferencing, corporate events and exhibitions. The O2 Arena in London is one such example and has a large staffing infrastructure to accommodate its shows and wider business activities. Working in a venue may provide a greater degree of financial security, but personal flexibility is required, often working unsociable hours and being able to adapt to a wide range of events that may not always include music.

The permanent entertainment venue is often a costly building to run; it is often large and remains empty for most of the time, as concerts run primarily in the evening. Venues often have expensive council rates and fees to pay if situated in a city centre; they also have to maintain a 'public liability' insurance policy in case a customer is injured on the premises and a claim ensues. As venues do not run concerts every night of the week throughout the year, many require a degree of sponsorship from private enterprise sources, the local council or government arts funding initiatives. Understanding the financial implications in running a large venue will explain why employment opportunities in large theatres can be sporadic. For those that work in the theatre domain, the connection with music may not always be to individual taste, but working in the sector provides a worthwhile step towards understanding the wider entertainment industry: how it works and survives. The venue will need an occasional workforce whenever an event takes place, which often includes the following staff:

- Door monitoring staff and ticket collection: Part-time staff will be brought in as required and there may be a crossover with external security employed on door monitoring. The size of the event will dictate the extra amount of personnel required.

- Enhanced security: Often a local company or agency will supply the required amount of trained and licensed security personnel with experience of conflict management, in consideration of the expected audience numbers.

- Theatre lighting technician: When large external lighting rigs are not brought in or needed by larger scale shows, the theatre's own onstage lighting will suffice, operated by in-house technicians.

- In-house sound engineer: On smaller events that do not require a large hired sound re-enforcement concert system, the venue would supply its own sound engineers to operate the venue sound rig, which is often much smaller than a full concert system (see section below 'Sound re-enforcement: Live sound engineer, front-of-house').

- In-house technicians: Maintenance and testing of the venue's lighting, sound and power, ensuring all meets current health and safety regulations.

- Stage and floor management: Ensuring that performers and crew set equipment in the right places and do not block safety exits. The movements of performers onstage and road crew are regulated in accordance with venue rules and health and safety regulations. Generally there will be venue staff that assist and may advise the incoming performers and road crew to ensure successful co-operation and collaboration in staging the show. Some of these duties may fall to technicians or other personnel working in the venue; this often depends on venue size and audience capacity.

- Food and beverages managers and bar staff: The number of part-time staff employed varies depending on the occasion. Larger audiences demand more refreshments, so this is sometimes a lucrative area for the venue.

There are distinct similarities in the roles associated with the venue and the roles involved in taking a concert 'on the road', so earning work experience in a venue will assist in understanding the logistics of the road tour. The concert promoter ultimately brings the live touring show into the venue. A 'life on the road' – working in association with the touring concert – may prove an attractive employment option; its infrastructure is outlined in the remaining sections of this chapter.

CONCERT PROMOTIONS

The music concert has grown in significance and importance through the 2000s, providing crucial income for the music industry in respect of its ongoing survival. This is due to the rise in interest from audiences and the concert going public. Concert promoters that stage good quality events find little trouble in selling tickets, as consumer values shift from the recorded product to the live performance. Concert promoters may range from small 'sole trader' entities to large companies, such as Live Nation, that have redefined the traditional music industry business model and taken it into new territories. Just as record companies themselves have diversified their activities, becoming 'music companies', the moniker of the large concert promoter has also drifted towards 'music company' status. Larger concert promoters have demonstrated a greater financial involvement in the artist, diversifying their trading interests by selling recorded works or merchandise at the concerts they promote. This model would have been unheard of in the past, but Live Nation is one such large international company. Live Nation claims to be the largest live entertainment company in the world, with offices worldwide and a strong presence in the UK. In 2009, Live Nation declared their music business strategy:

> Our core business is producing, marketing and selling live concerts for artists via our global concert pipe. Live Nation is the largest producer of live concerts in the world, annually producing over 16,000 concerts for 1,500 artists in 57 countries. The company sells over 45 million concert tickets a year and expects to drive over 60 million unique visitors to LiveNation.com in 2008. Live Nation is transforming the concert business by expanding its concert platform into ticketing and building the industry's first artist-to-fan vertically integrated concert platform.
>
> (www.livenation.com, 2009)

Such global mission statements demonstrate that large corporate music entertainment companies such as Live Nation are changing the boundaries of the traditional music industry model. However, the principles behind large or small concert promotion are largely the same, other than the level of investment and risk involved.

Scales of risk for the concert promoter

A small concert promoter simply stages musical events and may promote singular shows or many more dates by more than one artist. Music entrepreneurs with the right attributes, who are prepared to take financial risk, could enter the concert promotions industry with relative ease on a small scale. At grassroots level, it is possible to find local artists who seek promotional opportunities to perform, and if the act seems likely to provide a return on investment, such 'profit' confidence provides perhaps one of the best reasons to promote. Investment would constitute sourcing a suitable performance venue and date for the act, then publicising the date and selling tickets beforehand and at the venue on the night. A performance fee can be agreed with the act; the act may perform for a percentage of the door takings, or perhaps a set performance fee can be negotiated. The risk for any concert promoter, having spent money staging the event, is that audience does not materialise; the risks associated with concert promotion can be enormous when executed on a large scale. Artists with a large public profile, brand and proven track record of selling out huge venues (such as rock outfit Kings of Leon) will demand a greater fee for big concerts and tours, through their booking agent. This would correlate to higher ticket prices to cover such fees and the huge infrastructure required to support such large concerts. Staging a gig at a local bar is a far less risky business, but losses will still occur where there is a lack of audience, as bars rely on sales of alcohol to fund their entertainment. Guaranteeing consumer interest is not always an exact science, so any concert promoter must take good promotional steps to ensure the public is aware that the event is taking place. However, even the most expensive promotional campaigns may fall foul of other external factors affecting the designated date, for example, a bigger event may take place on the same day, in the same town, steering audience the wrong way. This would require careful planning and research on the part of the concert promoter to maximise the chances of healthy ticket sales for the specific event. Careful strengths, weaknesses, opportunities and threats (SWOT) analysis would assist in this regard (see Chapter 11, in the section 'Strategic positioning: The SWOT').

Concert values

Due to the growth and renewed level of interest in 'gig going' in the UK and Europe, there are audiences that are prepared to pay excessive amounts for the 'right' concert ticket. As value held in recorded music has decreased, the value consumers place on the concert ticket has clearly increased, especially in comparison with the ticket prices of the past. As sound re-enforcement technology has improved, concert sound has also seen a marked improvement, enhancing the 'concert going' experience for audiences. Skills concerning event management and staging of the live show have also greatly improved, with many shows boasting extensive lighting enhancement, stage and set design. The 'spectacle' has now become the common expectation for audiences. Conceptualisation of the event and strong themes now run through many popular music concerts in comparison with relatively basic sound and lighting set ups of the 1960s and 1970s. The concert promoter must consider the rising costs associated with the new greater 'audio and visual' requirement and be prepared to invest more heavily in the show. Due to the huge staging and logistical costs, large tours often do not fall into profit until their closing stages. Historically, many tours and concerts have made losses, but they are often executed to provide a promotional platform for new acts. Other losses are simply due to concerts or outdoor festivals affected by 'acts of god' such as a rain storm and no fault of the concert promoter directly. Concert insurance can be taken out to cover some of these eventualities. For supporting acts to appear on the bill of a large tour, it is commonplace for 'pay-to-play' schemes to operate. The support act's management or record company pays the concert promoter to appear on the bill. Pay-to-play fees can run into thousands, but the supporting artist gains hugely from being exposed to a new large audience, effectively 'tapping into' an existing established fan base.

At this stage it is important to realise where the concert promoter sits in its relationship with the venue. Concert promoters do not own or maintain venues; they simply hire them, sometimes on a semi-permanent basis (e.g. AEG's arrangement with O2 Arena, London). AEG has a team of employees that oversee the concert process, from sourcing the artist through agents and promoters, to ensuring that the event takes place. O2 Arena employs its own permanent staff in the running and maintenance of the venue, but will work with the freelance staff of AEG also in the staging of concerts. It has become commonplace for large concert promoters such as AEG and Live Nation to inhabit a venue permanently. For instance, Live Nation stages pop concerts at Southampton City Guildhall, UK, and runs its fully staffed operation from its offices there.

The new concert promoter

The new evolution of some concert promoters into 'music' companies is interesting to observe; in the past, record companies concentrated on the creative and artistic development of the artist, coupled with the marketing of recorded musical works by the artist. Record companies would leave concert promotion, live activities and artist performance matters to the concert promoter. Music companies now seek to maximise incomes from music in all its forms, both live and recorded. New exploitation models in music have changed the way that traditional music industry structures operate. In 2009 Live Nation also announced that:

New music division Artist Nation has signed superstars such as Jay Z, Shakira and Nickelback, and manages their record releases, merchandise, tours, and sponsoring.

(www.livenation.com 2009)

Live Nation's intentions may make good music business sense, but one would need to question the musical acts signed to Artist Nation and those around them to assess whether this new model will produce sustained benefit to all parties. Live Nation's business strategy bears witness to continuing changes in the music industry; the notion of a concert promotions agency becoming a 'one-stop' music label would have been unheard of in the past. Yet there never were any laws to govern the framework of the music industry and the form it should take, although it is widely accepted that public perceptions of it are immersed in the evolution of recorded products. Taking care of all of the artist's revenue streams in these new business models is regarded as a '360-degree deal', whereby an artist signs to one company to look after all key business interests. The amount of 'degrees' may be reduced depending on the amount of business interests covered; for example, 180-degree deals may include live and recorded revenues, but not music publishing and merchandise income streams. Traditionalists may argue against this, but survival of the greater music industry will always be paramount and it will always find new ways to generate as much income as possible. With these new accepted structures in place, additional routes open up for the entrepreneur. Past 'music venturists' starting their own independent record label would source a band then go to the recording studio first, replicate the recorded works and seek to market them to the public, using radio as the ultimate marketing tool. Live Nation's business model would suggest the entrepreneur can source talent and promote in the venue first, cultivating an audience and fan base, then selling recorded works at the venue, alongside merchandise.

Getting independent experience in concert or gig promotion on a smaller scale is not particularly hard, especially at a local level. Small venues are often open to the idea of a well promoted gig night that will draw a good crowd – especially on quieter nights in the week when it is harder to fill the venue. Smaller venues with lower capacities can often provide successful gig nights; a small venue with a capacity of fifty people, when full, may hold a rewarding experience. Promoter, artists and audience will all benefit from the atmosphere in a small venue full to capacity, rather than fifty people present in a large, spacious venue; in this scenario, the concert promoter has only sold fifty tickets to experience success. Applying a commercial theoretical strategy, such as 'the four Ps', may assist in planning – exploring potential through Product, Place, Price and Promotion. Using this method will help the independent concert promoter assess the feasibility of the event in the initial phase (see Chapter 11 for more on the four Ps). Staging the correct act, hiring the correct venue and pitching tickets at the correct price for audience should be the primary concerns. Applying the four Ps concept to a larger event, we could exemplify the following scenario: if international rock act Green Day were staged at the 20,000 audience capacity O2 Arena in London, with tickets priced at £40, a potential sell-out will return ticket sales at £800,000. Add merchandise and CD sales to this as by-product income from audience and an estimated £20,000 could be added to the financial returns. However, the costs to stage such an event in hiring a large venue with all necessary technical requirements, paying all staff associated with it and paying the concert promoters share, often leaves a profit margin lower than expected. Keeping the same event in one place for several nights is more likely to return a healthier profit due to no costs associated with the logistical touring movement of the show. Larger scale shows involving greater investment in venue and act may return larger profits, but the risks of low audience attendance give rise to much larger potential losses. Often tours are cancelled when tickets simply do not sell quite enough. It is easier to 'bail out' than continue with a failing business venture – although often there are contracted 'cancellation penalties' applied when larger, fully professional concert tours are called off.

Expanding concert promotions

If large concert promotions companies became the new recording companies of the future, it is assumed that they would need a similar business infrastructure to that of established music labels. This would include having A&R departments to consider new talent acquisitions and so forth. At time of writing, Live Nation is the major exponent of the 'concert promoter as music label' business model. Artists who wish to approach concert promoters to further their careers should look to secure a reputable concert agent first, who could then try to get the act on to a good concert bill. After the act has proven its live abilities and further built reputation, it would then be the agent who could deal with the concert promoter to forge further opportunities. In order to grow its artist liaison and acquisition, Live Nation, as noted above, formed a new division called Artist Nation; in 2008 United Business Media commented on Artist Nation's activity:

> Artist Nation, headquartered in Miami, Florida, has a streamlined infrastructure in place to execute on these additional revenue streams. In total, Artist Nation currently has over 300 employees around the world and relationships with more than 500 artists. As the Artist Nation division continues to grow, its infrastructure will be supplemented to provide artists with the best service possible while maintaining an efficient cost structure.
>
> (www.prnewswire.com, 2009)

Artist Nation boasts an estimated 500 artist relationships, and its clear intention is to increase revenue streams by challenging the music business models of the past, with a new competitive way of exploiting music – primarily through the 'live' conduit. Although larger concert promoters may threaten to merge the boundaries between live and recorded music by representing artists in 360-degree contracts, they are the exception rather than the rule. At the time of writing, smaller concert promoters in the UK do not have any involvement with selling recorded music or merchandise on behalf of the touring artist at the concerts or beyond in the wider music market.

The Concert Promoters Association

In the UK the Concert Promoters Association (CPA) is a useful organisation for all serious concert promoters and outlines its mission as follows:

> Formed in 1986 by successful promoter Harvey Goldsmith, the Concert Promoters Association has worked to represent and promote the interests of its members and to provide a forum for discussion of issues of concern.
> (concertpromotersassociation.co.uk, 2009)

Campaigning for reasonable ticket prices for audiences, resolving disputes with the Performing Right Society for Music (PRS for Music), ticket touting, lobbying radio, discussions with music associations, event policing and venue licences have all been issues addressed by the CPA. Its forty-nine company members are currently 'established active promoters of concerts, concert tours and events/festivals by contemporary musical artists'.

Joining the CPA may not be appropriate for the smaller gig promoter, but the principles by which the CPA stands will effect smaller promoters down the concert chain. Essentially an organisation such as this is formed with the good intention to provide a voice for its professional members and to monitor the issues and greater politics of the industry that exists around it. The CPA deals with ongoing issues concerning concert promotion and lists the following example in a 'Health and Safety' campaign demonstrating its usefulness:

> Since the inception of the Association, various individual members of the Association have worked tirelessly to achieve benefits for all promoters. Lengthy consultation with the Health and Safety Executive resulted in the 1993 publication of a workable successor to the GLC Pop Code in the form of the Guide to Health, Safety and Welfare at Pop Concerts and Other Outdoor Events.
> (concertpromotersassociation.co.uk, 2009)

A full up-to-date list of UK concert promoters who are members of the CPA can be found on its website.

Seeking work in concert promotions and event management

Live Nation is one of the world's largest concert promoters and offers internships for appropriate individuals who would wish to enter the profession. AEG is also a large worldwide concert promotions company, alongside SJM Concerts and

Metropolis Music who are two of the largest concert promotions companies in the UK. Following this are many smaller concert promotions agents ranging from sole trader entities to companies that may employ only a few people, contracting affairs to other concert services. If seeking employment with a UK concert promoter, the CPA website is a good place to research its company members: www.concert promotersassociation.co.uk.

The Association of Independent Festivals

Another useful association that can supply information for organisers of festivals in the UK is the Association of Independent Festivals (AIF). AIF was formed in the UK by Ben Turner of Graphite Media and Rob Da Bank (developer of UK festival concept, Bestival) and states its primary function:

> The Association of Independent Festivals is a non-profit trade association created to represent UK independent music festivals. The aim is to help the businesses of our individual members, and help the needs of the independent festival sector.
>
> (www.aiforg.com, 2009)

AIF promotes the business of UK festivals and aims to enhance the audience experience through sharing information provided by its members. The AIF website outlines its further obligations and provides a member 'map', which is useful in researching the key outdoor UK festivals that occur primarily between May and September each year.

Legal aspects and the concert promoter

The professional concert promoter will have many legal aspects to consider and will need to employ a lawyer to ensure agreements and avoid litigation wherever possible. The lawyer will ensure commercial and public liability insurance is in place and will oversee contractual financial agreements with the artist, agent and venue. The concert promoter is involved in a great deal of risk and the expense of preventing such risk is a costly process. The CPA advises that any persons wishing to enter concert promotion should look for work experience opportunities and 'learn the ropes' first. In summary, the essential duties of the concert promoter include:

- liaison with the concert artist agency in the setting up of the concert or tour
- negotiation of fees between concert agency (representing the act) and concert promoter
- finding and hiring suitable venues for the concert
- assessing the costs of hiring the venue and any linked venue publicity

- hiring suitable venues and paying the 'venue deposit' to secure the concert dates
- addressing 'public liability' insurance fees
- addressing 'act non-appearance' insurance fees
- researching the current market value of concert tickets
- providing a 'cash flow' prediction for potential ticket sales
- providing an account of all necessary expenses to stage the concert
- funding additional promotion in association with the venue and concert dates
- paying any Value Added Tax in association with the concert
- paying performance royalties to PRS for Music (if in UK territory) in association with music used in the performances.

The CPA advises that a concert promotions business can carry a great deal of risk, and often the profit margins that they work to are very slim. Touring contracts entered into with major artists are often negotiated as 90/10 or even a 95/05 per cent split – with the larger share in this due to the artist and their management. This example highlights that with such tight profit margins the concert promoter really needs to guarantee that the tour will actually work logistically and financially. This demonstrates why concert promoters want to work with known quantities; artists that can simply 'sell out' in any given venue.

THE TOUR MANAGER

The primary role of the tour manager is to control logistical operations 'on the road' and to ensure the smooth running of the tour. The tour manager must be personable and a good communicator, as this multifaceted role provides the first point of contact between the artist and supporting road crew. This is coupled with the needs of the act while on tour, which can often add complexity. Common duties for the concert tour manager include:

- Ensuring artists and musicians have a daily 'tour schedule'. The schedule will include transport details to ensure all personnel are delivered to the venue and transported to hotels at the correct times.
- Addressing catering needs for the artists and crew and ensuring that artist 'riders' are adhered to. 'Riders' appear in artist contracts and often include additional hospitality packages for artists, such as certain dietary or beverage requirements.
- Scheduling rest for artists and crew in association with the tour schedule.
- Monitoring tour finances and keeping records of logistical expenditure on the road.

- Providing a central point of liaison between promoters, stage designers, venue managers and ticket agents.

- Ensuring organised meetings with public relations and media in support of promotion of the tour takes place with the artist.

- On smaller tours, collection of box office monies will become the responsibility of the tour manager, so good accounting and record-keeping skills will be required.

- If the tour leaves the country, the tour manager will liaise with travel agents and ensure the act and all tour personnel arrive at airports on time; the road crew also must arrive in time to meet the scheduled concert, if transported by another means.

Immediately, it can be seen that anyone wishing to consider this role as a profession will need to be highly flexible with good organisational skills. The tour manager must be a skilled negotiator as they oversee and address the daily issues that occur on the road between all parties. Due to this, the tour manager will often work longer hours than any other personnel on the tour and must be contactable at all times. Many tour managers have worked their way into the profession gradually through a variety of routes working elsewhere in the sector. At times this role may be highly stressful, as music artist personalities may not always be the easiest to deal with; the work is often tiring, tedious and physically demanding in realisation of the show. Dealing with personal issues may require the ability to counsel and persuade those with problems to do their best at low moments on the road. The tour manager is an experienced person; it would be rare to find a young individual in major tour management, unless in an assistant role, which may be common in the larger tour scenario. Professional concert tour managers earn their posts by being 'tried and trusted', having worked for the artist's management previously; this is not an occupation that can be entered into without prior experience of handling acts on tour.

When considering the potential salary, young tour managers may work for very little initially and purely work for expenses while learning their trade; an established freelance concert tour manager on a major tour with a solid reputation will earn good rates of pay. Artist managers, record companies and concert agents may all source and subsequently employ a tour manager when required, or certainly recommend a known, reliable person for the role. In seeking a route into tour management, it is worthwhile researching a variety of music companies that would typically employ concert tour managers; these could be record companies or concert promoters. Typically, as in many music industry roles, they are not advertised, so sourcing a suitable apprenticeship opportunity in the role would be necessary. Getting experience working in a good-sized city concert venue would permit closer observation of the tour manager and what the role entails when a tour visits; getting close to the role may lead to valuable information and making the right contacts. However, working on any tour will provide an insight into the world of touring even if starting on a very small level assisting a band. Travelling across the country to just a few towns or cities will provide enough experience to demonstrate the key principles involved.

Tour managing is all about being assertive and not being afraid to be so; also, the tour manager may not get a night 'off' when on tour, as there is so much ongoing organisation. When things go wrong, the tour manager will need to know and be there to assist in solving the problem. Although tour managing is a very active and varied occupation, the enormity of it will largely be decided by the size of the tour and the number of personnel employed on it. On occasion, it may actually be the artist's personal manager who adopts this role; on small-scale tours, this is more than likely to be the case.

THE 'CONCERT-GOING' EXPERIENCE

As music events have grown in the UK in recent years, so has the ability of stage production 'creatives' to increase the spectacle of 'the show'. In today's concert ticket market, do audiences actually demand a bigger, better, more colourful atmospheric show when they purchase a ticket through the box office? Music futurists David Kusek and Gerd Leonhard argue that audiences do not pay for their seat, but merely pay for their concert experience (2005:114–117). Yet audiences actually ask few questions at the box office other than where the best seats are, and how much will they cost. As audiences are drawn to the brand name of the act, or sometimes the sales concept behind the show, it is difficult for any audience to ascertain exactly what they will get for their money beforehand. Buying access to a show is an 'unknown', unlike tangible goods that one can obviously view and inspect in a shop – in the case of the live show, it is often a poster or advertisement that tells the audience that the event is due to take place. Websites such as YouTube may help a little in advance, visually informing audience about performance capabilities. As most known acts have video clips and footage of their live performances uploaded to YouTube, a taster is provided for those interested to see and hear the band play live. Many audiences purely trust that the 'headliners' associated with the concert will deliver value for money based on reputation. If audiences estimated that the sound would be poor; the seating or standing arrangements inadequate; the viewing of the act difficult to see; the close proximity of other people uncomfortable; the air quality poor; and limited lighting and special visual effects lacking – would they still buy a ticket to see the band? The answer is that fans buy tickets in advance without any real knowledge of possible factors that may dampen their experiences. If audiences experience some of these negative aspects and perhaps do not enjoy the concert as much as expected – it is rare for audiences to complain and demand a refund, except in the case of non-appearance by the artists themselves. This phenomenon would not always occur in a retail situation where hard goods are purchased; perhaps there is an understanding by audiences that these factors may be commonplace in some concerts, therefore a 'forgiveness' level exists in the audience. Many just want to see their favourite act perform – purchasing audiences and fans in all situations have a pre-engaged 'trust' when buying concert tickets. Where concert promoters and stage production managers invest less in the 'show' there could be greater profits available, and conversely, in a large stage show, there are fewer profits available to the concert promoters. It would appear that a good live show or musical 'spectacle' attracts greater audiences in the long term, however, largely through show reputation; audiences 'talk'. Audiences attending impressive shows will tell their friends, peers and colleagues – both verbally and through social media on sites such as Facebook, perpetuating the reputation of the act far and wide. This human communication phenomenon known as 'viral marketing' is an important tool; all financially associated with the act respect its value, so the concert going experience cannot be neglected. Consider in addition the revenue streams produced by sales of DVD recordings of the live performance and it would therefore be hugely beneficial to produce the largest music spectacle, wherever appropriate and where budgets allow. Due to this, the role of the concert production manager has become increasingly important in devising the modern-day music show.

CONCEPTUALISING THE EVENT

Smaller gigs that take place in pubs, bars or other smaller capacity venues with an approximate audience capacity of up to 50 persons would not generally require a large stage production. A simple lighting rig would suffice and the act would normally supply their own PA (public address) speaker system and perhaps lighting, though the venue may have this equipment already 'in-house'. Additional items to promote the band, such as using a 'back-drop' with the band name emblazoned on it, may be useful, especially for the unknown band. Largely, this type of gig or performance may not have a door entry fee and the act may play for very little, if anything at all. A large stage show is not expected with such a low budget and the act performance should supply all that is needed in this scenario.

However, there are no set rules to prohibit a band from exploiting their situation to full effect. 'Conceptualising' a smaller music night or event is a relatively easy exercise; it requires very little financial investment and essentially relies on one main ingredient – a good idea. This notion is production management on a small scale; learning to entice and excite an audience visually. Placing a strong sense of value in the minds of an audience becomes an 'imperative', and if the promotion and timing of this goes well, curiosity will encourage improved chances of audience attendance. Conceptualising requires developing a theme around the event; this may start with the simple creation of a unique title for it. There are many music events that occur in most cities on a Saturday night, so making an event more special than the others will set the event apart from the competition. Attracting audiences using a strong theme and by being both different and attractive is a precursor to success.

Production managing an event on a large scale is similar in nature to that of production managing on a small scale. The obvious difference is the budget, increased financial risk and the experience required to manage a large-scale production. Where the venue is larger, there are many more production items to consider, such as large screens to relay images to the audience situated further back in the venue. A larger concert public address sound system and sound re-enforcement requirements are needed alongside more special visual effects and image or video projection. Often pyrotechnics, stage backdrops and curtains, costume design and sometimes dancers and choreographers are used in pop music shows. The organisation and subcontracting of these services will become the job of the production manager. Some of these creative specifics may be requested by the act themselves, the artist management or record company as directed. In many cases, the production manager may not make creative decisions but will recruit services as directed by whoever requests them for the show. In the case of major touring rock artists such as the Rolling Stones, they may request using their own production team on tour and pay them from their own budget, rather than allowing the concert promoter to source the production manager independently. This example demonstrates how various structures in the live music business sector may be subverted at the request of the artists themselves, the artist's management company or the artist's contracted music label. Good event conceptualising can produce a concert that audiences will find visually and sonically stimulating; but when larger, ambitious creative ideas can be financed, the production manager can deliver a show that provides a more memorable experience that will encourage returning audiences.

THE PRODUCTION MANAGER

While the tour manager handles on-the-road logistics, the production manager will handle creative 'on stage' logistics concerning the show itself. To learn production management, it would be advisable to gain experience in a production discipline. Production opportunities exist through many UK education courses and there are many ways to build live production experience at a local level in small venues, working with local artists. Larger production management companies often do not survive by working on music shows alone; many of these companies survive producing corporate events and other shows. A production manager's job is to create atmosphere first and foremost and create an event that audiences will find memorable and will want to discuss with those around them. Creating the right setting can vastly improve the performance given by the music artist and can create atmospheric interaction with the audience. Technology has greatly improved visual matters for audiences; the introduction of digitally controlled LED lighting systems and screens has revolutionised the 'live visual' experience for audiences. Compare this with lighting technologies of the 1970s concert and the visual improvements are many. In the 1970s and 1980s it was commonplace to see arrays of heat-producing parabolic aluminised reflector (PAR) cans hung from scaffolding and a simple black curtain backdrop with the band name and logo. An early example of this basic concert set up is demonstrated in Led Zeppelin's 1976 film release *The Song Remains the Same* – live footage taken from their 1973 dates playing at Madison Square Garden in New York also saw the early use of lasers as part of the light show spectacular. Prior to the seventies era, the technology was even more limited, with pure reliance on the performance of the artist. A modest lighting rig can be seen in YouTube footage featuring The Beatles, 15 August 1965, playing at Shea Stadium in the US or Jimi Hendrix playing at the Woodstock Festival in the US in 1969. To create onstage spectacle certain rock acts would use 'thunder flashes', pyrotechnics and large 'inflatables'. In the case of metal outfit Motörhead's 1980 'Bomber' tour, a large 30-foot inflatable aeroplane was hung out above the audience. A variety of dry-ice, smoke, flame effects or laser lighting could also be seen in many concerts from the 1980s onwards. These additions to the show would get audiences talking; fans would buy further tickets to witness these shows again. Creating and boosting this interest is the responsibility of the concert stage production manager, ensuring that night after night these creative effects and additions will work in the right way and precisely at the right moment.

Digital lighting panels and video effects are used more so in today's live show spectacle. Health and safety directives have changed vastly since the 1960s and 1970s; larger scale music performances attract 'risk assessment' procedures that have become a necessity for many stage production managers. Often they will employ production and engineering staff who are registered and trained by the International Powered Access Federation (IPAF), an organisation set up in 1983 that 'promotes the safe and effective use of powered access worldwide' (IPAF, 2009). The work of the IPAF is an essential part of assembling the large stage show today, particularly in the case of festivals with large outdoor stages.

The Music Managers Forum

Managers working in the live music industry sector can join the Music Managers Forum (MMF). Further discussion and detail on this association, affiliated to the IMMF (International Music Managers Forum) can be found in Chapter 7.

THE CONCERT AGENT

The role of the concert agent lies between the live performance affairs of the artist and the concert promoter. Smaller scale agents can acquire gigs for acts playing pubs, clubs and smaller venues, while bigger agents negotiate fees for large concert tours with the concert promoter. Artists are not usually signed to an agent exclusively for a lifetime of performances, but agreements will exist for one-off dates or a series of concert dates. Smaller agents expect anything from 10–15 per cent commission of the total agreed gig fee for securing a gig date for the act. The act pays commission to the agent after the gig has taken place, unless the agent has been paid directly by the venue; in that case, the agent will then deduct commission and forward payment to the artist. Concert agents negotiating on behalf of artists playing on a larger scale can expect commission rates of 10–20 per cent for fixing the best rates with the concert promoter. It is advisable for bands and artists to search for and appoint a reputable agent to secure performances in venues of a higher calibre. Sometimes agents can secure a lucrative support slot for a new act, if it has a good reputation and fan base. In searching for an appropriate agent in the UK artists should research The Agents Association of Great Britain (AAGB) website, which documents a list of its members online. It should also be noted that agents will work in association with the artist's personal management company when arranging matters with the concert promoter. Artists should consider the benefits of having personal management representation that can act on their behalf and appoint a concert agent, remembering that the concert agent only negotiates the live performance contract with the concert promoter. Artists with larger reputations can demand fees in advance, and these would be negotiated by the agent. Contracts are subsequently issued covering cancellation fees in case a concert promoter may renege on obligations. There are agents of all sizes, appropriate to the needs of acts and their commercial reputation. Professional concert agents have ongoing relationships with concert promoters and festival bookers; new acts should seek an appropriate agent, if looking to play a variety of stages.

The Agents Association

The organisation that represents the affairs of agents in the UK is the AAGB. Formed in 1927 it exists to promote the interests of agent members, protecting their welfare. Further aims are:

> . . . to induce unity of action; to prevent abuses by all reasonable means; to promote and maintain a friendly, professional and harmonious relationship between fellow members and with musicians, artistes, other performers and all buyers of talent and entertainment services.
>
> (www.agents-uk.com, 2009)

A comprehensive list of the obligations that The Agents Association continues to administer on behalf of its many UK members is listed on its website. The AAGB has approximately 400 members and lists contact details of its members online. This is a good source for those artists researching agency representation in the UK and a place to gain a greater understanding of the work carried out by the artist agent.

EVENT PUBLICITY, PROMOTION AND PUBLIC RELATIONS IN LIVE ENTERTAINMENT

When concert dates have been secured by an agent and the concert promoter is ready to stage the events, effective event publicity, promotion and PR must be employed. It is worth considering the distinct types of promotion and publicity appropriate to the live staged event, other than services associated with recorded music promotion. Event publicity, promotion and PR must be planned in advance long before the live event is due to take place, to allow maximum lead time on ticket sales. Publicity is often generated by those with an interest in the act – the record company, the venue, the concert promoter and the agent. A public relations officer is often nominated for larger events, who will co-ordinate the press and promotion effort in respect of the performance. Professional promotion in respect of the live event usually includes a range of strategies such as the following:

- flyers
- banners
- posters
- social media networking
- invitations
- mail-outs
- e-marketing
- personal appearances by the artist in the region of the upcoming show
- media interviews with press and radio.

Lists of further appropriate media 'hit lists' are prepared in the pursuit of key journalists in appropriate newspapers and periodicals, venue and tourist brochures, 'gig guides' and listings. Press releases are distributed to media in order to maximise audience awareness of the event. Advertising the event through broadcast media will have the biggest impact but is the most expensive form of promotion. In the build up to an event, 'street teams' are often deployed to distribute publicity and event information legally. A fine may be imposed against the concert promoter if a street team acts illegally by 'fly-posting' in city centres and causing litter; an invoice may also be issued by the local council, due to the clean-up operation. Data protection and possible defamatory remarks or slogans are also items for consideration when creating and distributing publicity material.

Getting the timing right in the run up to the event will be a key feature of any event publicity campaign – not 'peaking' too early, or getting notice out to potential audiences too late. Good publicity will be meticulously planned and should never be overlooked: if audiences are not aware of the forthcoming event, they will simply not be there; a comprehensive publicity campaign is an essential budget consideration when staging any live music event.

SOUND RE-ENFORCEMENT

Live sound engineer, front-of-house

The 'front-of-house' (FOH) sound engineer mixes sound while facing the act on stage. Largely, the FOH mixer and personnel are situated in the audience, midway towards the back of the venue. Stage microphones around the performers are plugged into a multi-socket stage box, signals are fed to the FOH mixer through a multi-core or 'snake'. The mixed signals are amplified and routed through the large speaker stacks and arrays that are placed either side of the stage. The act should be visible in front of the live sound engineer – in order to assess the panning of the stereo sound field left and right and to attain the correct audible fader volume balance of each onstage microphone. Often, several live sound engineers may be present at larger music events, which require more 'mixing' – such as an outdoor festival with a number of major acts on the event roster. Each act may provide its own personal sound engineer, as that specific engineer will have worked with the band in the past and knows the sound requirements. They know the band set list, live mix changes and specific dynamics in association with the certain songs. It is commonplace for an act playing in front of a live audience to feel nervous before

FIGURE 3.1
Sound engineers working front-of-house at Hyde Park, London. Photo courtesy Dave Robinson, *PSNE*.

a performance, regardless of how musically capable the act may be. A trusted live sound engineer will assist the performer in attaining the best possible sound; this assistance improves confidence for the performer. Getting to know what the performer prefers and 'feels' from the sound on stage requires skill, training and experience. Many professional sound engineers working with established bands have been working with them from their early days. Canadian rock outfit Nickelback have retained road crew that were with them from the outset; the 'roadies' know the band's touring requirements well and vice-versa. Artists often just want to stick with the roadies that know them best, sound-wise, technically and socially. This model would suggest a good starting point for anyone wishing to become a live sound engineer. Making contact with a suitable local band that needs a live sound engineer provides the opportunity to learn the live sound craft, alongside getting to know a band, how it functions and what the sound requirement is on stage.

The life of a professional touring sound engineer entails working many long hours, often arriving at the venue early in the morning for setting up. 'Sound-check' duties are usually undertaken prior to the performance in the afternoon, then engineering the front-of-house mix for the evening's live performance duration. Assisting in the dismantling of equipment after the performance will constitute a late finish. The journey to the next venue often will occur overnight, ready to start setting up again early the next day at 9 a.m. in the following venue. Taking a tour on the road is a very costly business, and usually gaps between venue dates are kept small by the concert promoter in order to keep tour running costs and wages down. It is not unusual for a sound engineer to be away from home for many months when on a large world tour with a major musical act. There is a distinct occupational difference here between the nature of live sound for touring rock bands and live sound for live shows and musicals. Musicals are often static, placed in one theatre location for many nights, so a resident sound engineer based in a London theatre need not endure such arduous travelling. The musical theatre show may prove an interesting challenge for some sound engineers, often with many more onstage microphones worn by a multitude of singers and dancers. Couple this with a large 'pit- orchestra' and there is a large amount of sound to be controlled and sonically treated. The live sound engineer may also be involved in technician duties where electrical problems occur in the sound system. An ability to trace and establish wiring faults and electrical connection problems will fall into the lap of the sound engineer. Faults that occur at the last minute may unsettle those without the ability and confidence to trace them quickly, so the live environment can be a very pressured and stressful one when equipment stops working.

The nature of this occupation will always dictate that wherever the show goes, the live sound engineer must follow. There are roadies who welcome the irregularity of the hours and duties offered by this occupation and to be associated with the performance of music in its most natural form – live. Those wishing to get into this profession can start at grassroots level and aim to understand the intricacies of live sound and what is required by working with local artists and performers first. It is important to build confidence using larger mixing consoles and attain greater sound skills and understanding. Getting in contact with both small and large sound hire companies that supply concert sound re-enforcement touring rigs and seeking work experience is a good first step. Prospective sound engineers should also research venues and find out from venue managers how sound is provided therein. Smaller venues may have just one sound engineer who covers front-of-house duties, microphone placement, onstage engineering, sound monitor engineering and maintenance duties. Some sound engineers build up their own PA system from scratch and learn their craft using it; when confident they then hire their rig and sound services to local venues and artists. If successful, the business can build into a much larger concern; this is how most large, established PA companies started out.

It is also worth considering audio for live broadcast through the television medium, as many sound engineers who work in television and post-production may have involvement with mixing live music, depending on their department. Live broadcast audio is another area for prospective job role investigation, through independent TV production companies or the BBC, who employ sound specialists and technicians.

There are many courses in the UK that teach sound in both technical and creative ways, yet there is no set way into the live sound engineer occupation. Both artists and live sound hire companies with good commercial reputations are unlikely to allow a novice to take control of their live sound equipment, so the ability to understand and manage the live sound environment confidently would be an essential pre-requisite for employment. Carefully building experience, knowledge and interpersonal skills from the ground up are also necessary attributes for the live sound engineer.

Monitor engineer

Generally, a dedicated monitor engineer will only be required for larger live music performances and sound stage set ups. The monitor engineer will usually reside to the side of the stage and controls the audible onstage mix for the act known as 'fold-back', as the sound is 'folded back' to the band. This amplified mix will differ from the FOH mix, as the audience does not hear the monitor mix. A separate onstage speaker system usually consisting of 'wedges', cabinets and bass bins, which has its own independent amplification system, provides a mix for the onstage performers. The mix requested by onstage performers is often 'dry', having little reverb or echo applied to the sound, unlike the FOH mix. In more recent years, 'in ear' monitoring systems have been developed, reducing the need for larger speaker systems on the stage areas. This 'headphone style' monitoring is sometimes preferred, while many other performers still prefer a speaker on the stage beside them. On a large stage, performers are often some distance from each other and need to hear and 'feel' the music clearly, hence why a monitor mix is fed back to the performers onstage. The monitor engineer will control the mix sent to the performers on stage; as some artists work at higher volumes on larger stages, the monitor engineer is an essential component in assisting the performance of the act. As the monitor engineer is required for larger shows, the same attributes are required as in the FOH engineer role. When a monitor engineer gains a good reputation for their work, they may be requested by the same band for many more tours. The monitor engineer should have a good understanding of the performer's sonic requirements and must be prepared to empathise with the needs of each individual performer on stage.

ROADIES: ROAD CREW ASSISTANTS

The 'roadies' or road crew that assists in setting up the live performance and show have many varied duties. The term 'roadie' may include all those on the road, such as the tour manager and technical crew, but sometimes the term is reserved for the road crew assistants. Many of the roadie's jobs involve heavy physical work, starting with collecting and loading flight-cased equipment from the PA hire company on to the trucks that will transport the show. Although venues are used to receiving large quantities of equipment from shows on a daily basis, often access can be limited and the venue stage ramps are steep. Support crew usually have to wait until the venue opens on the morning of arrival before offloading all band instruments, PA and lighting. Setting up the equipment can be precarious – climbing ladders, assembling scaffold, hanging arrays of PA speakers and setting the stage. Assisting the sound engineers to position equipment and setting up backline and instruments for the band are also necessary duties of the support crew. The roadies often have the longest hours to endure; from early morning 'load in' to the venue, working most of the day setting up the show – to the eventual dismantling, flight case packing, stowing and reloading back into the transport late at night. Road crew may also be required to drive large articulated vehicles and will require an HGV licence in order to do so. Having a practical aptitude and physical fitness is required in this role; in many circumstances also a 'head for heights' and good knowledge of Health and Safety legislation are required. Some venues will draft in local road crew assistants and helpers where extra persons are needed at 'load-in' and 'load-out' to get equipment on and off stage more quickly. Local agencies supply this additional freelance crew; researching local venues and finding out crewing requirements from the venue manager will reveal possible employment routes into this line of work. Getting in touch with PA hire companies and concert logistic companies listed in magazines such as *Pro Sound News Europe* will also provide information. Websites such as www.roadie.net will provide a more collective social insight into the life of the roadie and possible online networking opportunities.

INSTRUMENT TECHNICIAN

The instrument technicians, who may be known individually as guitar techs, bass techs, drum techs or computer techs, are responsible for the setting up of individual band member instruments. Further to that, instrument technicians maintain the instruments, changing strings, rectifying amplifier problems or changing drum heads as required and ensuring the equipment will prove to be reliable on stage. At the sound-check, the same technicians may test the instruments as amplified through the full sound system, to establish levels for FOH and monitor mixes prior to the arrival of the performers. Instrument technicians are often accomplished musicians themselves, with the technical know-how to maintain instruments or computer technology confidently on the road. Instrument technicians are used on larger tours; while on smaller tours instrument technicians double in other roles, helping with load in/out and other road crew duties. Professional instrument technicians may be known to the performer personally prior to the band being a large touring concern, or sometimes the work has materialised through the hire company that provides instruments for the tour. Pursuing such an occupation would require a greater knowledge of the tour requirements of instruments and getting in contact with tour management companies to establish the needs of individual performers and how the road crew supports network functions.

C@SE STUDY

THE LIVE SOUND INDUSTRY – A VIEW

Dave Robinson, *Pro Sound News Europe*

Dave Robinson has been editor of Pro Sound News Europe, *the leading news-based monthly title for the entire European audio industry, for ten years. Before that he was deputy editor on* Future Music *magazine. In this section Dave comments on the health of the live sound industry as a result of focused specialist research carried out by* PSNE *and, in addition, highlights issues facing the sector.*

There was an understandable cloud of uncertainty concerning the short-to-midterm future of the live sound industry in the summer of 2009. But a year later, those in the business, be they venues, manufacturers or PA companies, had regained their fire and their spirit. According to a research study undertaken by *PSNLive – Pro Sound News Europe*'s annual in-depth report into the live sound market 2010 – the upbeat mood became particularly apparent among audio manufacturers, with nearly 90 per cent of participants who expected their sales to increase during the rest of 2010. The very healthy average growth forecast of 19 per cent (plus) confirmed the resilience of audio manufacturers, who continued to bring significant new products and technologies to the live market despite the wider global turmoil.

Companies such as DiGiCo, Soundcraft, Avid and Midas continued to refine digital mixing desk technologies – once a rarity, now pretty much de rigueur on a major tour. Meanwhile, the likes of Audinate, Harman, Riedel and Optocore are continuing to develop networking protocols that reduce 'fat' multi-core cables of old to a few thin strands of copper or fibre. Manufacturers were also further encouraged in their endeavours by *PSNLive*'s rental company overview in the survey, which found a near 10 per cent shift in favour of expenditure on stock expansion following the emphasis on consolidation that characterised the mood of 2009. Once again, the overall outlook became more positive with 56 per cent of companies predicting an increase in the overall value of their work through 2010.

An identical percentage of live sound engineers expected their workload to increase in 2010, although that part of the survey was more notable for its evidence of a willingness to incorporate the latest technologies into event workflows. For example, over 60 per cent of live sound engineers considered themselves to be very up-to-date with technological developments in audio, while 67 per cent thought that networking would have a significant impact on their day-to-day working lives in the next decade. No part of the survey was without its caveats, of course, and these were arguably most apparent in the venues section. While the largest single share of participants (45 per cent) expected their live music income to increase in 2010, there were concerns about pricing structures and rising ticket prices. Britain's live music sector, argued *PSNLive*'s sister title *Music Week*, 'was bracing itself for a downturn in the market for 2010'. Trade publication *Pollstar* had reported US headline acts' revenues for the first half of 2010 down nearly $200 million (€150 million), while the biggest promoter, Live Nation, talked about a 12–15 per cent drop in sales. But there was little sign of a corresponding slowdown in Europe in the future. 'We've just had one of our busiest Septembers', the MD of one of the UK's largest PA companies was quoted. While he saw fewer stadium shows – 'and the fact is, there aren't that many acts who can fill a stadium these days' – he reported 'lots of smaller business, with a huge number of acts doing smaller venues'.

Another audio managing director – while noting that trading circumstances were harder at the beginning of 2010 – wondered whether there was an element of the audio press trying to manufacture news. 'We're busier than ever with both stadium and arena gigs', said the head of sound at another rental house. But there's a change in perception. Back when tours were a promotional expense aimed at selling albums, record companies would spend money to get the best, and expect top prices. Now the gig *is* the money-making opportunity and record companies

C@SE STUDY

C@SE STUDY

want to make as much as possible, meaning that the touring costs are seen as having a bottom line impact rather than being viewed as an advertising cost. That puts pressure on suppliers. There are also warning signs. Perhaps the downturn in traditional record sales has forced acts on to the road and makes them over-exposed. Promoter Live Nation has reportedly told artists and agents 'the big, upfront paydays of the past are over . . . we're not going to pay you that much because we don't feel we can sell enough tickets at that amount'. Inevitably, touring costs will be targeted as the acts try to make up the shortfall.

Less profit margin in the future, perhaps, but probably no less work – if acts can't sell records, they have to tour. The O2 Arena, the world's most successful venue, boldly predicted 'a stellar year' for its immediate future.

SUPPORT SERVICES TO THE LIVE MUSIC INDUSTRY

There are many other services that work to support the logistics of the live music industry sector; these services may work within the venue or be subcontracted, depending on the production, venue or touring concert scenario. Many of these roles fall on the peripheries of the music industry and, arguably, are not an integral part of the live music industry, but they provide essential structure and services to it. The rest of this chapter highlights some of these roles.

Security and policing at live music events

Security and marshalling is a huge part of many festival operations, ensuring public safety and monitoring ticketing, access and boundary control. Professional event security personnel are trained in crowd control, venue information, licensing, health and safety, first aid and many other diplomatic means of dealing with the general public. The association that exists in support of licensing security affairs is the Security Industry Authority (SIA). Information directly from the SIA states:

> The SIA manages the licensing of the private security industry as set out in the Private Security Industry Act 2001. We also aim to raise standards of professionalism and skills within the private security industry and to promote and spread best practice.
>
> (www.the-sia.org.uk, 2009)

In the UK the SIA works to improve standards in concert security; some may consider this a good area in which to attain experience by observing logistics in the staging of larger events. Approaching concert security companies or security agencies may prove worthwhile as they may employ many more staff around the event than actual production and road crew in connection with the performance. Seeing large events firsthand will provide valuable experience; networking in person and learning how the venue and event is policed will provide valuable information concerning concert logistics and managing audiences. It is worth noting that there are many listed concert security companies working 'behind the scenes' in a supporting role; knowledge of marshalling and security at large events would be an essential requirement for the budding concert promoter.

Merchandise, catering and trading at music events

Merchandise has become an increasing feature at concert events whereby the opportunity to make extra money is maximised when a large audience is present. When audiences are enthused by an event, in all probability there will be a certain percentage of fans or gig-goers that will by product on offer. Profits are increased when there are a suitable range of goods on offer, such as CDs, T-shirts, and clothing with other branded merchandise and memorabilia. Ensuring that the right amount of stock is available at the right time is crucial to successful merchandising; producing too much stock could see the merchandiser seriously out of pocket. In today's world of 360-degree music contracts, the artist's merchandise and subsequent profits are often administered by the music company to which the artist is signed. On a small, independent scale it is relatively easy for artists to produce their own merchandise, duplicating low numbers of CDs for instance that can be sold at gigs to enhance income. Merchandise should also be made available from the artist website, so that suitably impressed fans can purchase memorabilia after the event. It is important to design merchandise that promotes the artist brand, but also be of good enough quality and visual aesthetic to entice audiences to buy. At large music festivals merchandise and goods are sold in large number to the captive audiences in attendance; today there is a greater awareness of the trading potential associated with music fans at events and their penchant for clothing. As revenues have decreased in the sale of recorded products through the 2000s, artists and their labels have looked to merchandising to make up the shortfall in profits, particularly at concerts.

Catering and trading

Where large audiences gather, there is often a legal requirement to feed and water them. Providing sufficient food and beverages is another valid requirement in connection with the live event, and there are businesses that profit from this in the live sector. Many venues have their own food and beverage managers. The catering role may fall once again on the peripheries of expectation in the music industry but once again may facilitate a valuable experience for those interested in it. Event catering will often mean very long hours from taking delivery of supplies early in the morning, preparing food and serving most of the day, usually into the small hours of the following day. Event catering ranges from simple fast-food to large-scale kitchen systems and dining marquees that are hired into the event. Large kitchen systems will have their own infrastructure with electricians, technicians and health and safety personnel. Once again, on a large scale this will be logistically demanding and will require good management to ensure the food and beverages are delivered on time and that there are enough supplies to service the event customer. UK caterers now recognise the diverse catering needs of the public and offer a much greater range of food choice at larger festival gatherings. There is often a great appreciation for new styles of catering at large events; at Glastonbury Festival in 2009, from over 400 onsite retailers, a caterer won the festival's top accolade:

> Catering supplier 'Hurly Burly' won a Gold Award; for their commitment to serving up healthy fairtrade and organic food to hungry festival-goers from their solar-powered van.
>
> (www.glastonburyfestivals.co.uk, 2009)

This indicates a positive step forward in event catering and that there is a requirement for new ways of thinking about festival catering and food consumption. Although the tried, trusted and humble 'hot dog' van may always have a presence, festival-goers are always on the look out for something different. It should be noted that the commercial kitchen will require licensing to trade in various areas. Late hours catering licences (catering between the hours of 11 p.m. and 5 a.m.) may be required through local councils, and there will be a trading fee applicable for those wishing to trade at large events. Trading fees are determined by the festival organisers or the venue managers, and although the costs to traders of all descriptions may seem large, there is good profit to be made from large numbers festival-goers. Prices for food beverages and other retail goods can be expensive at festivals and events; in contrast, the rental and licence fees payable in order to trade legally may also be very high – the trader only has a small time window in which to recoup the fees and make profit. Although trading and catering at large events may be thought of as very peripheral support role to the live sector, caterers are also contracted to service the needs of crew and artists. The catering and trading industry has a positive connection in servicing the entertainment industry; for some this will afford access to the event arena and provide valuable observation concerning these operations.

Other roles

There are many more peripheral job roles in the live music industry sector that are important to its successful operation. The following occupations may provide new areas for further research:

- ticketing services, external box office and secondary ticketing
- tour travel agents
- tour equipment and personnel transport
- tour coaches (sleepers) and luxury artist travel, driving and chauffeuring
- flight casing and custom equipment packing and electronic support logistics
- technician services
- aircraft charter services
- sound (audio-visual) and lighting hire (wet or dry)
- stage and marquee hire (outdoor and indoor)
- mobile recording studios and audio post-production services
- TV and video recording services with post-production
- costume design and wardrobe
- stage design and event conceptualising
- event publicity design
- pyrotechnics, indoor and outdoor fireworks
- immigration and work permit services
- rehearsal studios for live pre-production.

There may be many individuals who would wish to work in the live music industry sector, but may not see a clear way into it. Many of these posts are not freely advertised, but there are in fact many alternate ways in which to connect with this industry. Being involved in some of the live music industry peripheral job roles and responsibilities may not be the preferred choice of occupation or an ideal career destination for some, but the opportunities afforded by these roles to observe the industry at closer quarters and make valuable career contacts and judgments cannot be overlooked.

REFERENCES AND FURTHER READING
Books

Barrow, T. and Newby, J., *Inside the Music Business* (London: Routledge, 1995), pp. 132–148, 186–195.

Baskerville, D. and Baskerville, T., *Music Business Handbook and Career Guide: Ninth Edition* (London: Sage, 2010), pp. 223–239.

Beattie, W., *The Rock and Roll Times Guide to the Music Industry* (Oxford: Spring Hill, 2007), pp. 194–213.

Britten, A., *Working in the Music Industry: How to Find an Exciting and Varied Career in the World of Music* (Oxford: How to Books, 2004).

Chesnutt, K., *Showcase International Music Book* (London: Showcase Ltd, 2010).

Davis, G. and Jones, R., *Sound Reinforcement Handbook* (New York: Hal Leonard, 1999).

Davis, S. and Laing, D., *The Guerrilla Guide to the Music Business* (New York: Continuum, 2006), pp. 3–141.

Gelfand, M., *Strategies for Success: Self Promotion Secrets for Musicians* (New York: Schirmer, 2005), pp. 123–138.

Gibson, B., *Ultimate Live Sound Operator's Handbook* (Music Pro Guides) (New York: Hal Leonard, 2007).

Hull, P.G., *The Recording Industry: Second Edition* (New York: Routledge, 2004), pp. 97–120.

Kusek, D. and Leonhard, G., *The Future of Music: Manifesto for the Digital Music Revolution* (Boston: Berklee Press, 2005), pp. 114–117.

Lathrop, T., *This Business of Music Marketing and Promotion* (New York: Billboard, 2003), pp. 199–210.

Nunziata, S., *Music Business International* (London: Miller Freeman, 2009).

Passman, D.S., *All You Need to Know About the Music Business*: Sixth Edition (London: Penguin, 2008), pp. 421–463.

Schwartz, D.D., *I Don't Need a Record Deal: Your Survival Guide for the Indie Music Revolution* (New York: Billboard, 2005), pp. 222–288.

Stark, S.S., *Live Sound Reinforcement* (Cengage Educational) (London: Course Technology Inc., 2005).

Summers, J., *Making and Marketing Music* (New York: Allworth, 1999), pp. 103–205.

Talbot, M., *Music Week Directory* (London: Tower, 2010).

White, P., *Basic Live Sound* (London: Sanctuary, 2000).

Periodicals

Music Week. Available at: www.musicweek.com (accessed 18 January 2011).

Pro Sound News Europe. Available at: www.prosoundnewseurope.com (accessed 4 September 2010).

PSNLive. Available at: www.prosoundnewseurope.com/psnlive (accessed 18 January 2011).

Sound On Sound Magazine. Available at: www.soundonsound.com (accessed 4 August 2009).

Associations and organisations (online)

The Agents Association (Great Britain). Available at: www.agents-uk.com/aims.html (accessed 17 August 2010).

Association of Independent Festivals (UK). Available at: www.aiforg.com (accessed 17 August 2010).

Concert Promoters Association Ltd. Available at: www.concert promotersassociation.co.uk/about.aspx (accessed 14 September 2010).

International Powered Access Federation. Available at: www.ipaf.org (accessed 9 September 2010).

Music Managers Forum. Available at: www.themmf.net/showscreen. php?site_id=55&screentype=site&screenid=55 (accessed 17 August 2010).

Security Industry Authority. Available at: www.the-sia.org.uk/home (accessed 8 September 2010).

Online resources

Concert tour personnel travel agents. Available at: www.thedeparturelounge.com
(accessed 10 July 2010).

Glastonbury official site. Available at: www.glastonburyfestivals.co.uk
(accessed 10 September 2010).

Live Nation official site. Available at: www.livenation.co.uk/aboutus
(accessed 10 September 2010).

Pollstar official site. Available at: www.pollstar.com (accessed 10 March 2011).

Roadie news. Available at: www.roadie.net/portal/html/modules/news
(accessed 10 July 2010).

The Beatles play Shea Stadium 1965. Available at:
www.youtube.com/watch?v=_mUXwnEWEnE (accessed 21 July 2009).

The Song Remains the Same (Led Zeppelin concert movie). Available at:
www.youtube.com/watch?v=4KfkC9fmMR0&feature=PlayList&p=D162C0625F
E23EFF&playnext=1&playnext_from=PL&index=17 (accessed 15 August 2010).

Work permits for live performers. Available at: www.tandsimmigration.co.uk
(accessed 16 August 2010).

CHAPTER 4

Music ownership into copyright

Paul Rutter

ADMINISTERING MUSIC

This chapter examines the administration of the musical work, ownership in the song, its inherent copyright and its potential to earn money, in relation to the range of media in which the song may reside. Understanding ownership, intellectual property and copyright are the first steps required in building a foundation of knowledge that will enable music creators, music publishers and music venturists to begin to understand the foundations of music law. Monetisation of 'the song' and its surrounding components can produce global income streams that are often subject to legal issues, as a result of their success. A deeper understanding of these issues provides a basis on which to confidently set up in business and trade as a music business entity.

DEFINING 'THE SONG'

Music creators, composers and songwriters often encounter difficulties when approaching music copyright issues. For music creators, understanding music copyright is at odds with the creative process of music making; musicians, composers and songwriters prefer to get on with the business of having fun with music creation and take less time to understand the mechanics of music law and copyright issues within music. This chapter aims to simplify the divisions within music ownership, which naturally leads into copyright in the musical work. The musical 'work' can be defined using the following criteria, but this is by no means exclusive to all musical works. Examples of the musical work or composition may be defined as follows:

- A solo vocal composition without any accompaniment.

- Music and lyrics combined: A composed musical backing arrangement with vocals sung or spoken.

- A 'top-line' melody: A simple melody played one note at a time on an instrument.

- An instrumental backing track: A musical arrangement produced to accompany other instrumentalists or vocalists.

- A symphony: A large musical piece written with many parts to be played by an orchestra.

Before the music creator considers copyright in the work, it should be considered what type of composition the song actually is and, importantly, exactly who is involved in creating the piece. There have been many examples of past court and litigation cases arguing against who actually wrote the song and its parts, who was it that created the music and what musical copyrights have been infringed. Many lessons can be learned from these previous infringements and advice to music creators would be to address issues of musical ownership at the earliest possible stage. Because ownership has not been addressed at the outset, in the case study examples that will follow, litigation has occurred, often resulting in expensive court and legal costs.

ADDRESSING OWNERSHIP

It would be better to think about ownership in music in very simple terms, looking at common types of popular music creation and how the share should be divided will aid understanding of it. Historically, music royalty collection organisations in the UK such as PRS for Music will expect musical works to be divided in terms of composer, author and arranger; applying this concept to the musical work helps to divide the music ownership share and subsequently understand applied copyright in the musical work.

The singer-songwriter

The solo singer-songwriter who plays acoustic guitar and writes their own songs provides a good example of a 'one-stop' music creation entity. In this regard, the songwriter writes lyrics, strums simple chords and sings over the top of the chords. The lyrics that are written are regarded legally as literary works; the backing chords form a musical arrangement and provide a foundation for the vocal melody that is sung over the backing. This sung vocal melody can be classified as the 'top-line' melody or 'tune'. Other tunes may be invented within the guitar backing also, playing distinct separate notes, but usually it is the vocal melody that carries the

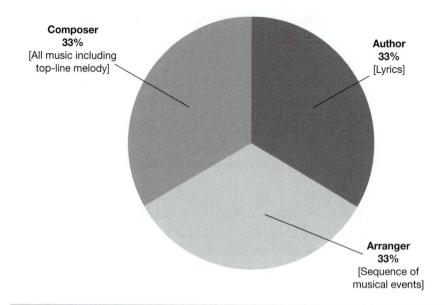

Composer
33%
[All music including
top-line melody]

Author
33%
[Lyrics]

Arranger
33%
[Sequence of
musical events]

FIGURE 4.1
Solo songwriting – potential shares

'tune'. The musical arrangement could further consist of introductions, verses, choruses, middle-eight sections and solo sections. However, in the first example this song is written and constructed by one person, but it can be seen where musical division exists in the work (Figure 4.1).

In the song (Figure 4.1), it is easy to understand this division of musical items. It could be argued that song divisions are set to one third in each responsibility (yet this share is not necessarily 'cast in stone'): composer, author, arranger. If one person writes the song, then it would simply follow that the writer owns 100 per cent in the whole song share and owns 100 per cent of this musical work. If the songwriter is signed to a music publisher, a business percentage of the song would certainly be shared with the publisher, depending on the agreement entered into (in order not to complicate this example, we will assume that the writer here is unpublished). Where the songwriter owns 100 per cent in each part of the musical composition or work, the writer may then decide what to do with their work. If other musical collaborators join and contribute to any of the apportioned areas, then the share may alter according to the level of contribution from the collaborator. For instance, if the lyrics were re-written by another author, the new collaborator could earn a 50 per cent share in the song – as musical works are often split 50/50, composer and author. These anomalies are by no means set in stone, therefore it is up to the collective songwriters to agree how songs will be divided and shared when the song is finalised.

Band and group songwriting

In the case of a song composed by a band, song division can be more complex and has proved to be controversial in the past. If a four-piece band were to compose a song, the song division could look like that seen in Figure 4.2.

Figure 4.2 adds complication for the song in the 'who wrote what' stakes. If a bass player invents a bass line in accompaniment, it could be argued that this becomes a part of the song share, contributing to the song as a composed integral melody; however, the band may disagree. This would also apply to a drummer playing a rhythm part, not being melodic in effect, but an essential part of the arrangement, in order to facilitate the finished song. Other additional musicians may run into similar 'contribution issues' in assembly of the song; all musical contributors would need to argue their case for a share in the newly created musical work. At the 'song creation' stage, artists and groups should crucially consider the level of importance of their musical participation; however, this has often proved not to be the case. Usually, the lead songwriters in a band bring the primary ideas to rehearsal, engaging the band in trying out new ideas in an experimental approach; the remaining band members then contribute. However, the remaining band members are often sidelined in the creative process and are not credited for their part in formation of the song. Legally, the main songwriters can actually claim ownership in the song

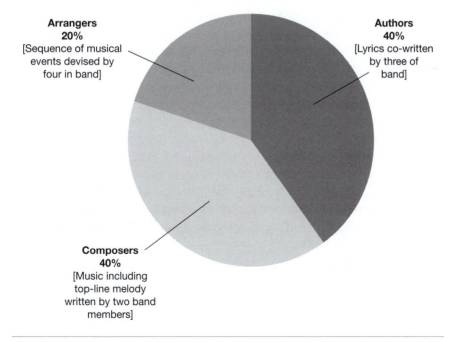

Arrangers
20%
[Sequence of musical events devised by four in band]

Authors
40%
[Lyrics co-written by three of band]

Composers
40%
[Music including top-line melody written by two band members]

FIGURE 4.2
Collaborative band songwriting – potential shares

if the music, chord arrangement and lyrics are created solely by them. Often, the songs are vocalised by a singer in the band who has a distinctive tone and delivery that will help market the song; yet they may be excluded from the songwriting credit and share, if they did not write the lyrics or backing music. However, some bands and groups agree amicably that, where a new song is finalised by the whole band, that an equal share in songwriting will occur. As an example, 1970s rock outfit Deep Purple agreed to equal band shares in some of their early musical works and credit 'all titles composed by Blackmore-Gillan-Glover-Lord-Paice' on their recorded media. This may occur even though members have not actually contributed equally to the song. 'Smoke On the Water' by Deep Purple (1972) demonstrates one of the most iconic and memorable rock guitar riffs composed of all time, which has been canonised by aspiring guitarists playing it incessantly all over the world; yet the opening 'riff' played by Ritchie Blackmore is in a song credited to the whole band. The financial and legal implications of this are that when this distinctive opening guitar riff is heard on air (e.g. when used in synchronisation with many TV adverts), the whole band receive royalties for the duration of the piece being used on air – as they are equally credited in the composition of 'Smoke On The Water'. Other 1970s outfits such as Queen also became aware of the songwriting divide and agreed equal ownership share in musical works between all core members. However, there have been many cases of litigation and band splits following disproportionate song royalty division as a result of ownership issues. John Lennon and Paul McCartney of The Beatles famously wrote 90 per cent of the band's original song catalogue individually, yet divided royalty shares equally in their early writing careers regardless of 'who wrote what' in the song. They relied on the fact that each may benefit from the other's writing success, and critics claim that for this reason alone, it brought stability to The Beatles. Songwriters who are acutely aware of ownership areas in songs may wish to retain as much of the ownership share as possible, keeping other passive contributors to the song out of the royalty share. This has been demonstrated many times in the past; as outlined in Frith and Marshall, members of 1980s pop outfit Spandau Ballet went to court in 1999 (*Hadley vs. Kemp*) to claim their alleged shares in songs that were credited solely to their main songwriter but consequently lost their case. Frith goes on to argue that Spandau Ballet's earnings were '. . . decided not by an investigation of the messy collective processes in which pop music is actually made, but by an examination of what rights were embedded in what contracts' (2004:100).

Where songs produce little or no royalty returns there is rarely litigious activity; but where a song becomes a long-term 'copyright' making many thousands of pounds for the credited songwriters, aggrieved band members may take legal advice and pursue a royalty share they believe to be theirs. The fundamental long-term issues that follow songwriting ownership arguments and individual monies made have an effect on the longevity and stability of successful bands and their ability to stay together. Followers of successful acts often wonder why they cease to perform and tour (over time) and are perplexed as to why their favourite group has split up; unfortunately, for many bands, issues associated with song ownership, royalty division, and subsequent financial remuneration between members causes their ultimate demise.

Sample songwriting and the DJ

The final example (Figure 4.3) has increased complexity and looks at the hybridised writing style of the DJ music producer. This concept of music creation has evolved through the conceptual acceleration and development of digital music sampling technologies, emerging in the 1980s and onwards. One of the first records to exploit this method of music making was '19' by Paul Hardcastle, released globally in 1985. From this moment on, the music hardware 'sampler' played a prominent role in songwriting, whereby music creators would sample segments from existing records, CDs, musical works or external sounds. The art of sampling is by no means a new one, as samples have been used in synchronisation with audio post-production techniques in film making for many years, where a short segment of recorded audio accompanies a visual element. The term DJ originated from the

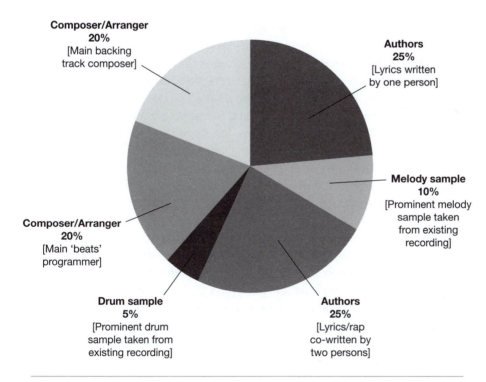

FIGURE 4.3
Sample songwriting production – potential share example

word 'disc jockey', not used in its full form today, but the job title given to radio personnel playing records to passive consumers via broadcast. The world's first disc jockey, Ray Newby, originated in California and broadcast on a spark transmitter in 1909. Today, DJs who work in nightclubs often create their own mixes at home and in studios using sampling software to create songs and remixes that can be distributed to the nightclub circuit and dance radio broadcasts. The creation of songs by the DJ songwriter is interlaced with music recording and production, as often the DJ will start with a collection of samples from various sources. Many samples may be obtained online or purchased as sample CDs, MP3s, vinyl records, other music file types (such as WAV or AIFF) and many other sources, which produce a selection of sounds in order to create a foundation for the songwriting. Working with a palette of sounds in this way permits 'collage' style music making, with music software and hardware used to assemble and edit the samples. The songwriter may then add top-line vocal melodies, electronic instrument sounds or phrases and anything from vocal 'raps' to acoustic instruments in the process. The resultant complex collage of musical arrangement and production in the final song can prove very difficult in identifying exactly 'who wrote what?'; any musical samples used in a new recording, without exclusive permission granted by the original owners, will give rise to ownership infringements, depending on who owns the copyright and how it has been administered.

Where a drum phrase or 'loop' is sampled from a vinyl record, the actual song sampled will be owned by someone; hence taking a drum loop without permission demonstrates two copyright infringements, one in uncleared use of the song and another in the uncleared use of the original recorded work. Looking closely at who participated in the songwriting in all samples used will produce a long list of credited participants. To avoid imminent litigation in a successful commercial work that has 'borrowed' samples in composition, it may be necessary to 'remake', rewrite or reproduce the samples used in the final song. Sample songwriting is often executed without thought or awareness of who wrote the original song and who owns the copyright in the original recording; publishers usually own and administer the song while the music label owns and administers the tangible music source. The drive in this style of music construction is simply to produce a good commercial release, yet the legal implications of sampling from sources with inherent copyright complicates the process, splitting the song many ways through a long list of credited songwriters. DJ sample songwriters often produce the recording first and worry about copyright clearances later; the clearances could be obtained in retrospect if the DJ producer is signed to a reputable record label or publisher. Where sample clearances are not fully investigated, litigation could easily occur if the song is released and accrues royalties through airplay and sales of product. As copyright clearance has caused issues in this style of songwriting and 'music borrowing', websites such as Creative Commons provides downloadable samples for use by others. Finding licensed works that can be shared, remixed and re-used legally provides music sample creators with greater freedom and many new creative commons media sites permit sample usage and sharing (see www.creativecommons. org). Terms and limitations are applied to the sample at the discretion of the owner, but new areas of music creation and exploitation are questioning traditional methods of ownership and copyright, largely due to this style of music creation and production. However, one of the most used drum rhythm samples, which has appeared on countless recordings, was taken from the b-side of a vinyl record by The Winstons released in 1969 entitled 'Amen, Brother'. This six-second drum solo 'break', was sampled in the late 1980s onwards and became one of the world's most widely known drum loops, used in 'drum-and-bass', 'hip hop' and 'jungle' dance music genres. As The Winstons never engaged legal proceedings against infringers using the sample illegally, the drum loop went on to earn iconic 'sample' status.

Scoring music

Where composers score musical pieces for many instruments using traditional forms of notation, ownership again can be dissected by looking at 'who scored what' in terms of the main body of the musical piece. Additionally, lyricists and soloists may add their part in creation of the composition. Arrangements and new musical parts may be scored by additional composers; each separate composition should be credited to its key contributors and writer shares divided accordingly. However, scoring a horn or string part, for example, over the top of an existing written or established composition, may not necessarily entitle these additional writers to a share in the original established musical work.

External contributions to songs from session musicians and guests

Litigation can occur when a successful recording session subsequently results in a hit record being produced and the session musician is involved. For example, a session musician or session vocalist is paid for their part in a hit record; the fee is agreed with the session player who adds their musical expertise and creation into the original song arrangement. This could take the form of a new 'hook', top-line melody, or distinctive musical solo part; here, the producer has sought to enhance the original song and recording by using the expertise of a guest musician. This valuable musical addition could become intrinsic to the song. Such distinctive creative contributions may not however entitle the session musician to a writing 'credit' in the song, as the session musician is paid a set fee for their contribution. Historically, there have been many songs that have become hits containing distinctive musical contributions from session players. When the songs become extremely successful and have earned thousands for the credited songwriters, the session musician can resurface to claim their share of the writing credit. One such example occurred in the UK concerning the 1971 hit song 'Maggie May' written by Rod Stewart, when session player Ray Jackson made news headlines with his claim that he was never properly credited in the songwriting some fourteen years after its original release. The song was subsequently sampled and repeatedly broadcast in a national advert for a major finance company in the UK featuring Jackson's solo mandolin part. Jackson claimed he was only paid £15 for the original recording session and not even credited in the original song, even though he was asked to play creatively in the song. It is arguable whether Jackson's distinctive mandolin part contributed to the ultimate success of 'Maggie May', but also arguably the song has proved financially lucrative for its publisher and the original writers – guitarist Martin Quittenton and Rod Stewart. Ray Jackson has since campaigned to earn a writing credit for his work and recoup claimed lost royalties.

In light of these experiences, the session musician or any musician who is invited to appear as a guest on a recorded work should be clear about exactly what is required in the recording session. If the music producer requests original creative musical contribution from the guest there should be a possibility of writing credit. If, however, the guest part is already scored, written or mapped, the session player should not expect a songwriting credit if played as directed. Creative contributors to the song should seek advice and consider the legal perspectives to avoid problems if the song generates a large songwriting income stream as a result of a huge commercial success.

Music borrowing and litigation

Borrowing melodies, song parts or samples may prove costly to songwriters, bands and record companies, even when copyright ownership clearances are put in place before releasing recorded product. In 1997, UK rock act The Verve released the ironically titled 'Bitter Sweet Symphony', which subsequently became a worldwide hit. The song adapted sampled content from The Andrew Oldham Orchestra's 1965 vinyl release entitled *The Rolling Stones Songbook*, which consisted of an orchestral arrangement of the famous Rolling Stones song 'The Last Time' originally released in 1965 and credited to Mick Jagger and Keith Richards. Sample clearances were put in place, but The Rolling Stones' manager Allen Klein (deceased 2009) invoked legal proceedings arguing that too much of the sample had been used and breached the sample agreement. In losing the case, The Verve relinquished 100 per cent of the song ownership to Jagger and Richards. In this case, even though 'Bitter Sweet Symphony' was constructed around the Stones' original ostinato, the original lyrics writer Richard Ashcroft also lost his songwriting credit due to this legal case. The Rolling Stones have also received criticism in that the song was originally influenced by a traditional gospel song 'This May Be The Last Time' originally released in the US in 1955 by The Staple Singers. In the 1960s it was not uncommon for pop bands to take influence, melodies or lyrical content from traditional American blues songs.

Music lawyers would advise sampling with due care and attention using 'creative commons' methods or putting clearances in place from the original copyright owners to avoid costly litigious activity in the future. Addressing issues of ownership at the earliest stage by dividing songs fairly in defining individual creative contribution is not to be overlooked, yet many young creative songwriters avoid this imperative. There are many case histories concerning copyright infringement in songs, since music publishing and the monetising of music began. Repeated litigation concerning songwriting, creative contributions and due writer credits demonstrate that, historically, addressing issues of ownership for songwriters and producers at the early stage has not always been clearly defined or apportioned correctly.

UNDERSTANDING COPYRIGHT IN MUSIC AND MUSIC PRODUCTS

To understand copyright in music, it is necessary to understand issues of ownership, as outlined in the first part of this chapter. When ownership in the music parts, sub-parts, lyrics, arrangement and samples (if used) is established, it is easier to understand what copyright is actually being applied to. Copyright can be complex to understand and the concept of copyright may also differ in various global territories; music law may also update and change in these territories so it would be advisable to investigate music copyright law in a world territorial context (see www.copyrighthistory.org); this chapter will discuss UK copyright law and procedures primarily.

The importance of copyright

The introduction of the Copyright Act in the UK has provided a mechanism by which creative authors and musicians may first protect their creations, through the intellectual property ownership right, and second mark out a starting point to administer music. Without copyright in place, a third party could inadvertently 'copy' the original work and exploit this for financial gain to the detriment of the original creator. The right to copy musical works and lyrical creations rests with the copyright owner, who initially are the musicians and lyricists who have created the work in the first instance (see previous section). The musical creation can surface in a myriad of ways, with sample song style creation providing more complex ownership and copyright issues. Those that own copyright can assign copyright; 'assigning' could be thought of as 'leasing' rights to a third party – in the music industry, this would usually be a music publisher. When ownership in songs and song division is clearly demarcated, it is then possible to pinpoint how this is apportioned and exactly *what* copyright is applied to. It is commonplace for some songwriters to collaborate on musical works but be signed individually to different music publishers; each publisher then has a vested interest in the copyright of the song through their respective writers.

Copyright history and music copyright law

In the creating modern intellectual property (IP) law, the copyright act was introduced when the British Parliament invoked the very first copyright statute – the copyright act of 1709, known as the Statute of Anne. Prior to this, many other worldwide territories were active in the pursuit of protecting the act of 'copying' printed books, manuscripts and other written matter –as early as the year 560 AD. The Statute of Anne copyright act was originally limited to books and literary materials; this early enactment has since been revised and expanded many times to include sound recordings and musical, dramatic, artistic, film and typographical works. In 1886 the Berne Convention for the protection of literary and artistic works provided a bi-lateral agreement with America to provide reciprocal protection of British and United States authors, in recognition of growing global exploitation of the literary work (Intellectual Property Office 2010). The next key revision in copyright law in the UK took place on 1 July 1912 when the Copyright Act of 1911 came into force; this was the first time sound recordings, perforated rolls and records gained protection through the revised British law. The 1912 revision saw the abolition of the need to register copyright in works with Stationers Hall, London – a fundamental principle of the Berne Convention that had been a requirement previously in Britain (Intellectual Property Office, 2010). The Copyright Act of 1956 then came into force on 1 June 1957, which produced further amendments to the UK bill to include films and broadcasts, in consideration of Britain's accession to the Universal Copyright Convention of 1952 in Geneva, in recognition of worldwide copyright law (UNESCO, 2010). The United Nations Educational, Scientific and Cultural Organisation (UNESCO) has become a principal guiding influence concerning in international copyright law and today re-enforces its commitment towards copyright protection since its inception in 1952 (UNESCO, 2010). UNESCO holds regular inter-governmental conventions at its headquarters in Paris to discuss global issues concerning the cultural creative industries and levels of global enforcement of copyright law. As large-scale copyright infringement becomes a worldwide concern with an ever growing onset of digital technologies, UNESCO's 200 international member states have become instrumental in the political discourse of global piracy. UNESCO's presence would also indicate that future global policy concerning copyright is conceived and modernised on an international level through its member states and therefore is less an individual country's responsibility to devise. On 1 August 1989 the Copyright, Designs and Patents Act came into force in the UK and is still in place, taking into account amendments from European directives and updates, still maintaining this title with the addition of '(as amended)' to include such new revisions in its title. Each global territory may develop its own individual revisions in copyright law, which can be investigated further, but with differing infringement types across global digital economies, intellectual property law revisions steer largely to the same outcomes and destinations. Official revisions and new updates to UK copyright law can be found by accessing the Intellectual Property Office (IPO) website (www.ipo.gov.uk).

COPYRIGHT IN SONGS – COPYRIGHT IN RECORDINGS

Understanding the origins of copyright law and intellectual property rights can be complex in itself, but understanding how these are implemented in music is essential to music creators in order to facilitate an awareness of where 'income stream' administration begins. Income streams are collectively known as the monetary returns produced as a result of exploitation of the musical work. The term 'exploitation' is used in relation to music usage (in a non-predatory manner) and usually simply means the musical work has received radio airplay, or has been released or sold on a format, such as MP3. What makes music IP law difficult to understand is often the confusion that exists between the copyright that exists in songs and the copyright that exists in recordings. These are two separate rights and should not be confused with each other, as the term of copyright differs in each. Each right produces separate income streams, giving rise to further confusion concerning earnings from sound recordings. Legally owning copyright permits the owner of the work 'the right to do'.

Copyright in songs and the copyright term

The agreed ownership in the song title may decide 'who will earn what', in percentage terms of any subsequent song income streams; but in title, the song is subject to and governed by the copyright laws that surround it. In the UK the IPO officially defines copyright existent in the song:

> If you are the composer of the music you will be the author of the musical work and will have copyright in that music. The lyrics of the song are protected separately by copyright as a literary work and will usually be owned by the person who wrote them.
>
> (IPO, 2010)

Furthermore, the duration of ownership or the 'term' of copyright applied to the song is 'the creator's life plus 70 years from the end of the year in which he/she dies' (IPO, 2010). One additional consideration is that in a joint song collaboration, the term of copyright would last seventy years from the last remaining author's death. After the seventy-year expiration of copyright, the right to copy the work by others without consent of the original authors or publishers would come into effect. This would mean the song could be re-recorded or 'covered' and released without permission, whereas any song that remains in copyright requires permission from the copyright owner before it can be legally exploited.

Exploiting the song and generating royalties

Exploitation of the song could manifest itself as using the song on any duplicated tangible media such as CDs, electronic music files, MP3 or used in synchronisation with visual media on DVD. When songs are used in this way, a *mechanical* royalty is generated; in the UK this is administered by an organisation known as the Mechanical Copyright Protection Society (MCPS) (see section on the MCPS, later in this chapter).

Where the same song is *performed* through radio or TV airplay, or is played in a large venue to a ticketed audience, an organisation known as the Performing Right Society (the PRS for Music) will collect royalties on behalf of the copyright owner for performance of the song, on air or live. At this stage it should be noted that whoever created the song and has a vested interest in its copyright should be aware of the key royalty collection societies that operate in the UK. The importance of the MCPS and PRS are discussed later in this chapter. It is worth noting that the original song creators (composers, authors and arrangers) own the song by default, unless they decide to sign over their intellectual property rights to a third party, which would usually be a dedicated music publisher (see section on music publishers).

Copyright in recordings and the legal copyright term

Having addressed complex copyright and ownership issues in songs, it is perhaps easier to understand copyright existing in the recorded work. Music recordings could constitute a range of tangible items such as CDs, vinyl, tapes (digital and analogue), hard disc or digital music files (MP3, AIFF, WAV and many more). Through the studio recording production process, a finished version of the song will be edited and mixed, known as a 'master'. The master is a source for further duplication or replication of copies of the musical production. The owner of the master can usually be defined as the person that has paid and arranged for the recording to take place; this is often the record company as outlined by the BPI in the UK:

> Under the Copyright, Designs and Patents Act 1988, the 'author' of a sound recording is the producer, but it is generally accepted that the copyright owner will be the person who made the arrangements for the recording to be made – typically a record company.
>
> (BPI, 2010)

The British Phonograph Industry highlights that, regardless of the personnel that have taken part in the recording (recording engineer, producer, musicians, songwriters), whoever pays the studio bill largely owns the copyright ('right to copy') in the final master. It is, however, possible that the label has negotiated contracts with those involved in the recording to include the producer (known as the author of the work and first copyright owner) in a percentage share of sales of the replicated work. As a larger record label would seek to exploit the 'master recording' in replicating and selling the work, it would seek to preserve this exclusive right in a contract with the record producer. Smaller independent producers of music (bedroom to garage producers) provide and fund their own studio time, so naturally own copyright in their own musical recordings. Recording and mixing between different studios can cause further confusion where ownership in the recorded work may shift as a result of collaboration in the production authoring and who has paid for or provided most 'studio time' to arrive at the final product.

The copyright term for recordings differs from that of songs, with the term running for fifty years from the end of the year in which it was made. The Intellectual Property Office highlights further issues that affect the term of applied copyright in connection with publishing of the work, which would be worth investigating if the recorded work is to be published (see www.ipo.gov.uk). In order to claim copyright in the sound recording, the music itself need not be original (e.g. a recorded cover version of an old song), but if the new sound recording includes samples from other copyright sound recordings, the new work cannot be classed as new. Using samples in this way would require permission from the original owners of the sampled recordings; often a complex process, this provides a reason why many creators will re-make or re-record their own sound samples before including them in their own new works. Re-mastering a recording made and owned by others would therefore not constitute a new work and therefore would not have copyright protection (IPO, 2010). In the case of compilation albums that are re-mastered and contain separate tracks from a variety of labels, the releasing record company would need to obtain a licence from the owners of the original sound recordings before inclusion on the compilation. This type of licensing deal would usually involve a payment to the owners of the recordings, often a small amount, with a licensing contract to determine the terms of use and exploitation. A common statement of ownership in the sound recording is often clearly printed or marked on tangible products as follows and is recommended by legal bodies:

> The copyright in this sound recording is owned by (label name). All rights of the manufacturer and of the work prohibited. Unauthorised copying, lending, public performance and broadcasting of the recorded work prohibited.
>
> (IPO, 2010)

This statement may appear on the CD body itself in small print or may appear printed on any accompanying inlay booklets; if an electronic release, the statement may still appear visibly in connection with the sound recording. Although not a legal requirement, the statement of declared copyright establishes ownership by the sound recording owner and displays a visible awareness of the label's intellectual property claim.

THE ISRC CODE: IDENTIFYING SOUND RECORDINGS

A system called the International System for the Identification of Sound Recordings (ISRC) has been instigated in order to provide a unique digital identifier that can

FIGURE 4.4
Applying ISRC codes in the recorded music work, courtesy the author

be permanently encoded into a sound recording or music video. A computer software program can be used to embed the code into the sound recording at the time of final mastering, before the replication stage, and this is done for each and every separate sound recording. The purpose of the code is to provide identification in each unique sound recording, which, in turn, creates a link to its creator and ensures revenue payments are directed to the rightful owner. In the UK, Phonographic Performance Limited (PPL) is the sole agency appointed to issue the ISRC code; a UK music producer or music label can join PPL as a record company member who is then issued with an ISRC system (PPL, 2010). The system allows generation of the unique international code, attributing the sound recording back to the releasing label and subsequent owner in the work; ISRC provides a unique and useful tool for rights administration and identification concerning the distribution of electronic media. The International Federation of the Phonograph Industry (IFPI) advises that all producers and owners of sound recordings should use the ISRC system to identify their works; other global territories have similar agencies to PPL who can provide labels with the ISRC system. In the UK there is little or no cost to apply ISRC, so any music label, regardless of size, should take steps to address positive identification of its recorded works as part of the mastering process.

INTELLECTUAL PROPERTY

The term 'intellectual property' exists within copyright, and the World Intellectual Property Organisation (WIPO), which is a specialised agency of the United Nations based in Geneva, Switzerland, defines IP succinctly:

> Intellectual property (IP) refers to creations of the mind: inventions, literary and artistic works, and symbols, names, images, and designs used in commerce.
>
> (WIPO, 2010)

The WIPO exists to develop an accessible and balanced international IP system and provides further in-depth definitions of IP while seeking to safeguard the public interest. As developed countries are becoming more IP aware, due to global creative economic development, the WIPO has grown in significance. Kidd, in Coyer *et al.*, highlights the call for a new world economic order through global IP control concluding that 'the new global movement to democratise communications follows a long trajectory' (2007:247–248).

It should be noted that two categories of IP exist, first copyright, which includes musical works, lyrics, poems and plays, films, artistic works such as photographs, paintings, drawings, architectural designs and sculptures; and second, inventions (patents), industrial designs and industrial property. Furthermore, WIPO re-enforces IP in terms of music as follows:

> A clear distinction is made in relation to rights related to copyright, including those of performing artists in their performances, producers of phonograms in their recordings, and those of broadcasters in their radio and television programs.
>
> (WIPO, 2010)

Intellectual property in music is broadly generated as a result of musical creations that occur from the human mind, but such creations need to exist in a tangible form for copyright legislation to take effect. In respect of music creations, these tangible forms may constitute sound recordings on CD, lyrics on paper or music notation scored and printed. Electronic files that are generated as a result of creative musical thought processes are also recognised as acceptable formats in which intellectual property can be realised. The type of IP protection required will depend on exactly what musical article has been created; there are four main types of IP protection that can be used to protect creations or inventions (IPO, 2010):

- Patents: A patent will protect how things work, not applied to songs or recordings but perhaps applied where a new musical instrument is invented and the inventor wants to protect the idea.
- Designs: IP exists in the design of artefacts, for example, in a music product this could be a new CD gatefold case design.

- Trade Marks: A company logo may exist in promotion of a record label's brand name in a website.

- Copyright: The automatic right that exists when a musical work is fixed; written or recorded in a format. Note that separate copyrights exist in both songs and recordings, and if photographs or artwork is used in conjunction with promotion of a musical work (e.g. a CD cover or inlay), this holds its own IP right too.

Looking at these four distinct areas of IP should assist in understanding where protection needs to be applied, and for new independent labels or producers of music commodities, attention to trade mark IP should be considered. In this regard, knowing clearly where IP exists, and who created items or materials in each, allows scope for protection to be applied in these key areas of original creation and invention surrounding the music project.

Copyright: The automatic right

In the UK and many other world territories there is no official requirement for an original work to be registered with an official body. Through international IP conventions and treaties, IP has evolved to provide an automatic right of ownership in a newly created original work. Simply put, when a work has been created and 'fixed' in a format, copyright protection applies. In the UK, the Intellectual Property Office advises that in order to establish copyright and to help to protect the work, a small symbol may be applied to the work (c), alongside the name of the copyright owner and the year in which the work was created. Taking these steps, however, is not essential, but it will indicate if the term of copyright has expired in respect of the original date of creation. Should others wish to use or reproduce the work, the details will indicate who the owner is and where permissions need to be obtained in order to use or reproduce the work.

Protecting intellectual property

Popular misconceptions exist in the 'copyrighting' of a musical work, its protection and subsequent copyright infringement, whereby independent music producers and creators of music seek to understand how to protect new and original musical works. Knowing exactly where original ownership lies in the song, separate rights in the recorded work (files or CDs) and any accompanying items such as artwork, photographs, brand identities and websites would be the first step to understanding all IP existing in the music venture. Separate copyright processes need not necessarily be entered into in order to 'copyright' the whole music package creation, as the automatic right exists in the package when created, but it would be worthwhile looking at the values held in all components of the package: 'who did what' and where specific areas of ownership lie in the new musical 'package'.

When this can be quantified and listed, several actions are then possible in order to claim IP rights and the right to 'copy' components in the music package. There are a range of popular methods available to indicate 'possession of works':

- Music creators can post the music package and components to themselves via recorded mail or special delivery format in a firmly sealed envelope. The sealed package is signed for and dated, then stored in a safe place and remains unopened. The package can then be produced and opened in court in the event of an IP infringement case.

- Music creators can lodge the music package with a solicitor or bank. The package would be date stamped and stored in a safe or vault in the bank or solicitor's premises, remaining unopened, unless required in court to prove IP ownership.

- Independent online IP companies offer to accept the package as files, for example, music as MP3, JPEG images and lyrics as text files. For a fee they will send a dated certificate in receipt of the files. If IP infringement occurs the certificate can be produced. Using this method requires periodic certificate renewal, so may not prove to be the most cost-effective option. Fees charged per song can be expensive.

It is important to realise that using any method above does not necessarily prove that the musical work is original or has actually been created by the person claiming IP possession in all components. However, many music creators have entered into these processes in anticipation of possible future infringements, preferring to have a date stamped package that can be produced in a court of law proving their IP ownership and assisting in any resultant claims. It should be noted that, in the case of commercial musical works that gain mass media exposure over long periods of time, it would be much more difficult for a new infringer to wrongly claim IP in such works due to the establishing presence of the work. As soon as the musical work enters the public domain (such as uploading to YouTube), its arrival in the public sphere denotes its IP presence – as long as the work is original and has not been plagiarised from another source.

Intellectual property infringement

When a song or any part of its components are copied and distributed by a person or company without permission to do so from the copyright owner, an infringement has taken place. The IP owner is responsible for enforcing copyright, so if the musical work is unpublished, the IP owner would need to decide what action to take. Consultation with legal advisors may be necessary in order to claim for damages or to invoke an injunction, but employing legal advisors and attorneys to take action is costly so obtaining an initial estimate of the costs involved would be recommended. Negotiating a solution with the infringer 'out of court' would be a more cost-effective solution, assuming the infringer is open to negotiation and admits to the infringement. If an infringement occurs and the work has no proof of ownership (e.g. a dated, sealed and registered envelope posted to oneself containing the work), it may be difficult to pin-point how the work has been exploited unlawfully. Where a trade mark has been infringed (e.g. a record label logo) and it has not been officially registered, the common law of 'passing off' allows action to be taken. However, it must be proven that: a reputation has been built up in the trade mark, ownership in the trade mark can be proven and harm has occurred as a result of use of the mark. As it is difficult to prove a 'passing off' action, it would be advisable for a serious music label business concern to register its mark with the Intellectual Property Office (www.ipo.gov.uk). Paying to register one's distinctive trade mark is not a legal requirement when setting up a music label, but there are production and music company owners who may feel this is a worthwhile move (IPO, 2010).

Assigning song copyright to a music publisher

Understanding the ownership and subsequent IP rights that surround the song is important for composers and songwriters, especially if assigning those rights to a music publisher. Music creators should consider the value of signing to a music publisher and exactly what benefits may occur as a result. The music publisher role is largely to administer songs and music compositions and collect the income streams associated with them, when exploitation occurs. In addition, the publisher role should promote the musical works and relieve the administration and legal issues for the composer, permitting more time for musical creation. When a songwriter or music creator assigns an original work to a publisher, the rights then belong to the publisher under the terms of the contract entered into; some writers choose not to sign to a publisher and retain their rights, others seek the support of a publisher in promotion of the catalogue of musical works. It should be pointed out that sound recordings are owned and administered by recording companies (or the music producer), while the publisher collects monies on behalf of the writer for the song only. There are, however, hybrid music recording agreements offered by recording and production companies that may ask the writer for a share in the music publishing. Modern music companies today continually seek additional revenues, but historically, publishing, recording and management deals were regarded as separate entities. For the 'singer-songwriter' recording artist, signing all three revenue stream areas to one single company was always regarded as unethical. Today the 360-degree deal is more commonplace, but the pitfalls of signing all music rights to one company should be seriously considered by the music creator.

REFERENCES AND FURTHER READING
Books

Barrow, T. and Newby, J., *Inside the Music Business* (London: Routledge, 1995), pp. 167–175.

Baskerville, D. and Baskerville, T., *Music Business Handbook and Career Guide: Ninth Edition* (London: Sage, 2010), pp. 25–46, 79–125.

Beattie, W., *The Rock and Roll Times Guide to the Music Industry* (Oxford: Spring Hill, 2007), pp. 214–219.

Biermans, H., *The Music Industry: The Practical Guide to Understanding the Essentials* (London: DSS, 2007), pp. 20–24.

Demers, J., *Steal This Music: How Intellectual Property Law Affects Musical Creativity* (Athens, GA: University of Georgia Press, 2006).

Frith, S. and Marshall, L., *Music and Copyright: Second Edition* (Edinburgh: Edinburgh University Press, 2004), p. 100.

Hull, P.G., *The Recording Industry: Second Edition* (New York: Routledge, 2004), pp. 27–77.

Kidd, D. (in Coyer, K., Dowmunt, T. and Fountain, A., eds), *The Alternative Media Handbook* (Oxford: Routledge, 2007).

Leach, J., *Music Copyright Basics* (London: Alfred, 2003).

Passman, D.S., *All You Need to Know About the Music Business*: Sixth Edition (London: Penguin, 2008), pp. 241–246.

Schwartz, D.D., *I Don't Need a Record Deal: Your Survival Guide for the Indie Music Revolution* (New York: Billboard, 2005), pp. 96–100.

Walker, Jr., L.J., *This Business of Urban Music: A Practical Guide to Achieving Success in the Industry, from Gospel to Funk to R&B and Hip-Hop* (New York: Billboard, 2008), pp. 155–247.

Wikström, P., *The Music Industry: Digital Media and Society Series* (Cambridge: Polity Press, 2009), pp. 12–46.

Online resources

Bently, L. and Kretschmer, M. (eds), *Primary Sources on Copyright (1450–1900)*. Available at: www.copyrighthistory.org (accessed 20 August 2010).

Davies, W., 'Allen Klein, the Manager Fans Blamed for Beatles Break-up, Dies at 77', *Mail Online* (5 July 2009). Available at: www.dailymail.co.uk/news/article-1197584/Allen-Klein-manager-fans-blamed-Beatles-break-dies-77.html (accessed 13 August 2010).

Global performing rights organisations. Available at: www.bmi.com/international/entry/C2258 (accessed 20 August 2010).

'How Long Copyright Lasts – Sound Recordings', Intellectual Property Office. Available at: www.ipo.gov.uk/types/copy/c-duration/c-soundrecordings.htm (accessed 20 August 2010).

Intellectual Property Office (IPO). Available at: www.ipo.gov.uk (accessed 20 September 2010).

'MCPS Royalty Schemes', PRS for Music. Available at: www.prsformusic.com/creators/membership/MCPSroyalties/mcpsroyalty sources/Pages/MCPSroyaltysources.aspx (accessed 20 August 2010).

'Music Business – Copyright', British Phonographic Industry (BPI). Available at: www.bpi.co.uk/music-business/article/copyright.aspx (accessed 20 August 2010).

Phonographic Performance Limited (PPL). Available at: www.ppluk.com (accessed 20 August 2010).

PRS for Music (Performing Right Society UK). Available at: www.prsformusic.com (accessed 20 August 2010).

'Rod Faces Maggie May Action', BBC News online (3 March 2003). Available at: http://news.bbc.co.uk/1/hi/england/2816253.stm (accessed 12 September 2010).

United Nations Educational, Scientific and Cultural Organization (UNESCO). Available at: www.unesco.org/new/en/unesco (accessed 20 August 2010).

World Intellectual Property Office (WIPO). Available at: www.wipo.int (accessed 20 August 2010).

CHAPTER 5

Music publishing

Paul Rutter

MANAGING THE CREATIVE OUTPUT OF THE SONGWRITER

This section outlines how music is managed in terms of the actual creative output from artists, songwriters, composers and lyricists. There are legal considerations applied concerning the creation of songs, 'copyright' being the main vehicle by which income can be generated from the song. The earlier chapter on music ownership, copyright and intellectual property law outlines the legal perspectives in connection with the musical work. Understanding music ownership and copyright will aid the clear understanding of music publishing and its function in respect of 'song management' through publishing means. Songwriters and composers may question whether or not they need a publisher and the same question could be asked concerning the need for personal management. There are, however, specific songwriter managers in existence, but this extra layer of management is usually only reserved for the most successful composers. When artists become successful and have a manager, the publishing contract is usually negotiated by the personal manager. But if the songwriter does not perform the songs live and only records material as a composer, then the assigned publisher could be thought of purely as the 'administrator' of the work of the songwriter. The creative musician who starts with the intention of becoming a well known artist often realises that the commercial worth in their songs often holds a greater value than first thought. The songwriter environment is far less pressured than that of the 'high profile' performing artist. The career of the songwriter can be very lucrative, with the right promotion and management of their creative music catalogue, and these duties could fall to a good music publisher. Those that compose or arrange music, write lyrics in accompaniment, devise melodies or author words for songs could be referred to as 'songwriters'.

MUSIC PUBLISHING: A BRIEF HISTORY

The Music Publishers Association (MPA) claims that the UK's publishing market is 'the world's 4th largest music publishing market – making for 10 per cent of worldwide revenues and is second only to the USA as a source of repertoire' (MPA, 2010).

Music publishing provides a lucrative income stream for those that can promote and administer music works to full effect, as has been the case for many years. Before recorded music products became popular at the turn of the century, Barrow and Newby point out that, 'music publishing *was* the music business' (1995:44). Primary music industry income was generated by the music publisher who paid a fee to the composer to acquire the copyright in their musical compositions and sell the works to performers who needed songs. Sheet music was sought after, returning greater revenues from show and stage song catalogues; lucrative returns from radio and stage performance permitted the publisher to pay a 'royalty' percentage back to the composer. Today the publisher seeks out the established artist, singer-songwriter or band; artists who enjoy mainstream media success and write their own songs have the potential to cultivate the highest publishing revenue through performing musical works on and in a variety of media. Publishers will bid for established songwriter artists through favourable royalty contract strategies and advances; the most attractive major publishing deals are reserved for those that command the largest audience. For the new songwriter, there are thousands of publishers who can sign their works and administer their work, but proceeding with care and targeting songs to appropriate publishers would be advisable. The following section summarises and describes what the songwriter may encounter and provides discussion for those that want to know more about the work of the music publisher.

INDEPENDENT MUSIC PUBLISHING

Not all songwriters need or want a music publisher; as in personal artist management, this would depend on the level at which the songwriter is working, at that particular moment in their career. At grassroots amateur level, musicians can compose original music at home and may not seek to exploit their musical works, simply composing for pleasure as 'hobbyists', to play music at home or to friends. The original material composed is still subject to applied copyright by default, and although there may be earning potential in the song, its creator simply seeks not to exploit or promote it. In the UK, the songwriter could join song royalty collection societies PRS for Music and the MCPS in order to register these works in anticipation of future commercial exploitation, but doing this serves little purpose unless promotion and exploitation of the works is a future aim. No royalties are generated from original songs that are purely written and not performed to the wider public, or released on a recorded format into the 'public sphere'. Some amateur composers are concerned about their work being plagiarised, when in fact their songs receive little or no exposure and are not being actively 'pitched' or promoted in music industry circles. However, if a songwriter uploads material to popular online music streaming platforms such as MySpace, it would be well worth joining royalty collection societies PRS for Music and MCPS, and gaining IP copyright knowledge is then advisable, as these media platforms expose the songs to a global audience. Further measures can be taken by the songwriter to register proof of ownership in their musical works, and this can be done simply by the songwriter (see chapter on song ownership). A publisher makes money from the exploitation of songs, so the small independent songwriter may wish to consider whether the level of local exposure given to their catalogue is worth sharing with a publisher. Songwriters can publish their own songs, join key royalty collection societies, collect their own royalties through these societies and promote their own music catalogue independently without a publisher, if they so wish. Although the songwriter can set up their own publishing company to publish their own songs, they cannot publish the musical works of others, unless they register formally as a music publisher with the PRS and MCPS in the UK. Registering as a publisher, however, costs more than if self-publishing. When a songwriter collaborates and there is a shared writer credit in the work, the writer can only publish their part of the song, so if a writer writes half of the song, they can register the song title with PRS and MCPS, but must declare their 50 per cent stake in the songwriting share.

SONGWRITERS AND SMALL PUBLISHERS: THE PITFALLS

Simply having a publisher take an interest in a particular song or catalogue is not reason enough for a songwriter to sign a contract with them. It may be hard for the songwriter to identify and quantify exactly what the publisher can do for them; checking the track record of a publisher may help, but once the song is assigned to the publisher, the publisher can do as much or as little as they feel, in promotional terms. A flow of new songwriters is always approaching publishers, so publishers may subsequently prioritise and promote new songs that have come to their attention, instead of material already signed. New writers may want to take the risk and gamble their songs with publishers who offer promise, but it would be advisable to negotiate a set time clause on the song promotion. For a single-song publishing agreement, a limited term of one year (possibly up to five years) would be reasonable; if the song is not covered by an artist within the set period, the song copyright reverts back to the original writer. Some publishers are open to this arrangement, while other publishers feel that if they promote a particular song title for around six months, that their efforts warrant keeping the song for 'life copyright' in the hope that one day the song will be commercially exploited. This agreement favours the publisher; writers who cannot agree a time-limit clause with the publisher on single-song assignments should consider self-publishing. If a song is locked in agreement with a publisher, the writer can also join forces and actively promote the work collaboratively via websites and mailings, but perhaps the writer needs to then consider why they have assigned a publisher in the first place. Songwriters may feel flattered that their catalogue has been signed, yet uncommitted publishers often 'blanket sign' songs to their catalogue, in the belief that the more songs they have signed, the greater chance that one of those songs will become a hit out of hundreds signed. Ideally, songwriters will receive rigorous promotion of their works and longstanding commitment from their publishers.

Often, a publishing contract for the up and coming songwriter offers no advance, a 50/50 royalty split and publisher ownership of the song copyright for life. There are hundreds of publishers listed in music industry contact books and online, but many are inactive. Some publishers are set up to administer a single music catalogue, a vanity publishing imprint or simply hope to sign an elusive hit by chance. It could be argued that no person could be more passionate about the new musical work than the person who wrote it, and many songwriters are capable of being tenacious promoters in pursuit of their own goals. Promotion of songs involves the management of music catalogues, so careful targeting of works that are appropriate to the right artists, through their management and A&R teams, would be advisable. Research, detective work and approaching song promotion in a professional way would be a prerequisite. The independent may find difficulty in getting songs to well known artists, as they are approached by many publishers and writers with a track record, but songs that sound like obvious 'hits' often do get listened to and can 'bubble-up' to the surface. If a songwriter can create a buzz through their material, the publishers will soon follow; it may well be worth signing to a publisher, but only if the terms are fair. Specialist legal advice would highlight the pitfalls and issues in any weak agreement.

MAJOR MUSIC PUBLISHING CONTRACTS

In publishing, it is the value of the music catalogue that determines the financial worth and size of the publisher, thus determining if the publisher is a 'major'. The main attraction of signing to a larger reputable publisher is that they have the infrastructure and industry contacts to generate commercial success for the songwriter; however, there are no guarantees of success even after being signed – this is merely a starting point. In the industry there are many more major music publishers than major record labels in existence and each major record label has its own separate music publishing company. But signing to EMI records does not necessarily mean an automatic publishing agreement will be signed in tandem with EMI's music publishing division. Historically, this move would be seen as a conflict of business interests with the artist or songwriter's personal manager, who would negotiate the best possible deal for the songwriter elsewhere, offering the publishing to the highest bidder. Progressive business models in the music industry today have eroded some of these past business models, largely due to reduced income streams from recorded products. The 360-degree deal has one company to administer all rights on behalf of the artist – from recording and publishing through to touring and merchandise revenues. Warner Music Group has exemplified this business model in an effort to harness music income revenue streams, whereby publishing can be included in deals as a lucrative part of the artist income. There are industry professionals today, however, who would still argue against the 360-degree deal model and would wish to separate negotiation and contracts in each key artist income stream.

Major music publishers can supply advances and finance for the artist or songwriter to facilitate concentration on the creation of songs. Typically, new songwriters are likely to get far less than established bands or artists who can attract larger publishing advances due to the potential value of their ongoing mainstream media exposure: through TV and radio (generating PRS royalties); recorded music sales (generating MCPS royalties); and in some cases printed music catalogue sales. Named and signed recording artists have the potential to generate income beyond these streams in synchronisation agreements, for example, pop videos, music to accompany film and TV programmes. All of these factors mean major publishers will risk greater investment in respect of the advance offered to the artist. When a record is released and promoted by a major label, publishing revenues will follow naturally, leaving the publisher to administer and collect royalties. Territorially, the collection society PRS has reciprocal arrangements in other countries to collect abroad, but MCPS royalties are specific to the UK, so to collect 'mechanical' royalties abroad requires a publisher to collect these in their own territory; in the US, companies such as the Harry Fox Agency perform a similar function. For the UK artist releasing product abroad, their 'home publisher' has a relationship with publishers in each global territory, known as a sub-publisher; the sub-publisher collects the mechanicals and distributes royalties back to the UK publisher. In the case of the mechanical royalty, this is where being signed to a major publisher can increase revenue streams for the songwriter, as it has a global publisher network to administer and collect these royalties. For the songwriter who self-publishes, setting up sub-publishing agreements with designated foreign publishers would prove very difficult and time consuming, although if the song catalogue is of real worth abroad, it would be worth creating agreements with publishers to collect foreign 'mechanicals'. The artist-songwriter becomes all powerful when they become well known and can generate worldwide hits; unless they sign a very long exclusive 'staff writer' agreement with a major publisher, the artist is in a strong position to negotiate. New songwriters may be presented with a 50/50 share contract, but artists signed to major recording labels can negotiate 80/20 deals in their favour or even greater. The named artist songwriter can set up their own publishing company imprint to retain control of their music catalogue and can then offer the publishing out to a major publisher for a sizeable advance. The publisher can then use its global infrastructure to collect the maximum amount of revenue. Usually these kinds of contract would be negotiated by the songwriter's personal management, so legal representation would be an essential part of the process. Allowing a major publisher to administer the catalogue in this way releases funds back to the artist (and manager), by default, and maximises earning potential from the song; these agreements can be reviewed periodically, perhaps between albums.

REVIVING FORTUNES IN MUSIC PUBLISHING

Harnessing digital music media exploitation through streaming and downloading has presented new challenges for royalty collection societies and music publishers. Often, the publishing revenues associated with digital media and the internet are smaller revenues, so publishers and collection societies continually seek new ways to maximise digital income. The most lucrative income streams in publishing are still generated from traditional media: TV and radio airplay, recorded music sales and synchronisation in media. The major music publishers administer income streams in all of these areas to great effect, with harder working publishers constantly promoting their catalogue of works. Songs can encounter a revival of interest, such as an older song that has been selected for a product advertising campaign, and it can then go on to get increased radio airplay as a result and make re-appearances in national charts. If the advertisement is global, the song also can enjoy further global success; in 2010 the song 'Don't Stop Believin'' by US group Journey enjoyed renewed radio and chart success. The song was originally released in the US in 1981 and although it reached number nine in the *Billboard 100* chart, it only peaked at number 62 following its UK release in 1982. As a result of download culture and use of the song in numerous synchronisation agreements in film, TV, sport and use in the video music game *Rock Band*, the song became a cult hit. Revived download sales ensued in December 2009; the song reached a chart position of number six and retained its chart status throughout 2010. In addition to sales of the song allegedly totalling 75 million worldwide, Journey's original songwriters Jonathan Cain, Steve Perry and Neil Schon have enjoyed hugely revived publishing revenues: 'Among the beneficiaries will be Perry's own Lacey Boulevard Music and Schon and Cain's Weed High Nightmare Music, administered by Wixen Music Publishing' (Hau, 2007).

Examples such as this demonstrate the need for fair publishing contracts. It is difficult to predict when a song will be successful and what may activate its ultimate earning potential over time. 'Don't Stop Believin'' bears witness to the unpredictable nature of music in synchronisation with media and how popular songs can create a groundswell effect, resulting in continuous and recurring exploitation. Many publishers are aware of this factor, as the publisher's wealth is inherent in their music catalogue whether dormant or active. Music catalogues are often bought and sold as in any other company or business commodity. Business bartering over Northern Songs, publishers of around 180 songs in the Beatles' repertoire, bears witness to the acrimony that can ensue as a result of buying and selling the artist's work. Patrik Wikström recounts: 'In a series of unfortunate events the Beatles lost control of Northern Songs when Associated Television (ATV) acquired a majority stake in the company in 1969' (2009:82). Northern Songs was founded in 1963, and one of its principle songwriters, Paul McCartney, has endeavoured to acquire the ownership of 180 Beatles songs several times, only to be outbid. High profile publicity has surrounded the recurrent sale of this publishing entity, with the Michael Jackson Family Trust now co-owning Northern Songs with Sony ATV. The Northern Songs catalogue is alleged to be worth over one billion pounds and is the third-largest music publisher in the world.

In the 1960s to the late 1990s there was little music industry advice, knowledge or education available for the new artist and songwriter; unfair contractual agreements were not uncommon, although they are still on offer today from unscrupulous publishers. Songwriters, artists and managers who understand ownership in music, principles of IP law and basic agreements in music publishing can increase their music industry awareness in preparation for potential contract offers, therefore safeguarding against the potential malpractices that have occurred in the past.

PUBLISHING AGREEMENTS

Two primary types of agreement exist in publishing terms for the songwriter. Both agreements should cover similar clauses and obligations; the 'single song assignment' is an agreement that covers just one song at a time, and the other type, the 'staff-writer agreement' contracts everything the writer does over a set period. A synchronisation agreement is another classification of agreement and would be issued to composers who are writing for a specific purpose, for example, film, TV programmes or accompaniment to an electronic media product perhaps. When assigning any popular music song to a publisher, provision for synchronisation purposes is usually taken into account, as pop songs are often expected to have an accompanying video made for promotional purposes. The following section outlines common clauses and structures that often appear in songwriter agreements. If offered any publishing agreement, the songwriter should always seek independent legal advice in support of their career aims and objectives from an experienced music lawyer. Observing the key clauses that appear in agreements will aid understanding of the contractual obligations that both songwriter and publisher should adhere to. The following overview of clauses and structures may be found in many music publishing agreements and will appear in the 360-degree contract – if the artist agrees that publishing shares are included.

The single song assignment

- Dated agreement between parties: The contract sets out all those that are entering into the agreement, the songwriter(s) being one party and the publisher being the counter-part. If the composition is co-written and involves lyrical content, the writers may collectively sign one agreement, or they may also sign separate agreements dependent on how the publisher issues their contracts. In any event, all parties should retain their own copies of the agreement for future reference; should any breach of agreement occur, each signee can check the contract for anomalies.

- Details of the work: The name of composition (and any sub-name) is included alongside specific names of writer participants and their addresses. At this stage ownership in the work must be clear and concise (see chapter regarding song ownership issues). The importance of clear ownership cannot be overemphasised.

- Introduction: This section may outline any advances payable. In a single song assignment the advances are often small and for the songwriter/ producer advances can be offered to cover the recording costs. Where an advance has been paid, the publisher would seek to recoup the advance amount before the writer gets paid from any royalties due as a result of exploitation of the song. The warranties in this section will affirm that the songwriter is able to assign the 'whole and entire' copyright in their particular musical work, to the publisher. If the publisher sells his future catalogue (which would include the assigned song), this section will usually state that the song ownership will transfer to the publisher's successors, without the need for signing perpetual agreements. The writer must also warrant that the agreement is binding on their own heirs and executors; should the writer die, the contract is still binding in respect of copyright law and the 'term' or duration agreed in the contract.

- Territory: Most publishers will request publishing for 'the world', but managers or songwriters may wish to restrict this territory, if the publisher will accept this. Territorial negotiation could occur specific to UK and North America for instance, allowing further negotiation in other territories, if the song succeeded overseas.

- Songwriter warranties (a): The songwriter would agree to sign any further documents that may be necessary, in addition to the primary agreement, to facilitate assignment of copyrights in relation to the song.

- Songwriter warranties (b): The songwriter declares that the song is an original work, does not infringe the copyright in any other work (has not plagiarised any part that occurs in the song). If the song has sampled or borrowed parts from other musical works this would have to be declared. A songwriter cannot assign rights that they do not own; often songwriters who 'sample' in order to compose pop songs encounter many issues in this area (see 'ownership' sections in Chapter 4).

- Songwriter warranties (c): The songwriter declares that they have not already assigned the work to another publisher, person, firm or company and is free to assign the full rights that they hold in the work.

- Songwriter warranties (d): The songwriter declares that the work is not defamatory of any person, firm or company. If a work is regarded as 'defamatory', the publisher could be sued for libel; to safeguard matters the publisher may include this clause.

- Songwriter indemnity: If the songwriter breached a, b, c or d above, the songwriter would indemnify the publisher against all claims, damages and costs that may occur, in the event of a claim made against the publisher. The indemnity clause encourages the songwriter to be truthful about the musical work they are assigning, as the songwriter will have to compensate the publisher if litigation occurs as a result of the false declarations made.

- Publisher warranties (a), promoting the song: 'The publisher will use all reasonable endeavours to exploit the work'. This crucial clause in the contract summarises what the publisher will do for the writer in respect of the promotion of the song to others in the music industry: managers, artists, record labels, etc. For the writer, knowing exactly who, what and where is essential. The promotional role of the publisher is crucial to the songwriter and although often difficult to quantify, without accurate definition of 'reasonable endeavours', the publisher could actually effect little promotion on behalf of the writer.

- Publisher warranties (b), adaptations and moral rights: Once the song is assigned to the publisher, new adaptations of the work may occur, for example, if the work was to be used in a film, new orchestrations of the work could be produced. The writer waives the moral right, authorising the publisher to make alterations, changes, new arrangements and lyrical translations in the work. The writer may wish to negotiate limitations in this clause, requesting consultation prior to and after the alterations.

- Publisher warranties (c), royalty statements: Many standard publishing contracts usually agree that royalty statements are issued twice yearly at six-monthly intervals. The publisher may add more time (around 60 days) to each period, which would delay the very first royalty payment by two months.

- Publisher warranties (d), infringement: Where the musical work is 'infringed', the publisher will undertake to institute legal proceedings against the infringer. For the songwriter, this clause offers security because the publisher, as the assigned copyright owner, would instigate prosecution proceedings. Any resultant compensation or payments are split between the publisher and writer, after deduction of any costs (which the publisher would pay for in advance).

- Remedies: If the publisher or songwriter breaches the agreement in respect of any clause (such as the publisher exceeding time limits on a late royalty payment to the writer), the remedy clause sets a timeframe to remedy the breach. Usually the innocent party must serve notice (sent by recorded delivery) to remedy the breach (usually within thirty days). This gives time to rectify the breach, without instigating legal proceedings, which could ultimately ensue if the breach is not remedied.

- Territorial legal abidance: The contract will state in which country of origin it is signed and agreed; if signed in the UK, the contract is construed in accordance with English law and all parties must submit to the jurisdiction of the English court.

- Royalty schedule: All key income streams that return the publishing royalty should be outlined in the contract. In each income stream, the percentages may vary and could be dependent on advances issued. Songwriters should expect a favourable share of between 60–85 per cent in most streams, but sheet music royalties are often far less; examples are set below.

- Royalty shares on sheet music: The publisher usually pays a lower royalty rate at around 10 per cent of the retail purchase price, for each copy of printed sheet music sold. Inclusion of printed music in catalogues is also often 10 per cent. Where copies of printed music are given away by the publisher in respect of promoting the work, no royalty would be payable. Sheet music royalty rates are only set at around 10 per cent as the publisher has to risk all printing and manufacturing costs. This could be compared to a record company who takes on board the risk and investment in manufacturing recorded products, hence the percentage offered in recording agreements can be plus or minus 10 per cent.

- Royalty shares on performing and broadcast fees: Usually, this income stream is the most lucrative in publishing terms as all monies collected by PRS for Music generated from radio broadcasts, TV, live performance and internet performance usage are returned to the publisher. This affords a higher royalty percentage for the songwriter, usually 60–85 per cent. If the songwriter is a PRS member, the royalty share is distributed directly to the writer and the publisher is paid its share separately by the PRS. In this regard the PRS writer-member receives money at the same time as the publisher, rather than the writer allowing the publisher to collect royalties from PRS and wait six months or more for the publisher to distribute royalties back to the writer.

- Royalty shares on 'mechanicals': When the song is used in a sound recording (e.g. CD or MP3 format), a mechanical royalty is due for each copy made by the record label. The writer's share could be agreed as between 60–85 per cent of this income. It is received from the Mechanical Copyright Protection Society (MCPS) in the UK. The songwriter can also join MCPS, but in this scenario the publisher collects the 'mechanicals' and distributes to the writer. If the song is sold in other global territories, the publisher will appoint sub-publishers to collect the 'mechanicals' in that specific territory. If the contract covers 'the world' and the song is eventually released in all territories, collection and distribution of this income can take a year or two to filter back to the writer, depending on the efficiency of the sub-publisher and its territorial mechanical collection society. In the US, the Harry Fox Agency collects in a similar way to the UK counterpart, MCPS.

- Royalty shares in synchronisation fees: Where the song is used in connection with a video, TV programme or film, the writer should expect 60–85 per cent of the royalties returned. Publishers can negotiate a primary synchronisation fee for the use of the song in connection with these mediums; commercials can generate a 'synch' fee from one to thousands of pounds for the exclusive use of the composition. In a TV broadcast, the songwriter can benefit in two ways – first from a share in the 'synch' fee and second from the PRS royalties returned when the commercial is aired.

- Royalty shares on other fees: The advent of new technologies has demanded a blanket clause to cover exploitation of the song in connection with emergent mediums. Some of these forms have not yet been invented, but the song may be used in connection with them when they arrive. From 60–85 per cent of fees should also be expected when the work is used in connection with new media or hardware technology, such as mobile phone ringtones, 'start up' melodies and embedded music in electronic devices.

- Term: A set term should be granted to the publisher by which the publisher is given time to promote the work properly and display commitment to the writer's work. For a single song assignment, a period of one year should suffice, though some publishers prefer up to five years in which to attain successful commercial placement for the song.

- Signatories: In respect of all clauses the contract is signed and witnessed.

Staff-writer agreements

In the staff-writer agreement similar clauses will ensue. The main differences will be in the term, the amount of musical works assigned and the advance. If a major publisher advances a large sum to the writer, the publisher will want to retain control of the writer's catalogue for as long as possible. Every song the writer produces within the contract term will be subject to the rules of the contract. Some writers may feel stifled by a staff-writer agreement, particularly if they are not pleased with the service the publisher is providing. For other writers, the staff-writer agreement often permits the freedom to concentrate on writing songs for a long time period while they endeavour to establish their songwriting careers. More high profile artist songwriters naturally attract more lucrative publishing agreements and have greater negotiating power. New songwriters offered staff-writer publishing agreements by small independents should be aware of the pitfalls. Consulting legal representatives will help, but the track record of the publisher is all important, alongside 'get-out' clauses and shorter 'terms', until the publisher can prove that it can cultivate success in promoting the writer's work.

SETTING UP IN BUSINESS AS A MUSIC PUBLISHER

Going into business as a publisher is a relatively easy process for those who understand basic music law and have a tenacious capacity for the promotion of musical works, and, given success, the income can be lucrative. Other than deciding on a suitable publishing imprint brand, companies in the UK would need to join PRS for Music and the MCPS as a publisher member (the costs to join as a publisher are greater than that of a songwriter member). The key issue for the would-be publisher is the effectiveness of their song promotion. Taking over copyright possession in the works of talented songwriters can provide the feeling of potential business wealth, but if the songs are not covered or exploited in any way, they are of little use to the publisher unless the original writer undertakes to promote their own work through live performance or other means. The music publisher's job of managing and promoting a new music catalogue to A&R departments is often thankless and unrewarding. There are many more songs available in the market than major artists looking to record them. Many major artists write or co-write their own material or have a close network of 'creatives' around them to ring-fence any potential lucrative income from guaranteed music sales. Many of these issues make life difficult for the new publisher who may not have appropriate songs or connections in the music industry. The most encouraging aspect for publishers and songwriters is that music consumption is vast on a global scale and the turnaround of songs in the modern-day chart system is very quick. Perpetual consumer appetite demands a constant stream of good 'hit' songs. Writers and publishers alike who can cultivate, create and facilitate certain 'sure-fire' hit material, whatever the genre, can feel optimistic about the likelihood of financial gain through music publishing.

THE MUSIC PUBLISHERS ASSOCIATION

The music publishing association that exists in the UK in support of publishers both independent and major is known as the MPA. Nine UK music publishers formed the original Music Publishers Association in 1881, in an effort to fight against the piracy of sheet music copying. The intention of the organisation was to 'watch over the general interests of the music trade' and to 'communicate with the proper authorities on all matters connected with copyright whether home, colonial or international' (MPA, 2010). Today the MPA provides a collective voice for music publishers and the writers that are signed to them; in doing so it acts to promote and safeguard the wider interests of the publisher. The MPA makes representations to the music industry, government and the media, claiming to promote a greater understanding of music publishing and the value of music copyright to the public. This collective forum is instrumental in creating policy papers that are submitted on behalf of its songwriter and publisher members through the umbrella organisation, UK Music. Many of the policies it has campaigned for are in direct relation to the evolving technologies that have produced new revenue streams for its members, from sheet music and early wax drums through to MP3. The association works closely with other UK music societies – PRS for Music, MCPS and the British Association of Song Composers and Authors (BASCA). Today the MPA survives as a 'not-for-profit' organisation and provides business services such as draft contracts, educational events, professional development and lobbying on behalf of its members. New publishers would be advised to consider MPA membership, as this could provide advantageous networking opportunities and valuable information in pursuit of enhanced publisher knowledge.

The association campaigns on behalf of its 250 publisher members and represents all music genres, stating the benefits of good songwriter and publisher liaison in all genres:

> A good publisher seeks out great music and great composers and songwriters, and supports composers and songwriters in the creative process, promotes their catalogues across a variety of platforms, manages the business exploitation of the catalogues (including the registration of works and the collection and onward payment of all due royalties) and generally seeks to protect and enhance the value of their works with passion and professional commitment.
>
> (MPA, 2010)

COPYRIGHT CONTROL AND THE WORK OF THE PUBLISHER AND SUB-PUBLISHING OVERSEAS

Music creators do not need a music publisher to control their own copyright; the declaration 'copyright control' can be printed on copies of the work to demonstrate the creator is administering their own songs. However, if a song is released on a worldwide basis, there may be a requirement for sub-publishing agreements in other territories. Sub-publishing agreements will ensure copyright monitoring and policing in territories far from home, a difficult task for a small, home music composer. If musical works exploited abroad are administered correctly by the sub-publisher, foreign income revenue streams can be greatly improved. Publishers that are committed to their composers and music catalogues should provide the following:

- Registering assigned musical works with appropriate royalty collection societies.
- Royalty collection and distribution to the composer.

- Assisting in the costs of recording song demos, studio time, facilities and professional song production.

- Providing an A&R mechanism to create collaborations with other good songwriters and allowing time for writers to develop their talent.

- Seeking commissions for new works from artists and other areas such as synchronisation to other media forms, such as TV, films and commercials.

- Licensing and producing printed sheet music and music catalogues.

- Assisting in the production of materials that will promote the composer's works and music catalogues.

- Licensing the music in world territories and ensuring efficient monitoring in the exploitation of the works.

- Assisting in the worldwide promotion of signed composers to record companies, commercial users of music, performers and broadcasters.

- Working with new emergent media forms to generate further licensing revenues.

- Policing IP in the assigned work and invoking legal proceedings where infringements occur.

TO PUBLISH OR NOT TO PUBLISH – THAT IS THE QUESTION

Smaller publishers limited by finance may not be able to provide all of the above, but the majority of publishers can provide a mechanism for royalty collection and distribution. Key points listed above may also be covered in any contract entered into between songwriter and publisher, setting out what the publisher will endeavour to do for the composer. The songwriter may earn an advance from larger publishers on signing a contract; a percentage share is due on any royalties earned. Typical percentage shares can start at 60/40 (composer/publisher) for a single song assignment, although this could be improved significantly with negotiation. Independent composers and songwriters need to decide whether they feel the need for a music publisher; where a writer clearly understands ownership, IP and legal implications, it is possible to self-administer the song and retain a 100 per cent share in the work. However, self-publishing will require the songwriter to promote their own songs; they may lack the contacts and networking opportunities to increase their chances of commercial exploitation. Composers can join the two primary collection societies, PRS for Music and the MCPS, in the UK. Music publishers are also members of these societies and will collect income streams accordingly. If a songwriter is signed to a music publisher, achieves airplay and is a member of PRS for Music, the writer will receive the royalty share directly from PRS for Music. The PRS royalty share will not go through the publisher account, but the publisher will get their contracted share direct from the PRS at the same time of royalty distribution. However, in respect of any MCPS royalties generated, they will go to the publisher first, so even if the writer is an MCPS member, the writer will need to wait until the publisher distributes the payment.

Songwriters should consider the flow of income, who is collecting it and how this distribution works; essentially composers should join these two societies in the UK in respect of their songs whether signed or not, especially if commercial exploitation is at the core of their aims. The benefits of signing to a publisher can be wholly significant for the composer, but only if the publisher can create enough income and opportunity as a result of licensing and promoting the musical work. As the publisher makes a living from the composer, it is in the publisher interest to persevere with the promotion of their songs in an effort to maximise the value of their catalogue.

THE ROLE OF THE PERFORMING RIGHT SOCIETY

PRS for Music exists as one of three key agencies in the UK, and it specifically collects royalty income on behalf of songwriters, composers, music publishers or song copyright owners. In other global territories similar collection societies exist; in the US the American Society of Composers Authors and Publishers (ASCAP) performs a similar function (www.ascap.com). A current full list of global collection societies or performing rights organisations (PROs) can be found on the Broadcast Music Inc (BMI) website (www.bmi.com). Although it is not always necessary to join all overseas societies (as these agencies have international reciprocal agreements), joining the PRS in the UK on home territory would permit royalty collection and liaison with ASCAP, should a song enjoy radio airplay in the US.

The world's first performing rights organisation was founded in France in 1851; the PRS was founded in the UK on 6 March 1914 by songwriters, composers and publishers to assist them in the administration and collection of royalties for live performances. The PRS formed the MCPS-PRS Alliance in 1997 and adopted the name 'PRS for Music' in 2009. It should be noted that the MCPS collects a different income stream from that of the 'performing right'; the MCPS is discussed in the next section. The 'performing right' income stream consists of royalty income in consideration of public performances of the musical work, examples as follows:

- Songs and compositions used in radio broadcasts on a timed basis, for example, royalties are paid based on the duration that the song is played on air.

- Songs and compositions broadcast on television on a timed basis, usually in synchronisation with a programme or film. Each TV programme or film may be accompanied by a cue sheet detailing the exact length of musical works used in synchronisation and who the composers were. PRS should have a copy of the cue sheet on file.

- Songs and compositions used in live performance. For ticketed venues, a cue sheet may be supplied in respect of the musical works performed, their duration and who the composers were.

- Blanket licence revenues. Although it is difficult to pinpoint 'who composed what' and 'what was played' in this revenue stream, PRS will collect licence fees from a variety of premises allowing them the right to play music to the general public en masse; for example, theatres, festivals, music venues, pubs, nightclubs, social clubs bars, supermarkets, shopping malls, hotels, restaurants, hairdressers, gyms, workplaces, offices, car workshops, religious buildings, colleges, universities and any known public place where music may be played to the public.

The 'public performance right' exists as a key element of copyright, so when someone wants to play a musical composition in public, the PRS will try to obtain a royalty in respect of the usage as set out in their tariff. Where a music composition becomes a worldwide commercial success, the four aforementioned areas of revenue can generate large sums for the composer or assigned publisher. Joining PRS for Music as a composer or publisher member is a straightforward process and can be done for a relatively modest fee. Any composer who is 'self-publishing' their own music and seeking airplay exploitation through media forms such as radio, should ensure they are members of PRS. They may then formally register their original songs and compositions with the Society. The song title and its credited composer(s) will be required by PRS (see ownership and song share section), and if lyricists and arrangers are an intrinsic part of the share, this should be addressed in the credited ownership attribution.

> When a music creator becomes a member of PRS for Music, they give us exclusive permission to licence the public performance of their works. Therefore, you can't get a licence to play those works from anyone else.
>
> (PRS for Music, 2010)

The society makes regular royalty payment distributions to its members, but surprisingly, not all of its 60,000 members receive the high revenues one may expect; in 2007, a £1 royalty distribution breakdown was declared by PRS for Music (see Figure 5.1).

The research provided from PRS for Music shown demonstrates the small proportion of members who achieved earnings of over £20,000 in 2007, at just 4.7 per cent (Figure 5.2). This figure could be representative of composers who are experiencing increased airplay and media exploitation due to a worldwide hit occurring. Composer and publisher members who represent catalogues of established global hit material often earn substantial continual revenues; this has largely been the case in respect of the lion's share of PRS monies distributed. The PRS advises that 'in 2007 nearly 90 per cent of the PRS membership earned less than £5000' (PRS for Music, 2010).

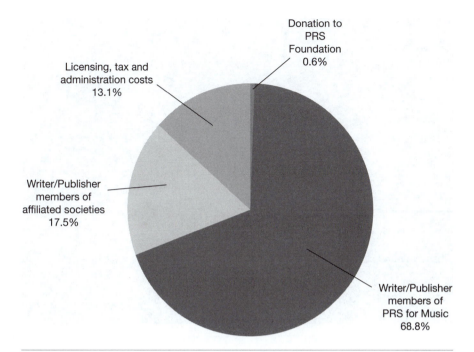

FIGURE 5.1
A breakdown of the PRS £1.00 distribution

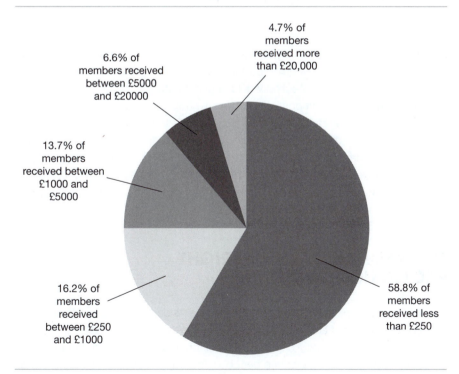

FIGURE 5.2
Distribution share in per cent of monies received by PRS membership

FIGURE 5.3
Performing rights royalties are due to songwriters playing to larger 'ticketed' public audiences. Photo courtesy Dave Robinson, *PSNE*.

In the UK, there is no other agency alternative to PRS for collecting performing rights revenue. Composers could opt out and try to collect their own royalties, but on a global scale, royalty collection would appear impossible by the individual. PRS for Music does have its composer critics, too, who would argue that blanket licence collection monies are impossible to direct back to the original writers – that is, unspecified original music used in pubs, clubs and bars. Small businesses with few employees have also contested paying their PRS music licence fee; buying permission to use a radio in a public place of work; or needing PRS licence to play music that has already been purchased, then played in a gym to perhaps one or two individuals.

THE MECHANICAL COPYRIGHT PROTECTION SOCIETY

The area of mechanical copyright is easier to understand when separated from the concept of the aforementioned performing right. When a composition or song is mechanically reproduced by copying onto a format, for example, a song pressed on CD – a royalty is then generated per copy, known as a 'mechanical'. The MCPS was founded in the UK in 1924 and operated independently of the PRS; individual music works and compositions would be registered by its members with each separate society. In 1997 the shared database of compositions became a focus for the formation of the MCPS-PRS Alliance, with a subsequent name change in 2007 to 'PRS for Music'.

The 1988 copyright act states that the fundamental right of IP in a song or composition grants the owner the right to 'do' – copying the song onto a format for public consumption is fundamental in providing income for songwriters and publishers. If a musical work is replicated in tangible media form such as CD, a fee is due per copy of the song, to the MCPS. At the time of writing the fee collected is 8.5 per cent (excluding tax) of the published price to dealer (PPD); a published list of MCPS royalty schemes is available at www.prsformusic.com. If a record company intends to release an album with thirteen songs on it, an MCPS fee is due for each song on the album, multiplied by the amount of pressings required. The record company will contact the MCPS to declare the replication and full song data, MCPS issues a demand for payment and in return, an MCPS licence is granted to the record company to go ahead and duplicate; many duplication companies will not press large numbers of CDs or physical media without the licence in place first. When MCPS receives the licence fee, a small operating percentage is taken, then the balance is paid to the copyright holder in the original songs for use of the compositions in the replicated product. MCPS fees can be applied to a range of music products:

- music CDs and CD-ROMs
- vinyl records and audio products
- music used in games and multimedia
- downloads
- free CDs in music giveaways and cover-mounts (CDs on magazines and newspapers)
- novelty products (music used in toys and cards)
- music in synchronisation released on DVD
- online and mobile products (ringtones)
- music in films
- bundled music on MP3 players and USB devices: a full list of updated qualifying products can be found by visiting the MCPS section at the PRS for Music website (www.prsformusic.com).

If the composition or song exploited is published, the publisher member will receive any fees due then pay the composer under the terms of the composer-publisher agreement. Where a songwriter retains copyright, is 'self-published' and runs their own record label and intends to replicate copies of their own album for sale, there is still a requirement to organise a licence from the MCPS. In this case the writer can obtain an MCPS exclusion agreement for their music release as they are, in effect, the record company; however, the writer/label owner must be an MCPS member.

The two organisations, MCPS and PRS, provide two distinct revenue streams in association with use of the song and demonstrate its earning potential in association with its media exploitation. Clear understanding of each stream permits an understanding of the legal obligations in subsequent music publishing agreements that may arise. However, registering songs with PRS for Music and MCPS does not prove copyright ownership in the works alone or provide protection from plagiarism and litigation. Policies and procedure updates for both societies are available at www.prsformusic.com.

REFERENCES AND FURTHER READING
Books

Barrow, T. and Newby, J., *Inside the Music Business* (London: Routledge, 1995), pp. 44–55.

Baskerville, D. and Baskerville, T., *Music Business Handbook and Career Guide: Ninth Edition* (London: Sage, 2010), pp. 49–75.

Beattie, W., *The Rock and Roll Times Guide to the Music Industry* (Oxford: Spring Hill, 2007), pp. 43–54.

Bessler, I., (ed.), *2007 Songwriter's Market* (Ohio: F+W, 2006).

Biermans, H., *The Music Industry: The Practical Guide to Understanding the Essentials* (London: DSS, 2007), pp. 28–72.

Davis, S. and Laing, D., *The Guerrilla Guide to the Music Business* (New York: Continuum, 2006), pp. 387–396.

Hull, P.G., *The Recording Industry: Second Edition* (New York: Routledge, 2004), pp. 69–96.

Passman, D.S., *All You Need to Know About the Music Business: Sixth Edition* (London: Penguin, 2008), pp. 253–388.

Schwartz, D.D., *I Don't Need a Record Deal: Your Survival Guide for the Indie Music Revolution* (New York: Billboard, 2005), pp. 193–199.

Schwartz, D.D., *Start and Run Your Own Record Label* (New York: Billboard, 2009), p. 100.

Sobel, R. and Weissman, D., *Music Publishing: The Roadmap to Royalties* (Abingdon: Routledge, 2008).

Walker, Jr., L.J., *This Business of Urban Music: A Practical Guide to Achieving Success in the Industry, from Gospel to Funk to R&B and Hip-Hop* (New York: Billboard, 2008), pp. 196–235.

Wikström, P., *The Music Industry: Digital Media and Society Series* (Cambridge: Polity Press, 2009), pp. 46–84.

Wixen, D.R., *The Plain and Simple Guide to Music Publishing*: Second Edition (New York: Hal Leonard, 2010).

Online resources

British Association of Song Composers and Authors (BASCA). Available at: www.basca.org.uk (accessed 20 August 2010).

Hau, L., 'Journey's Happy Ending', *Forbes* (13 June 2007). Available at:
www.forbes.com/2007/06/13/sopranos-hbo-journey-biz-media-
cx_lh_0613journey.html (accessed 13 August 2010).

Music Publishers Association (MPA). Available at: www.mpaonline.org.uk
(accessed 20 August 2010).

PRS for Music (Performing Right Society UK) and the Mechanical Copyright
Protection Society (MCPS). Available at: www.prsformusic.com (accessed 20
August 2010).

UK Music. Available at: www.ukmusic.org (accessed 20 August 2010).

CHAPTER 6

The recorded music industry sector

Paul Rutter

INTRODUCTION

The recorded music industry sector has provided inspiration for modern music making, actively steering much of its progress and its place in popular culture since the formation of the first official recording company in 1889 by Edward D. Easton, of the Columbia Phonograph Company, US. Easton organised the mass production and selling of the first 'recorded format' in the shape of wax cylinders, reproducing music recorded by the United States Marine Band. Columbia subsequently produced the first record catalogue in 1890, listing cylinders released by Edison and Columbia. Since the late 1800s recorded music has endured numerous technological advancements and format developments, yet the impact of the recorded music format and its value remains unique in entertainment media culture. Record companies use their influence through passive consumption conduits – radio, TV and mainstream media – which in turn perpetuates music product demand and cultivates music business infrastructure. The live music industry sector feeds the recorded music industry sector and vice versa; artists play live, the consumer sees and buys the product or, the consumer hears the artist on radio then pays to see the artist live. Historically, record companies would 'break' acts through radio, TV and press before following up with a tour; more recently an act that debuts at a large festival goes on to enjoy greater success in the media having been seen prominently on the festival platform. The record company business model has had to adapt to change, largely as a result of new digital technologies and the way in which consumers choose to listen to and buy their music. New emerging challenges face the recorded industry sector; as digital futures accelerate, the traditional music industry model formed leading into the 1900s has been forced to seek alternative ways in which to harness revenues, new potential and emerging complex revenue streams and its future in general. Regardless of the changes that the industry has endured over the last century, the departments and principles existing in the structures of a music recording company remain largely the same, but with one or two new additions. This chapter examines the common structures that underpin the administration of the recorded product and the framework that allows it finally to reach its audience.

MAJOR RECORDING COMPANIES

The representative voice of the UK recorded music business is the British Phonograph Industry, and it describes the all-encompassing British music industry as follows:

> The UK music business is composed of rich, diverse and passionate organisations. Record companies are one part of a complex business that includes self employed individuals, small businesses and large multinational companies.
>
> (BPI, 2010)

From 1988 to 1998 the major recording companies consisted of six labels: Warner Music Group, EMI, Sony Music, BMG Music, Universal Music Group and Polygram. Subsequently, Polygram was absorbed into Universal Music Group in 1998 creating the 'big five', and Sony amalgamated with BMG in 2004 to form Sony BMG. BMG and Sony parted company in 2009 to leave the reformed Sony Music now part of the remaining 'big four' consisting of: Sony Music Entertainment, EMI Group, Warner Music Group and the largest of the four, Universal Music Group. The major labels typically operate under the control of a music group: a corporate umbrella organisation that is owned by a conglomerate holding company that may have non-music interests and divisions. The music group consists of a multitude of interests in music catalogues, music publishing, sound recording manufacture replication, distributors and labels. Constituent companies in a music group may also consist of manufacturers, distributors and labels; known as a record group, these companies are sometimes marketed as being 'divisions' of the group. The presence of these large companies in the music market is significant; in 2005 the 'big four' controlled over 70 per cent of the global music market and, in the US, around 80 per cent of all music sales.

INDEPENDENT LABELS AND ACQUISITIONS

Independent labels could generally be defined as any label that releases non-mainstream music regardless of its corporate structure; such labels would not be under the direct control of the 'big four', sourcing their own distribution network and empowered with the ability to make their own creative decisions. Historically, many 'indies' have grown to become larger corporate structures, whereby their artists have become successful through healthy consumer interest. Major music companies also work with successful independents to 'upscale' their operations; the majors' powerful promotion and distribution mechanisms facilitate greater product exposure for a percentage of the proceeds. The independent will often discover, develop and produce the artist then license its product to the major. Licensing deals with independents are commonplace in the music industry; the artist development work undertaken by the 'indie' will save the major valuable time and investment. Majors also 'buy out' independents with a successful roster of acts and then add the label imprint to its collection. Independent labels with an extensive, valuable back catalogue are often bought and sold – similar to the way in which successful music publishing catalogues are bought and sold. Here follows several examples of past successful UK independents and their artists:

- Beggars Banquet (established 1977): Artists include The Lurkers, Tubeway Army, Gary Numan, The Charlatans. Now referred to as the Beggars Group, this company has created a large umbrella independent. Beggars now incorporates other successful independents.

- 4AD (established 1979, now under The Beggars Group): Artists include Scott Walker, The Big Pink, Bon Iver, Camera Obscura, The National, TV on the Radio.

- XL (established 1982, now under The Beggars Group): Artists include Freeze, The Prodigy, Badly Drawn Boy, The White Stripes, Basement Jaxx, Dizzee Rascal, Radiohead, Vampire Weekend, Sigur Ros.

- Warp (established 1989): Artists include Aphex Twin, Autechre, Maximo Park, Squarepusher.

- Rough Trade (established 1978, now under The Beggars Group): Artists include The Smiths, Scritti Politti, The Strokes, The Libertines, Babyshambles, Belle & Sebastian.

- Factory Records (established 1978): Artists include Joy Division, New Order, Happy Mondays, James, Orchestral Manoeuvres in the Dark.

Major labels who have acquired independent labels and their catalogues continue to use the original label imprint and identity for their new releases – for example, Mute, which was acquired by EMI and continues to release artists in a post-punk electronic vein. Early Mute signings include Depeche Mode, Yazoo and Erasure; later signings Goldfrapp, Moby and Nick Cave continued the Mute tradition under EMI's ownership. Donald Passman states that 'A true independent is not owned by a major label, but rather is financed by its owners and/or investors' (2008:77); for the successful independent, selling music catalogues to the majors remains a temptation and part of an ongoing evolution in music industry and catalogue ownership globally. Chris Blackwell, founder of Island Records, sold the company to Polygram in 1989, Polygram was subsequently bought by Universal Music Group, which endeavours to retain the original label ethics, maintaining responsibility for rock group U2, among other new and established acts. The business of buying and selling recorded music catalogues is similar to the way in which publishers trade song catalogues – whether independent or major and regardless of the moral intention when the label was first conceived.

RESPONSIBILITIES OF THE INDEPENDENT

For the independent label, the responsibilities it must address to market the artist are similar to that of the major, although the independent has fewer resources at its disposal; similar departmental functions must be carried out, but with less staff and less finance. Often the director of the label is the A&R person who actually sources the talent and is also the executive producer of the music and promoter of the recorded catalogue. All other essential roles required in pursuit of music sales and marketing are 'contracted out' where the company owner needs additional expertise and support. Closely observing record company core functions and departments later in this chapter will clarify some of the necessary duties in running a music label. For an artist who is deciding who may be best to approach, major or indie – it is evident that, although the independent may have less to offer financially, it is easier to access those that make key artist decisions with the indie label. New artists looking for a contract who are carefully targeting their material, may find it easier to get noticed by an indie that is being approached by fewer artists and therefore may have fewer demonstration recordings to review. Although majors have a larger available mechanism for commercial exploitation, many artists signed to majors have found themselves in competition with a release schedule that prioritises higher profile artists sharing the roster. There are many other advantages and disadvantages to be argued for in each label type, but in essence, there have been countless acts that have moved through both avenues and been highly successful.

IMPRINTS AND SUB-LABELS

For the major, it is sometimes beneficial to mask larger corporate identity branding in association with certain acts. The major therefore creates a label 'imprint' that resonates with its artist and, more importantly, its consumers. The imprint has no legal business structure and therefore is deemed a company division or project operating under the wing of the major. The imprint concept is used widely in other commercial businesses; in the record industry, imprint labels are often invented or they may even be old label brands that were once successful. Label brands are acquired by majors and re-launched to create novelty, nostalgia and kudos for artist and consumer. For instance, the Harvest records imprint was created by EMI in 1969, releasing many rock and pop artists until around 1984 and then went on to become a re-issue sub label, Harvest Heritage, to revive music catalogues by seventies acts such as Barclay James Harvest, Deep Purple, Pink Floyd and The Electric Light Orchestra. The Harvest brand is reactivated whenever an artist release fits with the culture of the brand. Although Harvest does not have its own A&R department, EMI as parent owner would decide when to utilise the brand in appropriation with the act. Examples of sub-labels can be observed in the case of Island Records, whereby 4th and Broadway, a trademarked US subsidiary company owned by Island and established in 1984 (specialising primarily in hip hop), released product under Island's distribution network. The small print beneath 4th and Broadway releases revealed 'an Island records inc. company', establishing the parent label ownership. The complexity of brand ownership in the 4th and Broadway label increases due to subsequent corporate mergers that have occurred; the label, defunct in 1998, saw its parent – Island – subsequently bought by Polygram (in 1989); Polygram was then subsumed by Universal Music Group in 1998, now current owners of the catalogue. At the time of writing, current key sub-labels and ownership structures in the major UK and US recording industry are as follows:

- Universal Music Group: Mercury, Island, Def Jam (Lost Highway, Roadrunner), Interscope, A&M, MCA, Verve (GRP, Impulse!), Geffen, Universal Classics (Decca, Philips, Deutsche Grammaphon). Universal Music Group is a wholly owned subsidiary of international French media conglomerate Vivendi. UMG's head office is in New York.

- Sony Music Entertainment: Columbia, Epic, Jive, Zomba, J Records, 1965 Recordings, Syco Entertainment and Phonogenic. Sony Music Entertainment is owned wholly by the Sony Corporation of America.

- EMI: Angel, Astralwerks, Blue Note, Capitol, Capitol Latin, Capitol Nashville, EMI Classics, EMI CMG, EMI Records, EMI Records Nashville, Manhattan, Mute, Parlophone and Virgin. EMI is owned by private European investment company Terra Firma.

- Warner Music Group: Asylum, Atlantic, Bad Boy, Cordless, East West, Elektra, Nonesuch, Reprise, Rhino, Roadrunner, Rykodisc, Sire, Warner Bros. and Word. Warner is a standalone music group with its headquarters in New York.

The significance of the ownership in labels and sub-label structures by the majors demonstrates the huge amount of multinational catalogue held by these companies. Such catalogues represent much wealth and each time the catalogues are re-released and exploited through mainstream media, healthy income streams are perpetuated (e.g. EMI has continually re-released The Beatles' back catalogue on its Apple/Parlophone imprint). Although there is constant consumer hunger for new releases, back catalogue releases still produce very valuable returns for the majors. Globally, the major labels listed above may also have many more labels and imprints particular to various countries in which they will promote, distribute and exploit talent, relative to the territory and consumers.

VANITY LABELS

The term 'vanity label' is used when an artist carries their own imprint, and usually this is a small label that would suggest that the artist has full creative control in the recording processes and in the label image. Some artists launch their own label early on in their careers in an effort to establish a personal imprint and to bring their music before the public, and this may be with the assistance of others, such as personal managers. If the artist is subsequently offered a recording or licensing deal by a larger label, the distributing label may then allow the artist to keep the small imprint label, usually for 'kudos' reasons. In some cases the artist can be allowed more creative freedom releasing under their own imprint, whereas for some it may mean nothing more than having a greater say in the presentation of the recorded work. Ultimately, the licensor of the small imprint label will have control over the final output; for example, the now defunct Nothing Records set up by Trent Reznor of Nine Inch Nails, was administered by Interscope (now under the wing of Universal Music Group); Nothing Records still remains a strong vanity imprint. There are many examples of vanity labels including US artist Prince's Paisley Park and Madonna's Maverick Records, both formed under multinational, Warner Music. The artist may also part company with the vanity brand over time, as in the case of Madonna and Maverick, due to a multitude of reasons. Vanity brands both major and independent are often bought and sold; music labels and imprints represent a 'secondary' brand that simply follows the kudos of the artist and often creates a sense of additional product value for the consumer.

LABEL DOMINANCE IN THE MUSIC INDUSTRY

Ownership in the global music industry as a whole could be defined by the larger corporate structures that exist to dominate commercial creation, development and sale of recorded products, as opposed to smaller music producers and labels who release independently of these structures. Since the inception of the first official large recording company (The Columbia Phonograph Company in 1889), there have been many recording companies that have come and gone, and there are major companies that have proved themselves in retaining a heavy market share in recorded music. It is the majors who, to this day, remain steadfast in their domination of the music industry due to their powers of promotion and distribution – having a huge influence on what the music-buying public consumes. The conduits of mainstream media such as TV and radio remain largely the exclusive promotional territory of the majors. TV and radio producers respect the products released by the majors and endorse this by playing their product. Internet media has provided new opportunities for the independent music releaser to promote at little or no cost, but the majors can naturally use the internet tool to full effect, being able to purchase highly visible positions and net advertisements. In any promotional medium the majors prove consistently dominant, as there is enough investment, infrastructure and product respect to allow this to happen. Smaller independent labels limited by their financial position can only access a fraction of mainstream media to promote, compared to the majors. If, however, the indie is licensed to a major, the major can then use its promotional mechanisms to assist in the product placement.

THE SIGNIFICANCE OF THE MAJORS

The dominance of the major label mechanism in the UK is evidenced in the statistics provided by organisations such as the PPL, which, in its annual review 2009, published 'the people's pop chart'. The chart was compiled uniquely by PPL using radio airplay and public usage data (not recorded music sales); the diverse list of artists showed that in this top-twenty chart, each overriding music label brand was a major. Warner licensed one of the releases, EMI licensed two (including the number one position), Sony Music licensed seven and Universal Music represented half of the top twenty, with ten releases. The significance of this proves two salient points; first, although small independent labels may unite with a major to enjoy greater success, it is the major that ultimately has the finance, promotional tools and media influence to make a significant impact with the artist on a wider scale. Second, for the independent, simply using the internet as a promotional tool will not earn a placement in a mainstream top-twenty chart, such as PPL's people's chart, although electronic media and internet are a recognised effective global promotional tool. The PPL chart is significant, as the data that is collected is based on royalty returns from mainstream media; the chart is described as 'what the public was listening to in 2009'.

As the major label mechanism dominates mainstream media promotional routes, it could be argued that airplay charts would return very different results if the independent labels also had equal access and 'clout', concerning 'gatekeeper' producers in TV and radio mainstream media. However, with the total amount of new music product released each week (from both majors and independents), it is unlikely that the current infrastructure in mainstream media would have the resources to sift and select appropriate music for airplay.

Due to the 'music mass' that is perpetuated in these constant releases, the arrival of online technologies has provided a natural 'storage' home for the small independent. Streaming services that allow consumers to search for exactly the music they want from services such as We7 and Spotify permit and accelerate discovery for the consumer. However, not all consumers are investigative or 'active' in their use of new media; many still prefer to listen to music and discover new artists through older established mainstream media forms such as radio and television. The dominance of the majors in the music industry and therefore the resultant shape of industry is likely to remain intact, as long as consumers are passive in their consumption, discovering artists through TV and radio. Generally, it has been proven that consumers are happy to be guided in their music consumption habits by mainstream media output; this facilitates and enables control in music markets by companies that have exclusive access to this media. Although passive consumers can now stream a 'niche genre' radio station online, the level of investigation required is more complex and time consuming, as is researching and discovering new music through, say, MySpace. Investigative and active consumption online has provided new modes of consumption, but this is still a minority pursuit compared to the public at large, who still prefer to discover music through traditional radio and TV media. If the public en masse decided to search and listen to music via online investigation only and abandon mainstream media forms, it is predicted that the music landscape would look very different to the enduring model of today. Furthermore, if online media becomes future mainstream media in totality, as many predict, the question remains whether current passive consumers will actually become active consumers in their total discovery of music. Kusek and Leonhard predict that many future consumers will all possess a 'UMD' (universal mobile device) and that there will be streamed, 'anytime-anywhere access to music' on-the-road or at home, all for a small fee (2005:16).

OWNERSHIP IN RECORDINGS AND MUSIC PRODUCTIONS

Any person or company that chooses to fund recorded music in a studio and then creates a brand identity for that product could be known as a record or music label. Music labels are then responsible for the manufacture, distribution and promotion of the recordings that they own, under their label imprint. In legal terms, the first copyright owner in a recording is the producer, who is known as the author of the recording (this should not be confused with the separate copyright that resides in the song or composition). The producer is often contracted or commissioned by the record company to oversee and facilitate the recording. As the record company has paid for the studio time, the record label then becomes the copyright owner in the whole recording (see music ownership and copyright sections). Owning copyright in the master recording is crucial for any record company; protecting this copyright enables the record company to recoup any investment made in its producers and signed musical acts in the future and to remain solvent. Additionally it should be noted that the financial investment and promotion processes are often long and expensive before a record company sees any monetary return from its signed acts.

RECORDING COMPANY DIVISIONS AND CORE FUNCTIONS

Larger music recording companies have core functions that facilitate the acquisition, manufacture and sale of recorded products. Depending on company size, independents would also need to consider these roles and the framework required. It is easier to understand the internal workings of this model if divided into three key areas:

- Products division: Artistes & Repertoire, Production, Marketing & Product Management, Sales & Distribution.
- Promotion division: Press, Promotion, Digital Operations, Creative/Video.
- Administration: Managing Director, Legal and Business Affairs, Business Development, Finance, Human Resources.

The functions and roles in each division are discussed in detail in the next sections.

Products division: A&R

The Artistes & Repertoire department is primarily responsible for the acquisition of new emerging talent; the A&R function, when successful, provides the lifeblood for the label and should guarantee future revenue streams from successful acts – long-term income copyrights. The phrase A&R originates from pre-1950s music industry, whereby the job of the recording company was not only to source new artists, but also to find appropriate repertoire for them to play and sing (BBC, 2006). The methods employed in the selection of acts by the A&R department remain one of the music industry's great mysteries to musicians, artists, managers and publishers alike. There is no set formula for selection, other than the ultimate belief that the act singled out for signing and contractual obligation, has potential to succeed on behalf of the label and provide a revenue stream. Belief in the act often extends beyond the A&R department; many other personnel in the record company would need to endorse the discovery and signing and, more importantly, feel enthusiasm for the act and an empathy with it. The managing director, product division and promotion division will often be involved in the signing process as ultimately it is they who will be tasked with the investment in finance and labour in breaking and working the act. In addition, persons exterior to the company, such as family and friends of employees working at the label, may voice opinion on the potential signing. The market research carried out in the signing process has always proved to be relatively unrefined; A&R departments and labels often only measure their risk against a low sample or demography – this is usually the growing audience that a new act may attract. A&R looks for a 'buzz' surrounding potential new signings, which could constitute a large number of hits on a MySpace or YouTube site; enthusiastic audiences at gigs; or a 'word of mouth' propagating a viral presence concerning the act. In the past, current market trends have been noted by record companies and therefore 'manufactured' acts have been recruited to satisfy the demand, often assembled by managers and music moguls. The science of A&R is far from exact, but when the right act is discovered, the longevity of the label is often assured. Beyond the artist selection process, the A&R department is also responsible for selecting appropriate songs and producers for the artist, organising the studio recording and providing important interaction between the artist and the company, often liaising with the personal management of the artist. Larger music companies have a hierarchical structure, which begins with an A&R scout (who is tasked with searching for new talent), A&R managers and heads of A&R working at different levels of decision making and working with different styles of music.

Products division: Production department

The production department co-ordinates the manufacture of the physical product as essentially recorded products need to be in the right quantity at the right time in order to meet market demands. The market demands are instigated by the promotions department, who seek to create consumer demand through popular media. It is essential that product is available following the media promotion campaign. Gauging the correct amount of physical product has proved risky on many occasions, and although CDs and DVDs remain a popular format in supermarkets, the 'standby' format of the server-stored MP3 download undeniably saves on considerable production costs. The converse problem, however, is the lower profit margin associated with the download format. The production department liaises with pressing plants and ensures that they have all necessary components to press the tangible media form. Before replicating large amounts of CDs, an MCPS licence will be required; the record company will purchase this from MCPS, and the licence will be required by the pressing plant to prove that the record label has the necessary permission in place to replicate the musical works, songs or compositions (PRS for Music, 2010). Other components that need to be in place would constitute a red book CD master with ISRC coded tracks (PPL, 2010); artwork items (supplied in manufacturer format, for example, high-resolution image files); and directives on packaging specifications including inlay booklets and cards. CD duplication involves using a master copy to burn a disc's contents to another (often up to 1,000 copies); replication is defined by the cloning of a thousand or more CD copies, using a glass master created from the original (see www.discread. com). In the production of tangible music formats, replication and duplication plants provide full product specifications on their websites. Labels considering any forms of replication should observe key components when contemplating duplication as alteration at a later stage can prove very costly (see www.dischromatics.co.uk). Finished products replicated by the pressing plant are delivered to the distributor for propagation into music stores, supermarkets, wholesalers and retailers of music consumer and media products. Major labels such as EMI utilise their own distribution networks, but it is commonplace for many larger labels to franchise this task out to independent distribution networks.

Products division: Marketing and product management

The marketing and product management department works closely with the A&R team and the artist management to create a marketing strategy for each act signed to the label. Forging unique identities for artists carves a market niche, boosting appeal to music consumers and maximising potential in the act. Fashion stylists may be consulted also at this stage in order to finalise an image and fashion the artist. Product management also involves research and investigation into the demography and intended market the act may succeed in most. Gauging public perception at an early stage will dictate which media conduits to use, for example, a guitar band may feature in *NME* magazine or popular classics artists in Sunday newspaper magazines. This media process is known as market 'positioning', whereby the music company seeks to establish the act within its true consumer audience demographic. This liaison process will also involve consultation with other departments. In order to approach the market in the correct way, the product management team will also work with assigned artwork designers (for advertising and posters), photographers and pop video producers. It is important for the act to be noticed at the right place and right time, and it is equally important for the act to be seen in the correct light by the public. In short, the product managers must ensure that the artist sells. The marketing personnel liaises closely with the sales and distribution department, measuring the approach taken towards online and retail marketing approaches. Authorisation to manufacture is given only when this department agrees that the artist product is ready to be taken to audience in its entirety. If a subsidiary label is involved (whereby a smaller independent label is licensing its product to a major), the independent label may be very proactive in formulating image and marketing with the endorsement of the major. Often the independent will fund and provide the whole artist package as part of the licensing arrangement, however, previous to the major using its power and funds to market the product, certain marketing and image agreements may need to be adhered to by the independent. The issue of 'manufactured' acts provides further fuel for discourse; record companies often form acts with a preordained purpose in mind rather than recruit an act already formed. Authenticity and the original nature of the manufactured pop band is often called into question by certain consumers.

Products division: Sales and distribution

The sales and distribution department oversees the trading volumes of music that are destined for retail and online availability, whether tangible media or digital music product. Meeting the release date is a key priority, ensuring that any promotional work carried out prior to release matches with product availability to the consumer. This department will therefore liaise closely with any contracted external distributors to monitor sales data; not all labels distribute product themselves and often use other aggregators to distribute their music, for example, iTunes. The employees in music label sales teams often have a history in retail and therefore possess a good geographical knowledge of the music retail sector into which they are selling product. Although this department must identify new markets, the sales team can also identify consumer trends regionally; for example, heavy metal music markets may demonstrate success in certain locations. Targeting these markets using knowledge of regional buying tendencies will improve sales. The sales force will cultivate relationships with 'key' account customers – these are large buyers of musical product, such as large supermarket chains (ASDA, Sainsburys) or music retailers, such as HMV. The head office of these large retailers usually has a 'buying manager' who will decide on the quantity of product that they will purchase from the record company sales force. The buying departments will usually need to know details of the promotion plan that accompanies the act: the 'plot'. Buying departments do not want to stock products on shelves that do not have a strong promotional campaign behind them. Shelving or 'rack space' is always in high demand from many music distributors, so music product usually remains on shelves for six weeks, then new product is brought in to refresh the racks. The buying department will often produce a music chart for in-store displays to highlight to customers the current popularity of their music products. This chart, however, does not always correspond with national certified charts, but purely serves to reflect music products being promoted at that specific time. If the product does not sell within six weeks, it is often returned to the distributor when the product may be re-released at a future date or re-distributed. This method of retailing is known as 'sale or return' (SOR). When the product does not sell, the retailer may then return the product to the distributor to clear rack space, then subsequently issue an invoice back to the record company to reclaim what was paid for the unsold product. Accurately estimating the quantity of product that *might* sell is crucial when a 'sale or return' contract is in place. For instance, replicating 40,000 copies of a CD then having them returned could prove financially disastrous for many small record companies, so field and market research is essential before pressing huge quantities of tangible media. Key retail sales account customers (Tesco, etc.) provide the largest revenue for record companies, but this has come at an increasing price. Key account customers demand larger discounts on product, therefore buying and retailing product for less, driving down profit margins for record companies. The remaining argument for the recording company is that where the company loses profit, there is less to invest in new emergent talent. Regardless of these issues, essentially the sales and distribution department must ensure the product is available at the right time in the right place, in tandem with the label marketing and product management team.

Promotions division: Press

The personnel working in this department are known as press officers and will work closely with the product division. As the artists they work with are 'positioned' in the market by the music company, 'positioning' will often dictate the style of press that the artist requires. This is set by the marketing and product management team, so press officers can then ensure an appropriate press campaign. When an artist is recording a new work set for release (promoting existing catalogues, re-releases or playing live), the press officer will aim to ensure articles are written about the act. There is a requirement to ensure reviews, photos and interviews appear in key publications in the build up to the release, so the press office will often work many weeks and months ahead of this date. When a new release is imminent by an established artist, the press office raises awareness through a variety of means; celebrity magazines, timely appearances at show business parties or presenting at televised awards ceremonies. Other press tactics include, alternative 'gossip' and personal story lines (other than those purely concerning the artist's music) and utilising artist associations with external bodies, sponsorships and charities. Finding new ways to feature and discuss an artist in the press is a constant mission with each new record release. In the final analysis, all artists and labels strive for the same thing – publicity for their recorded works. An interesting or creative 'plot' increases the chances of 'column inches' in magazines and newspapers and is far more likely to succeed in 'grabbing headlines'. The artist may require additional regional attention, for example, Scottish or Irish regional press, although national press will give maximum exposure alongside glossy entertainment and music magazines. Online press promotion is also an ever expanding area for the press office. For those that seek work in this sector, perhaps the greatest attribute a press officer can possess (other than a wide range of contacts) is the power of persuasion. Each journalist that this press team deals with is important to the label, as the press articles they can secure will maximise publicity and contribute to the wider campaign, effectively 'making or breaking' the product. The press officer can also accompany the artist to interviews and photographic sessions, enabling opportunities to network with journalists and monitor the press campaign.

Promotions division: Radio and TV

Working closely with press officers, this particular division utilises more powerful mainstream media conduits in radio and television to raise the profile of the artist; TV is still regarded as the most effective way to reach the widest possible national audience. This type of promotion is known as 'plugging', and once again the positioning of the act in the market will determine the type of exposure required and which stations to approach. In the UK, the demise of weekly music programmes such as BBC's *Top of the Pops* and its weekly chart rundown has reduced national TV opportunities to promote popular chart music; however, a plethora of new 24-hour TV media cable music channels provide alternative platforms. Coupled with this are opportunities to promote and advertise artist videos online; consumers and fans can find out about their favourite acts' releases and see and hear product in seconds, compared with active and passive consumption methods of the past. The TV and radio plugger's ultimate goal is to achieve maximum exposure and airplay in both mediums. As this is such a huge task, additional independent pluggers may be contracted to work in separate areas of regional or national radio, for example, FM regional radio, BBC regional radio or national frequencies, such as BBC Radio One. The plugger will often have a long list of known contacts in radio or TV, which is the most important attribute for the plugger alongside excellent communication skills. Being signed to a major will greatly assist in getting noticed by radio and TV programme producers, but it is by no means an automatic right to airplay. Independents will often find this process even more difficult, as the funds required to enlist good pluggers on a national level will prove expensive, alongside not being able to sustain a long national campaign across two or three music releases. Majors will often 'lock into' a prolonged campaign in which to break a new artist to the public, costing many thousands of pounds – resources that small independents simply do not have. As online audiences and media expand, the TV and radio plugging department has many more digital avenues to pursue in respect of its artists, alongside these mainstream media formats. The department will 'outsource' promotion and public relations (PR) activity to ensure maximum exposure for the label's own targeted and prioritised acts, wherever the budget will allow.

Promotions division: Creative video

When a single release occurs via a major label, a video will be produced in support of the track to increase public awareness of the product, usually a forerunner to a pending album release. As the video medium has expanded through internet growth, the music video has become more crucial in accompaniment to single song releases. On 1 August 1981 at 12.01 am, Music Television (MTV) based in New York showed its first video, 'Video Killed the Radio Star' by British pop band The Buggles; MTV was the first to establish the concept of cable niche programming, reshaping music marketing and subsequently providing a new symbol for youth culture. MTV proved its popularity in its first year with 2.1 million households subscribing. Today MTV programmes less continuous music and primarily broadcasts a variety of reality TV and popular culture shows, targeted at adolescents and young adults. As many more cable music channels have developed worldwide (proving that entertainment consumers are prepared to pay for dedicated 24-hour music channels), record companies have seized the opportunity to promote heavily in this medium. The greatest successor to MTV is YouTube, an online video streaming service based in California and formed by Chad Hurley, Steve Chen and Jawed Karim, that uploaded its first video for internet viewing on 23 April 2005. Now that music consumers are able to search for and see their favourite artists whenever they want through mediums such as YouTube, consumers do not now need to wait to see music in mainstream media. In addition, the video file format and the ways it is disseminated to potential audiences online are ever increasing. The creative video department must respond to trends in this sector and will commission appropriate videos to accompany the single song release. The creative video department will select and appoint a director for the video and devise the content; a 'storyboard' for the video will be discussed, with the 'positioning' of the act and its potential market at the forefront. The video department may also take on other roles, from booking the location to overseeing the shooting of the video, ensuring that the artist is chaperoned and guided in the process.

Promotions division: Digital operations

Digital operations departments have increased in importance as online download sales have accelerated globally and become a much larger part of record company income streams. Market sales of 'single' song purchases in the UK now consist of nearly 100 per cent downloads with just a few per cent tangible media. This department is responsible for all aspects of internet marketing and sales; the digital operations department must promote artist release information and content to blogs, music portals, newspaper websites and social network channels. The digital operations department liaises with the creative team, who have 'positioned' the artist in the market; working further with the production division and A&R personnel to ensure that technological, communication and fan-base solutions are developed appropriately for the artist. As the digital medium is constantly renewing and evolving, the department must ensure widgets, applications, websites and social network profiles are continually developed for the artist. Digital content production requires a detailed knowledge of online public relations and digital marketing as the music label looks to maximise potential for its roster in this ever expanding area. Currently, fan-base projects increase customer awareness through methods used such as 'viral seeding', using blogging to promote artists through large social media sites such as Facebook, and also sharing comment and video on YouTube. Recording companies set fan-base targets of three, six and twelve months; artist presence and fan awareness is raised in a gradual, advancing way. Email marketing initiatives will always follow the release of new product, whether a new digital compilation of multi-artists, a mobile application or iTunes LP. The record company is constantly seeking innovation in the digital operations area in an effort to maximise the electronic media potential in its artists and subsequent revenue income streams.

Promotions division: Advertising and sponsorship

TV advertising is a proven way of increasing CD and tangible product sales, especially where the finances are available to deliver a strong campaign. This department negotiates advertising rates with national TV, radio, press and online media, in respect of national and regional advertising campaigns to raise product awareness for the artist. TV advertising is still regarded as the most effective means of raising product awareness. It has been proven by major labels many times that even when the overall music market is experiencing a downturn in sales (e.g. just after Christmas), launching a well-fuelled advertising campaign can boost individual artist sales by 20 per cent and more. For this reason alone, expensive TV advertising is still widely used for music products, providing an effective sales-boost strategy.

Advertising rates can vary; a national TV campaign that goes out across all ITV networks in the UK can cost from around £3,000 for one ten-second commercial broadcast at non-peak time, to nearly £30,000 and upwards for the same length commercial at standard peak times. In the UK, peak advertising periods usually constitute ad breaks between highly viewed soap operas with estimated viewing figures of around 10 million, depending on storylines. Music labels can tailor their TV campaigns to suit the artist demographic and available budget, but it can be seen that commercials running over one or two weeks are very expensive – costing thousands. In the commercial, 'tagging' is also common, whereby a specific retailer (e.g. a supermarket such as ASDA) is mentioned in tandem with the advert exclusively. In this regard the record company has a specific deal with the supermarket, ensuring enough stock is available, with the supermarket gaining publicity for its store. Advertising campaigns are important in selling product out to retailers as the ad campaign forms a huge part of the plot and must tie in with artist's appearances and interviews at the time of release. Adverts for product can run in all media, and usually the cost of advertising product outweighs the music production costs. Given this level of investment, new music venturists should be aware of the financial commitment when breaking new music products to a national public audience.

Advertising and sponsorship lie closely together in this department as sponsorship extends into advertising through the association of consumer products with the artist. In the history of the music industry, the association of brand and artist is a relatively new concept; however, it has proved successful in its promotional worth. In 2008 in the UK, pop outfit Girls Aloud (signed to Universal Music Group) entered into a lucrative sponsorship agreement with confectioner Nestlé and their Kit Kat brand to mutual benefit. Brand association such as this produces increased advertising and awareness for the artist and an additional revenue stream in respect of the artist's earnings. Many high profile concert tours also attract lucrative sponsorship agreements, allowing brands to popularise their commercial outputs in front of new demographics. Associating the wrong brand with an artist could, however, be damaging if brand ethics do not impress the fan-base of the artist. Personnel that work in this department must cultivate new business in seeking exterior bona fide commercial companies with a reputable history and profile. The brand association should enhance the career of the artist and essentially must be created appropriately.

Administration department: Managing director and team leaders

The Managing Director (MD) team leads all departmental managers in their business affairs. The MD sets out the company strategies, budgets and liaises with the BPI. Ultimately, the MD is accountable for the success of the label and is therefore required to participate in decisions that shape the label identity and its future in the marketplace. In the US, the status of chief executive officer (CEO) will often equal that of the managing director in the UK. Also in the US, large conglomerate labels often have presidents of each smaller label brand and further to that are vice presidents (VPs), occupying key roles in various departments. US terminology can also be used in the UK, but generally the title 'manager' is more common. As recorded music product incomes have decreased worldwide, many of the hierarchical structures that once existed in the record company have been re-organised to include fewer managers. Many job roles that once carried large responsibility and large wages have decreased in size, in tandem with an increasingly youthful team now managing many record company operations. Lower record company revenue streams have had an impact on long serving experienced music personnel also within the majors; a more youthful workforce is less expensive to maintain. Work experience interns demand even less in wages and have become a popular way to staff departments; the major record industry has evolved a new financial coping mechanism by which it can exist. It could be argued that this new hierarchy provides more opportunity for the youthful, enthusiastic and tenacious, even though much patience will often be required to become a permanent employee. The new record industry hierarchy is often criticised for its haemorrhaging and devaluation of forty-something, experienced record company executives; the average age of the new MD in most major labels and their subsidiaries is now around thirty. However, there has always been a trend for many experienced executives who leave or retire from the industry to go on and set up their own music companies. They utilise their contacts, reputation and status either to record, manage or publish music artists, as they are still passionate about the industry.

Administration department: Legal and business affairs

The legal and business affairs department liaises with the MD, A&R and the marketing department on behalf of all artists signed to the label. The department issues contracts and agreements, entering into negotiation with the artist and their appointed manager, lawyer or legal representative. The legal department employs qualified specialist music lawyers who have extensive knowledge of contractual objectives and practice. Where an advance is payable, the legal department will set out terms and conditions to be met; as contracting is a regular occurrence, an 'off the shelf' agreement is often tailored to the specific artist. The modern major recording company continually seeks to tap into new revenue streams and receipts from their artists; as a result, contracts have become more complex. If a full 360-degree deal is offered, which incorporates a wide range of artist income, this would demand a larger type of contract with many more clauses and conditions to be met. For the artist who is offered a recorded music contract it would be advisable to seek the services of a reputable music industry lawyer. Key clauses to be aware of are the term and length of the agreement and how the company will seek to recoup its investment. If publishing revenue is to be included in an all-inclusive agreement (see Chapter 5, in the section on contracts) with merchandise and live performance fees, contracts will be highly complex and difficult to understand for the novice. A larger advance would naturally be expected in return for a contract that included more artist revenue streams; ultimately the contract must be *worth* signing, and an experienced independent music lawyer can estimate what may constitute a reasonable and fair agreement.

The business affairs team sets out budgets for all record company projects and their artists, planning the business strategy under the guidance of the MD. Often, record companies look to 'back catalogue' and re-issues to bolster income, rather than the expense of multiple new artist signings. If a compilation album is to be released, the legal department is involved in negotiations with other labels for any music recordings they do not own, particularly if external licensed tracks are included. Often music recordings owned by the label are used in synchronisation with a film, advertisement or DVD project, so commissioning of tracks and clearing will be necessary with an accompanying agreement. The measured use of such material – percentages due, advances and timescales – will be subject to contract in each recorded work, and this would be negotiated by the legal team.

When music works owned by the record company are infringed, the legal team will be required to represent the label in court on behalf of the artist. The legal might of the majors provides their artists with a degree of security, knowing that a mechanism exists to fight possible infringements and plagiarising of their recorded works. However, the greatest challenge to legal departments has surfaced in the digital age. Policing mass file sharing among private music consumers and illegal copying of music has proved virtually impossible. Instigating prosecution proceedings, with such a large worldwide number of infringements, cannot be done by recording companies alone, so greater solutions are required. Record company legal departments and their music industry representative bodies (such as the British Phonograph Industry and UK Music) recognise the direct threat posed by the digital music revolution and the costly legal proceedings that occur as a result of it.

Administration department: Digital business development

The digital revolution has by default demanded a requirement to develop new business strategies in digital media. Emerging ways in which consumers wish to download music has provided challenges for this department: the growth of online digital delivery and new interactive mobile media such as Apple iPhones, iPads, and an ever increasing range of gadgetry. Although tangible music products still form an important part of music sales, the industry prediction is that the majority of all music sales will be digital in the future; innovation in new digital music business models and further harnessing of the online digital consumer will be the saviour of the large record company. Where music label product and catalogues are available through digital mediums, the digital operations department negotiates commission rates and percentages earned as the result of downloads from distributors, internet service providers (ISPs) and mobile phone companies.

Administration department: Human resources

If considering working for a major music label, approaching the human resources (HR) department to establish the individual company policy and how employment may obtained would be the first step. As increasing numbers of applicants seek to work with major labels, competition for places is often fierce. The HR department is responsible for all aspects of staffing, interviewing prospective employees and creating the contracts that bind employee to company. Although record companies may advertise in relevant press, magazines and websites such as *Music Week*, often a specialist London media employment agency such as Handle Recruitment will advertise on behalf of the music company. Where a greater level of expertise is required, HR will seek applicants with a proven track record, as would be the case in any other industry – a wider net may be cast in search of the most appropriate person, with the right credentials. For aspiring hopeful young music personnel, gaining contacts in the industry is a necessary process; networking is a key requirement and a proven ability to do the job, a pre-requisite. Many employees who now work for large music labels started out by working in sectors of the industry that surround and support it, such as retail sales, independent promotion, public relations or management. This is often the best way to get to know the major and network with the personnel that work in it; when a major record company job does become available, 'networkers' are the first to know. Many music companies, both large and small, provide internship opportunities; approaching these in a professional manner, with an appropriately informative and relevant CV, will aid the application process. To build industry experience, it is easier today to showcase talents on a small, independent scale – for example, providing visual proof through the development of online materials on MySpace and YouTube. Demonstrating proven involvement with artists, showing positive hit counter achievements and the ability to display individual effort and success can demonstrate inherent skills. Internship opportunities will vary from a few days to a few months working in support roles in various departments, and often these are unpaid placements. The 'work for free' ethic is commonplace in the entertainment industry – from radio to performance, the live music sector to the recorded music industry sector. Working without salary may lead to a full or part-time post in the industry; many are prepared to take the chance without any guarantees. Record companies often state their employment and HR policies on their company websites, which is an ideal place to start research for prospective applicants. Ultimately, the HR department must improve the effectiveness of the company by devising salary levels, training and staff development, staff advice, and employee communications, relations and performance management (UK Music, 2010).

> If you can demonstrate to key figures in the music industry, that you can do things well for yourself; for instance selling music and creating a buzz independently – others in industry will then ask you to do the same things for them.
>
> (Mike Smith, MD Columbia Records UK,
> personal correspondence, 2010)

MIKE SMITH, MANAGING DIRECTOR OF COLUMBIA RECORDS/SONY MUSIC UK

Mike Smith

Mike Smith is MD of Columbia Records UK, part of Sony Music. Mike describes how he got into the music industry. Originating from Merseyside and moving to London, having previously studied History and Politics at Manchester University, he then decided to follow a creative career pathway.

While at University I began working with bands in Manchester, helping them to find gigs and give them an audience. I worked briefly with Gareth Evans, a venue manager in Manchester, who also managed The Stone Roses, giving me early experience of working with bands that had commercial potential. I landed a post at MCA publishing in London and applied for many industry jobs while observing the processes behind A&R. While at MCA I was involved in signing Blur and The Smashing Pumpkins and eventually left to work at EMI Music Publishing, where I worked for fourteen years, working with the Creation Records roster as well as many others including Supergrass, The Verve, Primal Scream, Arctic Monkeys, White Stripes, Arcade Fire, Gorillaz and Robbie Williams.

As MD for Columbia, one is aware of the sense of history of the label, it being the oldest record label in the world. Working for a large multinational you find that large amounts of money are invested in the roster (Kasabian, Mark Ronson, Kings of Leon to name a few) and in new artists. The biggest challenge is getting your records onto the radio playlists and making sure the wider public gets to know about the artist. The record industry has faced many challenges in the last decade, but perhaps the greatest changes that have happened are the issues that surround income. Since around 2005 to 2010, income for the recorded music industry has halved and this can be attributed to some key factors.

First, when tracks became 'unbundled' from albums, consumers moved towards making single-track purchases, so instead of buying a whole album, consumers may now only buy a few songs. The second issue is piracy; 60–70 per cent of the industry's sales are lost through file sharing and illegal copying. Finally, supermarkets have driven down dealer prices of CDs. The impact has been huge across the industry, and it could be argued that the recorded music industry is two thirds the size it was in 2006.

The industry has found mechanisms by which it can survive and has generated a leaner business model to weather the recent storms by

PROFILE

finding new ways to staff and run the industry. Fortunately the public still respond well to reading about music, to live shows and to radio airplay, and it has been proven that many are happy to be 'guided' in music buying and prefer the wider endorsement of music through these means. As things stand, the labels can still create good reasons for people to consume music, which gives good reason for majors to hold a significant place in the music buying market.

Sometimes when small-scale entrepreneurs are given money to invest in the music industry this does not always work; so the important thing to consider is playing and being involved in music for pleasure and simply enjoying it first and foremost. And if you are thinking of working in the music industry, remember that aside from talent, your enthusiasm is the most important factor in impressing those you work for.

Administration department: Finance

The finance department handles the revenue streams that occur as a result of exploitation of the recorded product. Music labels seek new ways to harness income from their acts in the future and the finance department needs to consider administering complex new revenue streams in the digital revolution. This department must also cope with the converse, as expenditure has grown as a result of rising advertising and promotion costs, and so it must 'balance the books'. The finance department employs qualified accountants who will have knowledge of UK tax systems and liaise with the UK Inland Revenue and Customs and Excise (see www.hmrc.gov.uk). Smaller labels will sub-contract these duties to appropriate accountants, in place of larger 'in-house' operations that would monitor income and expenditure on a continual basis. Major music company accountants support senior management in weekly and monthly reporting tasks: balance sheet reconciliation, profitability studies, financial analysis and performance are important parts of the work. Three key collection societies operate in the UK in association with exploitation of the recorded work: the MCPS, PPL and Video Performance Limited (VPL) – the accounts department will liaise with these societies. Working in this sector will require financial acumen, necessary accounting skills and a thorough knowledge of music income stream generation.

MAKING MONEY FROM RECORDED PRODUCTS: PPL

Phonographic Performance Limited is a UK record company society that collects revenue on behalf of its record label and performer members. All record labels, independent, major or 'bedroom' status, can capitalise on recorded music income streams by being a PPL member – a key revenue stream in the exploitation of the recorded work. The PPL was formed in 1934 by EMI and Decca, following a prosecution case brought against a restaurant in Bristol that played recorded music to its customers; it was deemed by the courts that, in principle, those that were involved in the creation of a sound recording should be paid for the public performance and broadcasting of their work. The board of current PPL directors hail from a wide range of entertainment industry companies and music business interests. When record label members and performers join, they assign their legal rights to PPL in order that PPL can collect revenues from a variety of sources whenever the sound recordings are used in public media. The PPL largely divides revenues derived from playing music in public into two categories: playing music in association with a business; and playing music in association with broadcasting:

- Public playing of recorded music may occur in: Nightclubs, pubs, shops, hotels, gymnasiums, business waiting rooms, offices, factories and warehouses, exhibitions, music events and festivals, sports stadia, telephone 'hold-on' music, and jukeboxes.
- Broadcasting revenues may occur from the following sources: Radio broadcasting, TV broadcasting, public performance, online and mobile television, online and mobile radio, new media, music suppliers and international usage.

A record label or performer can join the PPL at no cost; it is advantageous for performers that are participating in recorded works to become PPL members alongside their releasing label or imprint, in doing so assigning PPL the right to collect and distribute valuable income. The PPL licenses thousands of performer members and record companies in the UK, enabling 'hundreds of thousands of shops, pubs and others to use recorded music in their business' (PPL, 2010). In addition to media transmission revenue streams such as TV, using recorded works publicly in association with any UK business is illegal, especially whereby playing the recorded work enhances the business space, for example, in a small waiting room, public house, bar or nightclub. Businesses can apply for a PPL licence and negotiate a yearly PPL fee based on specific music usage. The blanket fees collected from businesses are later distributed among its performer and record company members. Under the UK Copyright Designs and Patents Act of 1988, playing music in public (other than domestic use – playing music at home) is illegal. Without the PPL, businesses would need to contact the label owners in all music recordings before being able to play them in public lawfully. The PPL acts on behalf of thousands of record companies and performers, so a single licence from PPL will allow a business proprietor to use virtually all recorded music available in the UK. The PPL has reciprocal arrangements with twenty-four different worldwide territories. Arrangements with other similar foreign licensing organisations produces income from recorded works used overseas for both performer and record label members.

THE PPL

Fran Nevrkla, Chairman and CEO of the Phonographic Performance Limited

The music industry has never been a more exciting or vibrant place to be a part of. At PPL, we are continually adapting to these new challenges to ensure we retain our place as one of the world's leading rights management agencies.

PPL is the music licensing company that, on behalf of 45,000 performers and 5,750 record companies, licenses the use of recorded music in the UK. This enables TV and radio stations, online streaming services and hundreds of thousands of shops, pubs and others using music in their business to obtain a licence comprising millions of recordings. As a music industry service, we do not retain any profit for ourselves. The costs of collecting, processing and distributing the licence fees are taken from the gross revenues we collect, which are distributed and paid to all PPL's record company and performer members. These include featured artists as well as session musicians, ranging from orchestral players to percussionists and to singers (approximately 90 per cent of whom earn less than £16,000 per year from their profession). There are no joining fees or administration charges and we actively seek members. The cost-to-revenue ratio has remained constant for three years despite increasing investment in technology. In addition, we now collect international performance rights income for 80 per cent of our members, and this revenue stream is currently the fastest growing area of the company. PPL now has representation in twenty-five different countries around the world, which has resulted in forty-eight separate contracts with similar organisations, representing a further 4,000 overseas record companies and 21,000 performers.

PPL's role and remit increases year on year. The company receives details electronically on a weekly basis for an average of 6,500 new recordings. Once this data has been fed into PPL's databases, it is then passed on to PRS for Music for it to administer the relevant copying rights on behalf of the songwriters, composers and publishers. PPL also provides that data to the Official Charts Company for the purpose of the UK charts, and to the BPI and IFPI (International Federation of the Phonographic Industry) to assist with their anti-piracy activities. PPL also uniquely provides the music usage data for the highly successful series 'The People's Chart', which is broadcast on national radio. PPL's other areas of operation include VPL and PPL Video Store.

We firmly believe that music makes the world a better place, and we will always stand up for music rights.

PROFILE

The PPL is effectively owned by its members and claims only to draw an operational profit; in 2008 PPL distributed more than £110 million to its members. Fran Nevrkla is chairman and CEO of PPL and provides further information on the work of this organisation in the Profile opposite.

THE PPL AND ISRC CODES

Specifically for the record label, an important feature of PPL is that on joining, a unique digital registrant code is issued in order that the label and all of its recordings, whether audio or video, may be uniquely identified. An International Standard Recording Code (ISRC) is generated by the PPL; the twelve digit code identifies the country of origin, the PPL database code, the year of reference and the unique recording number. The ISRC number is embedded in the recording, usually at the digital mastering stage when all digital identities are finalised in the recorded product. Having an ISRC alone does not prohibit piracy of the recording, but should identify the owner of the recording and key information to trace the owner and origin of the recorded work, when necessary. All music labels that are releasing recorded products, regardless of company size, should become members of PPL in order to obtain ISRC codes and embed them into recordings at the mastering stage for identification purposes.

MAKING MONEY FROM RECORDED PRODUCTS: THE VPL

In the same way that PPL exists to collect royalties for the use of recorded music in public, Video Performance Limited (VPL) exists to collect revenue for the public use of video recordings. In promotional terms, the popular music video has become one of the most important tools available to record companies to break new music and perpetuate existing catalogues. The VPL was launched in 1984 to ensure that those who owned copyright in the music video recording could be paid whenever the video is exploited before an audience. The broadcast and online industries use music video extensively, alongside businesses that play music video to enhance their public spaces; bars, nightclubs, venues and the concert arena is a key area for usage. The VPL exists as a separate company from PPL, yet shares its central management team. Businesses that use music video require two licences, both for PPL and VPL, in order to use video in the business space (as detailed previously). For any record company that produces and owns copyright in their music videos, joining VPL will assure the 'video performance' income stream; a separate process is required to join VPL. Details of the video performance must be sent by the VPL member for database logging; recorded music and video recordings both reside on the same repertoire database with PPL and VPL. For performers participating in music videos, there is no requirement to join VPL, only PPL; this is because under UK copyright law, performers' music video rights are classified differently from that of their recorded music rights and therefore do not receive music video licensing income. However, if the artist releases their own material independently, commissioning and paying for a video for their sound recordings – and they own copyright in the video recording – the artist may join VPL as a record label, to capitalise on income derived from exploitation of the independent video. Artists who are contracted to labels often receive a percentage share of VPL income under the individual terms of their recording contract but other participating video performers, such as session musicians and actors, are often paid through 'buyout' arrangements, which may be negotiated collectively between the BPI, Musicians Union and Equity.

THE DIFFERENCE BETWEEN THE SOCIETIES

In summary, it is worth clarifying at this stage that PRS for Music and PPL/VPL are different collection societies; PRS for Music collects and distributes royalties for the use of music and lyrics on behalf of songwriters, composers and publishers; PPL collects and distributes royalties for the use of recorded music, on behalf of record companies and performers. In the UK, playing music in public will require a licence from both societies, PPL and PRS. Where a venue only plays live music and plays no recorded works, a PPL licence is not required, but a PRS licence is required to cover the musical and lyrical composition copyright usage. The value of music used in synchronisation with retail business cannot be overlooked: 'If given a choice, 90 per cent say they would select a high street store with music, rather than no music' (MusicWorks, 2010). Investigating how music is used in broadcast and business can uncover distinct and significant revenue streams for the music creator and music releasing company, so becoming a member of the societies that collect these revenue streams is a necessary measure.

THE BRITISH PHONOGRAPH INDUSTRY

In the UK, a central body, the BPI, exists in support of the recorded music industry. The key functions of this trade organisation are further discussed by Lynne McDowell, Public Affairs and Communications Executive, who provides a greater insight into the work of the BPI and its functions, central to the recorded music industry sector.

THE BPI

Lynne McDowell

At the forefront of an ever-changing music industry are a host of British record companies churning out quality music in a competitive global market. And at the core of this dynamic sector supporting the music-makers is the BPI.

The BPI is the representative voice of the UK recorded music business. We are a trade organisation funded by our members, which include hundreds of independent music companies and the UK's four major record labels – Universal Music, Sony Music, EMI and Warner Music. Our members account for approximately 90 per cent of all recorded music sold in the UK. Globally, the UK's recorded music market is the third-biggest behind the US and Japan. Since the incorporation of the BPI in 1973, we have been working tirelessly to tackle the widespread problems of physical – and more recently – digital copyright infringement. Our dedicated Anti-Piracy Unit (APU) has been at the forefront of action against all forms of illegal use of recorded music; seizing counterfeit goods, issuing take-down notices to websites that illegally host copyrighted material, and uncovering criminals who run profitable businesses at the expense of our member companies. The work of the Unit has become increasingly diverse as the illegal uses of music have become ever more complex. Informing the work of the APU and evaluating the impact of copyright infringement is the BPI's Research Department, which publishes the BPI's *Statistical Handbook*, prepares reports on the scale of illegal file-sharing and compiles information on changing attitudes to infringement. This, in turn, helps the industry navigate how to best tackle the issues at stake. The BPI believes in a three-pronged approach: education around copyright and how to make the most of digital music, the development of legal alternatives to unlawful file-sharing, and last of all, should the former solutions not be sufficiently effective, the enforcement of legislation. In this regard, our in-house Public Affairs team raises issues of concern, including copyright term extension, licensing and piracy with British and European policy-makers.

It's not all about illegal downloading, though. The BPI fights to bring about positive change for the industry, taking the lead on campaigns such as that to save the BBC digital radio station 6 Music from the axe. We strive to improve the industry's relationship with consumers and have recently developed the Music Matters Trustmark to help music fans locate legal digital music services and take advantage of what they offer.

At the heart of our work is our commitment to all our member companies, who continue to innovate and adapt to move the industry forward. Our international trade mission to Tokyo provides members with the opportunity to break into a new market and the annual visit to the

PROFILE

Los Angeles Sync-Licensing Mission has seen many of our members' music feature on Hollywood movie soundtracks and hit-US television series. Introducing our members to new markets leads to a diversified revenue stream, which is nowadays critical to success in the industry.

Behind the commercial, political and legal activities of the BPI is a strong will to support charitable and ethical initiatives. Since the inception of the BRIT Trust – the charitable arm of the BPI – in 1989, more than £14 million has been raised for worthy causes, chiefly through the BRIT Awards Ltd – the BPI's commercial body. The annual showcase of British talent donates the proceeds of the event to two main beneficiaries, the BRIT School and Nordoff-Robbins, in addition to a range of other charities.

As our member companies continue to navigate this challenging and rapidly changing global market, the BPI will continue to make itself heard with all key audiences. In doing so we will continue to convey three key messages: British music is the best in the world; British record companies are constantly developing new ways of meeting digital demand; and provided we have a strong, flexible copyright framework in place, the British recorded music industry can continue to evolve and grow.

REFERENCES AND FURTHER READING
Books

Barrow, T. and Newby, J., *Inside the Music Business* (London: Routledge, 1995), pp. 19–31.

Baskerville, D. and Baskerville, T., *Music Business Handbook and Career Guide: Ninth Edition* (London: Sage, 2010), pp. 199–321.

Beattie, W., *The Rock and Roll Times Guide to the Music Industry* (Oxford: Spring Hill, 2007), pp. 181–192.

Biermans, H., *The Music Industry: The Practical Guide to Understanding the Essentials* (London: DSS, 2007), pp. 73–92.

Davis, S. and Laing, D., *The Guerrilla Guide to the Music Business* (New York: Continuum, 2006), pp. 208–268.

Harrison, A., *Music: The Business: The Essential Guide to the Law and the Deals* (London: Virgin Books, 2008).

Hull, P.G., *The Recording Industry: Second Edition* (New York: Routledge, 2004), pp. 121–139.

Hutchison, T., Macy A. and Allen, P., *Record Label Marketing: Second Edition* (Oxford: Elsevier, 2010).

Kusek, D. and Leonhard, G., *The Future of Music: Manifesto for the Digital Music Revolution* (Boston: Berklee Press, 2005), pp. 16, 107–123.

Lathrop, T., *This Business of Music Marketing and Promotion* (New York: Billboard, 2003), pp. 46–128.

Passman, D.S., *All You Need to Know About the Music Business: Sixth Edition* (London: Penguin, 2008), pp. 73–237.

Schwartz, D.D., *I Don't Need a Record Deal: Your Survival Guide for the Indie Music Revolution* (New York: Billboard, 2005).

Schwartz, D.D., *Start and Run Your Own Record Label* (New York: Billboard, 2009), pp. 106–139.

Walker, Jr., L.J., *This Business of Urban Music: A Practical Guide to Achieving Success in the Industry, from Gospel to Funk to R&B and Hip-Hop* (New York: Billboard, 2008), pp. 97–162.

Wikström, P., *The Music Industry: Digital Media and Society Series* (Cambridge: Polity Press, 2009), pp. 46–84.

Wixen, D.R., *The Plain and Simple Guide to Music Publishing: Second Edition* (New York: Hal Leonard, 2010).

Online resources

'A&R – Trivia', BBC online (March 2006). Available at: www.bbc.co.uk/wales/justthejob/followyourdream/hits/a_trivia.shtml (accessed 20 August 2010).

British Phonograph Industry (BPI). Available at: www.bpi.co.uk (accessed 20 August 2010).

Columbia, the first record company. Available at: http://homepage.mac.com/oldtownman/recording/notes.html (accessed 29 January 2011).

Discread. Available at: www.discread.com (accessed 20 August 2010).

History of recorded music and audio. Available at: http://homepage.mac.com/oldtownman/recording/notes.html (accessed 29 January 2011).

International Standard Recording Codes (ISRCs). Available at: www.ppluk.com/en/performers/International-Standard-Recording-Code-ISRC (accessed 20 August 2010).

MCPS licenses for recorded works. Available at: www.prsformusic.com/creators/wanttojoin/membershipagreements/Pages/membershipagreements.aspx (accessed 20 August 2010).

Music Week Magazine. Available at: www.musicweek.com (accessed 10 March 2011).

MusicWorks: Making Music Work for You. Available at: www.musicworksforyou.com (accessed 20 August 2010).

Phonographic Performance Limited (PPL). Available at: www.ppluk.com (accessed 20 August 2010).

PRS for Music, 'Copyright, Performing Rights and Mechanical Rights'. Available at: www.prsformusic.com/Pages/Rights.aspx (accessed 10 March 2011).

UK Music. Available at: www.ukmusic.org (accessed 10 March 2011).

Multinational music companies online

EMI Music. Available at: www.emimusic.com (accessed 22 August 2010).

Sony Music. Available at: www.sonymusic.co.uk (accessed 22 August 2010).

Universal Music Group. Available at: www.universalmusic.com (accessed 22 August 2010).

Warner Music Group. Available at: www.wmg.com (accessed 22 August 2010).

Independent UK labels online

Beggars Group. Available at: www.beggars.com (accessed 22 August 2010).

Rough Trade Records. Available at: www.roughtraderecords.com (accessed 22 August 2010).

Warp Records. Available at: http://warp.net (accessed 22 August 2010).

CHAPTER 7

Managing music

Paul Rutter

INTRODUCTION

The management of music occurs in all areas of music exploitation, whether live or recorded. Managing and dealing with the 'recorded music product' is largely the job of music labels covered in the previous chapter, while managing and administering 'the song' falls largely to the music publisher. Looking after the daily affairs of the artist and guiding their professional career is the job of the personal manager. This chapter focuses on how music is managed in a number of ways, but primarily focuses on personal artist representation and management. The umbrella term 'music management' is usually only perceived as 'personal artist management' but this may include roles associated with 'tour managing' and in addition 'agencies', as outlined in Chapter 3.

PERSONAL MANAGEMENT

Personal managing involves guiding and maintaining a constant relationship with the artist; consistency for the artist will assure a more stable background in a precarious business, regardless of 'how high up the ladder' the manager and artist are working. Artists that work at a local level booking their own gigs and events are, in effect, managing themselves on a small-scale; they are facilitating performances exercising just some of the functions that the professional manager must use. The general attributes a music manager should have are: persistence, perseverance, determination, patience, insensitivity to criticism and an ability to have an undying faith in their artist and product, regardless of what others may say. Unknown artists may struggle to find a manager, but when a manager does undertake to represent the artist they both inherit the same potential disappointments, highs, lows and all in between.

ARTIST REPRESENTATION

Having a personal manager will free an artist to get on with the business of being creative; essentially creativity is what the artist is most comfortable with and would prefer to do. At grassroots level, the luxury of a personal manager may not be a possibility as there may be less financial remuneration involved, so a local band may wish to use the services of an entertainment agent to assist in 'getting the gigs'. Local entertainment agents usually work on a commission basis and expect between 10 and 15 per cent of the gross income from the gig or performance payment. Artists that seek personal management are usually those that are performing original material and want to widen their exposure and impact, increasing earning potential far beyond the local audience. Employing a reputable experienced personal manager operating at a high level in the music industry is often difficult to achieve for the new artist. For an artist to prove they have what it takes to succeed globally, they will need to go beyond merely having a MySpace artist page. Will Beattie comments on managers that work at grassroots level and how the industry refers to them: 'Amateur managers are often referred to as "baby managers"' (2007:67).

The 'baby manager' is an alternative to major management, and initially they are often 'volunteers' – a good friend, relative or fan of the artist who wants to be involved with the industry. This relationship can work very well when the manager proves their worth by securing good gigs and attracting interest from the wider entertainment industry. When the artist invests enough trust in the manager to let them take over running these affairs, initially this type of arrangement can work very well. Problems often occur with the amateur manager when success escalates for the artist. A greater requirement to understand the intricacies of the music industry will follow success; often, more experienced personnel are required to step in and take over the artist management. Joe Jackson, father of The Jacksons, demonstrated commercial success as a 'relative' manager. However not all 'friend' or 'relative' style personal management proves to be the right course of action, highlighting the need to incorporate increased emotional support and stability, other than concentrating purely on commercial success for the artist. Finding a person who is prepared to work on behalf of the unknown artist for little or no return is a compliment to the artist and their work; this also highlights the potential they may have. Where nobody at all is interested in helping a musician with their career, they may find it difficult to progress to the next level by purely 'self-managing'. The grassroots artist may feel comfortable without a manager and if they are facilitating their own career without one, this is not always a negative aspect. Yet when a large music company signs an act it usually prefers the artist to have good management; without good management, it is highly unlikely that the act will get signed and taken to media by the label. For the working artist, managing their music output or performances must occur at some stage; there is little wrong with self managing, being personally managed, or using the services of others to facilitate opportunity. It is purely a matter of the differing levels at which management may occur that needs consideration, as there are financial implications.

THE ROLE OF THE PERSONAL MANAGER

Good personal artist managers look after many daily duties on behalf of their acts, generally taking care of all business liaisons and financial aspects of their artist's career. For the new manager trying to launch a new artist the job may seem daunting:

- booking gigs and arranging publicity
- organising and promoting the artist and the performances
- liaising with local media; for example, radio, press and TV
- inviting music companies to see the artists play live; for example, labels, music publishers *et al.*
- arranging studio recordings of the artists
- ensuring a practice regime is in place
- assisting with image and styling suggestions
- photography sessions
- stagecraft comment and advice
- exploring networking opportunities through personal and social media
- ensuring a comprehensive press pack and web presence is available
- providing a realistic business plan, even if on a small scale.

Looking at this list of essentials, it is easy to estimate the amount of work involved and level of commitment required. Managers new to the industry have inherited perhaps one of the most time-consuming jobs they could have chosen, and moreover, it is a lifestyle choice. The manager's list of duties in this regard displays a blurring of lines; the manager must multitask and unless the manager has the finances to 'contract out' some of these services, the manager exists as promoter, production company, financial investor, friend and ally to the artist. Launching and supporting a new artist is virtually a full-time occupation even though the artist may have a shared input in some of these duties. Amateur managers can usually start relatively easily by showing their interest in a local artist and then proving their worth by helping with some of essential duties previously listed. If the artist then trusts the manager, they may let the manager act on their behalf with other essentials in helping to organise some of the live dates, website creation and social media promotion. All can be done with little investment, but there will come a time when even greater levels of commitment and service are required if things escalate for the act.

Because grassroots-level management is so time consuming, it has to be undertaken with the equal passion of the artist – as the trajectory and guarantees of success at a major level may be few. For many new managers, just being a part of the artist's live shows and occupying a managerial position in a niche genre may be reward enough. Many artists have retained successful longstanding business relationships with their 'baby managers'. Setting guidelines initially between artist and manager are advised, so if greater success is achieved, amateur managers know they have to rise to new challenges and be able to cope with them. Managing a local act is good way to learn about common local music industry issues and to obtain a wider experience in a number of interconnected multifaceted roles.

PROFESSIONAL MANAGERS AND MANAGEMENT COMPANIES

On a larger scale, the professional manager usually has a proven track record and due to this can attract the attention of wide-ranging contacts in the music industry. This can lead to securing greater opportunities for their artists. The professional manager is also approached by many artists, so the management company gets involved in their own A&R processes in assessment of commercial potential in the artist, before representation can occur. At this higher level, the manager makes a living solely from managing music and may already have a roster of acts successfully signed to music labels and so can generate publishing deals for the artist. The professional manager should aim to develop and advance the career of the artist, negotiating the best deals through lawyers and accountants. A great deal of trust is required from the artist's point of view; a good music manager will be open, honest and transparent. Rod Smallwood, longstanding manager of rock outfit Iron Maiden argues (in Beattie 2007:57): 'The days of the shark manager are over as it's a very professional business nowadays'. Music business history has witnessed many appalling examples of artists who have achieved major success but have received little in return, due to 'shark' management. Conversely, there have been managers who have worked tirelessly for their clients, only to find the artist has chosen to work with others when at the crossroads of success. The music industry is fraught with litigation in music management, as there is always scope for artists to seek better deals and managers to seek more profitable artists. Many relationships in the music industry are short lived, and many confuse emotional involvement (and music) with viable business prospect and decision. As in all other industries, personal relationships, emotion and business do not often mix well together. Loyalty on both sides, manager and artist, is a pre-requisite to fuel a solid work ethic in the pursuit of commercial success, but often common tenuous links are apparent in this arrangement. Management companies are generally a collection of professional managers who will work together, sharing in the commission of all the artists that they manage. The artist can still retain his own singular personal manager working in the company, but issues may arise if that manager leaves the company and the artist is passed to another manager working for the firm. As these companies hold strong financial positions they are often facilitators of music product, for instance, auditioning and putting together bands such as boy or girl band outfits. They sometimes adopt an 'intensive care' stance toward their artists' careers, conceptualising, planning and scheduling much of the artistic processes involved – from the artists projected daily image, through to song selection and total career concept. In the UK and the US, management companies such as 19 Management (founded by Simon Fuller in 1985) have demonstrated potential to conceptualise the artist. The company represented the Spice Girls and further cultivated lucrative interests in pop music TV with the 'Idol' franchise worldwide, having a large stable of artists, writers and producers to call upon to facilitate projects.

RESPONSIBILITIES OF THE PROFESSIONAL MANAGER

Professional managers, working at greater levels of commercial music exploitation, have many duties to perform in order to co-ordinate a variety of key aspects concerning the careers of their artists. The infrastructure required is greater than that of the grassroots amateur manager, which would include secretaries and management assistants; bigger contracts and wider exposure requires further duties in addition to those listed for amateur managers, as previously outlined in this chapter. When the artist has signed contracts with a music label the manager must consider:

- the creative freedom of the artist in association with the music label
- the support and assistance of the label's A&R department concerning creative artistic decisions
- large-scale public relations activity and how this fits with the artist's intention and public perception
- co-ordination of music release strategies and media campaigns in association with releases from the artist
- maximising artist potential, using music label infrastructure.

Where the manager is negotiating an exclusive music publishing agreement for the artist, there are business matters to take care of in this area:

- ensuring an appropriate advance is negotiated if the artist's musical works are signed in an exclusive agreement with the publisher

- ensuring that the publisher is using all reasonable endeavours to promote the catalogue of musical works by the artist to other artists (where appropriate)

- ensuring that contractual and legal obligations are being adhered to by the publisher

- ensuring that publishing revenue streams are expanded by negotiation of synchronisation agreements, whereby the artist's music can be used in films, TV, commercials or wider media.

Finally, in promotion of the recorded and published material a series of live concerts will usually ensue; a larger 'live' management infrastructure is required, so the professional manager will appoint the services of others. Chapter 3 details the execution of live music in greater depth; the personal manager must be mindful of the issues cultivated on-the-road and is instrumental in monitoring the live show proceedings as follows:

- co-ordinating promotion and PR affairs in respect of the live concert tour with the record company and artist

- working with the record label on appropriate release schedules and the artist's availability to tour and promote

- appointing a tour manager for on-the-road duties

- negotiating with concert promoters and agencies concerning venues and ticketing

- ensuring touring schedules and contract obligations are being met

- maintaining an oversight role on the tour promotion, production and can gauge ultimate success of the live appearances.

THE PERSONAL MANAGEMENT CONTRACT AGREEMENT

When signing representation rights to a management company, the artist can usually expect to pay a commission rate of between 15 and 20 per cent of earnings to the professional manager. At this stage it is worth pointing out that contracts are often complex and should be reviewed by a qualified music lawyer before signing them, in order that all clauses and issues may be closely examined. It is common for the agreed percentage to be deducted from gross earnings by the artist and not the net figure. To clarify this important point: if the artist is on a 20 per cent contractual agreement and gets paid £1,000 for an appearance, the manager will earn £200 commission. Although this may seem obvious at first, there may be costs and expenses incurred by the artist to appear, for example, transport and subsistence costs of £300, leaving a net figure of £700. It could be contested that the manager should be paid after these necessary costs have been deducted, say, a revised commission of £140 in this example (20 per cent of £700). If the overarching contracted commission rate in all revenue streams applies to the gross fees, the artist is far more likely to be worse off than if a 'net' deal is struck. In negotiation of the deal, 'capping' may be an option, whereby the manager may never earn more than a 50 per cent commission rate on live performances. Other contracts may include a lesser commission rate, such as 10 per cent applied to earnings from publishing and songwriting revenues. In many developed global territories with a music industry, the principles of management and contractual terms are similar; the following list provides common key considerations in negotiation of the manager contract:

- The manager share: The expected share is 15–20 per cent of gross or net income. New acts often pay a higher commission rate, as greater investment is required to launch the act.

- Touring revenues: Applying a net commission rate (after touring costs) is recommended as this encourages the manager to limit touring expense as a larger commission to the manager is returned. Touring costs may include sound, lighting, opening and supporting artists. Record company monies may be paid to the artist to compensate for losses made on tour.

- Exclusions and reductions: Reducing and excluding certain types of artist income from management percentages such as music publishing or areas where the artist is already established, for example, TV acting perhaps, or new revenue streams such as book writing. In such excluded areas, the manager is not bound to represent the artist.

- Further deductions: Monies that pass through the artist account (usually paid by the record company) purely to facilitate the artist's music production and are not classified as artist earnings; recording costs, advances paid to the music producer and the requirement for additional songwriters or musicians. These areas should not be commissionable by the manager.

- Expenses: The manager will incur expenses in acting on behalf of the artist, however, limiting these to a 'reasonable' amount is recommended. In some cases the artist may wish to approve management expenses, rather than have high 'entertaining' figures continually deducted from the artist account.

- Collection costs: Where the artist must sue a third party for non-payment of fees, for example, non-payment for a concert appearance, the manager will then only take commission on the amount recovered after any court costs incurred by the artist.

- Power of attorney: The artist may devolve certain powers to the manager to act in the absence of the artist – accepting and signing agreements, employing personnel and agreeing financial affairs. Authorising the management to take certain financial decisions without artist permission, could prove detrimental to the artist.

- Key person clause: Where the artist has a particular working relationship with one person in the management company, the 'key person' clause ensures this same persons acts on behalf of the artist. If the key person leaves the management company, becomes seriously ill or dies the contract terminates.

- The contract 'term': This is the set time period that the manager will act on behalf of the artist. The time period could be set from one to three years; sometimes this is geared to album release cycles, which could be one or three albums. Options to extend the contract will exist, but these should be with the consent of the artist. A contract term cancellation policy should also exist, should either party not adhere to the contract clauses.

- Termination and parting agreement: After the management contract expires or is terminated, there should be clear agreement on earnings 'after the term'. If the manager negotiates a successful recording contract, the music products may go on making money as a result; these recordings may be subject to manager's commission, even though the contract has ended.

- Closure agreement and 'sunset' provision: These clauses act to place a final closing term applied to monies earned after the manager contract has ceased. Publishing and recording revenues can be phased out gradually; a set termination date should be agreed for a complete end to these revenues as a newly appointed manager may require access to all income streams to assist in the new activities.

Many larger professional managers would argue that the fees they attract for their artists are much higher than if signed to a smaller, less influential manager, so thinking carefully about such rhetoric and the alleged opportunity would be advised before entering such agreements alongside checking the credentials of the manager. Many artists may be organised and capable of self-managing to a certain level but may not be able to progress further without the services of a professional manager. Passman details the work of the personal manager in the US with additional reference to the UK, providing a comprehensive example, 'A good personal manager can expand your career to its maximum potential, just as a bad one can rocket you into oblivion' (2008:32–48). In thinking about what is required from the manager and 'would-be' manager, all involved should demonstrate clarity and realism concerning what the manager can do for the artist; both parties should have the ability to re-examine the contract over time, to ensure each party's interests are both represented and protected. Management contracts are specific to artist requirements, often determined by the level at which the artist is working at that period in time, in their professional career.

COLIN LESTER, PROFESSIONAL ARTIST MANAGER

Colin Lester

Colin Lester is a seasoned professional artist manager and is CEO of Universal Music Group management company 'Twenty First Artists'. Colin formed Wildstar Records in 2001 and has managed a host of world renowned artists including Craig David, Arctic Monkeys, Travis, Connor Reeves and Brand New Heavies. Colin is a teaching fellow in the music industry and has overseen global record sales in excess of 25 million records. Noted for his passionate approach to the industry, Colin provides a candid view on the role of the personal manager.

$A + B = C$ ... Great song, plus radio airplay, equals potential hit record – that is the formula I have always endeavoured to work with, since being a professional music manager. This equation has not changed throughout the history of the music business. Obviously there have been many changes to 'C' over the years. For example, how the consumer receives music, overall sales volume and the digital revolution, which has changed the profit margins and the face of retail. The industry has also suffered terrible losses via internet theft, which has conveniently and incorrectly been called 'file sharing'. Section 1 of the Theft Act 1968, 'taking property with the intention of permanently depriving the owner of it', does not distinguish between physical or intellectual property. But this has not, until now, been upheld or distinguished by the courts and as such has cost the industry billions of dollars!

However, the most important relationship within the industry is, and still remains, the relationship between the artist and the fan. This must be nurtured, encouraged and protected by the artist and the manager. However, it is important to point out that if one person steals from another –that is, say, if the consumer illegally downloads product – then the relationship no longer exists as in the same way that, if an artist rips off his fans by overpriced records, tickets and merchandise costs he can no longer expect the loyalty and support of the fan.

Having passion and belief in your work as a manager, and an understanding of your artist's ability – talent is the single most important attribute that a manager needs to begin with. You will also need to be a control freak! Nothing must escape your attention and the buck always stops with you no matter where the fault or problem is.

Historically, in the 1970s, 1980s and 1990s, due to the revolution of the CD and the re-mastering and re-issuing of existing artists' catalogues, there was much more money in the industry. Today things are somewhat

PROFILE

different; due to the decline in revenue, record labels are signing far fewer acts and the manager often needs to look outside the music industry for investment from various private equity funds or government approved tax schemes that may be available, in addition to sponsors in order to fund projects. And even when the manager does secure a music deal or funding for an artist, that does not necessarily make them a good manager because that is when the real work starts! The manager has a duty to advance the artist's career commercially and creatively, at the same time as retaining artistic integrity. The artist has a duty to perform to the best of their ability and to fulfil what is required of them in order to sell records and concert tours. It is a certain type of partnership, which requires both parties – the artist and manager – to work closely together. The manager is not an employee of the artist and is generally not paid a salary. The manager's earnings are made from a percentage of the income generated, which is typically 20 per cent of the artist net income, but can vary subject to circumstance and levels of investment made by the manager.

In today's business it is essential for a manager to understand the model of the new music industry at an early age, engaging with new media guerrilla tactics, using new initiatives and innovative ways to sell music. The future of the music industry leans towards artist's doing more for themselves initially, so artists and managers need to be aware of this and capitalise on new media promotional methods. Management agreements are essential and should be taken seriously. All too often agreements that are not revised by specialist music lawyers are unenforceable due to previous case rulings known as case law or case history, which a general practitioner may not be aware of. So it would always be advisable to engage the services of professional music lawyers whenever possible. Unfortunately, where large sums of money are involved the lines and terms of engagement sometimes become blurred. Management agreements remove the ambiguity – and don't be fooled by relationships built on friendships! If you want loyalty buy a dog, for all other purposes get a fair agreement – for both parties – that way it will stand up in court!

PROFILE

FIGURE 7.1
Colin Lester, managing music (right-to-left: Colin Lester, Craig David, Paul Rutter). Courtesy Southampton Solent University.

THE INTERNATIONAL MUSIC MANAGERS FORUM

The IMMF comprises around eighteen affiliated global music manager forums, with each territorial MMF representing the moral, legal, economic and professional interests of managers and their 'featured artists'. The MMF lobbies government and official bodies on issues such as intellectual property value and copyright legislation, acting as a voice for the protection of cultural creators in music. The IMMF recognises that the featured artist is significant in the said production of 'over 95 per cent of the economic activity in the global music industry' and, as an organisation, supports comments from its members who uniquely negotiate artist affairs on a daily basis (IMMF, 2010).

In the UK, the regional MMF was formed in 1992 and has over 400 members; any UK manager, large or small, can join for a yearly fee that will provide networking opportunities to share opportunities and information. The organisation is an active participant in global conferences, forums and events such as MIDEM, Popkomm, Musexpo, CMJ New York, Folk Alliance and SXSW; the IMMF also makes representations to WIPO in Geneva, Switzerland. For new managers, the MMF provides an opportunity to network and learn more about all aspects of the music manager role, through its education programmes and forums. The IMMF regards the featured artist manager as the person most qualified to comment on the business of music, due to the manager's daily engagement with new challenges in the industry. Representing these views, the IMMF ensures that its members' interests are heard and where possible safeguarded against the emerging threats to the music manager or management company.

REFERENCES AND FURTHER READING
Books

Allen, P., *Artist Management for the Music Business: First Edition* (London: Focal Press, 2007).

Barrow, T. and Newby, J., *Inside the Music Business* (London: Routledge, 1995), pp. 32–43.

Baskerville, D. and Baskerville, T., *Music Business Handbook and Career Guide: Ninth Edition* (London: Sage, 2010), pp. 129–141 and 175–187.

Beattie, W., *The Rock and Roll Times Guide to the Music Industry* (Oxford: Spring Hill, 2007), pp. 55–69.

Davis, S. and Laing, D., *The Guerrilla Guide to the Music Business* (New York: Continuum, 2006), pp. 358–367.

Gelfand, M., *Strategies for Success: Self Promotion Secrets for Musicians* (New York: Schirmer, 2005).

Passman, D.S., *All You Need to Know About the Music Business: Sixth Edition* (London: Penguin, 2008), pp. 32–56.

Walker, Jr., L.J., *This Business of Urban Music: A Practical Guide to Achieving Success in the Industry, from Gospel to Funk to R&B and Hip-Hop* (New York: Billboard, 2008), p. 37.

Weiss, M. and Gaffney, P., *Managing Artists in Pop Music: What Every Artist and Manager Must Know to Succeed* (New York: Allworth Press, 2003).

Online resources

International Music Managers Forum (IMMF). Available at: www.immf.com (accessed 17 August 2010).

Music Managers Forum (MMF) UK. Available at: www.themmf.net (accessed 17 August 2010).

CHAPTER 8

Promoting music

Paul Rutter

MARKETING COMMUNICATIONS THROUGH PROMOTION, PUBLIC RELATIONS, PRESS AND MEDIA

This chapter focuses on the demand that may be stimulated for music products and performances and how they may be brought to public attention. Historically, the successful global profiling of many artists can be attributed to inspired promotional campaigns that have utilised professional marketing communications strategies in support of the artist's brand. However, there has been controversy surrounding some of the promotional methods used; generating an awareness of these controversies is an important consideration, alongside an awareness of the common tools used in music promotion theory. Marketing music can be compared to the marketing of any commodity, but whether the commodity ultimately succeeds or not is largely due to the consumer response. Selling music products or performances has proven that there is no secret formula for success; other businesses that sell products also need to find their niche consumer and music is no different in this respect. The recurrent problem facing most music companies is that only a small proportion of the many acts that are signed and invested in actually succeed. Music industry critics Kusek and Leonhard argue that in respect of past recorded products, 'only four percent of records ever sold enough copies to break even' (2005: 115). The promotion infrastructure, which includes public relations, press, advertising and wider media, is an expensive outlay for the major music company. In some cases, an artist promotion campaign has been known to cost millions, especially with global artists on an international campaign. The shrinkage of global music industry revenue has presented challenges to the major music company that must conserve funds; budgets for promotion have been put under stress, thus calling for more effective strategies and use of resources. For the independent, promotion means using all conceivable promotional methods that fall within financial reach, and in today's terms the internet is the promotional saviour of the independent.

PROMOTING THE MUSICAL WORK

For artists who are enterprising and want to bring their material before an audience and consumers, promotion begins just as soon as music has been created. In a performed musical work, promotion must occur prior to performance (see Chapter 3 on how promotion is administered in relation to events and concerts). For the independent producer of recorded music, promoting the work could be compartmentalised in several ways, initiating an awareness of one's music by sending it to others such as record labels, publishers, retailers, distributors and sub-sellers of the music. Simply getting music 'out there' via whatever means possible, could be described as communicating with the market, so placing the music within a wider promotional framework will maximise the commercial chances of the product or artist. The next sections will concentrate primarily on the concepts behind marketing communications in music, promotion of the recorded work, the tools that are available and the interconnecting roles associated with it.

MUSIC IN MEDIA: TELEVISION

Television exposure is enduring in its powerful capability to bring both music and artist to the widest possible audience; terrestrial TV is a medium that consumers en masse are continually drawn to, and music is a huge part of it. The relationship between popular culture and TV has endured well, with thousands of music programmes being broadcast each week through cable and terrestrial channels. Countless TV shows that feature, include and use music as its mainstay have grown in number, as have the amount of music channels worldwide. Waiting a whole week to watch iconic UK chart show music programmes such as BBC TV's *Top of the Pops* is no longer necessary; the demise of the programme was due in part to the competition from the onslaught of new music channels launched in the cable TV era. Even though there is an abundance of music television today, using television to advertise music products is a proven way of boosting sales; large music companies today still use this medium widely. Financially the majors can afford to exploit the TV advertising infrastructure; it is a sure-fire way of bringing music product before consumers without the need to secure artist appearances on music TV. Chat shows, reality TV, breakfast TV or any show that will entertain the record companies latest artist release are all television targets for the music label promotions department (see Chapter 6). Appearances on these shows is difficult to guarantee, as guest places are limited and even with a large promotional infrastructure, music companies can struggle to secure enough airtime to expose all their artist's releases to the public. TV shows largely do not pay the music companies for their artist's guest appearances on TV shows (unless a programme has been commissioned especially to feature that artist). In many cases the music company will fund a commissioned TV programme, made in respect of the artist's new music product (perhaps a DVD or album). The record company will then try to persuade the TV network to broadcast this at the same time as the artist product is released (e.g. aimed at the Christmas consumer market). If accepted, the TV network would pay the owners of the music show for its broadcast use; the songwriters and performers would also earn royalties and fees from the public TV performance. It should be noted that in guest show appearances the artist may get paid little or nothing other than a recommended standard guest fee, often set by Musicians Union or Equity in the UK. Performers do not get paid thousands for appearing on chat shows, in fact, both record company and artists are pleased that they can capitalise on the appearance. This is due to the vast amount of artists who are clamouring for the same TV opportunities in a crowded entertainment marketplace. TV appearances are often a coup for the artist, their music company and the supporting promotional infrastructure.

FIGURE 8.1
Music being recorded for TV broadcast. Courtesy Southampton Solent University, photo: www.paulmaple.com.

TV opportunities

High profile major artists and their public relations teams have a greater range of possible promotional opportunities to choose from in TV media to showcase their new releases, but unfortunately for the vast majority of music artists, terrestrial TV promotion is not an option. Music TV shows have their own complex infrastructure with a team of researchers who will be aware of what is happening on the music scene. They know which acts are breaking into mainstream media and who is creating interest among live audiences (e.g. the acts headlining large festivals). TV producers and researchers are approached by a mixture of individuals from the promotions stable; public relations and plugger personnel who work tirelessly to secure as many artist appearances as possible. In addition, large music labels usually assign a 'product manager' to the marketing campaign, who then employs promotions personnel they know can succeed in the task. Many TV producers often have ongoing relationships with music label PR teams; the music label is careful when employing PR personnel in this field, ensuring that they have a strong background in TV media. To work in the promotions sector requires a 'ground up' apprenticeship, working with established promoters and PR teams first and getting to know who makes 'booking' decisions in TV production circles. Because the TV promotions infrastructure is expensive to action and maintain, independent labels would need the licensing powers of a major in order to break into TV with any real impact. Producers that commission music for TV prefer to see a large committed promotional campaign behind a record release before they will book an artist appearance.

Artists are only seen on TV when they have a new or re-released music to promote, so major labels construct their release schedules in tandem with the TV shows that are in production. The infrastructure in place sets a precedent for the kind of music that is likely to appear on TV – this provides a filtering mechanism that only really sees artists signed to majors securing TV exposure. In the UK and the US particularly, the independent that is producing viable music products may see this as biased towards major powers; the only way independents can secure national television appearances is largely by being under the wing of a major. This disparity can vary in other territories, however, with national television exposure in the Irish Republic for instance, being slightly easier to achieve for the artist, primarily as there are far fewer weekly record releases than in the UK and US. Regional TV stations may also have differing policies in the screening of independent music.

The current TV music selection filtering mechanism that is in place promises to deliver the best in new music, due to mechanisms that are able to resource the very best acts for audience viewing consumption. Arguments have ensued between majors and independents concerning the artist selection processes of mainstream media and the methods applied. Today all recorded music can be made available quickly in an online downloadable format to satisfy unending consumer demand without the need for coordinated tangible stock in shops. For music labels both large and small the aim is to earn TV exposure to reach a music buying public and it could be argued that if the music is proven to be good, equal consideration should be given to both independent and major label music products regardless of label size or infrastructure.

Allowing the public to be 'the judge' is the ultimate barometer for gauging the popularity and success of the new artist and the 2000s saw the revival of the 'talent show' format. The talent show *Opportunity Knocks* was first broadcast on BBC radio in 1949 and moved to television in 1956, making its final broadcast in 1990 in the UK. The recent global surge in the renovated 'reality TV' talent show format has provided a new platform for many amateur vocalists (rather than bands and singer-songwriters with original material) to gain national and global exposure. Although these shows are still gate-kept by a series of producers in the selection process before singers get a chance to appear before a televised judging panel, there are thousands who crave the exposure and are happy to enter the process. For major labels associated with these shows, the talent show format has returned lucrative income and refreshed the artist roster. Syco TV's *X Factor* and *Britain's Got Talent* have been reported to account for a vast majority of Sony Music's profits since 2008, due to its associations with these talent shows.

Without national terrestrial TV exposure, artists and labels find it difficult to generate large-scale public interest in their music, so must look to other media and methods of promotion. TV remains a primary source of passive media consumption for its audiences and a proven successful promotions conduit for the record label.

MUSIC IN MEDIA: THE INTERNET

The internet has emerged as the primary vehicle for music promotion for all artists and record labels. The popularity of music and social networking sites such as MySpace and Facebook have given independents in particular an open platform to promote their music without the gate-kept promotional restrictions existing in primary media, TV and radio exposure. YouTube has grown into a respected internet streaming medium by which any artist or label can make their music video available to the world – but only if potential viewers have internet access. The greatest problem with this type of music promotion is leading the audience and consumers to it, as the sheer quantity of music available on sites such as YouTube, holds millions of music videos. As music videos do not stream continuously and 'passively' (the audience needs to 'look up' an individual video first before playing it), the mechanics of *finding* needs to be carefully designed. Product manager at YouTube, Jamie Davidson, has highlighted 'lean-back' consumption developments: 'We're looking at how to push users into passive-consumption mode, a lean-back experience' (in Stross, 2010) 'Lean-back' streaming links YouTube video programmes together in 'webisodes' similar to the continuous experience of traditional TV. Streaming service developments such as these brings web media ever nearer to the passive TV consumption model that in time could provide tools of even greater importance for the online music promoter.

Posting links on social networking sites such as Facebook, generating larger fan networks that will encourage music consumers to 'search and discover' will help to promote interest in the artist. Those with the greatest ingenuity can often achieve the maximum amount of exposure and consequently may generate sales, especially if linked to a digital download aggregation service or 'one-stop' platform such as iTunes. Major labels use the internet heavily to promote; they have the financial means to pay for internet advertisements and banner ads and can pay for prioritisation of their music products. Advertising artist product on key websites increases artist 'visibility' and leads the consumers to more links, searches and engagement with their products. Record company promotions managers use their digital departments in tandem with popular internet sites that can feature or advertise music. This will ensure that their products are 'positioned' correctly and visible to the passing surfer; their PR teams generate current artist news stories which become features that change on a daily basis. Increasing artist visibility in other media forms such as national TV, naturally advances the internet 'hit rate', prolonging and increasing consumer awareness. The downside in this free medium for both labels and artists is that when the general public decides to upload their own footage taken from camera phones at major concerts, issues occur. Protecting the image and sound of the artist (where copyright in sound and image is under contract) is difficult to police by the record label; uploaded footage to YouTube demonstrates image and sound quality that is often very poor. This phenomenon provides benefits and potential liabilities for the artist; the public is promoting the artist online for free, but this is without the permission of the label and poor uploaded content may be tarnishing the image of the artist. This is in itself an illegal act but the practice is so widespread globally that it is difficult to stem the flow of such mass public uploading as prosecuting each and every infringing member of the public would prove impossible. Independent artists should be aware that uploading poor audiovisual material to the internet may be damaging in the early stages of their career, especially if in pursuit of serious attention from the wider music industry. As the wider music industry (A&R, press, recording companies and wider media) uses the internet as its primary source to identify artists and gather information, it is worth noting that it may be impossible to remove damaging substandard online material, which can remain on some sites for many years.

Artist websites often contain an electronic press kit (EPK), a downloadable file with a selection of edited material available to media. The EPK could contain a combination of edited items; a full artist biography, news releases, music samplers, video files, artist video interviews and online links to other material. Using an EPK to get accurate good quality information over is an essential tool for the professional artist and label alike. Music companies sow promotional seeds weeks ahead of an impending release; singles or 'taster' tracks will precede the album, increasing artist visibility through advancing counter 'hit' rates and chart appearances. Creating news items, emailing fan subscribers, alerting online communities, artist discussion groups and offering new merchandise, will generally build the online buzz. Artists can develop a 'one-to-one' relationship with their fans by involving themselves in a blogging process, through sites such as Twitter. Using multi-artist sites and online niche music stores also provides ever increasing ways to reach the right consumer demographic.

Today, artists must increase their web presence beyond simply having their own personal website in order to sell music from it. Building a strong web presence means appearing in as many credible places as the artist can possibly manage, persuading users to navigate their way to their information and music with the minimum amount of clicks. Keeping surfers affixed to the content for as long as possible is the greatest ongoing challenge for the web designer, artist or label. Record labels now use online research companies to determine the best possible sites to advertise on, marrying their demographic with their website analytics.

Music hunting: Active and passive music consumption

The inherent problem in using internet promotion is that this medium is still largely reliant on the 'active' consumer. Demographically, younger users are prepared to search in an active way to find their music of choice and are more 'net aware', having more time to devote to the pastime of 'music hunting'. Popular sites that provide a more passive form of music discovery are sites such as Spotify and LastFM; users can choose to stream a genre and the site will automatically pick music that is in a similar vein for the listener using a form of 'music recommendation'. Listeners can also tune into internet radio stations, many of which play a mixture of major and independent music releases providing the passive medium. For the consumer prepared to do the detective work, there is a global world of new music to discover online; as time progresses, online search engines and navigation strategies make it easier and quicker to find these services. As the internet continues to grow in stature and dominance, this medium could take over in the future as the primary source of passive music consumption. In this regard, old media forms such as terrestrial radio could be subsumed into an online world, which would change the passive music landscape as we now know it.

MUSIC IN MEDIA: RADIO

Radio has endured as a key promotional tool for labels over the years, with the only looming threat to it, posed by the internet, even though virtually all commercial radio stations now stream their broadcasts online. Figures suggest that only around three per cent of all national listeners stream their stations online, yet many smaller UK regional stations report an online listenership of around 10 per cent. Where a radio station holds credibility within its niche, radio becomes a powerful tool for the record company. Radio licences are granted to stations individually to supply a specific type of entertainment to the region they cover; the radio station must largely stick to the mandate set out by the licensing authorities. Terrestrial radio stations are costly to maintain, in the UK BBC radio stations are funded by the public through a television licence fee, which funds national and regional television *and* a vast national and regional BBC radio network. Independent local radio (ILR) is funded by advertisers in the main. A licence is not required to listen to a radio, but is compulsory for all TV owners in the UK. The BBC's primary music stations have national music coverage, primarily through Radio 1 and 2 (popular music) and Radio 3 and 4 (talk and classical output). Music labels largely look towards Radio 1 and 2 and the independent commercial music radio sector to promote its product; there are hundreds of licensed FM stations in the UK to include smaller community radio entities. For a commercial radio station to remain solvent it must remain popular, so many small stations subscribe to the UK radio research organisation Radio Joint Audience Research Limited (RAJAR), which surveys national and regional radio closely in defining its listenership and ultimately, station popularity (see www.rajar.co.uk). The obsession radio has with its listenership is key in providing a future for the station, commercial radio can only survive through popularity and is understandably fiercely protective of it. Popular radio shows attract advertisers and those that pay radio to advertise need to know the demographic they are reaching and how many, which is why RAJAR is so important. This radio construct sets a precedent for the music audiences are likely to hear on radio; commercial radio needs maximum listeners and commercial pop music needs to fit with the radio requirement.

Creating 'the playlist'

When radio stations create playlists, the radio playlist manager knows that the most popular artists generally attract the most listeners, so the music selection formula for radio is set. It could be argued that the BBC does not need to meet commercial targets as it has no advertisers and therefore need not worry about audience figures. Yet the BBC also craves popularity and so daytime playlisting follows a similar pattern to commercial radio. Many commercial radio stations observe the playlists of the BBC and other large commercial stations to then copy the playlist in pursuit of popularity. Independent labels often argue that it is harder and in many cases impossible, to attract airtime on daytime radio playlists in favour of high profile artists signed to larger labels that attract a large disproportionate share of airplay. Some regional stations will playlist local talent or give spot plays to new independents, but largely these are in non-prime evening slots when the listenership is at its lowest. With so much music being promoted to radio and so many artists competing for airtime, it is commonplace for even major signed artists to struggle to get airtime. Artists who are 'in fashion', 'cool' or 'happening' becomes a major feature in playlist management and music choice tactics. The playlisting decisions made by commercial radio are primarily financial; radio needs large audiences to survive, unless it has low overheads and is merely an online broadcast entity. The national terrestrial radio construct does not generally make provision for independents making potential hit records; therefore they struggle to get airplay. Radio stations are often criticised for playlisting decisions, but radio cannot play everything that is thrown at it. Many stations are owned by conglomerates – in the UK there are two major owners Global and Bauer; in addition, in 2010 RAJAR measured that independent local radio (ILR) was losing popularity, holding a share of just over 40 per cent of the overall market, and ILR has been criticised for losing its 'localness'.

The media juke box

In respect of these conglomerates the playlists are decided by a head office and distributed down to many of their national stations, who will all broadcast the same playlist without regional considerations. For independents to earn playlisting on popular mainstream radio in the UK, signing or licensing credible 'hit' records to a major is the way to start the journey through to the daytime playlist. Today in radio, DJs do not hear an artist and champion their music on the basis that they believe the song could be a hit; playlists are business decisions made based on statistical evidence that will minimise risk for the station. Risk means losing listeners and subsequent advertising revenues, which could lead ultimately to a station closure. The primary radio construct in the UK and US follows in the footsteps of national TV in its prioritisation of which music they choose to exploit, essentially using larger music labels to service the 'media juke box'. Today, the way in which radio showcases new music has evolved into a two tier system; terrestrial radio can argue that it devotes ample airtime to new music. First, larger radio stations play new songs released by major artists and also songs by new acts that are signed to larger labels. The primary concern for radio is that these releases have a good promotional 'plot' behind them in wider TV and other media. In this regard the radio station is not isolated in its support of the release and so has the confidence to include it in the primary daytime playlist. Another way that radio showcases new music is by smaller stations (usually regional radio) providing spot plays for the independent; much of this occurs in slots other than primetime for fear of losing listeners due to unfamiliar material. For instance, dance music remixes are played off-peak on Friday and Saturday evenings and often feature new artists, but would generally not be played during the day at peak listening times. The promotional plot is not such a large concern in this case, as the music is unlikely to make regular playlisting; BBC regional radio will frequently feature new artists in specialist music or niche genre shows. National BBC Radio 1 will showcase new independent artists appropriate to their playlist, most however are non-primetime slots. Globally this policy can vary, but as radio stations become more commercial and 'market research led' in the survey orientated information age, record labels must be more aware of the needs of the radio station, prior to plugging their next release. In the US in the past, conglomerate radio executives have been known to suggest to music labels what they would like to hear on their own stations. Major labels now conduct more market research concerning trends in public music consumption, rather than releasing a record and hoping everyone will like it, just because all the record company staff do. With the huge amount of time and investment required to promote new music to radio, record labels have always been measured in their approach to this medium and with ever increasing commercial returns due in radio, the new label and artist may find it increasingly difficult to achieve airplay in this arena.

'Plugging' in radio: Impressing producers

Understanding how radio infrastructure operates has a direct bearing on how music is selected for airplay and public consumption. It is the job of the radio promoter or plugger to get the record release into radio and ultimately, onto the playlist. Usually, the record company marketing department will employ a freelance plugger who specialises in the music genres appropriate to the release, to go to radio with the recording. The influence the plugger has is carried in their proven ability to achieve airplay success, and this depends on the contacts that the plugger has developed and how well 'networked' they are. Pluggers that have strong relationships with producers and the playlist managers that make key decisions in radio are valuable to the music label. As radio stations are spread far and wide geographically, pluggers cannot call in to each individual station, hence some of the plugging may be done remotely. Depending on the type of release, CDs may be distributed to regional stations by post, but increasingly music is sent by electronic delivery methods. Releases that are selected for airplay consideration are presented at a playlist meeting where radio producers meet frequently to finalise weekly playlists. A shortlist of releases will go onto an 'A' or 'B' playlist rotation, with the 'A' list getting the biggest rotation of plays across the week. Releases can travel up or down the playlist depending on factors such as the length of the record company's promotional campaign, artist appearances and the chart position of the music. Marketing music in modern day terms means scheduling promotional activities long before the music is available to the consumer; a six week radio airplay build up before actual release is common. Maximising music exposure this way ensures that when the record is released there is a surge in buying when the consumer downloads or purchases a single at the moment of release.

Sales of tangible CD singles have fallen away dramatically in the UK and US due to preferred MP3 downloading; although the demise of the single has been passionately debated by media and music industry, the 'single' is still regarded as the best tool to promote a new artist or draw attention to the album on which the song appears. Many pluggers and radio promoters work independently, so it is possible for an independent label or artist to employ a plugger to go to radio with their release. This can be a costly exercise, depending on the reputation of the plugger. Often, a plugger may not be willing to take on a music project, if the release is inappropriate to their music promotions specialism, or the release is of poor quality and could damage their reputation. Full-scale promotional packages are costly exercises, so the independent must be confident in the reputation of the plugger and the realistic nature of what can actually be achieved. Targeting the release is crucial; with the correct music genre being plugged to the right radio station, going to the correct producer and most appropriate show. With all these provisos in place, there is still no guarantee of airplay, much of it due to radio infrastructure and prioritisation of valued major product that can retain listeners. For the well organised and professional independent artist, off-peak spot-plays may be achievable without the services of a plugger in regional radio. For well-funded promotional campaigns plugging is purely a part of the marketing plan. Radio stations examine the release campaign and judge accordingly; perhaps the release has already achieved healthy success elsewhere (e.g. a hit in North America), before it is considered for playlisting. For the independent label, building a buzz through smaller networks where appropriate and online is advisable when starting out. To work in the radio plugging profession, there are many tenacious attributes that are required alongside the ability to network keenly throughout the music industry; newcomers to plugging would need to work with an established record promoter to learn the ropes first.

Persuading radio: Payola

The term 'payola' emerged in the US in the 1950s; it means the practice of giving gifts or paying radio personnel or a radio station in exchange for playing and promoting records. The widespread controversial practice of commercial bribery in music began in the early 1900s when music publishers would pay key artists to perform their works in theatres, subsequently increasing their sheet music sales figures. The activity was not deemed illegal until the first US payola prosecution case brought many years later in 1960, against DJ Alan Freed. Freed pleaded guilty to two counts of commercial bribery and was fined $300, issued with a suspended sentence and fired from his position at WNBC. Due to the illegality of the practice, music companies sought methods to disguise commercial bribery by using independent promoters; a 'third party loophole' was developed to issue 'promotion payments' to radio, masking payola. But as recently as 2005 and 2006, out of court settlements were reached with Sony BMG, Warner Music, Universal Music Group and EMI respectively, in settlement of payola-related activities in the US (Babington, 2007). Increased legal scrutiny and subsequent prosecutions have caused many US media conglomerates, such as Clear Channel Radio, to disassociate from this method of independent promotion. Many artists who were signed and promoted by majors were unaware of the practice; the general public perceived artists and their music as being popular, when in fact unethical commercial persuasion methods had been used by corporate structures to bring music to the fore. In the UK, the concept of payola has not surfaced in media headlines as in the US, but the practice of 'hyping' records has been commonplace in the UK music industry, outlined later in this chapter.

It is not unknown for music labels to strengthen their relationships with radio by offering free tickets to concerts, entertaining radio personnel via attractive invites to enhanced artist showcases where record company executives and promoters can meet. Both radio and music company may see this as a normal business relationship, as in many other industries. The practice of granting expenses and high quality entertaining has proved a powerful ingredient in persuading radio in the past. However, there are those artists and labels that view this practice as unethical, given the unfair financial advantage as small independents do not have the resources to persuade mainstream radio in this way. In the UK, radio stations pay PRS and PPL fees to use music and some radio executives argue that this is a one-way street: artists gain promotion; songwriters and record companies get paid by radio for use of their music; labels gain profit from all music sold as a result. The recompense for radio is that they get supplied with credible music that will retain a listener base and ultimately provide a level of financial security for the station. The major radio conglomerate values its relationship with the primary labels that consistently supply music, which in turn preserves their listenership; they are far more likely to develop a mutually beneficial relationship with these labels and prioritise their releases. Independent internet radio stations legally charge labels and artists for a certain amount of plays, a legal type of online payola, a practice that has been criticised by both labels and artists. Early statistics regarding the success of this phenomenon is limited, but the practice could help to raise the profile of an artist with payment being made for a nominal amount of plays, for example, a thousand online plays.

In conclusion, the centralisation of programming by commercial radio conglomerates has now changed the way in which music is playlisted; the constant measurement of statistical information coupled with the survival of the radio industry are key factors that ultimately influence what the passive consumer gets to hear.

MUSIC PROMOTION: CHART SYSTEMS

The British Phonograph Industry and the Entertainment Retailers Association jointly operate the Official Charts Company (OCC), providing the foremost chart information in the UK (see www.theofficialcharts.com). All charts are published weekly each Sunday, covering a wide range of music product sales from the preceding week; to qualify for a chart placing, OCC set official criteria that must be met, to include bar coding of the music product. The music charts were first conceived in the US when *Billboard* magazine published the *Hit Parade* in 1936, exemplifying the idea of a music popularity system that later became known as the *Hot 100*. In the UK the first official chart followed some years later in 1952 with the publication of the *New Musical Express* (*NME*) chart. Other music magazines such as *Melody Maker* also began listing their own top twelve records with *NME*'s chart being given credence by its weekly rundown on Radio Luxembourg. Several companies have since instigated music popularity charts culminating in the Official Chart Company's canonised status in the late 1990s as *the* UK official music sales compiler. Charting music in this way has served as an important promotional tool; consumers can purchase music through the OCC charts website, allowing consumers to purchase chart content via a link. The importance of the charts has changed in more recent years, particularly as a result of global online music consumption and the amount of new and differing charts that have been conceived in the pursuit of music promotion. Music television programmes, both cable and terrestrial, constantly manufacture their own chart rundown shows to make an entertaining programme, rather than reflecting which music sells most. The canonisation of the music chart throughout the last fifty years has served to make consumers 'music curious' on a competitive level. Through the 1970s in particular, the BBC programme *Top of the Pops* became a major source of interest for families who would be curious to know, on a weekly basis, who was 'number one'. The chart rundown's broadcast on BBC Radio 1 and on the independent radio network added to the competitive nature of music listening and buying for the consumer. It could be argued that in the online and cable television age of new media, the chart has expanded its horizons but in doing so has diluted its presence somewhat changing the way in which the consumer now values it. However, a strong 'chart placing' creates further promotional opportunities for a single; a top ten record will go on to earn more widespread airplay and in doing so canonise its place in music chart history. The chart is still important to the recording industry promotional vehicle, even if slightly less impressive to the current music consumer.

Competitive music

The charting of records provides the notion that because a certain record is selling well it somehow tells the public that the record is superior to those songs that are not selling as well. In such a subjective medium, the number one record in the chart provides a message to the consumer that the record release is a winner, as in a sport. In sport, the winner is the first over the line and undeniably the best, but in music the winning record selling the most copies is certainly not the best in subjective listening or consumer terms. Not all consumers look to charts in guidance of what they should buy; charts assist the passive consumption concept, as they are broadcast on terrestrial radio, seen in newspapers and shops. As market research over many years in music consumption has proved, the 'passer-by' consumer is far more likely to take notice of who is number one, than who is number fifty seven, in the supermarket chart. Although the Official Charts Company provides primary record sales information through all genres and regions, supermarkets run their own chart systems (with charts being sent from head office to the regional branches), largely to connect with the amount of product they have bought in that particular week from music suppliers. As rack space is limited, CD albums are moved around within the store's own chart (with consideration and priority given to releases that also appear in the national album charts), but also tying in with the record company promotional campaign. The common goal for record labels and music retailers is the same, to sell as many copies as possible; this is where the retailer assists in helping to promote the artist via its in-store displays and accompanying charting system. The chart today provides a loose system for measuring mainstream music success for the single song, but is largely momentary, only making music visible to the public for a short period of time. Vinyl records of the past could linger in the top ten for many weeks, but in the digital download age, the proliferation of music product is greater and turnover is faster; today, many music releases often only make brief appearances in music charts, regardless of their high position.

Chart controversy: Hyping

Just as radio has been subject to payola and bribery, the importance of the music chart to the music industry has given way to the practice of record 'hyping' in the past. Hyping involves achieving a chart position by subverting what would be ordinarily a natural flow of music purchases from consumers. After the music chart was first conceived in the UK, labels would look at ways of achieving the highest possible chart placing, as this in turn would guarantee appearances on music-orientated shows such as *Top of the Pops* or other weekly terrestrial TV chart shows, screened up to the early 2000s. Throughout this time, the chart was compiled by selected record stores; store personnel would then report retail record sales back to the official national UK chart compiler at that time. Although designated 'chart return' shops were supposed to be anonymous, record labels and distributors quickly learned which key record stores made up chart returns and subsequently discovered methods to hype records into the national chart. Various hyping methods evolved; record labels gave product incentives to chart record stores including free music or merchandise, in return for guaranteed chart placement. Buying teams employed by labels would visit stores and actively buy their own product to effect a chart placement. Good record promotion and a strong fan base would naturally aid chart positions, but for new artists, charting for the first time would prove more difficult. The UK chart canon in 1985 was Gallup; their chart manager Godfrey Rust warned that labels caught hyping would experience chart exclusions as a penalty ('UK Chart Hyping Targeted', 1985). The demise of the CD single in recent times has been due to the vast reduction in sales in favour of MP3 single downloads; MP3 is counted as part of weekly record sales, with iTunes providing significant download data. In today's digitally orientated chart, the practice of hyping still occurs; in December 2009, the general public banded together through social networking to mass purchase downloads of 'Killing in the Name' by rock outfit Rage Against The Machine. The purpose was to deprive an *X Factor* talent show winner of the assured Christmas number one slot. In this case the hype was perpetrated by the public on supposedly moral grounds, rather than a label, even though the beneficiary in the whole affair was Sony Music – the parent label of *both* competing artists. Wherever labels and artists strive for visibility through the chart medium, there will always be the temptation to subvert the system in return for instant recognition, airplay and a return on the large investment outlay that music companies have to make, in pursuit of success. The chart is a powerful tool, and it is still reliably used by consumers and music companies alike in recognition of the value that is attributed to music.

PUBLICISTS AND PUBLIC RELATIONS: PRINT MEDIA

Publicising music through printed materials is an important part of the marketing plan for artists and labels that want to increase their visibility and add to the record release campaign. Music promotion in print is less effective in its wider impact than TV and radio, yet a good press campaign launched in tandem with TV and radio will enhance the marketing communication and maximise impact. Print media publicity is not to be underestimated and is also the easiest type of press to obtain at a local level, especially for the independent. There are several key areas of print media that music promoters and independent music makers should be aware of:

- daily newspapers or magazines (national and regional)
- lifestyle, music and pop culture magazines
- genre-based magazines
- hobbyist magazines
- trade publications
- web publication (e-zines, webzines, A/V net publications)
- newsweeklies and free music guides.

Music companies with a good promotional budget will employ an independent public relations company or person to endeavour to secure articles in print media; a good music publicist will have an ongoing relationship with entertainments features editors and be able to secure appropriate press articles and interviews. For major labels, when an artist of stature has an upcoming release, artist stories and photos may be leaked to daily press a month or two before the product release date. Press will also be invited to concerts to review artists on tour and comment on their performances in support of new product releases. For the small independent, it will be virtually impossible to attract articles in the national daily press without a track record and without having a known publicist who is well 'networked' in the press industry. Approaching local press is worthwhile as usually there is an ongoing interest in the local music scene; finding out exactly who the correct features editors are is a necessity. As in radio and TV, targeting key journalists and publications that specialise in certain genres makes the job of getting press easier, but there are only so many 'column inches' available and given the sheer amount of approaches daily print media gets, editors will look for the best and most credible artists to feature. A major problem associated with artists seeking print media publicity, is that they *all* have the same story to tell; they are all selling music and want the public to take as much notice as possible. For journalists and editors, seeking a good 'plot' will always take precedence; all artists will want to say that their music is good and they will want journalists to agree. In this regard, music reviews can often be damaging, if a performance is not up to scratch or an album is not as good as its predecessor; a negative press review could have a damaging effect on sales. Many music journalists 'write as they find', so artists should be aware of whom their music is being sent to and be wary of their critics. Other than the costs to employ a publicist in pursuit of press promotion, print media does not usually charge the music label for the printing of featured articles. Where many promotional avenues for the new artist prove impossible to achieve, such as TV and radio, print media often presents opportunity. This is largely due to many publications that rely on a constant supply of subject matter to write about. Print media is regarded as an effective way to build artist profiles, even in a world of enormous electronic media growth.

DIGITAL MEDIA: E-PRINT

The internet has had a huge impact on print media, which in turn has experienced a significant downturn in sales of many popular music publications. Forced mergers and closures have ensued to create a more economic print media climate. In the information age, magazines and newspapers upload their daily content to the web, so readers do not necessarily need to buy popular publications; they simply go online to read the content. The positive aspect of this for artists is that online articles are retrievable due to the huge amount of press material archived. When fans search for information on an artist, they can access past articles and reviews whereas at one time the printed matter would have been consigned to the bin. In extension to this, artists and fans can involve themselves actively in print publicity, contributing and participating in forums and blogs. The artist can define and control biographies, photos and the exact printed material that they want to be uploaded to various sites. Where the artist is in control of their own printed web materials, for example, on a MySpace page, blogs and comments can also be gate-kept by the artist to ensure positive messages are conveyed about their music. The downside is a lack of control on other sites where negative comments may arise against the artist, which may influence audiences and consumers (e.g. comment blogs on a newspaper website). PR companies and promoters increasingly use online print to create a buzz for their clients; usually the benefits far outweigh the negatives, especially as the costs to create online articles are relatively cheap in comparison with other media forms.

THE ELECTRONIC PRESS KIT

Due to the ever increasing electronic media components that are used in music promotion, artists and labels now unite these materials in one package that can be sent to wider media. The EPK has become an important tool that can be comprehensively used to inform media about a wide range of aspects concerning the artist. The EPK should include all that is needed by the print journalist, unless they wish to conduct an artist interview, which is usually conducted over the phone. The EPK contains press releases, photos and MP3s and any well produced video clips of performances or up-close interviews. A professional quality DVD can be produced to contain the EPK, or the EPK can be made available online at the artist's website for downloading. These materials can also be sent electronically to publicists and features editors; today there is little need for hard copies of materials to be posted unless specifically requested by journalists and wider media. However, exclusive CD copies are still often requested by some media personnel. Independent artists sending tangible promotional materials should be aware that any CDs sent out should be of full professional presentation, should include a bar code, with accompanying press release, artist biography and scanned photo. In the past, music reviews in print could only describe the music to the reader and the only way readers could verify journalistic critique and comment was to hear the record on radio or to buy it. Now in the 'new media age', readers of online articles can link to information quickly – to actually hear the artists music and make informed 'buying' decisions for themselves. The advent of 'convergence media' has changed the decision making process for consumers, in effect now speeding up their personal discovery and assessment of new music through electronic linking.

MUSIC IN MEDIA: CONVERGENCE

New media, as opposed to older tangible media forms, presents new opportunities for music exploitation. The integration of tangible print media, online print and digital audio visual material promises democratisation in new media through linking and integrated communication. Artists, labels and those who wish to work in the music industry must be aware of the changes that have occurred in media and the opportunities it presents; new skills are required to facilitate music promotion, using new media to its full capacity. New music consumers now expect more than old media forms and expect the integrated communication afforded by new media. The visual stimulation of high definition (HD) video images, a high quality publishing and photograph aesthetic, graphic tags and web links are now part of the new 'music in media' experience. Consumers expect instant digital delivery followed by an empowered ability to feedback interactively on the product they have just purchased by entering into global discussion about it. In new media terms, consumption of music has been redefined, from the simple act of buying and listening to a record, to the interlocking of many new technologies and concepts.

Terminology known as the 'three Cs' – Computing, Communications and Content – defines media convergence, which interweaves information technology with telecommunications and content providers, using electronic publishing. Works that are 'published' to the internet today include a full range of media (music, TV, radio, magazines, films and newspapers). Traditional paper print media alone cannot cover all the bases when compared with new media such as mobile delivery, video, web TV, user-generated content and multimedia messaging. Print media has crossed over into convergence through human and technological interactivity – and the music arena has provided an ideal environment in which music and print can thrive.

NIGHT CLUB PROMOTION AND REMIXES

On a national level in the UK, the night club establishment is well attended, especially at weekends. Labels working in the dance genre will instigate a national club promotion campaign in an effort to generate interest from the club-going demographic. A dance release that is well received on the club scene can escalate, encouraging specialist dance radio shows to play it. Sometimes a dance track can spend a year or more being played in night clubs before growing into a full-scale national release. Dance remixes of established hit songs are a popular feature in clubs which increases consumer visibility in the club-going demographic. Specialist promotions agencies that are well 'networked' on the dance club circuit are aware of underground radio shows that will also air club music. The dance market has been lucrative in the UK since the 1980s and with the right songs or remixes, a solid promotional campaign in the clubs is a good way to launch new music in the genre. Independents that are prepared to do the 'leg work' and promote fiercely in this market can create a buzz concerning their music, even if only on a regional level. Having the means to give much music away to DJs for free, networking with them and getting feedback is useful in the process. Audiences get to know club music very much on a passive level, as they do not necessarily request it, but dance audiences are a good consumer demographic as they will often purchase songs that motivate them and accompany their social activity, especially when out at weekends or on holiday. Field research in the genre and its buying demographic is necessary to identify what motivates consumers at any given moment, due to the trend based nature of the 'scene' and its fast turnover of product.

AWARD SHOWS: CONGRATULATING MUSIC

Some forms of music promotion are not outwardly thought of as promotion to the passive consumer; congratulating music through award shows would fall into this category. Award shows began with music magazine publications recognising various categories of music, artists and other items associated with music in published yearly accolades. The *NME* 'Poll Winners Concert' was first held in 1953, shortly after the founding of the magazine. Other successful music magazines, such as *Melody Maker* and *Sounds*, followed in the footsteps of *NME*, recognising the achievements of music artists annually. *Sounds* later produced the spin off metal genre magazine *Kerrang*, which today hosts a televised metal music awards show. In the UK, the largest televised award show, which attracts the largest national audience, is the Brits, hosted annually and originally developed by the British Phonograph Industry in 1977. The Brits is a national showcase for high profile artists in the main and has had several sponsors in the past but is now largely sponsored by the major recording industry. Other UK award shows of note are:

- The MOBOs: The British R&B focused 'Music Of Black Origin' awards launched in 1996.
- The Ivors: Songwriting awards sponsored by the British Association of Song Composers and Authors and PRS for Music, in the name of Cardiff-born composer Ivor Novello.
- The Mercury Prize: Celebrating all UK and Irish music genres, focusing on album releases, sponsored by a large credit card conglomerate.
- The UK Music Video Awards: Recognising creativity and innovation in music video.

Regionally these award shows recognise differing achievements in music, but in relation to marketing communications, when televised, award ceremonies provide a recognised promotional tool, carrying huge endorsement potential for the music product. Exactly how votes are cast and how data is gathered to produce an award show winner is sometimes controversial; often, the reasons why one artist is nominated or chosen over another can cause further newsworthy press comment after the ceremony. Record labels know well in advance if any of their artists are winners in televised award shows such as the Brits. The major then has commercials at the ready featuring the product, which will appear in advert breaks when the show is transmitted, capitalising on the recognition; compilation albums of collective show winners are also advertised as being available during and after the show. A by-product of the Brits is to raise money for charity to fund music projects, promoting the positive aspects of the award show other than celebration and promotional objectives. In the US there are several high profile award ceremonies that take place to acknowledge international music achievement, three of which are:

- the American Music Awards
- the Grammys
- the Country Music Awards (CMAs).

Cable music television pop shows also host and broadcast award ceremonies for music such as the MTV Europe Music Awards. In 2009, the show hosted in Berlin produced thirteen high profile winners in its main categories; however, eight of its winners were from the US market, while Turkey, Germany and Ireland produced one winner each, with the UK producing the remaining two winners. Such results demonstrate the clear benefit of extended televised international promotion for US high profile artists in a 'European' branded award show context (see http://ema. mtv.tv/winners).

The World Music Awards (WMAs) 2010 took place in Monaco; the WMAs were founded in 1989 and use sales figures from the International Federation of the Phonographic Industry to produce winners from many global territories. The show is broadcast in 160 countries and boasts a potential audience of one billion viewers. Campaigning against illegal downloading practice, its show chairman stated in 2010:

> A recent study generated by IFPI demonstrated that it takes about US $1 million to break an artist to the top of the charts in a major market. With a better legal environment it will be easier for labels to secure a return on that investment and plough money into discovering, nurturing and promoting the next generation of talent.
>
> (John Kennedy, IFPI, 2010)

Each year, the World Music Awards traditionally produces a strong succession of US winners, due to the global visibility of the major US pop artist through huge promotional investment and music that appeals to a mass demography. An award show of this magnitude has the potential to extend far beyond the traditional artist promotion campaign, exemplifying this in its charitable activities. Although music award shows only occur annually they serve as an additional promotional boost and a chance to pit artists against their rivals, thus provoking competitive discussion between music fans and ultimately, selling more music.

GIVING MUSIC AWAY: 'FREE'

A trend has emerged in recent years whereby established high profile artists give their music away free. This is all part of a wider promotional plan to attract a larger audience and sometimes this method can work in favour of the artist and issuing label. In July 2007 and July 2010, US artist Prince authorised the free distribution of two of his albums. The giveaway formed part of the media press plot, and the promotional benefits were huge as, in 2007, national news networks reported on the giveaway in primetime TV slots. The 2010 album (20TEN) consisted of 2.5m copies being given away free in UK newspapers; this marketing approach also marked the beginning of an international tour, thus aiding concert promotion even further. Even though the album was included in national newspapers, an alleged sum over £500,000 was paid by the newspaper to cover the licensing and marketing costs for the free distribution in 2007. In this regard the album actually made a financial return for the artist and was not actually free to fans, as they would need to purchase a newspaper to get the album. There are many examples of established artists using 'free' tactics to increase fans and guide them towards other products they may have to offer online. The notion of 'free' works for artists with an established value in the market; for the new independent, devaluing product before it even has a commercial value is not necessarily the best way to start. Often what appears 'free' is simply a part of the promotional campaign. If something appears free, it draws consumers to it, and in respect the global artist, 'free' attracts wider media attention.

SECONDARY PROMOTION

Music in the ether

Music played in bars, social clubs, shops, restaurants, hairdressers, the workplace, hotels, 'lift' music, weddings, juke boxes and social occasions provides additional promotion for labels and artists. Although perhaps less publicly prominent, this music is 'passively' consumed through 'background' delivery. When a business owner chooses music and plays it to enhance their business space, music is inadvertently passively consumed. Music can be selected to promote a good sales atmosphere and add a 'feel good factor' to a shop when buying clothes for instance, encouraging the buyer to be more relaxed and enhance customers buying experience. Recognisable music is often chosen for this purpose with the music gaining a promotional boost in turn, from this type of public exposure. Although the number of persons hearing background music are lower in small businesses, this could be far more significant when heard in a major supermarket chain. Historically, record retailers would always play new releases in store, drawing public attention to the records they wanted to sell. As supermarkets are now the largest retailers of tangible CDs, it is highly likely that they will play music in-store if they have stocked it and want to increase sales. Blanket licenses issued by PRS and PPL permit the store to play the music publicly, but there is a promotional benefit – placing the music in the psyche of the consumer. Consumers do not request or choose the music in these environments; it arrives at the ears of the consumer passively. Often the music is likely to be from a primary label, unless genre specific to certain retailers, for example, anonymous 'chill-out' music being played to create a more tranquil atmosphere in a coffee bar. At a social function, such as a birthday or wedding, independent DJs are likely to play well known music to larger gatherings; music that carries a sentimental attachment is often purchased following exposure at such events. In these environments, business owners are actually 'paying to promote' the labels and songwriters music, through their business premises blanket licence payments to PRS and PPL; yet as the business space is being enhanced with music, the business owner often feels this is a worthwhile investment. A song such as 'Celebration' by Kool and the Gang is probably one of the best known middle-of-the-road 'party' songs, which has been played at countless parties and sporting events since its release in 1980. With music residing in the 'ether', the real benefit to the label and artists is the increase in product familiarity and awareness to the passive consumer. This often leads to the ultimate canonisation of their music in the long term, through this often overlooked promotional medium.

Tribute acts, cover bands and new pop musicals

Another form of secondary promotion exists for music, which is also often overlooked, yet keeps music promoted largely through smaller venues, pubs, bars, clubs and theatres. The recent up-swell in bands that cover well known songs has increased in recent years; the 'tribute act' has become a growing feature in UK live entertainment. For the original act that made the music famous in the first place, their works are perpetuated and further canonised as a result of those who cover the material. Many original creators of hit material have ceased touring, have split with their band, or are simply too aged to deliver a performance. Others are too canonised or could not stage a tour due to a lack of financial sponsors. Seeing opportunity, the tribute act simply steps in and takes well known popular music to an audience that still craves it; in doing so, the music catalogue of the original writers and performers is promoted. In music publishing terms this is not a new phenomenon; shows that are staged in theatrical districts such as the West End or Broadway have perpetuated popular music works for many years, but largely the music was designed for musical theatre. There has been a steady growth in familiar pop music commissioned for use in West End and theatre shows in the UK since the 1990s. The music of popular rock outfit Queen, used in the stage show *We Will Rock You* and the music of Michael Jackson in *Thriller Live* have proved to be successful in attracting pop music listeners to the theatre. Writing shows around an 'already established' popular music soundtrack, capitalises on audiences that are familiar with hit material, hence it is easier to sell tickets for the show. Using music in this live context re-enforces fan relationships and where the wider family attends, a new younger consumer is introduced to the music. Large shows, tribute acts and cabaret performances have the ability to perpetuate hit material, keeping the music 'familiar' and in the minds of the public. In this regard, songwriters, artists and labels may not necessarily know where or when their works are being heard from a grassroots level upwards; although their catalogue is being promoted through this medium, it is simply as 'music in the ether'.

REFERENCES AND FURTHER READING
Books

Barrow, T. and Newby, J., *Inside the Music Business* (London: Routledge, 1995), pp. 103–156.
Baskerville, D. and Baskerville, T., *Music Business Handbook and Career Guide: Ninth Edition* (London: Sage, 2010), pp. 287–321.

Beattie, W., *The Rock and Roll Times Guide to the Music Industry* (Oxford: Spring Hill, 2007), pp. 75–80 and 168–177.

Biermans, H., *The Music Industry: The Practical Guide to Understanding the Essentials* (London: DSS, 2007), pp. 133–165.

Davis, S. and Laing, D., *The Guerrilla Guide to the Music Business* (New York: Continuum, 2006), pp. 210–240.

Gelfand, M., *Strategies for Success: Self Promotion Secrets for Musicians* (New York: Schirmer, 2005).

Hull, P.G., *The Recording Industry: Second Edition* (New York: Routledge, 2004), pp. 231–266.

Hutchison, T., Macy, A. and Allen, P., *Record Label Marketing: Second Edition* (Oxford: Elsevier, 2010), pp. 167–250.

King, M., *Music Marketing: Press, Promotion, Distribution, and Retail* (Boston: Berklee Press, 2009).

Kusek, D. and Leonhard, G., *The Future of Music: Manifesto for the Digital Music Revolution* (Boston: Berklee Press, 2005), p. 115.

Lathrop, T., *This Business of Music Marketing and Promotion* (New York: Billboard, 2003).

May, T. and Weissman, D., *Promoting Your Music: The Lovin' of the Game* (Oxford: Routledge, 2007).

Schwartz, D.D., *I Don't Need a Record Deal: Your Survival Guide for the Indie Music Revolution* (New York: Billboard, 2005), pp. 122–172.

Schwartz, D.D., *Start and Run Your Own Record Label* (New York: Billboard, 2009), pp. 185–269.

Spellman, P., *The Self-promoting Musician: Strategies for Independent Music Success* (New York: Berklee Press, 2000).

Summers, J., *Making and Marketing Music* (New York: Allworth, 1999).

Walker, Jr., L.J., *This Business of Urban Music: A Practical Guide to Achieving Success in the Industry, from Gospel to Funk to R&B and Hip-Hop* (New York: Billboard, 2008), pp. 255–285.

Wikström, P., *The Music Industry: Digital Media and Society Series* (Cambridge: Polity Press, 2009), pp. 46–84.

Online resources

Babington, C., 'Big Radio Settles Payola Charges', *Washington Post* (6 March 2007). Available at: www.washingtonpost.com/wpdyn/content/article/2007/03/05/AR2007030501286.html (accessed 24 August 2010).

BBC Radio 1. Available at: www.bbc.co.uk/radio1 (accessed 1 October 2010).

Greenslade, R., 'Mirror and Record to Give Away Prince Album', *The Guardian* (29 June 2010). Available at: www.guardian.co.uk/media/greenslade/2010/jun/29/daily-mirror-prince (accessed 25 August 2010).

Hazard, B., 'Is a Last.fm Powerplay Campaign Right for You?', *Music Think Tank* (1 April 2009). Available at: www.musicthinktank.com/blog/is-a-lastfm-powerplay-campaign-right-for-you.html (accessed 23 August 2010).

Kennedy, J., 'The World Music Awards: IFPI Statement', (9 April 2010). Available at: www.worldmusicawards.com (accessed 25 August 2010).

Lindvall, H., 'Payola: Once a Dirty Word, Now the Basis of Internet Radio', *The Guardian* (16 April 2009). Available at: www.guardian.co.uk/music/musicblog/2009/apr/16/payola-internet-radio (accessed 23 August 2010).

MTV Europe Awards Show. Available at: http://ema.mtv.tv/winners (accessed 25 August 2010).

Official Charts Company (OCC) UK. Available at: www.theofficialcharts.com (accessed 25 August 2010).

Radio 2, 'The Inventor of Rock and Roll: The Alan Freed Story', BBC. Available at: www.bbc.co.uk/programmes/b00pqb52 (accessed 24 August 2010).

Radio Joint Audience Research (RAJAR). Available at: www.rajar.co.uk (accessed 1 October 2010).

Reynolds, J., 'Prince Album Adds 27% to Mirror Sales', *Media Week* (13 July 2010). Available at: www.mediaweek.co.uk/news/rss/1015668/Prince-album-adds-27-Mirror-sales (accessed 25 August 2010).

Simpson, R. and Nathan, S., 'Rage Against The Machine Sells Half a Million Copies to Pip Joe McElderry (and Simon Cowell) to the Christmas No. 1 Spot', *Daily Mail* (21 December 2009). Available at: www.dailymail.co.uk/tvshowbiz/article-1237332/Rage-Against-The-Machine-beat-Joe-McElderry-claim-Christmas-number-one.html (accessed 24 August 2010).

Stoller, T., 'Independent Radio's Demise Began When It Lost Its Localness', *The Guardian* (24 May 2010). Available at: www.guardian.co.uk/media/2010/may/24/independent-local-radio-demise (accessed 20 August 2010).

Stross, R., 'YouTube Wants to Sit and Stay a While', *New York Times* (30 May 2010). Available at: www.nytimes.com/2010/05/30/business/30digi.html (accessed 25 August 2010).

'UK Chart Hyping Targeted', *Billboard* (3 August 1985), p. 4. Available at: http://books.google.co.uk/books?id=uSQEAAAAMBAJ&pg=PT8&lpg=PT8&dq=chart+hyping&source=bl&ots=ZvXrAr4jJ&sig=gGypc2IaUoVs69RT29S8IsQ9hmo&hl=en&ei=kP9OTIb5BITw0wS86diQBw&sa=X&oi=book_result&ct=result&resnum=4&ved=0CCIQ6AEwAw#v=onepage&q=chart%20hyping&f=false (accessed 24 August 2010).

CHAPTER 9

Music synchronisation and non-music brands

Stu Lambert[1]

MUSIC IN MOVIES, TV, ADVERTISING, GAMES AND NON-MUSIC BRANDS

This chapter explores ways in which music can make money, apart from its two main streams of a record release and live performance, and the royalty collections associated with those two key products. The two further principal revenue streams are: synchronisation, which is payment for the use of recorded music with visual images; and the involvement of non-music brands, principally associated with live events.

Money isn't the only consideration, particularly from the artist's side. The linking of music with a product brings in another set of values or associations, with the prospect of changing the carefully built perceptions of the artist, developed in their own media campaigns. The non-music partner in one of these deals is often buying a cultural message through their music choice, while the artist contemplates a link with a product that is equally culturally loaded. Sponsorship of live events is no longer a simple exchange of display space for money; the brand is looking for a high level of attraction between the bulk of the act's fans and the product, sufficient to get the fans registering, interacting and maybe even becoming brand ambassadors.

SYNCHRONISATION

Synchronisation, commonly known as 'sync' within the music industry, includes the use of music with movies, television shows, television advertising and electronic games. The rights administrators for the master right – the specific recording to be used – and for the underlying composition, are called the 'licensors', as they are asked to grant a license for the use of the work they control. The user applying for the license is called the 'licensee'. Because the work requested has usually been commercially released, all licenses are non-exclusive and limited to specified uses with the visual media. This is important, to avoid the possibility of an unscrupulous licensee releasing the track commercially or otherwise using it in ways that would cause disadvantage to the licensor or existing licensees.

Each type of use has requirements that shape the deals, but all have factors in common. The deal is a straightforward, who-needs-who commercial negotiation, unlike, for example, mechanical rights, which are all paid at a set percentage of product price. There are no immediate competitors to affect the negotiated rate, as there might be in a record contract, as it's not likely that a particular piece of music will be wanted for more than one film, advert or game use at the same time. This means that any recent deals are highly commercially sensitive and most industry experts will only give a range of figures within which deals are made. Equally, the budget available from the licensees and the scale of the projects or campaigns vary enormously, as does the prestige and bargaining power of the licensors.

The value of the music to the visual medium is also measured by the importance of the music within the work. While the term 'incidental' has not been clearly defined, music used incidentally, either as a short excerpt or giving little specific emphasis to the visuals, is worth much less than a more prominent use, which either has a strong context within the visuals, or is used as a theme or recurrently. It is widely agreed in the music industry that sync fees have dwindled, principally because the market has matured and has customary practices and because the licensees are now fully aware of their value and bargaining power.

As with all contracts, the clever bit lies in anticipating all possible needs during the term of the agreement before it is signed. To come back and ask for an extension of the uses requested for a work, when there is no option but to use that work because it is already tied in to your visual product, is a position in which no negotiator would wish to work. At the same time, it is costly to ask for more than is needed, so negotiators don't ask for world rights for a work that is unlikely to be commercially used outside its country of origin, or for a lifetime licence for music used in a three-month advertising campaign.

Effect on record sales

All media that use pre-recorded music have at some time shown clear effects on sales of records and therefore on artist profile. (Some examples of clear effects are given below, in each category of use.) A significant effect on sales will probably bring more revenue to the composer and performer than the sync licence itself. The great age of sync-related chart hits was the 1980s, for adverts, and early 1990s, for songs used in films. Sales and success related to TV programme and video game use were most obvious in the 2000s, with signs that the effects have weakened, become less frequent, or died away by 2010.

The principle of why people buy music that isn't new is the same now as in the 1980s: it finds a new audience, preferably one that doesn't habitually buy much music. The audience for a blockbuster movie is not only wider than that for soft rock (Bryan Adams) or sanitised soul (Whitney Houston), but will have different music purchasing habits. At the time, a cross-promotional strategy between the record release and the movie gave a clear buying opportunity, when acquiring new music was relatively difficult and coincided with shopping trips, giving a tight buying pattern that yielded the familiar virtuous circle of chart success, radio and TV play leading to a clear sales effect.

In today's climate of ubiquitous music and on-demand streaming, and with an audience super-saturated with media messages that constantly mine music's heritage, such mass buying in a short time is very difficult to stimulate. However, it is the digital age of music that has made music companies so keen to get sync deals; as consumer sales fall, any reliable business-to-business payment is welcome, particularly when it comes in the form of a buyout. A buyout constitutes a single payment covering all uses, rather than enduring the negative effects of accounting delays and deductions of royalties on music sales.

An effect on sales is often caused by the sync use introducing the music to a new audience sector, as the target audience for the original record release is expected to have bought, or at least be aware of, the music at its time of release. Using an old hit, such as Chanel's use of Nina Simone's 'My Baby Just Cares For Me' in 1987, introduces a younger age group, who may not have even been alive when the track was first released. Using an underground track, as Citroen did with 'Jacques Your Body' by Les Rhythmes Digitales for their dancing car advert in 2005, introduces the track to a broader audience than club play and dance radio could ever hope to do.

The big results, though, come from uses that motivate people who don't habitually buy much music. As the music acquisition of keen buyers – NME readers, Radio 1 evening listeners and the 16–24 age group in general, for example – has become ever more dispersed among different releases, between new material and catalogue and now between sales, subscriptions and illegal downloads, the effect of that audience's buying on sales of a particular record reactivated by a use in visual media has become more and more muted. Drawing the attention of the much greater number of occasional record buyers to one track begins another virtuous circle of sales, chart position, airplay and more sales. This set of circumstances isn't unique to sync; compilation albums for Valentine's Day and Mother's Day, charity singles and talent show artists such as Susan Boyle all benefit from the same stampede effect. These, though, are all backed by a planned release and promotion campaign. A sync use is effectively promoted by the licensee's work – the ad, movie, game, etc. – and, now that almost all single sales are downloads, there isn't even a need to make sure there is stock in shops. As Simon Goffe, of Gilles Peterson's Brownswood Recordings, says: 'It's money from heaven'.

The usefulness of sync to acts and authors varies greatly and, in many cases, doesn't achieve a lot more than the in-house promotion strategy for the music's first release. If the work is being actively promoted at the same time as the media release, it is difficult to separate the effects of the movie, ad or game from the effects of radio play, internet promotion or touring. The clearest cases come from a new use of a work that has achieved all of its sales potential through existing channels.

How to get sync rights for your music

There has been much debate about whether music can be explicitly pitched to potential licensees for sync uses. Some licensors with sync business say that the best one can hope to achieve is to keep clients updated and well serviced with reminders of the catalogue. Others believe that it is possible to work a specific track, act or catalogue around the community of clients, with a good chance of getting business from the effort. A large publishing company with hundreds of thousands of copyrights is likely to have enough business to keep a sync officer busy with negotiations and licences, while a smaller player may feel a great effort to establish a catalogue in the minds of potential clients offers the chance of relatively large rewards.

Often, a music supervisor's or creative director's reason for using a certain work is oblique; it creates an atmosphere, maybe gives a quirky take on the visuals to get the audience's attention, or indicates something about a particular character. Specialists in this field, such as Roxanne Oldham, co-founder of Mix-tape Music, regularly receive requests issued by music supervisors and agencies. Oldham suggests that, to get sync business for your act, you use a dedicated agency rather than set about contacting potential clients such as advertising agencies or film companies, due to the number of connections you would need to make in order to find a client for your music at exactly the right time. The fast turnaround on most requests is better handled by someone who does a lot of business in that area, rather than all aspects of artists' careers. 'It's about saving time for your contacts when they reach out to you', says Oldham. 'If a company has a roster that makes you think they will like what you are promoting, find out if they prefer CDs or MP3, package your music thoughtfully and see what they say'.

If you are intending to seek sync business directly rather than through an intermediary, Stephanie Perrin, Creative Licensing Manager at HannaH Management/BarBera Music, advises:

> A sync business takes a lot of pursuing. It's about networking, knowing the right places to go, the right people to talk to. You need to get the music out there, by getting in touch with editors, producers, independent music supervisors

and consultancies. Set up meetings, do research into who puts the music into TV, ads, films and games. Pay attention to names at the end of shows.

You can choose to concentrate on a specific track, or general awareness of your music. Oldham advises:

> Find out the right contact at the business then it's up to you to win them over with your music and meet their deadlines, so they come to you as a reliable source when a search comes up. Achieve a relationship with the client and then they will email you directly with a brief or send the brief to their contact email list of music providers.

She doesn't recommend subscribing to paid-for bulletins.

A lot of the business is about quick turnaround and making it easy for the clients. There are practical details such as, for digital files, including meta-information – contact details, keywords and lyrics. Oldham says: 'On a CD, make sure the track names come up on iTunes when the CD is put in, not to have that is an instant turnoff for many companies, and also that you print contact details on the CD and the CD package has a spine, so that it can easily be found again'. These apparently small details can make a big difference, because fast turnaround is a known characteristic of this sector; the clients want the music right away.

There is no clear trend about whether licensees prefer music that is set to be released or promoted during the time the track will be exposed in their ad or TV show – films and games have a much longer trajectory and are not likely to worry about that. Some prefer unreleased music, to show that they are 'out there' and in touch with talent; others hope for some level of cross-promotion, where record plays increase the awareness of the sync use and vice versa. They will be reading music blogs, looking for press coverage of the act. Some will specify in the brief that the piece must be six months old at most, for example. The TV series *Skins* tries to work closely with artists' release schedules, according to Stephanie Perrin.

MOVIES

The use of music in a film is the responsibility of the music supervisor, who may compose or commission original music for the film and also negotiate for the use of any pre-recorded music. Major film studios often 'encourage' the use of music from their associated record labels and the director may also have ideas for music, so the supervisor's job is not one of unrestricted creative choice. Music deals are often done late in the film's trajectory, because – as anyone who watches DVD extras will know – scenes are shot that are not used in the final cut, and it would be a waste of time and money to set up deals for music that isn't going to be used. Music supervisors then complain that they get the crumbs of the budget, most of which has been used for shooting, and their spending power is reduced.

Terms of contracts

Movies remain as cultural artefacts for decades – the daytime TV schedules establish that old age or poor quality are no barrier – and are distributed globally. Their longevity means that even extra-terrestrial use needs to be thought of, so the standard term of deals is 'in perpetuity' and the territory is 'the world and territories beyond'.

Different uses are held to be of differing importance. Music requested for the title sequence of the film gives the licensor the idea that their contribution would not be easy to substitute, so a high price can be asked. Similarly, if the piece of music appears 'out of context' with its use in the body of the film, such as in the trailer, it will have many more exposures and have a strong association with the identity of the film, so this request too will cost more than a use of the music when only used in context. Sometimes the trailer may be made by a completely different production company to those engaged on the film, so separate negotiations are essential. It's also important to establish whether the music is diegetic – music that the characters in the film can hear, such as a radio they are listening to, which is comparatively rare – or non-diegetic, often called incidental, music, which is not part of the dramatic scene and is used to create emphasis, such as suspense, humour or violence.

Of course, movies have a life beyond cinema distribution and we are now approaching the point where streaming of movies will take over from renting DVD as the delivery method for home entertainment. All potential uses such as these need to be factored in to the deal. If an original soundtrack album (OST) is to be released, a different set of licences covering mechanical reproductions must be obtained.

Effects on sales

The film industry was responsible for the disappointment of many would-be chart-toppers in the early 1990s, as a hat-trick of ballads from blockbuster movies hogged the number one spot. Bryan Adams set the as-yet unbeaten record for a stay at the top of the chart with 'Everything I Do (I Do It For You)', the theme from *Robin Hood Prince of Thieves*, which spent sixteen consecutive weeks at number one from June 1991, with a total of twenty-five weeks in the chart. The theme song from *The Bodyguard*, Whitney Houston's full-throated version of Dolly Parton's 'I Will Always Love You', hit number one in November 1992, stayed on top for ten weeks and racked up twenty-nine chart weeks. *Four Weddings and a Funeral* put Wet Wet Wet's version of an old Troggs song, 'Love Is All Around', at number one in May 1994, where it stayed for fifteen weeks of a massive thirty-seven week (almost nine months) chart stay. By 2000, such clear examples had mostly disappeared and it is now rare for a movie use to generate even a chart placing for a song, though MIA's 'Paper Planes' gained a lot of momentum from its use in the soundtrack and trailer of *Pineapple Express* and subsequently in *Slumdog Millionaire*. The rarity of sales spikes nowadays is perhaps because, twenty years on, the age group corresponding to the one that was stimulated to buy a record by hearing it in a film is still strongly engaged with music, influenced perhaps more by BBC's 6 Music or *Later with Jools Holland*, and therefore in no need of a big media message to discover new artists. An exception, which demonstrates the potential of the marginal market of record buyers in a different way, was the *Hannah Montana* movie of 2009. The sub-teen or 'tweens' sector flocked to the movie spin-off of the *Hannah Montana* TV show and took the soundtrack album to the top of the *Billboard Top 200* albums chart in the US and high positions in over twenty album charts worldwide.

TV PROGRAMMES

The huge amount of music used incidentally in British TV programmes, particularly factual programmes such as gardening or property shows, is possible because blanket licences have been negotiated between the record and music publishing industries and the programme makers. This means that the programme maker needs not enter into a specific negotiation every time a piece of music is used. A fee, typically under £100, is paid for this type of use. The fee is higher for commercial broadcasters than for the BBC, but is a set amount. Fees are administered by PRS for the publishing side and PPL for the master right. There is no blanket licence arrangement in the US, where each buyout is individually negotiated. This means that it can be worth the effort of plugging material to American TV shows; Brownswood Recordings has plugged successfully to shows like *CSI Miami*.

When the music becomes more significant in the programme, the licences are negotiated on a buyout basis and fees can run into thousands of dollars or pounds. As with movies, use of a piece of music for the trailer influences the fee.

Effect on sales

Significant effects on the sales of records used in TV shows are so rare that they are almost all noteworthy. Alexandra Patsavas' work as a music supervisor on US shows such as *The O.C.* and *Grey's Anatomy* is credited with bringing underground and foreign artists to the attention of a young adult, record-buying audience in the US. Imogen Heap's US profile leapt significantly when her track 'Hide-and-Seek' was used for the closing credits of the final series of *The O.C.* In the UK, a similar demographic tuned into Bristol-based teen drama *Skins*, enticed by a trailer featuring The Gossip's 'Standing In the Way of Control', which gave the band its only Top 20 entry, peaking at number seven in November 2006.

ADVERTISING

The choice of music for an advert is usually made by the creative department of the advertising agency, or the director of the filmed advert. It has long been held that music with words that refer closely to what is being advertised is a coarse, clunky choice, but that doesn't stop sync departments compiling lists of keywords from the song lyrics, in case it attracts the attention of a potential client. The choice of music for adverts can be borderline eccentric: DFS sofas ran consecutive ads featuring The La's 'There She Goes' and The Ethiopians' ska classic 'Train to Skaville', over fairly standard visuals of people trying out sofas. This demonstrates that the choice of catalogue music in adverts is not always driven by a desire to create an enthusiasm for the music in the public; there is a risk of creating the reverse effect of reducing brand recall by making the creative values too striking, so that the public recall the visuals and the music, but not the product being advertised.

Terms of contracts

One advert can be shown at differing lengths, depending on the timing within the campaign or the desired booking cost, so each extract of music used will have to be agreed. Most frequently, adverts are made for consumption in one country, so a licence for that country alone is often requested. Adverts run for a limited time, typically one, three or six months; restricting the length of the licence requested helps to reduce costs. An option to continue the use is often included in the contract, with a fee payable if the option is taken up.

There have been exceptions to the single-territory agreement. Global brands such as Pepsi Cola have run global campaigns and have enlisted super-celebs such as Michael Jackson, Madonna and Britney Spears – usually with unlooked-for publicity side-effects, which may explain why this is not current practice.

Effects on sales

The milestone moment when it was clear that the use of a pop tune in an advert could generate sales was in 1985, when male model Nick Kamen created a sensation as he stripped to his boxer shorts in a launderette to wash his Levis jeans, accompanied by Marvin Gaye's 'I Heard It Through the Grapevine'. Gaye's track, originally released in 1968, had no other promotion at the time, yet it reached number eight in the singles chart. Levis followed up this success with other classic tracks: Sam Cooke's 'Wonderful World' and Percy Sledge's 'When a Man Loves a Woman' reached number two in 1986 and 1987, 'C'mon Everybody' by Eddie Cochran and 'The Joker' by the Steve Miller Band were used, the latter going to number one. Levis then moved into using new music, creating a string of chart-toppers until 1999.

The success of the classic tracks, which was copied by several other brands, sits in the context of the times. The arrival of the CD had brought about a boom in back catalogue sales, as vinyl owners updated their collections, and pop acts including Paul Young and Phil Collins had recently had hits with classic soul tracks.

More recent examples of sync-driven sales boosts have included Cadbury's gorilla-suited drummer playing Phil Collins' 'In the Air Tonight' in 2007, reactivating the 1981 track to a number fourteen chart position, and Jose Gonzalez' 'Heartbeats', used on a 2008 Sony Bravia commercial. This featured 250,000 coloured balls bouncing down a hill in San Francisco, which took an artist almost unknown in the UK to number eight and thirty-three weeks in the chart.

If there is a common feature to most of these examples, which distinguishes them from other advertising sync uses that haven't created sales success, it is that there is little or no voice-over or product demonstration. The visuals and music are given space until the necessary message at the end. Many other catalogue tracks are used in commercials, but with the music in a weaker role as a 'soundbed' to people wandering around DIY stores, sitting on sofas and so on while a voice-over dominates the soundtrack; no concentrated sales boost is evident in these cases. Arguably, the attentiveness that the first format commands helps to enlist people to buy the music.

GAMES

The use of music in electronic games is the success story of sync over the last ten years. From *FIFA '99* for Playstation, where Fatboy Slim's name lit up the edges of the pitch when a goal was scored and a celebratory clip of 'Rockafeller Skank' played, to the participatory music games such as *Singstar*, *Guitar Hero* and *Rock Band*, with a huge number of available tracks, music's importance to gaming has been consistently on the rise and, correspondingly, a popular game introduces new audiences to the music it features.

Terms of contracts

As with movies, the importance of the piece of music within the game is important in negotiation. The hot spot is music that plays during menus; players can spend a lot of time sorting out what their characters look like, wear, kill monsters with and so on. This gives the music a chance to seep into their brain but also, arguably, less impulse actually to buy and own it as they hear it so much. Next in the rankings is gameplay, while title sequences are low-status, since gamers often skip them altogether.

Licences tend to be worldwide or there can be separate licences for the US and the rest of the world, as games are globally distributed. The term of the licence needs to be long enough to cover the viable sales life of the game, but expire around the time that technological advance consigns either the game or the host machine to the junkheap. A typical request is for fifteen years. However, as the online components of games bring increasing standardisation, licences are being sought in perpetuity, as for films and DVDs. A unit royalty payment is very rare: almost all business is on a buyout basis. Fees vary so much that a big-name artist's track occupying a prominent place on a premium game may attract 100 times as much as a new act's track used incidentally on a lower-profile release.

Video games have been part of the marketing mix for music for at least ten years. It has been the participatory music games such as *Singstar*, the *Guitar Hero* and *Rock Band* series and *DJ Hero* that have shown clear effects on sales. Sergio Pimentel, International Music & Licensing Manager at Activision Blizzard, which produces the *Guitar Hero* and *DJ Hero* games, says that his company sees:

> Huge sales spikes for catalogue tracks, for example around Christmas, when consoles and games are bought. We are seeing new audiences exposed to music in two ways: young kids, who wouldn't have listened to their parents' records, are interacting with the tracks and getting into them, while their parents may acquire a taste for r'n'b or other artists and genres they haven't been familiar with.

USA Today noted that sales of UK metal band DragonForce's CDs and downloads rose considerably after their track 'Through the Fire and Flames' was featured on *Guitar Hero III: Legends of Rock*. Digital sales of the track itself rose from a typical 2,000 per week to a high of over 37,000 just after Christmas 2007. Nielsen Soundscan tracked sixty-two of the seventy featured songs on *Guitar Hero III* and found that sales increased on all of them following the release of the game. Previous releases of *Guitar Hero* had featured cover versions rather than original tracks, but even these boosted sales of the original records, much as the performances on *Glee* and *X Factor* have done. As rock is almost always performed by the composers, a cover version still gives the act considerable benefit from publishing income – and, should they own their own catalogue, they get to keep almost all of the money.

There are indications that the effect on sales has flattened, along with sales of the music games themselves. There were no increases in digital sales for *Guitar Hero 5*, *Band Hero* or *DJ Hero* after their releases in 2009. However, Activision Blizzard claimed in 2007 that two-thirds of non-musicians exposed to music games planned to take up a musical instrument, and that sales of guitars and amps in the US rose by over a quarter in the same year. So the overall benefit to the broad music industry continues, and sales of the games and music across the world may show cumulative financial benefits for a longer time than a saturated market such as the US.

Becoming a legend of rock, even a small legend like DragonForce, is not something one can fully plan for, but there is scope for new acts to be included in the lucrative sync market for games. Activision Blizzard holds an annual listening session at the Midem trade fair in Cannes, to find new and even unsigned bands for its games.

'Though we keep our ear to the ground, in Europe and the US, it's worth making contact as there is so much great music that hasn't been discovered', Pimentel says.

Though budgets are shrinking, sync is still one of the good ways for a lesser-known act to make a mark. 'The money might not seem like much to a big act, but, if you own your own rights, one ad fee could fund a whole album for some artists', Roxanne Oldham says. However, it is rare that the sync use can be factored into a commercial development strategy for music, as clients choose music from across the decades and genres, for reasons which are not compatible with the music industry's set of values.

SPONSORSHIP AND BRAND INVOLVEMENT

A report by Will Page and Chris Carey of PRS for Music in August 2010 found that advertising and sponsorship brought £89.9 million to the UK music industry in 2009, out of a total income of £3.86 billion. Live music sponsorship grew 29.4 per cent to £30.8 million, while the live music industry was worth £1.54 billion. As those shares represent less than 2.5 per cent of total revenue in an industry that has, for at least ten years, courted sponsors obsessively, Page perhaps unsurprisingly concluded that there is room for growth in this revenue stream, but stated that, though the market appears static in value, the fact that it has weathered difficult conditions so well means that there could be capacity for growth, if the music industry can come up with innovative offers. The report also confirms what brand managers have been saying for two or three years, that the amount of work involved in setting up the relationship requires a better consumer relationship to be founded – more than just a product giveaway or space for a banner at a show. The best partnerships now go far beyond this simple deal.

Larger festivals and arena concerts have shown booming business since 2000, while small festivals and theatre and club shows have had trickier times; the first category of events can offset their high production costs by attracting a steady stream of sponsorship and advertising income. Mobile phones and alcoholic drinks, to some the twin curses of the modern age, have been a particular blessing for live music through their backing of festivals, club nights, talent shows and more.

The top line of sponsorship, most consistent and most visible, is venue and event branding. The O2 brand is now synonymous with the former Millennium Dome in East London, known just as 'The O2', and O2 branding is also present at the chain of Academy venues across the UK. These were branded as Carling Academy venues until 2008. Venue naming, particularly for large theatres and arenas, was common many years before O2's participation, carrying either beer branding or backed by a local radio station or newspaper.

The relationship between the music and the brand in live music sponsorship has different qualities to those in a synchronisation relationship. In event sponsorship, the brand is associated with the primary business focus – the event – while the sync relationship is secondary to the music interest, after the record release. However, the sync relates to specifically-chosen titles, each of which is paid for the use, while sponsorship is typically for a venue, a series of concerts, or a stage at a festival, though some tours, usually by high-profile artists, are also sponsored. Record releases very rarely, if ever, carry branding; a record has a very long lifespan, so that control over the way the brand is represented is lost with time: the brand message could come to seem very dated, the image or reputation of the music act could change, which makes recordings an unattractive prospect for sponsorship, though this is changing, as we will see later in the chapter.

Sync use in advertising doesn't usually work by trying to make viewers think that because, for example, they like Peter, Bjorn and John, therefore they may like the Homebase products that are advertised using their music. In event sponsorship, this association is exactly what is sought, with varying degrees of directness. The term 'positioning' is used often; the meanings of this have expanded. Initially, it means having the brand on display in the right way, whether that is Bacardi girls or Bluetooth media, in the right environment – somewhere that attracts people who might buy a pint of something different or upgrade their phone and change phone company at the same time. The more developed meaning of positioning is to become part of the music scene that the target audience enjoys. O2 became a key music brand through the high-profile shows by Led Zeppelin, Prince and others, even before it extended its reach through the Academy chain. Big artists are often attractive to sponsors but these acts don't deliver the right context for youth brands. Some brands are supporting new and developing talent, to gain the approval of the more adventurous fans.

Top Man clothing's offer to music fans, Topman CTRL, gives a good idea of the commitment needed by the brand to succeed with a modern music sponsorship. Topman CTRL is a series of monthly live shows, supported by a strongly music-focused website. Each month a 'controller' – a band or artist – curates a show, usually headlining, and choosing bands they are championing, which might be unsigned or recently signed. On the website, they talk about their tastes in music, film, books, or favourite places and make a 'scrapbook', which the site describes as: 'a guided tour around the mind of this month's controller'.

Jeremy Paterson, MD of Frukt Communications, manages Top Man's music activity. He says:

> There is nothing better than having a long-term relationship digitally and also in a physical involvement. CTRL is not a product endorsement; the bands don't wear the clothes. It's a media property and a live platform. Consumers can see Top Man supporting music positively, which creates a halo effect for brands who want to be a valid participant in the music industry.

The emphasis on clothing on the CTRL site is minimal: one frame at the bottom of the page, which isn't visible without scrolling down. Paterson says: 'Topman

CTRL relies on the power of word of mouth, stimulated by the digital content. We are using media to stimulate discussions, talking about a band playing on a stage paid for by the brand, not saying "buy this, I am great"'. Word of mouth is widely agreed to be still the most powerful way of spreading music and this factor gives great strength to offerings that can stimulate it. Visiting the CTRL site to get details of next month's gig gives the possibility of clicking to the scrapbook and finding something newsworthy to your mates, who will know that you found it out via Top Man. That gives a stronger impression than going to a gig that has merely been funded by a brewery or phone company. The alliance between live events and digital content is very productive; the audience may be driven to the site by its content, more likely the live event and perhaps most likely the feeds from their social media sites – mostly MySpace, Facebook and Twitter.

This introduces a key question for all 'soft' branding relationships: how does the client know that their money is well spent, that the campaign is working, if the drive towards their product is so subtle? Paterson does concede that, despite the wish to be seen as a music entity, one of the performance indicators for Top Man is 'footfall in store', with others deriving from webpage visits, sharing links with others and social media activity, and he says: 'It's a long-term game, not a short-term campaign'.

Topman CTRL sponsored a student tour in 2010 and students are a powerful demographic focus for other brands too. Student numbers grew sharply in the 2000s; they usually are web-and-phone-savvy and have high-speed internet access; and university does concentrate a large number of fairly recently independent consumers in one place, particularly at freshers' events. However demographically inconsistent the student body might be otherwise, it gives a nationally available gathering point for young music fans that can't easily be matched elsewhere.

Eastpak, a luggage and clothing company whose rucksacks are popular with students and backpackers, brands music events in different countries. As well as the Antidote tour, which took a traditional live format for a tour of twelve European countries in autumn 2010, with Sum 41 headlining, the Happy New Year tour unusually presented club nights for new students – the New Year in this case being in October, when university begins. The club connection arose because Eastpak products are widely used by DJs, who are taste leaders for the club scene musically, so could influence buying decisions for other products. This tour gives an example of a successful direct approach to a sponsor by a relatively new entrant to the music business, Dancing Robot Music (DRM). George James, a partner in DRM, had already been promoting 3D Raves while studying for his music degree. He approached Eastpak as part of a search for sponsorship for the raves. Instead, they were invited to run the Happy New Year event, receiving financial backing and taking 55 per cent of revenue. Social media feature highly on Eastpak's agenda: James says:

> Eastpak has 68,000 Facebook members, but only 400 in the UK, so part of our brief was to push users towards Facebook and Twitter and to get the

brand name out on university calendars and magazines. It was hard to move people who visit our sites over to Eastpak, but Twitter has been a wicked tool for connecting DJs with the brand in the mind of the audience. The DJs have been tweeting about the show, now it's kicking in, getting students to go online.

As well as the payment for the work, Dancing Robot Music is getting its own brand to the national student population alongside Eastpak's, and further sponsorship of their dance events is planned.

Students are also the focus for music sponsorship by Jack Wills, a casual clothing company that calls itself 'University Outfitters'. The Jack Wills Freshers Tour gives an illustration of a relationship with specific acts – three per tour – and the 2008 and 2009 tours were also badged 'JWunsigned'. The JWunsigned website, like Topman CTRL, goes beyond mere tour listings, including a blog, downloads, reviews and interviews and more music content. The manager of unsigned band I Only Date Models, Tom Overbury, was seeking more gig opportunities for his act and approached the promoter of the tour directly. After seeing a show at Rock City in Nottingham, I Only Date Models was added to the tour list. 'The image of being involved with such a brand will only ever look good', Overbury says. 'If you can say that you have a company or brand behind you, then new audiences will take you seriously. After all, a brand won't be interested in a rubbish band!' Overbury also notes free promotion for the band through the Jack Wills website, which is a very popular site with the band's target audience.

Jack Wills gives a heartening example of the accessibility of brand backing to new entrants in both the artist and music business communities. Overbury's comment also highlights the role of the brand, or its music industry representatives, as achieving some level of trust as gatekeepers, choosing a type and quality of music that aligns well with the music taste of the buyers or prospective buyers of the products in a broadly similar way to the branding of, for example, an *NME* tour. The brand may already be known to the audience and acts as one of the attractions of the event, so the function of the promotion is brand reinforcement, rather than introduction or change of allegiance. The JWunsigned 2009 tour was not actually branded as Jack Wills but as No. 350-4-842, which is Jack Wills' denim range, showing the level of expected familiarity with the brand even before attending a sponsored show.

All brands face the challenges of gaining new customers and of keeping customers over time. These wishes can work against each other, strongly so for a brand aiming at the popular music audience. Following trends may lose an audience as it gets older, while continuing to satisfy that audience may be unattractive to younger people, costing the brand new customers and credibility. The student market is, rightly, tempting to sponsors and advertisers, but the challenges are greater here too. Most students will change their lifestyle dramatically within less than three years of receiving a marketing message, as they take jobs or, in a growing number of cases, return to their home country. Political change shows rapid effects on the makeup of the student body: Higher Education places are cut during recession, EU expansion brings more students from Balkan and former Soviet countries. These are just the more visible examples of the need to adjust the campaign's values to keep recruiting a new audience. For Jeremy Paterson the pain of losing loyal customers is necessary: 'Brands must understand what their appeal is and renew the audience when it outgrows the product. They have to know when to stop marketing to people'. The music partners need to sign up with the brands that are succeeding in this, those that are on trend with the audience the label or venue wants to attract, not the one it already has and will at some time lose. For an artist or manager choosing a brand partner, the opposite choice could be better; to choose a brand that can keep an audience for as long as a successful artist career – several decades perhaps. An example might be Gaymers cider, which spends £5 million a year on its music campaigns. In 2009 Gaymers was the official cider of Glastonbury Festival, Download, Reading Festival and Camp Bestival, as well as taking profile in funky events like Camden Crawl and The Great Escape.

The pace of change in music makes it out of step with the strategic planning of music-related campaigns at the brands. Eighteen months' advance planning is typical of large campaigns; it's not possible to know where an act will want to be positioned so far ahead. This gives the choice of securing the campaign and risking a poor fit between artist and brand in the future, or waiting and scrambling for the opportunities that haven't been snapped up. Kim de Ruiter, digital and brand development specialist, formerly at Universal Music and now owner of music services company Solo Trader, where she manages brand relations for Defected Records and Anjunabeats, feels the differences in timing can make it 'hard to do something that looks good without it looking like a badging exercise. The campaign will try to shoehorn acts into what they are already doing, but that approach hasn't succeeded and the benefit is not strategic for the act'. She favours brand relationships that will always work well with music, such as audio companies B&W or Bose, and also likes working with music and fashion, which have a more natural fit in their timings.

Lucie Bartlett, blogging on the Synergy Sponsorship site, speculates that: 'people in 10 or 20 years might actually notice an absence of brand more than its presence' and are becoming inured to brand representations, seeing them as a normal and constant part of the entertainment economy. If so, then the new deftness of the sponsors' positioning plays a strong part in such a level of acceptance.

Early in the life of sponsored music events, there was a fear of resentment from the audience that a brand, with no other interest in music than to sell clothes, beer or other products, was intruding on their party, 'cashing in'. People may now be more accepting of commercialism and profit, yet they are also more used to participatory music communities, particularly through social networking sites and the ready interactivity given by laptops, wireless hotspots and smartphones. If the advertiser or sponsor adds value to the community, its presence is accepted or welcomed. Rhodri Williams, commercial marketing manager at Gaymers, says:

> We're looking to enhance the consumer's experience whether it's at a festival or a live music venue. There's a lot more acceptance of brand involvement in music now, more so than five years ago. But consumers are still looking for a benefit. They need to feel that you're adding something to their event or enabling their enjoyment of a festival indirectly through your sponsorship of it.

The 'prommercial'

Since the late 2000s, brands have also become interested in recorded music and video. The most talked-about relationship is Groove Armada's with spirits company Bacardi. The act was engaged to play twenty-five dates internationally at Bacardi B-live events and record a four-track EP funded and released by Bacardi, which would also commission music from Groove Armada for its own marketing and media platforms. The band retains ownership of the master rights in its recordings. In August 2010, Faithless launched the video for new single 'Feelin' Good' via a three-minute 'prommercial' for the Fiat Punto Evo. Faithless got no money for the deal, but the cost of the video was borne by Fiat and the promotional reach of the car company gave a welcome boost to a band that, like Groove Armada, had recently parted company with a major label.

Partnerships such as this are likely to become more common, as mature acts that have an established fan base regain their own rights and seek to extend their audience, using the greater reach of their partner companies. The role of major labels has diminished market-wide and in any case is less necessary for acts that have established themselves and can run their own business through their managers. Such deals may serve to create brand distinctiveness and affinity and allow a band to piggyback the media operations of a global company; they also seem most likely to cause doubts in the audience. Once the pattern is seen, there can be a forgivable suspicion that an act forming such a partnership is squeezing the last drops from its career, that there is nothing left to do in promoting the act that can't be done by the marketing folk who sell cars and drinks.

The attractions of brand involvement include a prestigious association, extra marketing reach for the music and, of course, a secondary stream of money from existing activities. For venues and festivals, this is enough and the challenge lies in making the best partnerships. For artists, the inability to plan strategically presents more of a drawback, but only the most privileged are in a strong position to ignore the potential benefits. Jeremy Paterson feels similarly about brand involvement to Roxanne Oldham on sync. He says: 'Brands aren't the saviours of the music industry, though they contribute tens of millions of pounds a year – but are individual artists going to have their lives changed by this? Absolutely'.

COMPOSING FOR TV

Simon May, onscreen composer (www.simonmay.co.uk)

Simon May is a UK composer and visiting professor in education who graduated from Cambridge University and started his professional musical career by co-writing the stage musical 'Smike', which was later televised by the BBC. Simon has since composed music in synchronisation for television, film and broadcast since 1973 and created numerous TV themes and film compositions. TV themes such as Howards Way, Secrets of Enid Blyton, The Legend of Robin Hood *and* William Shatner's 'A Twist In The Tale' *are just a small part of his work. Simon also composed the iconic theme tune to the UK's* Eastenders, *noted for its powerful and dramatic drum score introduction and enduring melody, which has grown to become hugely memorable in popular British TV audience culture. Simon remains pro-active in his work as a music composer and describes his work in the TV synchronisation medium.*

When I was asked to write the *Eastenders* theme tune, the original instruction from the producers was to create a dark 'edgy' theme, but the final composition changed into a brighter more 'feel-good' piece and the tune became far more melodic than the original brief. Writing music for television today does not come without its issues, however. When off-screen announcers talk over end titles, this can spoil the relaxing effect of the music and resonance of the whole programme. Largely, this commentary is due to the increase in TV channels today, so the off-screen announcers are scripted to talk over end credit sequences in an effort to keep the viewer engaged with the channel and away from the remote. To draw an analogy, it's as if you are in a restaurant and just as you are finishing the last mouthful of your main course the waiter comes up, snatches your plate away and thrusts the desert menu in your face! When you have just finished watching your favourite TV programme and are digesting it and chatting about it to someone else, do you really need off-screen presentation 'yakking' on about the next programme, just because they are running scared you are going to hit your remote button and go to the adverts on ITV? This approach seems to be how broadcasters and networks think they can retain their viewing audience.

I would suggest that any composers that want to approach writing themes for TV programmes or moving image should be aware that a music theme must reflect the spirit of the show and should be more than just recognisable – it must also be memorable! It is absolutely essential that

PROFILE

the composer(s) actually meet the producer so that they get an accurate feel of what the show is about, in order to formulate ideas early and work in an imaginative and collaborative way.

Working with others can be inspiring, especially if there is a challenging brief. I have always enjoyed working on my own, but more often I actually prefer working with other writers. Simon Lockyer and John Brant are the other two members of the 'Musiconscreen' team and collaboration is a strategy I strongly recommend – because it increases and enriches the wide range of musical ideas that are needed when writing music to picture.

NOTE

1   With thanks to Simon Goffe, Stephanie Perrin, Roxanne Oldham, Sergio Pimentel, Jeremy Paterson, George James, Kim de Ruiter and Rhodri Williams, whose comments were obtained through private interview with the author.

REFERENCES AND FURTHER READING

Books

Karmen, S., *Through the Jingle Jungle: The Art and Business of Making Music for Commercials* (New York: Billboard Books, 1989).

Terlutter, R. *et al.* (eds), 'Music in advertising: effects on brand and endorser perception', in *Advances in Advertising Research 1: Cutting Edge International Research* (Wiesbaden, Germany: Gabler, Betriebswirt.-Vlg., 2010).

Periodicals

Black, J., 'So who's the bigger star?' *The Guardian* (6 March 2009). Available at: www.guardian.co.uk/music/2009/mar/06/pop-music-synchronisation-games (accessed 10 October 2010).

De Whalley, C., 'Regular sync survey', *Music Week* (7 October 2010).

Ducceford-Jones, M., 'Round table music marketing partnerships', *Marketing Week* (27 May 2010) pp. 24–27.

Online resources

Advert Music Database. Available at: www.theopenworld.com/music/adverts (accessed 10 October 2010).

Farley, M., 'Interview with Alexandra Patsavas, music supervisor for "The O.C."', Bullz-eye.com (11 August 2005) Available at: www.bullz-eye.com/cdreviews/3farley/alexandra_patsavas_interview.htm (accessed 10 October 2010).

'Fashioning your own brand of art: when publicity goes awry', The Silver Thread
    (August 2010). Available at: www.sparrowhall.com/blog/fashioning-your-own-
    brand-of-art-when-publicity-goes-awry (accessed 10 October 2010).

'Filmmaker Resources and Information – Music', Britfilms.com. Available at:
    www.britfilms.com/resources/music (accessed 10 October 2010).

JW Unsigned. Available at: www.jwunsigned.com/Home.aspx (accessed 12 March
    2011).

Neilsen Soundscan, 'Music'. Available at: www.nielsen.com/us/en/industries/
    media-entertainment/music.html (accessed 12 March 2011).

Page, W. and Carey, C., 'Adding up the music industry', PRS for Music (4 August
    2010). Available at: www.prsformusic.com/aboutus/press/latestpressreleases/
    Pages/PRSForMusicaddsuptheindustry.aspx (accessed 12 March 2011).

Robinson, A., 'Guitar Hero "reinvigorating" guitar sales', CVG (12 January 2009).
    Available at: www.computerandvideogames.com/article.php?id=205693
    (accessed 10 October 2010).

Smith, E.C., '10 pivotal moments in band/brand relationships', Flavorwire
    (13 October 2010). Available at: http://flavorwire.com/124129/10-pivotal-
    moments-in-bandbrand-relationships (accessed 10 October 2010).

Song of the Salesman: Music Used in UK TV Adverts & Commercials and Cinema.
    Available at: www.songofthesalesman.co.uk (accessed 10 October 2010).

Synergy Sponsorship. Available at: www.synergy-sponsorship.com (accessed
    12 March 2011).

Topman CTRL. Available at: www.topmanctrl.com (accessed 12 March 2011).

USA Today, 'Band's sales are feeling the "Guitar Hero" effect (Dragonforce)'.
    Available at: www.usatoday.com/tech/gaming/2008-02-14-guitar-hero-
    effect_N.htm (accessed 12 March 2011).

CHAPTER 10

The classical music business

Marius Carboni

INTRODUCTION

The best way to understand how the classical music business operates is to look at it pre- and post-1989. In the autumn of 1989 the classical music industry began a process of (unplanned) radical change. One major record company, EMI, put in place a pop-marketing campaign for a classical recording. Instead of promoting the recording (Vivaldi's *Four Seasons* performed by Nigel Kennedy) to just a classical music audience, it instead developed a strategy to reach the whole music market. In 1990 another record company, Decca, released a recording of a concert given by three opera tenors to mark the final of the 1990 FIFA World Cup competition. The imagery of the singers performing in full concert dress in a football stadium captivated the global audience; the 'Three Tenors' phenomenon was born! Spearheaded by the major record companies, these two inspired initiatives altered, forever, the way the classical industry operated, and that remains the case today. In another area of development in the classical music business, that of online trading, it has been the vision of smaller, independent labels such as Chandos and Naxos who have led the way, with the majors following suit.

Popularising classical music is not new; prior to the *Four Seasons* release, one of the most successful series of recordings, which made classical music less of a mystique, was *Hooked on Classics*, a series first introduced in 1981.[1] The success followed the Electric Light Orchestra's fusion of arrangements of classical and pop melodies, personified, in particular, in the classic piece 'Roll over Beethoven'. Described as 'symphonic rock', recognisable extracts from classical music works were played over a continuous beat (similar to the London Symphony Orchestra's Classic Rock series). The popularity of this style of release was illustrated in a single from the first album, *Hooked on Classics*, reaching number two in the UK singles chart.[2] The series continued until 1989 and was a precursor to the widening of the context of classical music to the general consumer that took place in the 1990s.

A guide to the key influences and events that have had a major effect on the classical music business is set out below:

1989	Nigel Kennedy's recording of Vivaldi's *Four Seasons* released using pop marketing techniques.
1990	Puccini's 'Nessun dorma' aria used as theme tune by BBC for their 1990 FIFA World Cup competition programmes.
1990	The 'Three Tenors' concert at 1990 World Cup final.
1992	Launch of Classic FM including Classical CD Chart Show with Paul Gambaccini.
1993/4	Record companies recruit information technology (IT) catalogue managers.
2001	Creation of iTunes in January 2001.
2001	Apple iPod goes on sale October 2001.
2004	Napster becomes legal.
2004	iTunes launches itself as online retailer.
2004	Creation of the download chart.
2004	Creation of an integrated singles chart where downloads were counted as a sale for recordings as well as a physical recording.
2006	Apple reaches one billion music downloads since the launch of iTunes in February 2006.
2007	Statement from IFPI stating that digital sales accounted for approximately 10 per cent of the music market: 'Record labels have become digitally literate companies . . .' in January.
2007	Soprano Barbara Hendricks begins her third album campaign of selling over the internet without a fixed price.
2008	The number of households in the UK having internet access increases to 65 per cent.
2008	RAJAR/Ipsos survey shows 'almost 12 million people have claimed to listen to radio via the Internet'.
2009	Official Charts Company launches Specialist Classical Chart.
2009	The launch of violinist Tasmin Little's recording *The Naked Violin* on a pay-what-you-want structure wins 2008 Classic FM Gramophone Award for Audience Development and results in a follow-up project *Partners in Time*.
2010	BBC Radio 3 announces Chart Show.

Selective though this chart is, it nevertheless gives an idea of developments within the classical market over the last 20 years during which the most significant changes to the industry's business practices have taken place. Following pop marketing principles, and incorporating the internet for trade and marketing, have increased the exposure of the classical music genre to well outside its traditional buyer.

MARKETING

The breadth of the marketing campaign of the *Four Seasons* and *Three Tenors* releases was very different from what had been the traditional job specification for a record company classical music press officer. S/he would send out a monthly order form to national and regional classical reviewers of CDs (and before that LPs and cassettes), national papers, specific classical music magazines and various producers on BBC Radio 3. Once those forms had been returned, the record company press office would then fulfil some or all of those requests. Entertaining selected media in order to invite them to recording sessions and to meet the artists, or to feed through feature material ideas on artists and their new recordings was part of the role. Advertising would follow a similar pattern with occasional appearances in national newspapers but usually key releases restricted to some of the music magazines, displays in record stores and concert halls and adverts in concert programmes.

The turning point occurred in September 1989 with the EMI release of the *Four Seasons* and also the following July with the first of the *Three Tenors* CDs. Tracing the campaign twenty years on shows not only what distinctive campaigns these were, but also that the basic structure of the campaign has influenced subsequent campaigns. The *Four Seasons* campaign was devised by EMI's Barry McCann, marketing chief of the company's strategic marketing division (interestingly not from the company's classical division) and Kennedy's manager John Stanley (former manager of 1970s pop group The Bay City Rollers). This brought another dimension to the marketing campaign. Pop-style selling procedures were used, such as releasing a single (in this case the last movement of 'summer') in the preceding month to the full album going on sale. The work lent itself to a pop campaign with its short movements, which could be released as individual tracks. As a result the single was personally delivered to radio stations (as happens in pop campaigns) receiving airplay on Radios 1 and 2. This allowed the potential for a wider consumer base (attracting non-traditional listeners). Even music trade magazine *Music Week* devoted its front cover on 23 September 1989 to Nigel Kennedy and the EMI release (see Figure 10.1).

The range of advertising was markedly different from the (classical) norm; national and television co-op TV advertising, adverts on London radio station LBC, national press advertising in the *Guardian* and *Independent*, and adverts in monthly magazines

FIGURE 10.1
Music Week magazine cover, 23 September 1989, courtesy *MusicWeek*/EMI

Q, *20.20*, *The Face*, and *Blitz* (as well as in classical music magazines *Gramophone* and *CD Review*). Displays in record shops are another feature of marketing, regardless of the music genre. This was no different in this case, with the addition of an outdoor poster campaign around London including British Rail and London Underground sites.

This was an unparalleled campaign with an initial marketing spend of £100,000, unprecedented for a classical record marketing campaign. What made it feasible in the first place was the character of Nigel Kennedy. Not only was (and is) he a superb violinist, Kennedy is also a performer who can reach out to a broad audience. He writes and performs jazz, and is a supporter of Aston Villa football club, both of which he is very public about!

The release of the single was a month after Kennedy's appearance in the Prince's Trust televised concert with Sir George Martin conducting, and performing alongside big names in the entertainment world. Televisual exposure, near or at the same time as a new release becomes available, is the norm in pop and jazz. This is less feasible in classical music, especially when the use of an orchestra is involved. Further visual exposure via a Channel 4 film of Kennedy making the recording of the *Four Seasons* transmitted on Boxing Day and New Year's Day led to a March 1990 ITV broadcast of the programme *This Is Your Life* (with an audience reach of 12 million). And, as is normal procedure in the pop business, a UK tour featuring the *Four Seasons* followed. All this resulted in the album selling over 2 million copies, reaching not only number one in the classical album chart, but also number three in the pop charts and even garnering a mention in the Guinness Book of World Records! There have been four *Three Tenors* campaigns, each using visual impact and broad-based promotion as the key to high volume sales. For example, the third *Three Tenors* release of 1998 included an astonishing £750,000 spend, UK TV advertising (regional and national, including ITV and GMTV), 400 outdoor sites for poster displays, and advertising in national newspapers, trade and lifestyle magazines.

Compare this to the sales figures for most classical CDs and the difference is stark. Average sales figures reach between 800 and 1,000 CDs in their first year, and up to 500 to 750 in the subsequent two years. Well-known international artists, though, would sell significantly more. The chart below (Figure 10.2) from BPI and the Official Charts Company (OCC) shows the remarkable difference in sales when it comes to crossover material – not quite matching the *Four Seasons* and *Three Tenors* albums, but certainly significantly higher than straight-forward recordings of classical repertoire.

The unprecedented success of both the *Four Seasons* and the *Three Tenors* campaigns gave record companies cause to reflect. Perhaps classical music could be potential for a high return on investment than had been regarded in the past? This was further enhanced with the first *Three Tenors* concert featuring Domingo,

Pos	Title	Artist	Company	Digital%	Sales
1	Forever Vienna	Andre Rieu	Decca	1.1%	306,106
2	Tenor	Rolando Villazon	Decca	2.3%	43,139
3	The Ultimate Collection	Katherine Jenkins	Decca	5.3%	35,789
4	Nessun Dorma – Opera's Greatest Stars	Various Artists	Decca	3.9%	27,033
5	Classic Voices 2010	Various Artists	Decca	0.8%	18,277
6	Spirit of the Glen – Ultimate Collection	Royal Scots Dragoon Guards	Decca	2.0%	17,257
7	A Band for Britain	Dinnington Colliery Band	Decca	2.6%	15,458
8	Dreaming	Andre Rieu	Decca	0.1%	12,242
9	Second Nature	Katherine Jenkins	Decca	3.0%	10,875
10	Heroes	Coldstream Guards Band	Decca	4.3%	10,112
11	Highland Gathering	Royal Scots Dragoon Guards	Spectrum Music	0.2%	9,695
12	Living a Dream	Katherine Jenkins	Decca	3.2%	8,782
13	Fly Away	All Angels	Decca	10.3%	8,477
14	Camilla Kerslake	Camilla Kerslake	Mercury	9.7%	7,878
15	Harmony	Priests	Epic Label Group	2.4%	7,137
16	The Priests	Priests	Epic Label Group	2.0%	6,757
17	The Essential Collection	Pavarotti/Domingo/Carreras	The Red Box	–	6,343
18	100 Hits – Classical	Various Artists	100 Hits	–	6,095
19	Sacred Arias	Katherine Jenkins	Decca	8.8%	5,785
20	Nightbook	Ludovico Einaudi	Decca	25.5%	5,158

Source: OCC

FIGURE 10.2
Top 20 classical albums 2010 (Jan–April). By kind permission BPI/OCC

Album Sales by Type of Music (% units)

	2000	2001	2002	2003	2004	2005	2006	2007	2008	2009
Rock	25.9	27.9	31.0	29.2	30.8	40.0	41.5	37.2	35.7	31.0
Pop	32.4	31.6	30.3	31.2	27.9	19.8	20.8	22.3	25.3	29.0
R&B	8.5	8.8	7.4	8.4	8.8	7.6	8.7	10.3	10.5	9.6
MOR/Easy Listening	4.6	6.0	6.1	6.4	7.1	8.1	6.9	7.0	7.2	8.2
Dance	13.3	10.5	9.5	7.2	7.0	8.3	7.7	8.1	7.9	7.3
Hip Hop/Rap	3.9	4.2	5.1	5.5	6.4	5.6	3.2	2.7	2.2	4.3
Classical	4.0	4.2	3.5	3.8	3.4	3.3	3.4	3.6	3.7	3.2
Country	1.7	1.5	1.5	1.8	2.0	1.3	2.2	2.4	1.8	1.6
Jazz	1.0	1.1	2.0	2.6	3.2	2.1	1.9	2.4	1.7	1.5
Folk	1.1	1.1	1.4	1.2	1.2	1.2	1.2	1.2	1.2	1.4
Reggae	0.9	1.0	0.7	1.5	0.9	1.0	0.7	0.8	0.8	0.9
Blues	0.4	0.4	0.3	0.3	0.4	0.3	0.3	0.4	0.5	0.7
Childrens	0.5	0.6	0.3	0.2	0.2	0.5	0.5	0.8	0.5	0.4
World	0.6	0.4	0.4	0.5	0.5	0.5	0.6	0.6	0.5	0.4
Spoken Word	0.2	0.1	0.1	0.1	0.2	0.2	0.1	0.2	0.2	0.3
New Age	0.5	0.2	0.1	0.2	0.1	0.3	0.2	0.1	0.3	0.2
Other	0.5	0.4	0.3	–	–	–	–	–	–	–
Total	**100**	**100**	**100**	**100**	**100**	**100**	**100**	**100**	**100**	**100**

Source: BPI based on OCC data

FIGURE 10.3
Album sales by type of music (% units). By kind permission BPI/OCC

Pavarotti and Carreras at the final of the FIFA World Cup in Rome. Such was the reach through television of this extraordinary concert watched by millions worldwide, the CD became the biggest selling classical album of all time. Following the *Four Seasons* and the pop tradition, a single was released prior to the album going on full release. Placing classical music in the overall CD sales market over the last ten years (seen in the chart in Figure 10.3) is interesting. There is a gradual decline in market share to 3.2 per cent, way behind pop and rock but clearly above other specialist genres. Its small percentage reflects the uphill battle all areas of the classical music industry has (not just the recorded business) to further increase awareness, and through that growth, for the sector.

TV is a significant factor for the promotion of recordings that have the potential to sell in large numbers. The rest of the classical sector followed suit after the *Four Seasons* example. This can include artist interviews, advertising or in the case of Pavarotti, using a track from an album as the theme tune for a programme. In 1990 BBC TV sports programme *Grandstand* used the tenor's recording of 'Nessun Dorma' as the theme for all the World Cup programmes. The single alone sold over 500,000 copies and reached number one in the Top Twenty chart.

The combination of a pop marketing approach, coupled with the use of television when income projections are high, is now an integral part of the classical business. The resulting success of both the *Four Seasons* and the first *Three Tenors* albums saw the major companies re-structure their classical music divisions into a two-tiered system: one core classical and the other strategic classical. This meant that those in the strategic classical area were charged with drawing up classical music campaigns that would reach a consumer not necessarily (and unlikely to be) interested in the interpretation of the music itself; instead the spotlight was on either the artists themselves, or repertoire that could be easily listened to and did not require analysis. The potential extent of this market was larger than the core classical one and therefore would require further marketing investment into general media (rather than specific music media). This twin approach has remained in today's current classical music business practice. It is neatly summed up by François Colbert in his article on 'Entrepreneurship and Leadership in Marketing the Arts': 'it is said that high art has a product focus and popular art a market focus'. Colbert defines this by naming a product-orientated enterprise as a chamber music ensemble or modern dance company, and a Hollywood film project by way of a market-orientated example.[3]

The last twenty years have seen a range of products from the major record companies in this vein: In 2002 Warner Classics released a recording entitled *Monastery of Sound*. The title centred on a well-known clubbing enterprise, Ministry of Sound, based in London. *Monastery of Sound* sought to emulate the clientele associated with the original concept. It was based on Gregorian chants with a view to consumers buying it for late night listening, similar to ambient music. The marketing campaign targeted national newspapers, *Heat*, *Mixmag*, *Muzik* and *Time Out* magazines, Classic FM, Capital FM and Kiss 100 FM radio stations and outdoor fly-posting. This is a good example of both a marketing-focused product (because of the range of consumer the recording could potentially attract), and also product-focused, because the music itself was high art (that is, monks singing music to a high standard). The repertoire came from long deleted CDs of Gregorian chants on the Teldec label (part of Warner Music Group) so re-mastering the music was inexpensive. This is a clear example of a back-catalogue recording being re-issued and marketed to a non-classical consumer. This type of set-up continues today.

In the same year that Classic FM was launched (1992), the Polish composer Henryk Goreck's *3rd Symphony* sold 200,000 units in its first year in the UK, aided by

FIGURE 10.4
Sensual Classics, courtesy Warner Classics

Classic FM's 'sure shot' promotion. In 1994 the second *Three Tenors* concert and CD release took place (with a third in 1998). This was followed by the extraordinary phenomenon of a CD of Gregorian chants sung by the Benedictine Monks of Santo Domingo de Silos re-released and selling six million copies! In 1995 the EMI violinist Vanessa Mae released her album *The Violin Player*, a mixture of classical, pop and techno music promoted by a provocative and much talked about promotional video.

Another example of how far classical music marketing campaigns were changing was seen in the *Sensual Classics* 1993 campaign from Warner Classics devised by its then Director Bill Holland and seen on the CD sleeve (Figure 10.4). Its theme was well-known pieces of classical music taken from the Warner catalogue, placed on a CD with a provocative picture of an attractive-looking couple. Inside the booklet there were further pictures of the couple along with quotes from poets about the word 'passion'. The idea was to attract consumers of all persuasions with the picture on the front, and then encourage potential buyers to buy a CD with popular classical music.

Another example of a broader outlook for a classical artist is seen in Figure 10.5. It's from an HMV campaign with the aim of attracting consumers into their stores to buy violinist Nicola Benedetti's recording *My Inspiration*. The composer, Tchaikovsky, is popular, so it is appealing to both specialist and non-specialist music lovers. The marketing emphasises this with a quote from the violinist herself, placed prominently in the middle of the leaflet. To add weight, the album sleeve is also included in the advert along with the label that released it, Classic FM's own range. Branding the album with 'Classic FM' makes sense as the station is a populist broadcast medium with over six and a half million listeners.

Other artists have followed in the same mould as these singers. One example is Russell Watson, the English tenor, who sang Puccini's aria 'Nessun dorma' at the final of the Football Association's Premiership football final in 1999. This was the culmination of two previous public sport appearances: the Munich Memorial Game in 1998 also in Manchester, and at Wembley Stadium where he sang the National Anthem before the London versus Leeds Rugby League Cup Final spectators.[4] Exposure of classical music to audiences in a non-musical context has increased the accessibility of this genre.

These key events in the classical music business demonstrate a transformation in the way classical music has developed since 1989. It has continued to develop ever since. From Katherine Jenkins to Cecilia Bartoli, from Roberto Alagna to Andrea Bocelli, from Sir Paul McCartney to Kate Royal, from Placido Domingo to King's College Choir, Cambridge, from José Carreras to Julian Lloyd-Webber, from Aled Jones to Charlotte Church, from Russell Watson to Hayley Westenra, and many, many more, marketing a classical artist will never be the same again.

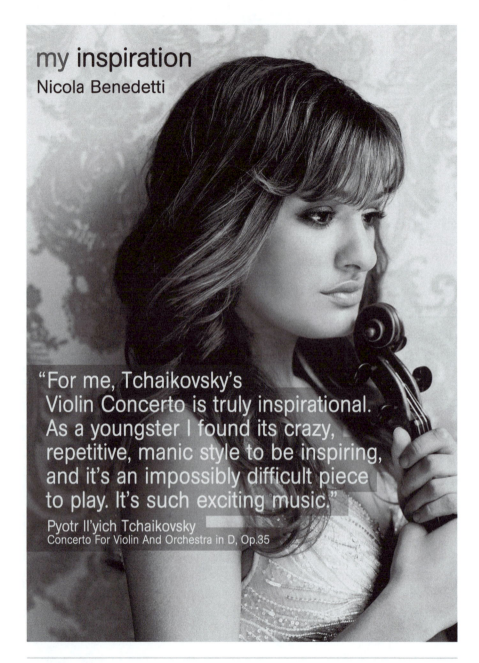

FIGURE 10.5
Nicola Benedetti, courtesy HMV/Classic FM (Photograph by Simon Fowler)

THE INTERNET AND SOCIAL NETWORKING IN THE CLASSICAL MUSIC INDUSTRY

The classical music industry is increasingly using online trade as part of its business model. The take up of broadband in the UK is important to the classical music sector. Easy and quick access to the internet encourages online trading. Music is a beneficiary of this growth; classical music more so because the nature of the music (compared to other genres) is very different. The works are longer and therefore fast speeds for downloading (possible via broadband) are required. During 2009, 70 per cent of UK households had access to the internet (over 18 million people), of which 63 per cent used broadband for their internet connection, a high penetration figure. This growth shows the potential for the classical music business. Additionally Jeremy Hunt, the Secretary of State for the Department for Culture, Media and Sport (DCMS), has already signalled in his first weeks in his new job the roll-out of a super fast broadband for the whole country.[5] The bigger the take up of broadband, the more potential there will be for downloads of classical music. The strength of the digital sector was underlined in the Digital Economy Bill published in the UK in November 2009 (and passed in April 2010), which commented that '. . . our digital economy accounts for nearly £1 in every £10 that the whole British economy produces each year . . . worth around 8 percent of GDP'.[6]

Figures for the division of formats of music sold in the music industry in 2009 are highlighted in Figure 10.6, from a presentation given by Kim Bayley, Director General of the Entertainment Retailers Association (ERA, the trade body for all retailers in entertainment) and the OCC. This is one piece of evidence that indicates that the use of the internet to access and to sell music has now become an established form of trading in the music industry.

The extent of the classical music sector's growth in its digital business is given by the IFPI's 2010 digital report. This document states that:

> . . . in 2009 globally, for the first time, more than one quarter of record companies' revenues come from digital channels . . . from download stores, streaming sites, subscription services, free-to-user sites, bundled with their broadband or a mobile phone handset'.[7]

The report goes on to state that music companies around the world grew their digital revenues by 12 per cent in 2009.[8]

To put the selling of classical music over the internet into context, the BPI and OCC's figures for 2009 show that the classical sector grew by 36 per cent in this field during 2009; this equates to a quarter of a million classical albums that were downloaded during the year, 64,000 more than in 2008. Although the music market as a whole increased sales digitally by 56 per cent, this is a sign of the classical sector moving its business model forward. The rise in digital sales is seen in the

Market Conditions – Album sales 2009 vs 2008

	Units			ASP			Value	
► All Albums	125.6m	–4.4%		£8.41	–		£1,056m	–4.4%
► Physical	112.9m	–8.5%		£8.52	+0.6%		£961.9m	–8.0%
► Digital	12.8m	+59.5%		£7.40	–		£94.4m	+59.5%

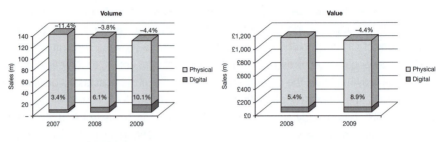

NB. All data includes identified digital sales only

FIGURE 10.6

Classical album sales, 2009 vs. 2008. Courtesy Entertainment Retailers Association (ERA).

3.8 per cent figure for 2008 increasing to 6.3 per cent for 2009. The pressure on internet sales is that much greater on the classical business because physical sales have been declining dramatically. The classical share of the market for 2009 was 3.2 per cent, itself down on the 3.8 per cent figure for 2008. And while the first few months of 2010 have shown a rise in the classical music market with sales up by more than 27 per cent according to the BPI and OCC, returning its share to 2008 levels, this is still far behind the peak of 11 per cent in 1990 (year of the first *Three Tenors* and year after the Nigel Kennedy *Four Seasons* recordings). The classical music business is now truly embracing the internet as a major source of revenue for selling, and increasing contact between itself and the consumer.

What the record labels are doing

Developments in online trade have been most noticeable since the mid-2000s. The withdrawal of Digital Rights Management (DRM) from the major record companies certainly increased online trade, but it was the smaller record companies who were the instruments in progressing online business. This is a shift from the dominance of the big companies to the smaller, independent companies, and more recently to the individual artists; Naxos and Chandos labels were the leaders in this field.

In 2006 independent label Chandos moved into online selling. In June 2006 it had three CD orders to every download. Another medium-sized indie, Hyperion, also launched its own download site, focusing on giving the consumer as much text information on the recording as possible. Pricing per second rather than per track, Hyperion offers a one-click purchase of a work. Booklet texts are free, and the company's whole catalogue is available online including material previously deleted.[9] Naxos, the largest of the budget classical labels, set up an online service, Classics Online, in 2007. This offered a dedicated classical music download service in respect of the company's classical music catalogue, accessible by sophisticated search engines optimised for classical music. The following year the company released the largest online collection of 320kbps, DRM-free classical music albums available for download. The company now boasts 29,000 albums and over half a million tracks covering classical jazz, blues, world music and folk genres.[10] The complete acceptance of new technology within the classical industry is seen in many of the smaller labels incorporating it into their business planning. A good example of this is the German company Hänssler Classics, which in 2008 released the complete works of Bach from the company's catalogue to mark the 75th birthday of its most high profile artist Helmut Rilling.[11] The music was made available in a 172-CD version retailing at £1,100 but significantly also pre-loaded onto a special edition 120GB iPod. This suggests that the generation who are perceived to buy the most classical music CDs and attend classical concerts are using new technology, which is encouraging.

As one might expect, the major labels are all adept at online trade. Deutsche Grammophon (DG) launched its DG Web Shop in November 2007, making 2,500 DRM-free albums obtainable in forty countries, sixty of which albums were not available on CD.[12] Timing was shrewd in being established in the run-up to the busy Christmas period. Its success was marked by reaching 50,000 registered customers by its first anniversary; following that milestone, the business expanded into mail order and prime quality downloads. This included an option to stream the album for seven days at 99 cents.[13] UCJ (of which DG is part of) has supplied over 100,000 titles on its website for download at 320kbps. New releases as well as already released recordings, video material, ringtones and concert dates are included.[14] Sony Music Entertainment has announced a high-quality 'lossless' download service for its classical repertoire with a provisional autumn 2010 launch. The company is negotiating with other major labels to add their material to its site, as is French label Qobuz. Qobuz sells download files in all existing formats and hopes to provide high quality albums of classical and jazz music from both the majors and independent companies (see www.qobuz.com).

Subscription models are a factor in digital projects from some of EMI's significant recording artists, which are being released only on digital format, or released digitally first and then in physical format later. One example is Sir Simon Rattle and the Berlin Philharmonic's recording of Mahler's *9th Symphony*, recorded specifically for a download release,[15] and works by composer Thomas Adès' including *Concentric Paths*. Pianist Ingrid Fliter made available for download some of the tracks of her new Chopin album two months prior to the full album release.[16] The company also has a Listening Club in which the consumer can stream music from the EMI and

Virgin Classics websites for free. Members are sent CDs with a software called Opendisc, which, when inserted into their computers, allows them to connect to the EMI and Virgin Classics Club.[17] A further model is found in Arkiv Music. The company offers not only currently available titles to order but also recordings that have been deleted. The music is burned onto CD with, where appropriate, the text or opera libretti. Up to 8,000 deleted recordings are now available.[18] Both founders of the company are experienced in recordings, having been employed by Tower Records, the now defunct American music retail chain with shops in the UK and US.

Artist empowerment

One of the most interesting aspects has been to observe the growth of the empowerment of the artist. With easier access to the market through internet developments, musicians themselves are using their own websites as a tool for selling recordings, concert tickets and merchandise as well as incorporating a social networking facet. Violinist Tasmin Little, singers Barbara Hendricks and Thomas Hampson, pianist Ben Grosvenor, and composer Peter Maxwell Davies are cases in point. The composer (and Master of the Queen's Music) Peter Maxwell Davies has been selling his music online since 2004, via his website www.maxOpus.com,[19] either via MP3 files or mail order on CD.

Tasmin Little represents a classical parallel with the 2007 *In Rainbows* campaign by pop band Radiohead. A brief resumé of the campaign is worth mentioning. *In Rainbows* was Radiohead's seventh album and the first to be released after a four-year gap, and without the support of a major label. The group began its marketing campaign with the banner of 'pay what you want' to download the new album. This was followed by the opportunity to order a deluxe box in time for Christmas. The release achieved worldwide media interest. Research by MCPS-PRS Alliance stated that there were 2.3 million downloads between 10 October and 3 November 2007.[20] This is a very high figure, helped by the worldwide media interest. The fact that the band was well established in the market added to the success rate. In fact figures from www.examiner.com show that three million purchases of *In Rainbows* were made from the band's website, disc boxes and the physical album release, a project that shows the breadth of sales tools now readily accessed by consumers.[21] A significant number though is the physical sales figure. The album sold 1.75 million physical copies, a major success with sales driven by the internet downloading campaign.[22] In a similar manner, another band, Coldplay, achieved 2 million downloads of its single 'Violet Hill', within one week of release. Taken from the band's album *Viva La Vida*, the single was available for a free download for seven days on the band's website. The band subsequently pursued the policy of 'something for nothing' by giving three free concerts in June 2008.[23]

Tasmin Little's album, entitled *The Naked Violin*, was initially made available as a free download with the release made available in an easy to access format on the artist's website, containing links to a range of music organisations and media outlets, as well as detailed material of the composers on the recording and a personal introduction about the new recording. The site extends an invitation to burn the CD free of charge at the top of the site;[24] unlike most other campaigns of this kind, there is no request for money at all. This is a prototype of how a professional classical musician has embraced technological developments in order to communicate with existing fans and to attract new ones. Little compounded the venture by releasing, in 2010, a second album *Partners in Time* using similar tactics.[25]

The model that soprano Barbara Hendricks follows is similar to Little's. On her website, Arte Verum, Hendricks comments that she:

> . . . created Arte Verum because it is possible for artists today to control their creative endeavours from the beginnings in the rehearsal room to the concert hall beyond, into the recording studio and then directly to the public. The technological advances that have made this step possible would have been unthinkable just ten years ago.[26]

This is a perfect example of how an artist can control what they release in terms of repertoire and marketing, while at the same time using the technological changes in the industry to their advantage. Hendricks' album *Endless Pleasure* is the third to be released on Arte Verum and the first to allow the purchaser to pay what they wish when downloading the release. As a clever marketing incentive, the purchaser is given the chance to download the previous two albums at the price they opt for buying the new release with the caveat that it must be the same or higher than €7. Download is DRM free and at 320kbps. In the first two months, 60 per cent of downloads paid for, were at an average price of €7.35 per album. The company states that many have chosen to download all three albums.[27]

The most recent recording, Schubert's *Die Schöne Müllerin*, extends the promotion with the offer of a bonus DVD.[28] Savvy marketing initiative can be seen in the special offers on six of her previous EMI recordings and her regular blog detailing the concerts she has performed at, or places she has visited as a way of adding a personal touch to her fan base.[29] These two artists offer examples of their business acumen, having full control of their musical enterprises, both in trading online and distributing on physical formats.

A further case is indicated by the baritone, Thomas Hampson, who has widened the role of his website to more than that of news, selling CDs and a concert schedule. Hampson has included a section on 'Books on Singing' that the performer has referred to often in his career, and a section of 'Essays and Projects'. The singer is also one of many to have his profile on social networking sites including Facebook, YouTube and Flickr.[30]

It is not only long-established musicians who are actively involved in selling their music content over the internet. The sixteen-year-old pianist Benjamin Grosvenor created a download-only album available in December 2008 working in partnership with the speaker manufacturer, Bowers & Wilkins. The sound quality is of particular importance because the download uses a 'lossless' sound, which is as good as the sound achievable on a CD. Benjamin's download was the first classical album on the Bowers & Wilkins roster, one on which sound quality is paramount. Four tracks of the album can be downloaded for free if the consumer joins the company's Music Club.[31] This example portrays a young classical music artist not only incorporating the use of the internet in his work but also collaborating with a major manufacturer in the process. The violinist Nicola Benedetti has shown ingenuity in this field by releasing a series of mobile phone ringtones available from her website. As with other artists, her website shows the violinist on Facebook and YouTube and she regularly posts a blog.[32]

The orchestral field

Social networking has moved into the orchestral and opera house worlds. Making Music has published data to support this. In May 2010 its magazine *Highnotes*, published useful statistics on social networking sites; in terms of their popularity for hits per month, Facebook achieves 1.2 billion, MySpace 820 million, YouTube 340 million and Twitter 55 million.[33] These are large numbers and explains the interest that music organisations have in using social networks to raise their profile. The LSO is one such organisation that uses social networking as a marketing tool. According to its research, an impressive 47 per cent of LSO supporters on Facebook are aged 18–24, compared to 40 per cent of those visiting the orchestra's website being over forty.[34] The LSO Facebook fans will receive regular updates on the work of the orchestra, and many are in an age category that gives potential for long-term growth.

The Royal Liverpool Philharmonic Orchestra's (RLPO) interactive experiment of 2007 was a unique project. Audiences around the globe were able to sit in a three-dimensional virtual version of Philharmonic Hall (its home) with ability to watch and listen 'live' to the opening concert of the new season. Even more inventive was the fact that listeners who had subscribed to the internet virtual world 'Second Life' were able to open dialogue with other listeners of the concert. After the concert the participants were able to communicate with the conductor Vasily Petrenko, among others at a virtual 'foyer bar' in the Philharmonic Hall. The initial trial was open to only 100 applicants to ensure transmission quality. Entrepreneurship and business acumen are evident in this example and show the industry taking the potential of the internet seriously. The Philharmonia was the first orchestra to podcast and run a webcast of a concert (in 2005), through its interactive project PLAY.orchestra. As with the RLPO's experiment, this was an interactive scheme. Placed on the PLAY.orchestra website were 56 plastic cubes and three hot spots laid out on a full size orchestra stage with each cube containing a light and a speaker. The listener chooses a cube, stand or sits on it to hear a specific instrument.

Up to a further fifty-eight friends can join you to listen to the full work. Two works were played, one a new commission by a young composer and the other a standard work from the classical repertoire.

In another linked initiative, the Philharmonia invited listeners to use Bluetooth to access Philharmonia-owned ring tones as well as a piece the listener could have created him/herself. This was a project that involved the public closely by using digital technology to the hilt. In 2008 the orchestra established a second interactive project: RE-RITE. This allowed members of the public to conduct, play and step inside the Philharmonia Orchestra with Esa-Pekka Salonen through audio and video projections of musicians performing Stravinsky's 'The Rite of Spring'. First opened to the public in November 2009, the project showed every section of the Orchestra performing 'The Rite of Spring' simultaneously 'as live'. The public were able to sit among the horn players, perform in the percussion section and take up the baton and control sections of the orchestra as they played. Selling recordings is a feature on most of the orchestras' websites. The procedure varies depending on the orchestra. The City of Birmingham Symphony Orchestra (CBSO) and BBC Symphony Orchestra (BBCSO), for example, list the recordings they have made. In the CBSO's case, there is an option to listen to a sample of the ones the consumer wishes to buy.[35] In the BBCSO's CD list, it includes the details of the recording and the company that recorded it.[36] Excerpts of the music are available if there is a CD that is recorded and which ties in with the repertoire of the concerts the orchestra is performing in that season. The BBCSO's website for March 2010, for example, features concert dates and music extracts of the symphonies by Martinů, which the orchestra was performing in concert.[37] The Philharmonia's website goes further and offers the chance not only to buy direct but also to listen to a part of a movement of the work in question.[38] This is also the case with the Royal Scottish National Orchestra (RSNO) and with the 'Listen to Music Online' section on its home page.[39]

Opera houses

Opera houses were equally alert to the benefits reaching consumers online. English National Opera (ENO) is one example. In 2007, the company set up a dedicated site for its, then, new production of *Carmen*, offering photos, news, rehearsal progress, booking details, video and music of specific parts of the opera, and various blogs from a number of key people involved in the production including the director of the production and ENO's Artistic Director.[40] Taking the process a stage further, ENO streamed a performance in its entirety on the Radio 3 website;[41] the first time that Radio 3 had video streamed an opera. The website also incorporated music excerpts taken from Chandos' catalogue (of opera recordings) and was made accessible through YouTube, Flickr and Facebook.

The Royal Opera (ROH) expanded the use of its website in 2008 by allowing the public to watch its productions via it. For example, Mozart's opera *Don Giovanni* was accessible via the website with access free of charge. Notes on the opera and a podcast of an interview with the director of that production were also made available.[42] This broadening of the company's website has continued. For instance, the March 2010 production of Handel's *Tamerlano* included an interview with Graham Vick about the production along with a brief synopsis of the opera. If the potential opera consumer joins the site and opens an account, then CDs of productions and a trailer of the relevant production are available to them. The web browser for this production is no longer available but an article in Classical Music Magazine confirms the detail.[43] The website also directs the browser to cinema productions of ROH productions around the country with background on all the opera plots and the venues at which they are being performed.[44]

Other live performance

Two models offering a variation on the above are St John's College and King's College, Cambridge. In 2008, the college launched a weekly webcast of its choral services, the first time a college has set up such a project.[45] This is significant because it demonstrates that it is not just large commercial classical music organisations exploring the breadth that the internet can offer. The St John's website includes previous evensongs with a choice of which music to listen to within the service itself.[46] King's College followed suit, albeit in a different mode, by broadcasting a performance of Handel's *Messiah* in April 2009. What made this event special was that the concert was broadcast live into cinemas around the world through the auspices of Arts Alliance Media.[47] A technological triumph, and a significant one, because it advanced classical music further into trading with new technology.

A further model is the British Library. A thousand pre-1958 recordings of music by Bach, Beethoven, Brahms, Haydn and Mozart are now available for streaming. These are all out of copyright and are comprehensive within its repertoire list of composers. For example, the site has every recording made before 1958 of Bach's orchestral suites, the *Brandenburg Concertos* and *Keyboard Concertos*.[48]

Further website usage

There are now a number of websites that provide listings of classical music events registered on the internet; www.concert-diary.com is one of the most user-friendly. All the details required for attracting a concert-goer are included: the price of ticket, venue, repertoire, artists performing and how to book. Another is www.classicalsource.com, which is similar and also includes reviews of live concerts and CDs. What is useful is that reviews are published within a couple of days, and their coverage of concerts is far wider than the national newspapers who allow a few reviews per week. Book, CD and festival reviews are also included in some, such as www.bachtrack.com, www.classical.net and www.opera-base.com. The classical world took music content on social networking site a stage further by using YouTube to establish a YouTube orchestra.[49] Players were chosen via videos uploaded onto the YouTube site for a premiere performance of a new work by Tan Dun suitably entitled *Internet Symphony No. 1, 'Eroica'*, conducted by Michael Tilson-Thomas in April 2009. [50]

Radio broadcasts

Another example where online activity is increasing is in the radio sector. RAJAR (the official research body that publishes listening figures and profiles of radio stations around the UK) in conjunction with Ipsos MORI (a leading market research company in the UK and Ireland) and RSMB (audience research company), published the findings of a survey of their research for the first quarter of 2010 up to March 2010. Reproduced in Figure 10.7, the chart shows that all digital listening has increased year-on-year with radio listening in general slipping slightly. In the classical music

RAJAR DATA RELEASE Quarter 1, 2010–May 13, 2010			
	Mar '09	**Dec '09**	**Mar '10**
All Radio Listening			
Weekly Reach ('000)	45,762	45,968	46,479
Weekly Reach (%)	90.2	89.6	90.6
Average hours per head	20.2	19.3	19.8
Average hours per listener	22.4	21.5	21.8
Total hours (millions)	1,025	988	1,013
All Radio Listening – Share Via Platform (%)			
AM/FM	67.5	66.6	66.7
All Digital	20.1	20.9	24.0
DAB	12.7	13.7	15.1
DTV	3.4	3.4	4.0
Internet	2.2	2.1	2.9
Digital Unspecified*	1.8	1.7	1.9
Unspecified*	12.5	12.5	9.3

*Inevitably, there is a certain amount of unspecified listening because either the respondent is unsure, or it is not always possible for them to know whether the station to which they are listening is being broadcast on analogue or digital, or via which platform. Every effort is made by RAJAR to ensure the instructions given to both interviewers and respondents elicit the highest possible volume of specified analogue/digital stations and platforms.
Source: RAJAR/Ipsos MORI/RSMB

FIGURE 10.7
RAJAR data release. RAJAR/Ipsos MORI/RSMB survey

sector, BBC Radio 3 engaged in a significant online experiment through its Beethoven broadcasts. Keeping within the BBC's regulatory considerations, the network conducted a major downloading experiment in 2005. Made available for free, around 1.4 million downloads of the complete Beethoven symphonies were made available over a two-week period. A second complete works project was announced over the Christmas period of 2005, the complete works of J.S. Bach. Subsequent complete cycles of works by Stravinsky, Chopin and Tchaikovsky followed. With an average listener's age of over fifty, this downloading endeavour was an initiative to keep pace with a changing business environment.

Other ventures

There are other areas of business that are expanding trade over the internet. Independent companies such as Classical World Ltd are buying into a licence to offer music for download. Founded in 2000 by Roger Press, a former EMI Executive Producer with DVD and TV responsibilities and former head of Polygram's (now UCJ) classical video division, recordings are available for on-demand streaming on its website www.classical.com. There are various deals for the consumer, from £6 per month to £60 a year. Classical.com has a catalogue of 450,000 titles on offer, including 1,200 labels covering jazz and world music, but particularly focused on classical.[51] This is a helpful model for the classical music industry because it gives an all-in-one point of access for the consumer, with the ability to listen to radio, browse books on music and buy music itself. A major selling point of Press's company is that it allows the music to be compatible with both the iPod and MP3 players. Subsequently digital rights have been withdrawn by the major record companies, allowing their products to be accessed on both formats as well, which is of benefit to the consumer. The company provides major international artists' recordings in their repertoire, including Alfred Brendel, Yo Yo Ma, Pinchas Zuckerman, Michael Tilson Thomas and Itzhak Perlman.[52]

Quality of sound

The bit rate for classical music downloading sites is an important area in the sector.

Music downloading sites for classical repertoire are leading the industry by offering above-CD quality downloads, which come at a premium price. Linn Records is an authority. Its website (www.linnrecords.com) gives an overview of what the company offers for classical music consumers:[53] Studio Master FLAC, Studio Master WMA, CD quality FLAC, CD quality WMA and MP3. Studio Master FLAC is the best for quality and interestingly is seen as offering the same standard of sound quality as Linn's SACD (Super Audio CD). FLAC files are lossless at high bit rates although not all PCs are compatible with this system. Studio Master WMA is similar to the Studio Master FLAC in that it offers what the company calls 'true "studio quality"' and is based on the production version of the CD release.[54] CD Quality FLAC is a lossless format that gives the best audio performance and has a file size half that of a normal CD.[55] Much the same is on offer with the CD Quality WMA; finally the MP3 file works with both PCs and Macs at a (high) 320kbps downloadable rate.

Other companies have strategies in place to combat a general lack of quality when downloading. Decca provides downloadable music at a rate of 320kbps, significantly higher than the standard of 128kbps. The company uses the WMA format, which offers the same quality of sound as iTunes' Audio Coding (AAC) files but with a higher transmission speed (iTunes has a bit rate of 128kbps).[56] Another is Universal. In 2009 Universal and Virgin Media broadband announced a partnership. Their subscription service allowed customers to stream and download music via Virgin Media's high speed 50Mbps.[57] This is significant because the Digital Britain report of 2009 sets a target of 2Mbps connection for broadband service providers by 2012 in order to encourage streaming and downloading at a higher quality rate.[58] By offering a much higher rate of downloading already, this is an attractive option for the classical music purchaser.[59] Music Research Consultants (see www.musicresearch.com) also comment that the introduction to the marketplace of MP3HD is leading to a comparable quality of sound between both formats, although it does continue to say that: 'these MP3HD files are not better than CD but are promising the same as CD sound, which is good'.[60]

BUSINESS ACTIVITY IN THE CLASSICAL MUSIC SECTOR

The classical music industry is highly business-orientated. But first one needs to place classical music in context of the music business as a whole. The PRS for Music's *Adding up the UK music industry for 2009* report[61] states that the music industry in the UK was worth £3.9 billion, up 5 per cent from 2008. The chart below, from Arts & Business's report, *Private Investment in Culture 2008/09: the art in the 'new normal'*, published in January 2010[62] shows that private investment in music has risen by 3 per cent, although opera has lost 12 per cent (the latter due to large one-off donations in 2007/2008 that were not expected to continue).[63] The 3 per cent recorded rise is a positive fact for the music business and classical music is a beneficiary contributing to that percentage increase.

Private investment was down by 7 per cent in 2008/09 from the previous year: business investment accounted for 24 per cent of private investment, 55 per cent came from individual contributions, with finally trusts and foundations making up the rest. Therefore the pressure to secure funding remains high. A&B matches projects created by arts organisations around the UK with business. Its annual awards give good examples of the classical music sector working with major businesses. There are many instances of commercial and classical music businesses working together. One clear example is the programme in 2008 between Mitchells

Table 10.1 Private investment by art form

Art form	Total (£/millions)	% change (above inflation)	Actual year-on-year change (£)	% of private investment
Arts centre	18.1	23	3,696,265	3
Arts services	25.1	−16	−3,901,686	4
Community arts	12.4	−23	−3,266,818	2
Crafts	0.4	−21	−107,741	0
Dance	21.8	−10	−1,831,053	3
Festival	23.8	−2	155,607*	4
Film & video	12.3	−7	−662,816	2
Heritage	225.2	6	17,997,605	34
Library/archives**	6.5	−23	−1,755,576	1
Literature/poetry	3.3	−26	−1,037,038	1
Museums	80.8	−37	−43,523,604	12
Music	37.9	3	2,019,181	6
Opera	27	−12	−2,979,419	4
Other combined arts	38.7	22	7,775,687	6
Other single art form	5.7	−55	−6,558,657	1
Theatre/drama	45.9	−16	−7,701,063	7
Visual arts/galleries	68.6	15	10,213,748	10
Total	**653.5**	**−7**	**−31,467,379**	**100**

& Butlers and the City of Birmingham Symphony Orchestra (CBSO), which, over a six-year period, developed support for an annual mainstream concert, while also providing funds for a community concert series (as well as endowing a musician's chair within the orchestra). The success of this partnership is seen in the figure of over 3,500 people benefitting from these performances in 2008.[64] The Mitchells & Butler and CBSO partnership is one practicable example of the types of projects that help classical music organisations stay afloat, especially with a downturn in the UK economy that has been underway since 2007. Successive governments, and especially since the first Thatcher Conservative Government of 1979, have not matched what classical music organisations require to survive financially, so these companies have had to look for, attract and then keep an income stream from individuals as well as public grants.

Another clear example is the partnership between Takeda Pharmaceutical Company and the London Symphony Orchestra (also on the short list for the 2009 A&B awards), demonstrating the collaboration of two global organisations with strong brands.[65] The partnership, which raises the profile of both brands, took music to wider audiences by sponsoring over 200 of its concerts around the world. A further initiative included the 'Musicians on Call' initiative that took music to the housebound or those in hospitals; again this was a global project and appropriate for a business involved in health care.[66]

BBC

Nowhere is the contrast between commercial and non-commercial activity more clearly defined than in the broadcasting field in the UK. From a classical perspective, this is identified through BBC Radio 3 and Classic FM. Radio 3 (funded by the licence fee) receives £51.5 million from the licence fee, of which £25 million is spent per year on paying for the classical musicians and administrative support of their six 'live' performance groups (BBC Symphony and BBC Philharmonic Orchestras, BBC National Orchestra of Wales, BBC Scottish and BBC Concert Orchestras and BBC Singers).[67] The money is from the taxpayer, and therefore the organisation has an obligation to provide a range of services and programmes through its Public Service Broadcasting (PSB) remit. Its commercial counterpart is Classic FM, which relies on advertising and commercial deals to fund its activities (and staff).

The BBC Proms are a superb example of what can be achieved with public money. It is a form of music patronage in the UK and its success is repeated each year. The BBC's published statistics for the 2010 season are impressive: 92 per cent average attendance for the main evening concerts, achieving an average of 4,000 people attending each of the seventy-six Royal Albert Hall Prom concerts, forty-nine of them completely sold out. Significant for the future growth of the classical music business, 39,500 bought tickets for the first time and more than 7,500 under the age of sixteen attended (up from 5,000 in 2009). It has a high profile through live Radio 3 broadcasts, a number of concerts transmitted on five BBC television networks, streamed live online via BBC iPlayer and available on-demand for seven days. Patronage is also seen in the inclusion of thirteen new commissions and premieres, fourteen of which were BBC commissions. This offers opportunity for living composers to have their works performed in a high-scale arena. Other programmes related to the Proms and televised highlights of the *Proms in The Park* events show classical music extending its core reach and appealing to a wide cross section of the community.

Classic FM

Classic FM is commercially operated and receives no public money. One indicator of Classic FM's successful reliance on commercial activity is through its wide range of advertising. The station broadcasts promotional deals as other (non-classical) commercial stations do, as a matter of course. One example was a campaign released in 2006; a six month £900,000 promotional deal was signed with Medicom to push Sky Digital channels during Classic FM's breakfast show, being the most-listened to breakfast show in London with a former Radio 1 DJ as its host, the deal allowed DJ Simon Bates to choose his pick of the Sky programmes being transmitted on Sky each day at 11.15 a.m. This type of deal shows large, global companies such as Sky being prepared to be part of the classical music sector.[68]

Another case in point is the ability to entice listeners into becoming more involved with the company and as an incentive to be eligible to win a prize. In January 2010 mobile phone company TalkTalk ran a joint campaign with Classic FM to encourage listeners to tune in to the radio station's *Hall of Fame* programme, and in the process have an opportunity to win a Roberts digital radio.[69] In this instance there are two companies working commercially with Classic FM – TalkTalk and Roberts Radio.

A further promotional area concerning Classic FM is the station's *Box Office* feature, which is an innovative and highly successful promotional tool. When the station was newly established, arts venues and performers were encouraged to send in details of their forthcoming concerts and a selection was then read out by each presenter. This did have a tangible result on ticket sales, so much so that the station now charges for the air space. This has become a lucrative opportunity for the station. Clients can now choose between three price options ranging from £4,000 to over £12,000. Each of the price options allows the company a specific number of acknowledgements (called 'spots') per week for their particular campaign. The organisation is given a minimum of forty seconds to portray the essence of the opera series, concert, recording or relevant art form they are promoting. These illustrations offer a comment on one classical music company operating in clearly defined business terms, proving in the process how successful it can be.

Combining brands

Joint brand promotion is also evident in the classical music field. 2009 saw a deal between Classic FM and High Street retailer Marks & Spencer. The clothing and food retail chain has now stocked CDs for the first time, and significantly it is classical music that is being offered for purchase rather than pop. A third brand, record company Universal, is providing the repertoire.[70] There are twelve titles in the initial batch retailing at an affordable price of £8. The synergy is evident between the companies: all three are in the life-style and entertainment business with retail price at the mid to low range. This makes it not only easily affordable but will engage those purchasers wishing to sample a CD without too much financial outlay. And interestingly, classical music is following a pop music initiative in a similar project between the Heart radio stations (also owned by Classic FM's owner Global Radio) and Universal Records.[71]

Further examples include the Royal Opera House and the *Sun* newspaper campaign of 2008. Here *Sun* readers were able to apply for tickets for the opening night of Royal Opera House's season.[72] The 2009/10 season repeated the promotion with two nights, one to watch *Carmen*.[73] Scottish Opera followed suit and offered readers of *The Sun* £9.50 tickets for the opening night of its production of *La Bohéme*.[74] In this particular case, the accessibility of the genre through a tabloid newspaper to reach a non-traditional audience is made achievable by the newspaper's readership.

An additional illustration is from the retailer HMV. In 2008, joined by the classical labels on Universal (Decca, Philips and Deutsche Grammophon) and Classic FM, the three organisations launched the series *Full Works*. This was a range of repertoire to build a library of the most well-known classical pieces.[75] The success over the first year has led to the series capturing a 10 per cent average share of the classical market, selling over 250,000 albums.[76] The target has now exceeded 500,000 unit sales. The incentive for the buyer is trust. The trio are long-established and trusted brands, the campaign's product is priced cheaply (at £5.99) with over 150 titles by a range of acknowledged classical musicians. For the businesses involved, HMV provides a national outlet to sell re-branded back catalogue from the record company; Classic FM offers a major media partner that can provide national coverage over the airwaves as well as through its affiliated magazine, *Classic FM Magazine*. Universal furnishes the repertoire.

The classical music business relies on a number of forms of patronage to survive, crucially for a niche area. Aside from the BBC, one of the most important is Arts Council England (ACE). In 2009/10, ACE invested £625 million from the government and National Lottery, of which £344.6 million went to what is termed grant-in-aid to 880 arts organisations (such as Birmingham Royal Ballet, the Royal Opera House and the Bournemouth Symphony Orchestra). Under their category Grants for the Arts, ACE gave out just under £65 million to nearly 2,800 groups and organisations.[77] This source of funding is for all art forms; classical music is only one part of this area and would have to compete with other arts categories. Royal patronage such as the position of official Harpist to HRH The Prince of Wales,[78] trusts such as the Keyboard Charitable Trust[79] or the Countess of Munster Trust,[80] provide the financial means of developing performers' careers. Foundations such as The Jerwood Charitable,[81] Paul Hamlyn,[82] Esmée Fairbairn[83] and Clore Duffield[84] Foundations are especially relevant in this sector. There are other organisations of equal importance to furthering and enabling the classical music sector to continue: local authorities, Royal Philharmonic Society,[85] PRS Foundation,[86] Youth Music[87] and the British Council[88] are some of the key ones. The pressure on all these areas will increase.

Ultimately classical music uses broader marketing strategies in order to reach two consumer bases, those who define themselves as core classical and those outside the classical field. Selling concert tickets or a CD is just one facet of an organisation's *modus operandi*. The musical world has three participants: the listener (or consumer), the musician (or performer) and the music company (be it a record company, broadcaster, promoter, publisher or venue) and the classical music industry is no different in this respect. Musicians and consumers have become more independent of the industry itself through advances in new technology, and the classical sector developing its business model through wider-focused marketing tools.

In 2007, at Pavarotti's funeral the aria that catapulted the singer to world fame ('Nessun dorma') was played; at the same time the Italian air force flew over Modena Cathedral where his funeral service was taking place. This portrays the summation of not only an example of the acceptance of classical market in a mass-market environment, but an acknowledgement to one of its instigators.

NOTES

1   www.face-the-music.de/louis_e.html
2   www.economicexpert.com/a/1981:in:music.htm
3   Colbert, F., 'Entrepreneurship and Leadership in Marketing the Arts', *International Journal of Arts Management*, 6, 1 (Autumn 2003), p. 30, Appendix 4.
4   www.prideofmanchester.com/music/RussellWatson
5   www.culture.gov.uk/news/ministers_speeches/7132.aspx
6   www.culture.gov.uk/reference_library/media_releases/6447.aspx
7   Kennedy, J., 'Music How, When, Where You Want It – But Not Without Addressing Piracy', *IFPI Digital Music Report 2010* (London: IFPI Ltd, 2010), p. 3.
8   Ibid., p. 10.
9   www.hyperion-records.co.uk
10   www.classicsonline.com/AboutUs.aspx
11   www.haenssler-classic.de
12   Kennedy, J., 'A new deal for consumers', *IFPI Digital Music Report 2008* (London: IFPI Ltd, 2010), p. 11.
13   Sommerich, P., 'Yellow label pushed the boat out online', *Classical Music Magazine* (20 December 2008), p. 9.
14   www.classicsandjazz.co.uk/page/aboutus
15   www.stereophile.com/news/100107emi/#
16   Email from Sophie Jefferies, former Director of Artist Relations and Communications EMI Classics, 11 September 2007.
17   www.emiclassics.com/listeningclub/index.php
18   www.arkivmusic.com/classical/Page;jsessionid=1DA2CC44 AC03087607E0BF9A7FF12E3A?pageName=pages/about.jsp
19   www.maxopus.com
20   www.prsformusic.com/creators/news/research/Documents/Economic %20Insight%2010.pdf
21   www.examiner.comx-498-Music-Examiner-y2008m10d16
22   Email from Richard Mollet Director Public Affairs BPI, 4 March 2010.
23   http://news.bbc.co.uk/newsbeat/hi/music/newsid_7373000/7373466.stm
24   Ibid.
25   www.tasminlittle.org.uk/
26   www.arteverum.com/?page=presentation

27 www.arteverum.com/?page=press&id=8

28 www.arteverum.com/index.php?page=catalog&disc=10

29 www.arteverum.com/?page=editorials

30 www.hampsong.com

31 www.bowers-wilkins.com/display.aspx?infid=3550&terid=3554&qid=3898

32 www.nicolabenedetti.co.uk

33 www.makingmusic.org.uk

34 Clampin, F., 'Site reading', *Classical Music* (19 July 2008), p. 24.

35 www.cbso.co.uk

36 www.bbc.co.uk/orchestras/symphonyorchestra/cds

37 www.bbc.co.uk/orchestras/symphonyorchestra/performances/
    martinu/index.shtml

38 www.philharmonia.co.uk/shop

39 www.rsno.org.uk/index.php

40 www.eno.org/explore/explore.php

41 www.bbc.co.uk/pressoffice/pressreleases/stories/2007/10_october/
    26//carmen.shtml

42 www.roh.org.uk/discover/dongiovannifree.aspx

43 Quinn, M., 'Don Giovanni relaunches Covent Garden website', *Classical Music*
    (27 September 2008).

44 www.roh.org.uk/cinemas/opusarte/index.aspx

45 www.sjcchoir.co.uk/default.php?page=webcast_about

46 www.sjcchoir.co.uk/default.php?page=webcast&webcast=91#

47 www.artsalliancemedia.com/cinema

48 Lydon, T., 'British Library streams 1,000 "canonic" recordings', *Classical
    Music* (28 March 2009), p. 11.

49 www.youtube.com/symphony

50 Ibid.

51 www.classical.com

52 Ibid.

53 www.linnrecords.com/linn-formats.aspx

54 Ibid.

55 Ibid.

56 www.linnrecords.com/linn-download-quality-and-file-type.aspx

57 http://pressoffice.virginmedia.com/phoenix.zhtml?c=205406&p=irol- news
    Article_print&ID=1298879&highlight=

58 www.culture.gov.uk/reference_library/media_releases/6221.aspx

59 www.classicsandjazz.co.uk

60 www.musicresearch.com/blog/?tag=internet

61 www.prsformusic.com/creators/news/research/Documents/
    Economic%20Insight%2020%20web.pdf

62 www.aandb.org.uk/Media%20library/Files/Research/pics0809/
    pics0809_fullreport.pdf

63 Ibid., p. 38.

64 www.artsandbusiness.org.uk/Case-studies/2009/oct_dec/m_mitchellsbutlers_
    cbso.aspx

65 www.aandb.org.uk/News/2009/Jul_Sep/09jul_31staandbawards.
    aspx

66 www.aandb.org.uk/News/2009/nov/31stawards_international.aspx

67 www.bbc.co.uk/annualreport/exec/performance/radio/radio3.shtml

68 www.brandrepublic.com/MediaWeek/News

69 www.talktalk.co.uk/music/competitions/classic-fm.html

70 Cardew, B., 'Not just any deal ... Classic FM links up with retailer', *Music Week* (11 July 2009), p. 8.

71 Ibid.

72 www.musolife.com/roh-offers-don-giovanni-tickets-to-sun-readers.html

73 www.thesun.co.uk/sol/homepage/features/2686904/The-Sun-brings-classics-to-a-new-audience.html

74 Nickalls, S., 'Scottish Opera looks to the Sun for new audiences', *Classical Music* (30 January 2010), p. 9.

75 Sommerich, P., 'Canonic approach combats CD slump', *Classical Music* (11 April 2009), p. 11.

76 Ibid.

77 www.artscouncil.org.uk/media/uploads/AC_annual_review_a4_online_final.pdf, p. 6.

78 www.princeofwales.gov.uk/mediacentre/pressreleases/claire_jones_to_become_new_official_har pist_to_hrh_the_princ_2118212610.html

79 www.keyboardtrust.com

80 www.munstertrust.org.uk

81 www.jerwoodcharitablefoundation.org

82 www.phf.org.uk

83 www.esmeefairbairn.org.uk

84 www.cloreduffield.org.uk

85 www.royalphilharmonicsociety.org.uk/?page=about

86 www.prsformusicfoundation.com

87 www.youthmusic.org.uk/musicispower/index.html

88 www.britishcouncil.org/new

REFERENCES AND FURTHER READING

Books

Adorno, T.W., *The Culture Industry* (London: Routledge, 1991).

Adorno, T.W., *Essays on Music* (Los Angeles: University of California Press, 2002).

Anderson, C., *The Long Tail* (London: Hyperion, 2007, reprinted 2009).

Baines, P., Fill, C. and Page, K., *Marketing* (New York: OUP, 2008).

Barfe, L., *Where Have All the Good Times Gone? The Rise and Fall of the Record Industry* (London: Atlantic Books, 2004).

Benedict, R., *Patterns of Culture* (London: Routledge, 1971).

Born, G., *Uncertain Vision, Birt, Dyke and the Reinvention of the BBC* (London: Vintage, 2005).

Briggs, A. and Crosby, P., *The Media: An Introduction* (Harlow: Pearson Education Limited, 2002).

Carpenter, H., *The Envy of the World, Fifty Years of the BBC Third Programme and Radio 3* (London: Weidenfeld & Nicholson, 1997).

Clayton, M., Herbert, T. and Middleton, R., *The Cultural Study of Music: A Critical Introduction* (London: Routledge, 2003).

Curran, J. and Seaton, J., *Power Without Responsibility* (New York: Routledge, 2002).

Davis S. and Laing, D., *The Guerilla Guide to the Music Business* (London: Continuum, 2001, reprinted 2003).

Diggle, K., *Arts Marketing* (London: Rhinegold Publishing Limited, 1994).

Drummond, J., *Tainted by Experience, a Life in the Arts* (London: Faber & Faber, 2000).

Fineberg, J., *Classical Music, Why Bother?* (Abingdon: Routledge, 2006).

French, P. (ed.), *The Third Dimension, Voices from Radio Three* (London: The Stourton Press, 1983).

Godwin, P., *Television under the Tories, Broadcasting Policy 1979–1997* (London: British Film Institute, 1998).

Hill, N., *Marketing for Business* (Worcestershire: Peter Andrew, 1997).

Johnson, J., *Who Needs Classical Music? Cultural Choice And Musical Value* (Oxford: OUP, 2002).

Kenny, B. with Dyson, K., *Marketing In Small Businesses* (London: Routledge, 1989).

Knopper, S., *Appetite for Self-destruction* (London: Simon & Schuster, 2009).

Lebrecht, N., *When the Music Stops* (London: Simon & Schuster, 1996).

McCauley, M.P., *NPR: The Trials and Triumphs of National Public Radio* (Chichester: Columbia University Press, 2005).

Orga, A., *The Proms* (Aylesbury: David & Charles (Holdings) Limited, 1974).

Peacock, A., *Public Service Broadcasting Without the BBC?* (London: The Institute of Economic Affairs, 2004).

Potter, J., *Tenor, History of a Voice* (London: Yale University Press, 2009).

Raboy, M. (ed.), *Public Broadcasting for the 21st Century* (Luton: John Libbey Media, 2007).

Ranchhod, A. and Gurău, C., *Marketing Strategies: A Contemporary Approach* (Harlow: Pearson Education Ltd, 2007).

Strinati, D., *An Introduction to Theories of Popular Culture* (London: Routledge, 1998).

Supičić, I., *Music In Society, A Guide to the Sociology of Music* (New York: Pendragon Press, 1987).

Tusa, J., *Engaged With the Arts, Writings from the Frontline* (London: I.B. Tauris & Co Ltd, 2007).

Online resources

BBC Press office, 'Record-breaking season for BBC Proms'. Available at: www.bbc.co.uk/pressoffice/pressreleases/stories/2010/09_september/10/proms.shtml (accessed 12 March 2011).

British Phonograph Industry (BPI). Available at: www.bpi.co.uk (accessed 12 March 2011).

Entertainment Retailers Association (ERA). Available at: www.eraltd.org/content/home.asp (accessed 12 March 2011).

Official Charts Company (OCC). Available at: www.theofficialcharts.com (accessed 12 March 2011).

RAJAR. Available at: www.rajar.co.uk (accessed 12 March 2011).

The Royal Liverpool Philharmonic Orchestra (RLPO). Available at: www.liverpoolphil.com (accessed 12 March 2011).

CHAPTER 11

Music venture strategies

Paul Rutter

ENTREPRENEURSHIP IN THE MUSIC INDUSTRY

Entrepreneurship is derived from a French word, meaning 'those who invest finance and exercise business acumen to transform their innovative ideas into economic goods'. Entrepreneurship could involve developing a brand new business idea or the revitalisation of an older established business. Other types of conceptualised entrepreneurship not related to the formation of a business venture have emerged including political, social and knowledge entrepreneurship. This chapter is primarily concerned with new business 'startup' and venturing companies in music. Any new music venture will require funding, depending on the business intention, 'venture capital', 'angel funding' or 'seed money' may be required to launch and build the business. Using music business investors in this way would normally dictate that these investors want a return on their investment from a percentage of annual profits; they may also hold a controlling stake in the company and be involved in decision making processes. In the arts, there are generally limited financial incentives on offer for the would be musical entrepreneur, however, seeking opportunity through government agencies, arts council funding grants, arts competitions, trust funds, community projects and music societies should be investigated to identify opportunities. There are many thousands of successful entrepreneurs in the music industry, the music industry lends itself to entrepreneurship, as it is passion led; the blind faith held in a song, a talented artist or a new label concept brand is often enough to set the ball of investment rolling. Passion for the music project motivates business objectives, but this should be tempered with a sense of realism as all businesses face risk. In a BBC online article, high profile serial entrepreneur and investor Peter Jones describes business entrepreneurship as 'the new rock n' roll':

And just as in the world of rock'n'roll, not everyone will make it: building a successful company can be a long, hard slog and it's more than a remote possibility that you could lose your shirt and everything else on the way.

(Jones, 2005)

High profile music success is usually very visible, while losses at grassroots level encountered by smaller music entrepreneurs are rarely heard of, yet there are many casualties. Having the determination to invest in a music project and see it through to the bitter end does not necessarily mean it will succeed; proceeding with caution in any business, regardless of the venture, would be advised, taking the venture one step at a time and avoiding desperate measures at all costs. Often the urge to succeed in music outweighs the sober thought required to protect one's assets. Using theories of business and entrepreneurship in a cohesive way coupled with faith and passion in the project will aid the business decision making process greatly.

THE MICROPRENEUR

The vast majority of new independent music business ventures only involve a few persons; a solo artist with manager, a band or small label. The term 'micropreneur' addresses those that wish to remain a small business concern. Micropreneurs will still encounter business risk and uncertainty, but as they can remain small and economical over longer time periods, they can stay in control of business affairs and finance. Greater autonomy can be afforded in solo working, however certain tasks have to be 'subcontracted' to others who have the expertise and time to carry out roles efficiently – such as specialised music plugging or targeted promotional duties. Many freelancers in the music industry set up in business on their own (also known as 'solo-preneurs'), having previously gained their experience working for larger music concerns in a full-time position. The internet allows the micropreneur to work remotely from home premises, alleviating the need for expensive office space rental and excessive business overheads. Just as advanced recording technology has provided a vehicle to produce hit recordings that can be made in smaller home spaces; mobile communications makes managing music on the move easier. The new digital economy affords a landscape in which the micropreneur may flourish; a 'startup' platform without the need for huge initial investment. As digital opportunity has increased, so has the list of duties that is expected of the micropreneur.

ENTREPRENEURIAL BEHAVIOURS

Whether launching new recorded works or a live event by a particular artist, there are many key activities that must be addressed (previous chapters detail the essential tasks and structures). To make music happen commercially, the entrepreneur must consider what is realistically possible, particularly on a personal level. In the commercial world of music, raw talent alone is not enough; the way in which the artist is brought to public attention is complex, to say the least. Certain key attributes will be required of the music venturist and considering essential entrepreneurial behaviours will assist in making the right decisions; determination, tenaciousness, strong self-motivation and a will to succeed must all be tempered with a sense of realism. Entrepreneurs have reshaped societies through creation of their new economic ventures; business school professor David Rae argues that 'The effect of entrepreneurial ideas and investment has redefined political, social and technological changes in social environments' (1999:18). Given Rae's statement, music entrepreneurs can argue their case for the way in which they have shaped music cultures, in bringing their music to the wider public. A high profile example of UK music entrepreneurship is exemplified by Chris Blackwell, founder of Island Records, responsible for bringing Jamaican popular music to a global audience, signing Bob Marley to his label. Introducing Caribbean music culture to European pop consumers in the 1960s and 1970s proved to be both culturally significant and musically influential, especially to many new artists that incorporated reggae into pop. Island later diversified, signing U2 and many other successful mainstream artists, a label noted in the past for its risk taking and diversity in popular music, given the musical diversity of acts signed. Blackwell later sold his stake in Island records to Polygram in 1989. In the live music industry sector, promoters such as Harvey Goldsmith have co-ordinated countless concert artist appearances including Live Aid; Michael Eavis has succeeded in promoting musical diversity through the Glastonbury Festival brand. Behind every successful music label imprint or concert brand, there are a host of music entrepreneurs attributed to the success of these ventures. Researching exactly who is behind the music venture and the people who assume risk, invest and work to bring the music before an audience will reveal the entrepreneurial requirements. How exactly do entrepreneurs bring music to audience whether they are artists, managers, label owners or concert promoters? Many of the essential attributes required can be assessed by looking at common enterprise theory and typical business behaviours.

ENTERPRISE THEORY

Enterprise theory can guide those with initial business acumen into a stronger position; learning from others who have succeeded or failed in the music industry is valuable to any new music venturist. Examining the principles behind entrepreneurship facilitates a wider understanding of what may be required from the enterprising individual. In the music industry, the market is a busy place as many entrepreneurs strive to make their music visible to a global public. If the consumer is an active music 'finder', they may well discover the music product online perhaps, but if the consumer is passive the business of bringing music to audience becomes the main task. Early historical and primitive modes of entrepreneurship and behaviours have been examined common to all business, falling into four distinct categories:

- Sense of conquest: Seizing opportunity with a degree of force, for example, ruthless leaders that seize opportunity, such as warrior kings.

- Trading and exploring: Supplying an established market through exploring new world territories.

- Producing and inventing: Responding to the global economy and innovating, largely through the use of new technologies.

- Knowledge: Predicting the market trends and consumer requirements, through the utilisation of communications and technologies.

In these key modes of entrepreneurship, three fundamentals of human behaviour become apparent; fighting – through the quest for human dominance; trading – by selling, negotiating and haggling; discovering – learning to be successful through the exploration of a new venture. Although these historic principles demonstrate early human business behaviours, music entrepreneurs need to consider whether or not they are 'natural entrepreneurs' and how they can assess their positivity through personal confidence in the venture.

CONFIDENCE

Confidence can be built in the music venture, but this can often take longer than planned and can require more perseverance than first expected. The confident music entrepreneur believes that they can visualise the end result of their efforts through positive motivation and a non-failure approach. They also believe that they can achieve their personal goals through their own ideas, based on the success of their previous efforts and past performances. In contrast, those that have suffered previous failures and are 'self-doubting' may struggle to accumulate the confidence to launch a new music venture. Having a fear of failure, identifying with others who have failed and 'losing nerve' at the crucial moment when making key investment decisions will hamper progress. Being unable to complete music projects in time and being unable to honestly reflect on personal qualities, competencies or be able to criticise product or performance, would also demonstrate negatives that will ultimately hamper the venture. Taking the necessary steps to build confidence will become a major factor in exercising and establishing the qualities of entrepreneurship, required in any business.

In 1934 Austro-Hungarian economists Joseph Schumpeter and Israel Kirzner each argued in favour of two conceptual entrepreneurial beliefs respectively: innovation and trading. Innovation through focusing on new products, finding new markets, creating the 'new' and causing change through determination became Schumpeter's theory; Schumpeter added that profit is not a driving force, but a by-product of such innovation. Trading became the focus of Kirzner's theory, arguing that entrepreneurs are astute risk takers, motivated by profit, alert to opportunity and able to identify market opportunities (Sobel, 2008). It could be argued that music ventures require a mix of these two theories, dependent on the project embarked upon. Artists and musicians often become entrepreneurs by default, because they have to begin with a large 'time investment', learning their musical craft over many years to be able to perform or record their efforts. In addition to this they 'speculate to accumulate' by investing in musical instruments to play and perform music; many musicians in developed countries spend thousands on instruments in their musical lifetimes. Achieving semi-professional or professional status earning money from the music craft requires dedication in an unmeasurable quantity. Securing a steady flow of profitable work in a crowded market is a challenge for those self-managing; the first mode of human entrepreneurship 'fighting' (in the non-physical sense) becomes a requirement for those that must rise above the competition in order to survive. The second basic mode of human behavioural entrepreneurship can also be found in the music producer, through their repeated experimentation, discovering and learning new methods of music making. In addition, equipping studios both large and small to facilitate projects through the accumulation of equipment to realise the project can also cost thousands. For many, this is an ongoing lifetime commitment, a hobbyist can become a business person; producers often unwittingly exemplify the theories of Schumpeter and Kirzner; innovating through fresh new music creation or creating products for exploitation in a pre-existing market.

For those becoming new managers or promoters, investment in time, tenacity and determination will be required in equal measure to break their artist to audience, alongside the financial means to communicate their aims. Exercising the art of music as a profession has a physical and emotional price tag, through conquering adversity and not being discouraged by rejection or alienation. Whenever the new artist or manager is easily discouraged, they are far more likely to become hobbyists in music. Confidence can be built on a strong foundation, given time and talent, but in more cases than not, a career in music is a lifestyle choice. When metal outfit Motörhead's founder and bass player Lemmy Kilmister was questioned in a BBC TV documentary regarding why he still played metal though he is aged over sixty-five, he replied 'it's not what I do, it's who I am'.

If a formula was accessible to guarantee success in music, all music entrepreneurs would be using it. However, David Rea argues positively for recognising the ability to unlock value in the business venture through opportunity: creating new opportunities, recognising existing opportunities that do exist, assessing their potential then exploiting them (1999:146).

PERSONAL AND VENTURE VALUES

Unlocking value in one's own music business venture can be highly rewarding – creating something that one is in control of reflects personal enthusiasm and passion. Profitability in the business would be vital in order to survive and prosper and these values are crucially important. Value will manifest itself in several ways; first personal values and second perceived monetary values held in the prospect of sales or royalty returns from the music. Believing that the music produced is worth a considerable potential sum is the first step in the value chain, even though the level of success cannot be predicted; a good awareness of ownership and the concept of copyright will assist greatly. Direct music revenues may occur in distinct separate areas; live performance, music sales, media airplay royalties, mechanicals and other recorded music usage. Market awareness in each area and tracing income streams in music is the key to survival in the industry. For the newcomer starting out, earning from any of these streams provides encouragement through profit, even though the income may be small to start with. The values that entrepreneurs ascribe to their businesses empower them with a great sense of commitment, providing determination and resourcefulness in dealing with difficulties when they arise. Professional values also affect how entrepreneurs wish to be received by others, how they carry out the work and how they interact with bodies surrounding the business, including suppliers and potential funders or investors. For the new music venturist, making a list of what is valued on a personal level, then what is valued on a business level (in order of preference) provides a basis for venture assessment. Building a sustainable business can only be done by thinking about exactly what potential music customers *will* value; if others ascribe value to the music venture, a sustainable business could be built from their values in turn. Potential investors in any business need to see that there is value in a business idea and that their investment is worthwhile, for example, licensing music to a larger label will only occur if the larger label sees potential value in the venture.

THE MISSION STATEMENT: ARTICULATING COMPANY VISION AND STRATEGIC PLANNING

Being clear about what a music venture is setting out to achieve should be established at the outset; ascribed personal values are important and should be reflected in the 'mission statement'. The mission statement should be a clear concise summary of the business intention; informative in its standing as a reference for customers and inspirational in its undertakings for the business owner. Mission statements are displayed by most music companies and organisations online, in an 'about us' link. The mission statement should articulate the music company vision, be realistic and simply constitute a short paragraph; bullet pointed summaries may follow to clearly state the music companies main aims, objectives and services carried out. If setting up a night club music promotions company for instance; being specific about the exact genres or sub-genres of music and range of services supplied, such as accompanying PA equipment and geographic regions covered would be essential. Although this may seem obvious to some, not everybody would recognise the limitations of such businesses in a global online environment. Many large music companies distil their mission statements into a short executive summary, followed by a larger series of links into their core business interests, activities and services. The vision and drive the business owner has should be evident in the mission statement providing an outward confidence. The music venture 'mission' can be simply reasoned by using tools authored by business management theorists; Henry Mintzberg (2000) developed four key questions that could be asked, interrogating any proposed business model:

- Purpose: Why the business exists.
- Values: What the business owner and stakeholders believe in.
- Strategy and scope: What is offered and how the business will deliver.
- Standards and behaviours: The principles held by the business.

Mintzberg highlights the usefulness of the mission statement inasmuch as it provides incentive to implement future marketing plans. Media theorist Marshall McLuhan developed a model known as the 'Tetrad of media effects' (1988), which is often used in establishing new business strategies based on new emergent ideas or technologies:

- What does the venture enhance? e.g. Fresh music that adds to an existing genre.
- What does the venture replace or make less desirable? e.g. The venture may provide more appealing music in a certain genre, rendering other music less desirable.
- What does the venture retrieve? e.g. The venture may revive a certain music genre that already exists, recovering what was perhaps lost.
- What are the effects when the venture is pushed to extremes? e.g. Often in music a backlash is returned from early adopters and consumers when it becomes commercially successful, in effect 'selling out'.

McLuhan's tetrad is a useful tool in recognising the need to devise a workable business venture and in particular to think about the specific impact that the music venture will have through its initial mission statement (McLuhan & McLuhan 1988). Any new business venture must be of use in its field; particularly in music, the turnover of ventures can be large, as the very next music trend can take up 'pole position'. The opportunities that exist for music ventures in both live and recorded music globally are vast, but this is matched equally by the amount of competition in the field. Setting one's venture aside from the competition can save valuable time and resources in establishing the new music venture. Using established business tools to map the mission statement before rushing into unnecessary investment is a worthwhile exercise for the new music venturist.

A SENSE OF BRAND: WHAT'S IN A NAME?

Through the commodification of music, the artist becomes the brand; for instance, though deceased, Elvis Presley is still the brand. There are many canonised brand leaders in music such as, U2, The Rolling Stones or The Who; in a postmodern media world 'the band is the brand'. These acts are brand leaders simply because they are more well known than other artists and as in all other consumer branded products, not all consumers will agree that the brand leader is necessarily the best. Yet as a brand leader, consumers know who they are and recognise the goods therefore cultivating priority in the consumer domain. Brand value increases with rising consumer brand awareness. In supermarkets, washing powder brand leaders take pride of place on shelves. Tangible music products sold in stores are conceptually similar, with brand 'followers' (goods that are not brand leaders) being placed close to high profile music products to attract potential customers to them. In music, consumers grow to value a brand for a lifetime (e.g. long standing fans of U2) as long as the music has enduring appeal and they can maintain an emotional bond with the music. Fortunately for new music labels and new artists selling recorded music, brands can be built quickly online; if consumers like the music, fans may download it without needing to see the artist in concert first. There is still however a promotional price to pay in bringing the brand to the national audience; where a major label is releasing and establishing brand through mainstream media, the costs are extensive. Having a sense of brand is important, as music consumers automatically ascribe value to it on their 'first impression'; the same ethos occurs in all other commodities that fans own and define their individual personalities with. 'Cool' music brands are far more likely to attract young consumers; dance label Ministry Of Sound has exemplified this in their branded range of music products and themed live ventures. Building a brand is an essential addition to the mission statement and should communicate a strong visual message or semiotic to the intended music consumer. A logo, art design or name should communicate an instant visual aesthetic. If this cannot be achieved in-house, brand design should be contracted to someone who can articulate the vision on behalf of the music venture. The music brand is sensory, appealing to sight and sound, even though today 83 per cent of all commercial communication appeals to only one sense – the eyes, claims Brian Harrop of Brand Sense Agency. However, passive music consumers will hear music on radio (in a car for instance), so an audible brand is communicated to audience often long before the listener actually ties in the visual image; the audible imprint fuels the visual brand sense. When an artist falls out of favour with an audience, the brand health suffers, sales fall and consumers can actually reject the brand and disassociate with it alongside the media that assisted in its ascension. Commercial music *is* commodity and can suffer the same ails as any product. The credibility of fan opinion is vital in effective music marketing communications. Chris Fill highlights credibility issues when the fan begins to doubt the brand and engages in the proliferation of negative views and comments, brand damage can spread through viral conduits (2006:207). Avoiding brand damage in popular music is difficult, sometimes the artist brand falls 'out of favour' with its audience simply because it has not been heard or seen for a while. By the time the new release eventually comes out, the market has changed or has moved on to new cool brands with the necessary kudos that satisfy current appetite, just as in clothes fashion. In smaller niche-genres this is less likely to happen; in jazz, for instance, fans are likely to stay loyal to an artist throughout their career, investing a very distinct value in the genre and for a specific artist. The same could be said in blues and classical genres, where generally an older demographic are settled in their genre buying habits and would stay true to the Schubert or Beethoven brand, for instance – commodified by the perpetuation of posthumous covers of their published works. Just as brands are reviewed in consumer magazines such as *Which* and given star ratings, music journalists and the public review and rate music, communicating messages to the market through blogs and online endorsements, such as a Facebook 'like'. Unlike soap, or exotic cars, arguably there are no luxury brands in music, only brands that are more visible than others due to their market profile – good or bad music values simply reside in the subjective minds of listeners.

Brand design

Brand strategist Martin Lindstrom argues that the highest percentage of commercial communication is only absorbed by one sense – the eyes, leaving a small percentage left to appeal to the four remaining senses (2005:102). In music, the audible brand aspects are paramount, but choosing the right visual branding and positioning it carefully in a crowded music marketplace can be a difficult task. Choosing a fitting name at the outset for any business venture, can often be attributed to its success. Being concise, quirky, different, direct and in many cases, purely abstract, can often promote keen consumer interest in the brand. Past artists with unconventional 'contrived' artist brands such as Englebert Humperdinck in 1967 (who was born Arnold George Dorsey and adopted the name of a famous German Opera composer), or the ultra-simplistic brand of U2, have proved successful memorable music name brands for their artists. Choosing brands that are already established in the public psyche (e.g. 'The Police'), may help consumers retain names due to the brand's existence in other walks of life. Strong established music brand logos have proven their worth through simple conceptual design; for example, the tongue and red lips logo of The Rolling Stones, newspaper 'cut-out' text forming the Sex Pistols moniker and the sharp angular text fonts used in the design of hosts of metal genre music acts such as AC/DC, Kiss or Iron Maiden. Using angular text fonts in the metal genre communicates an instant visual semiotic to its consumer target; in the split second that band logos and names are seen, the subliminal visual message tells the metal consumer they are looking in the right place for products that match their interests. AC/DC have always retained their brand logo just as Motörhead have retained their fanged skull and angular fonts. Pink Floyd uses a simple prism on a dark background with colour spectrum; instant brand recognition through simple semiotics. These music brand examples have much in common; they have been in existence for many years and have had time to develop, largely by being seen and worn on the T-shirts of fans and on classic album covers in the media marketplace. Music brand is established through both audio and visual aspects of music; strong identities in these mediums are key considerations for the music venturist, ensuring that they communicate to the market clearly and distinctively.

Brand strategy: TALK

Developing one's own brand and realising this through the plethora of digital design art packages available today makes the visual part of brand design easier than in the past. The TALK strategy can be applied to thinking through the design in new brand; the mission statement should be drafted first, in full consideration of the business aims and objectives. Establishing the mission statement will fuel strategies to build the brand further through Target, Appeal, Legend and Kudos.

The brand should effectively 'talk' to the consumer instantly, saying as much as it can in a very limited time due to the attention span of the consumer and potentially, the enormous quantity of products available in the field. Brands featured in web domains and marked on tangible goods such as CDs, should look as professional as possible. New music venturists can measure their brands against established products in the market, due to the easy access to many thousands of music products, which can be disassembled to reveal brand presence and product construction from competitors. The CD release usually has several brand logos associated with it; label name, distributor, production company, artist management and the artist themselves often carry their own 'marks of distinction'. This information is also carried over into the web domains of all these separate entities. Displaying a variety of company brands tells the consumer that many professionals have been involved in the manufacture and production of the item, subliminally increasing value

Table 11.1 TALK brand strategy

TALK Brand strategy		Action
Target:	Who will the brand reach out to in the target market?	Investigate the consumer demographic the brand is aimed at.
Appeal:	How can the brand appeal to potential customers in a crowded market? How strong is the brand presence and visibility in its competitor environment?	Examine similar brands in the field and measure their ability to appeal through simple market research.
Legend:	What lasting message is communicated to the market through the brand? The longer a product stays visible in the market the legend will grow over time, affixing the brand position in the field.	Examine long-term plans for the brand and assess what the brand can convey. Research the scope and possibility for further brand development.
Kudos:	What can the brand acclaim and how is it cool? How is it better than or more unique than others in the market?	Poll potential consumers. Use field research and survey expedition to reveal public responses and to determine brand accolades.

in the minds of consumers. In many products additional logos can be contrived in order to give the impression that many companies have contributed to the product, when in fact there are far fewer bodies actually involved. This 'multi-branding' technique can be exercised to elevate the product in the eye of the consumer. Wherever the opportunity exists to increase product status and value through professional and memorable branding, this course of action should be taken.

CONCEPTUALISATION

Embarking on a 'concept' or strong theme in the music venture will often make it stand out from others and cut across the unique selling point (USP). In past commercial music exploitation and product design, often the concept has come before the music is created or contrived. The concept can be visible by means of the brand, for instance does the venture have a fun message or novelty factor, or is a serious message carried through all elements? Many genres are rooted to their business concept and ethics; appropriate images are in harmony with the product, married to audiences who relate to the concept. Folk music products often have associated natural environmental images in their art design; juxtaposed to this, metal genre acts would require stronger and perhaps darker visuals. When a children's comedy TV character releases a song, the characters lie at the heart of the concept and are the driving force; the music is a by-product that communicates the character concept to its young audience. Strong musical concepts in records,

FIGURE 11.1
Conceptualising the music event. Photo courtesy Dave Robinson, *PSNE*.

festivals and performances that convey interesting ideas can attract new audiences, even if momentarily. The concept is a major contributor to the 'unique selling point', discussed later in this section.

STRATEGIC POSITIONING: THE SWOT

A strategic team action planning model was developed in the US by university scholars in the 1960s to assist groups of business executives to manage change; the acronym SWOT was given to a 'situation analysis tool', which examines Strengths, Weaknesses, Opportunities and Threats. A SWOT analysis can be used to evaluate a project or business venture and pinpoint the strategic position of the venture, identifying internal and external factors that will impinge on business operations. Ultimately, the success of the music venture is often determined by both controllable internal factors, such as strengths and weaknesses and uncontrollable external forces, such as opportunities and threats. If perceived weakness can be steered towards strengths and threats turned into opportunities, the business stands on a stronger foundation. For a new independent recorded music release venture, a SWOT analysis example may look like this:

Table 11.2 SWOT analysis

Strengths (Internal Factors)	Weaknesses (Internal Factors)
Music is well produced. Music act is distinctive. Music act stands out in the genre. Strong image presence. Commercially viable product. Mainstream media appeal. Large fan base possible. Initial audience reaction to the product is very positive. Good knowledge of IP law. Ability to pinpoint all income streams.	No major outside investors. No 12″ vinyl remix is available. No tangible product distributor secured. Low royalty expected from initial sales. Artist cannot tour Europe, UK only. Online sales through digital aggregator only.
Opportunities (External Factors)	**Threats (External Factors)**
Remixes can be made for club audience. National club promotion is affordable. Promotion can be carried out independently. Possible radio airplay will generate new income. Extra income can be made through additional music publishing activity. Online presence can be increased through affordable video production and YouTube upload.	Huge competition in the genre. Other independent labels currently working in similar genre. Product could become dated if outside music trends change. Cash flow problems if product does not sell well enough initially. Co-ordination of tour is problematic concerning availability of venues and artist.

The SWOT analysis should address the potential of the business, promoting an understanding of what the business has clearly got to offer in association with the needs of the consumer. In 1979, Michael E. Porter of Harvard Business School also developed a technique known as the 'Five Forces Analysis', which extends the SWOT for increased interrogation concerning the threat of competition in the chosen business environment.

MARKET RESEARCH

Identifying the needs of music consumers requires a research strategy to be put in place prior to major investment; today major labels research the type of music that fans want to buy and the music that mainstream media will play. Smaller independents have a tendency to release music that is driven by their own passion, emotions and personal aims, rather than from market driven perspectives. Challenges exist for all music companies in finding out whether customers actually want the music that is being produced or performed using market research. However, in the music industry, as income is derived from a range of sources other than music sales and performances; understanding where these income streams lie (such as music publishing income) will help entrepreneurs setting up new ventures understand exactly where the market research should be undertaken. If peripheral services to the music industry are being offered, such as plugging or promoting – labels, artists and managers would then become the focus for further investigation, so that their business needs can be identified.

Researching all potential income and the feasibility of actual customer demand can be facilitated through an examination of the market. Knowing how music industry meets the demand of consumers and knowledge of how departments and structures work together in both live and recorded mediums will pinpoint where the research should be carried out. For new labels releasing music, customer satisfaction surveys can be carried out through fan sites and blogging, to gauge exactly what fans like best about the music. If there is enough meaningful data returned in this type of survey, the information could then guide the nature of the next release, effectively encouraging fans (or customers) to return. Listening to the needs of the consumer is important, as there are many new artists willing to step in and poach fans from artists who do not engage with their fan base or neglect them. Growing the fan base means continually appealing to demand, and as music is often transient, continually developing 'stock' through new recorded material can grow the fan base and attract new customers. Many of the world's most successful independent artists play live every week and sell music and merchandise at their shows. This is often a lifestyle choice and an ongoing occupation; although they play to smaller audiences on a regular basis, they are meeting grassroots consumer demand for music. Major artists tour far less, as setting up the tour presents huge costs having an expensive surrounding major infrastructure. Although successful major tours generate huge profits, fans may only get to see international major acts live once or twice, in the entire career of the artist.

Market research and detective work: Defining customers and fans

Before entering into various market research methods, the music entrepreneur should make a list of who exactly will buy the music product or use the music service on offer. Being able to estimate who they are and how many will want the service will give a good indication of where to start the research. Drafting a SWOT analysis business model, and thinking about the 'opportunity' heading carefully, should give clues as to exactly where other providers are not meeting product demand. The new venture should seek to provide a business solution to this. Potential income can then be examined or estimated as a result of 'filling a gap in the market'; perhaps providing a product or service that others do not or simply cannot (e.g. a club promotions service in a niche sub-genre). Organisations such as IFPI, BPI, PPL and PRS for Music work to provide market research figures and analysis, which will assist in identifying national and global consumer trends in the music marketplace.

Detective work: Desk research

The desk research method is probably the easiest form of detective work, simply by searching out the services and products of competitors online. This type of investigation can be carried out from home or using technology remotely and is a good way of finding out the market values of products and services. Looking at online product launches and reading follow up comments in blogs will help gauge the success of certain music products. Desk research can be used to fuel a SWOT analysis, showing exactly where the new business can devise opportunities and demonstrate where the new product or service is different from others operating in the field. A new business needs to price its products and services competitively. New entrepreneurs often investigate how much the competition is charging for their goods or services – then they launch their service, undercutting the competition by a small amount in an effort to attract trade. For instance, overpricing product in the early stages (such as a new 12″ dance club remix) will probably discourage new business, unless there is genuine inherent exclusivity contained within the product. A trend has emerged whereby initially, new music is given away free to would-be fans, in an effort to entice and encourage them to buy the releases that follow. Sometimes giving away free music proves to be counterproductive. When consumers do not pay for music, the value that they ascribe to it may change too – rendering the new artist, less important than music in the fan's collection that was purchased at full cost.

Published market research

The new music venture will need as much information at its disposal as possible in order to find out about the market it is launching itself into, so accessing published reports in the field will reveal the market trends. Some published reports can be accessed online free and many industry publications are released annually that can highlight statistical information that may be important. In the UK the BPI regularly publishes music statistics as an ongoing part of their role in the industry, the BPI regularly reports and releases public information on issues affecting the British recorded music industry (see www.bpi.co.uk). The umbrella organisation UK Music, represents the collective interests of the UK commercial music industry and also releases statistical information into the public sphere (see www.ukmusic.org). International statistics and global reports can be accessed at the IFPI website (see www.ifpi.org). Published statistics are useful in demonstrating how established markets have performed over time; this data can then inform future predictions in the market. Although many statistics are produced annually, trends in music can change very quickly. Being aware of the current music market will extend into blending methodologies together through published, field and desk research, to achieve the full picture. In the UK the National Statistics Office (see www.stastics. gov.uk) provides national statistics on contemporary society, publishing information on status lifestyles and behaviours. Independent research companies are also often commissioned to conduct investigations into the market and make their published findings available for a fee. Some research collections are highly specialised so obtaining such information can be expensive. Other published research can be accessed in reputable daily newspapers in online articles. Identifying and using reputable sources are essential in obtaining accurate information; many tabloid press papers are known for exaggerating articles and could not guarantee the provision of high quality information. Unofficial online statistics quoted in small websites and blogs may also be highly inaccurate, so unearthing official data carefully should be considered to ascertain the most accurate factual representation.

Field research

Field research involves collecting primary data rather than relying on published research materials. Particularly in the music industry, field research can produce the most useful and up to the minute information to inform the venture and will provide vital content for the SWOT analysis in all sections. The scope of the field research that needs to be conducted relies on the type of music venture embarked upon; sometimes the results of field research are immediate and obvious. For instance launching a new band and gauging audience reaction at the first live performance will produce a revealing visual and audible result. Polling the audience further – after the performance and following reaction using social networking sites – will add valuable insight into finding out how the audience perceive the act and what they thought. Attending music performances of competitors in the field and being able to measure their audience reaction through observation will inform *either* opportunities *or* threats in the SWOT analysis. Traditional business models would encourage gathering as much information as possible from customers and clients; as music is an emotive medium, ascertaining the reactions and feelings of fans towards the music should be done wherever possible.

Quantitative and qualitative research in the field

In using field, market and desk research, two distinct useful types of social research can reside within these methods. First quantitative data can be derived, which is measureable – for example, the amount of persons that attend a live performance and their demographic profile. The quantitative data could then produce a set of figures and calculations resulting in statistical information on the audience, perhaps further revealing their purchasing habits in music. Quantitative data analysis is used regularly throughout the live performance domain, where the concert promoter will consider this data measurement essential, in respect of the amount of tickets sold for their events.

The second useful social research type is 'qualitative'; qualitative research would be conducted to identify the thoughts, attitudes and feelings of consumers towards the product. Researching audience reaction by observing 'qualitative' comments, perhaps made through social networking or blogging, could assist in providing valuable information that may assist in improving future product performance; for example, polling audiences for their reaction after a concert has taken place. Qualitative summaries could also be produced as a result of interviewing consumers to find out what they like best about a product and how their suggestions can be used to enhance the product or performance. Adding further example, if the new business venture was a dance orientated nightclub event promoted by two DJs, field research would be carried out to find out the best clubs, their location and which DJs can draw the crowds. Hiring venues, entrance fees, publicity, equipment and the importance of a strong brand would all be factors to consider and this qualitative data could be summed and mapped in a SWOT analysis. Launching a professional music venture without considering quantitative and qualitative research in the field could compromise the business venture from the outset; realistic aims and objectives should be paramount, based on information gathered from the field.

THE UNIQUE SELLING POINT

All products or services should have a USP or unique selling point, devised by having a strong sense of concept in the venture. In this regard, interrogating the product or service will say something about the USP; exactly *how* is the product or music service unique in its field? If the venture is unique, a gap in the market is filled; hence it could be assumed that generating new customers and business should be relatively easy. The main issue in the music industry is that in the world today, there are more producers making and selling music and services associated with it than ever before. Yet the same could be said for many other industries and their proliferation of products too, due to increasing world populations alone. If the intended target for the music was mainstream media and audience (which has become increasingly homogenised in many world territories today), then the music must be fit for commercial exploitation, meaning that if the product was *too* unique, it would not be commercially viable. The music product would therefore need to be different enough to be distinctive and boast its own unique style, but similar enough to other 'market driven' commercial music heard in the mainstream, to be considered for airplay in the domain. If an independent artist wanted to expand their venture by licensing music to a larger label, they would need a strong USP before approaching the A&R team. A&R persons looking for new material in larger labels are acutely aware of what types of music are selling most in the current market, due to their own ongoing research, thus modern major label A&R has become increasingly market driven. Being unique *and* marketable would be the ideal business proposition, closely followed by realistic committed aims in promotion of the commodity to as many people as possible. The USP, however, often extends far beyond a hit recording to include elements such as image, style and a unique storyline to accompany the act. All music artists are selling the same commodity and want to be heard, but often what encourages media to write about the act is the story behind the act or 'plot'. Artists should think carefully about the plot in relation to the USP and what makes them different. High profile established artists together with their record companies and publicists change and develop their USPs throughout their careers, always looking for new ways to interest and attract new and existing consumers.

Developing the USP, press release and biography

If an artist is releasing music for sale or securing performances and gigs the USP reigns supreme and should be documented through the press release. The media press release is used to impress the recipient and re-enforces the artist mission, which could constitute potential performance venues, music companies, music publishers, newspapers or magazines. It should always accompany the music, whoever the music is sent to; a concise press release will outline who is behind the music and why they offer something of value to the field. If the music is being sent to independent radio or a magazine for review, station producers, DJs or journalists will need a starting point for discussion, rather than just to outline 'another' record release in a crowded market.

The press release should open with a brief artist biography, with achievements noted to date, such as where the act has been playing live or touring, followed by any past successes. An up-to-date news summary can be outlined with final details on where the music can be purchased or where the music is available online – particularly with reference to web addresses and contact details. The press release should also contain good resolution photographic representation of the artist, in case media needs to reproduce the images. Although CD copies of music product and printed press releases are still requested today for some promotional mail outs, most approaches to media are now made electronically – EPK or emailed MP3 plus press release attachment and JPEG images. Some recipients will simply like to access the press release from an emailed link to the artist website and would classify an unsolicited promotional email approach as junk mail, and so may delete accordingly. An efficient online presence for today's music venture is paramount; the construction of the artist website should contain embedded evidence of the USP, clearly setting out the aims and objectives in the press release. Professional managers generally advise approaching the artist's press release with care; if possible get a trusted outsider to write the press release as often this can produce more impressive results and recognise unseen qualities in the artist. Testing the press release for reactive comments in order to improve the USP from trusted professionals before posting online or mailing out is advisable, in order that the right impression can be created from the outset. Often, a venture can be damaged before it really 'gets off the ground', due to things such as poor visual aspects, evidenced through unprofessional photography. The values held in all areas of new projects and ventures should not be overlooked, especially during the initial launch stages. Most music consumers assess products in seconds, on their very first impression; in the web age of music, consumers often see before they hear and read. Many companies use the press release to communicate their current stories to media; it contributes vital information to the marketing communications strategy in the venture and re-enforces the USP wherever necessary.

THE SOLAADS FORMULA: CONSTRUCTING INFORMATION FOR MEDIA

When writing a media press release, it is easy to research how other good press releases have been constructed, by observing competitor websites and studying newspaper and magazine news stories. Often the media will alter a press release to resonate with the style of the publication or article, so it is important to get as much relevant information into the press release as possible. If the services of a public relations person are not being used, the SOLAADS rules can be used to construct the message conveyed in the press release. In public relations and marketing this seven point formula will assist in constructing effective media release information.

In construction of the press release many key components may be included in the opening section; the SOLAADS rules can guide a press release towards inclusion of the most relevant and concise facts. When loaded online, the press release should be updated alongside biographical information, company news items, photographic images and discographies.

Table 11.3 SOLAADS rules

SOLAADS Rules		Example
Subject:	What is the main subject of the story?	Artist launches new online EP and announces short promotional tour.
Organisation:	Which organisation is the story from?	Artist's own independent label brand.
Location:	In which region does the story apply?	UK, US and any English speaking global territories.
Advantages:	What are the benefits and what does the reader need to know?	Exclusive information is revealed, reporting on past success and new activities regarding product release.
Applications:	Who is this of use to and who will benefit?	Existing fans learn of the new product release. Potential new consumers are made aware of a product that may enhance their music collection.
Details:	What are the precise details?	If about a person or band, biographical details will be included; if a product or performance what, where, why and how.
Source:	The person or company behind the press release and contact information.	The details of the public relations agent, independent promoter or indie/artist label owner. Details such as email, web domain, address of the contact.

THE MUSIC MARKETING PLAN

In creating a prospective marketing plan for a new music venture, it would be worthwhile observing some of the common strategies outlined in this chapter. These essential elements can aid the construction of a comprehensive marketing plan, which also forms an integral part of the overall 'business plan'. A solid marketing strategy can be built for any product, service or brand using these tools. Bringing together these strategies in consideration of the mission statement, the brand, SWOT analysis and business objectives will demonstrate how the business plan can be implemented, controlled and measured.

Marketing music: The four Ps

In the 1950s and 1960s US marketing professors developed a strategic business tool known as the 'marketing mix'. This theoretical model effectively apportions essential elements of marketing into a programme of events, which then produces a comprehensive analysis of the venture. The marketing mix was later given a classification known as the 'four Ps': Product, Place, Price and Promotion. The marketing mix helps businesses to understand the connection with their potential customers; using this tool, a music venture example could be applied throughout the framework:

Product: A tangible item such as a CD or intangible media form such as an MP3 file. The product should appeal to the customer demographic and have a USP that, ideally, will result in repeat sales and return a fan base. Mastered high quality music production would be a pre-requisite and marketable 'innovation' a distinct advantage.

Place: The location where the product is available to customers. If tangible products are being sold, such as CDs and merchandise, appropriate physical store distribution would need to be appointed, unless self distributed or if the music is being sold at concerts. In order to make MP3 products available, digital distribution through virtual stores or music aggregators such as iTunes would need to be appointed. The quality and reliability of distribution would need research, alongside the costs and percentages deducted by the distributor.

Price: The amount the consumer pays for the product. The relationship between product price, production costs and ultimate profit in the venture must be considered. The product price should generate income; in the other three elements of the four Ps, expense can be identified and highlighted. Research in the field, examining markets and competitor prices, will give an indication of realistic pricing. If music is to be given away free in order to incentivise potential fans, a ceiling should be placed on free copies and profit futures calculated.

Promotion: Reaching the consumer through communicating elements of sales promotion, advertising, public relations and personal selling. Many music ventures rely on viral marketing or 'word of mouth' whereby fans discuss the artist person to person and through social networking. By using appropriate market research methods, the end user demography can be ascertained, informing the type of promotion required for the product in the marketplace. Sub-markets can be identified using 'market segmentation' analysis.

The extended marketing mix

In 1981 B.H. Booms and M.J. Bitner extended the marketing mix with a particular focus on service-based industries to include three further Ps; People, Process and Physical Environment – thus becoming the seven Ps. As today's market is increasingly more customer-orientated and major economic driving factors are fed by the service sector, the extra three Ps bear importance and relevance in the extended marketing mix. Continuing with a music venture example, the additional three Ps could apply to the following scenarios:

People: The provision of customer service. The service providers in this example could be the artists who serve fans. The direct relationship between artist behaviours and their audience will influence fan perception and product sales in reaction to performances. Customer satisfaction at concerts and gigs is a key factor that will influence future ticket sales, music sales and merchandise purchases. Customer care is a key consideration, executed by giving audiences exactly what they want.

Process: The procedures that are put in place to make the venture run effectively. Concerning the live performance of a band, this would mean having enough infrastructure around the band to make things run smoothly, such as good PA sound at concerts, enough supply of merchandise and CDs to sell and a process by which fans can access and download additional information or music. Qualitative research process methods could be employed in the process too, polling fans for reaction to music and performances in order to improve the fan experience as a result of the research.

Physical: Enhancing the customer experience by considering the physical environment in which the venture resides. This applies to virtual environments as well as the physical domain. Artists should have attractive websites that are current and easy to navigate. Consideration should be given to performance environments by appropriate 'themeing' and by conceptualising and dressing the staged area or venue through good concert production management. Enhancing the visual and atmospheric experience for concert-goers, however large or small the venue is, will demonstrate value and character for the consumer.

OTHER STRATEGIC BUSINESS ANALYSIS TOOLS

There are many other strategic tools that can be applied to the music venture business idea and are worthy of further investigation, and some of these are described in the next sections. Depending on the nature of the project, some of these methods can be used to test the validity of the venture, which could generate new ways of assessing potential success.

PEST or PESTLE analysis

Political, economic, social and technological (PEST) analysis is designed to gain greater understanding of the environment in which the business is operating. For instance, this analysis may be useful to a potential concert promotions business setting up a small outdoor festival:

Political:	Factors such as local authority legislation and law; for example, local licensing laws and the issues concerning the attainment of music licences for the small festival.
Economic:	Aspects affecting finance, such as borrowing funds to stage the event.
Social:	Local cultural aspects and the demographic of the potential paying audience.
Technological:	The essential requirements to provide adequate public address and sound for the concert.

PESTLE

In addition to the PEST analysis, the preferred addition of Legal and Environmental factors by some analysts furthers this macro-environmental business tool (continuing with the concert promotions example):

Legal:	Health and safety laws would need to be adhered to in staging the concert, alongside assessing other legal aspects, such as 'public liability' insurance being in place to cover potential accident risks and public safety.
Environmental:	Heavy weather would impact on an outdoor event. Due consideration would need to be given to environmental damage, too, with a 'clean up' operation in place. Further insurance cover may need to be put in place to cover legal environmental issues.

Market segmentation

Examining the market segment involves researching a particular demography in the market to identify specific customers. The segment is a subset in the marketplace; for example, research carried out into the purchasers of thrash metal genre music would reveal that the subset exists within the (somewhat broader) classification of heavy metal commercial popular music. A true market segment is distinct from other segments, but is homogenous within its subset. Further research can then begin into the subset, establishing the key demographic by investigating consumer age, gender, general interests and the price they would normally expect to pay for their products or concert-going habits. This strategy can provide commercial advantages through its positive identification of the intended target market through pure differentiation.

Other strategic business analysis tools

There are many further tools that have been devised to analyse business viability and performance. Those most appropriate to the type of music venture are worthy of further investigation and may be mapped to the business idea, some of these include:

- Scenario planning: A strategic thinking method, with its developmental origins rooted in military operations. The method is used to develop a flexible yet detailed long-term company plan.

- Critical success factor (CSF) analysis: This technique involves the identification of one or more factors that are crucial to the success of the business. A list of vital elements can be derived that will determine how the venture will outperform its competition in the field. CSFs may include cash flow, audience response, the quality of performances and products, good product distribution and number of tickets to be sold in a music business venture.

- Competitor analysis: This method can be used to enhance the SWOT analysis, providing essential content in the opportunities and threats headed areas. The competitive position of the business is summarised by examining and rating the success of similar business competitors and their key success factors. Comparisons can then be drawn to create defensive strategic actions; detailed knowledge of business rivals can enhance the competitive edge of a business. A live music promotions company may, for instance, attend other events and examine the key factors that make other events a success in comparison to their own efforts.

- Project planning – the Gantt chart: The Gantt chart can illustrate a project schedule in a 'bar chart' type format. Although developed by US engineer Henry Gantt in 1917, it is still used today as a production control tool to demonstrate both scheduled and completed work. The Gantt chart is useful in tracking projects in a music venture. Various Gantt chart examples can be found online (such as at www.projectsmart.co.uk).

USING BUSINESS TOOLS

The strategies, theories, thinking and writings that now surround business entrepreneurship are vast. Early music venturists did not have the benefit of this knowledge, amassed through the experiential successes of global enterprises, small businesses and the documented analysis of researched business practice in teaching institutions worldwide. Using just some of these tools can serve to create a stronger foundation in the potential music venture and assess its potential. More succinctly, when music is monetised, somebody must assume an entrepreneurial role; for example, for many music artists, someone must address securing gigs; without this, there is little career for the artist. Where artists prefer to be purely artistic and avoid entrepreneurial duties – agents and managers must then engage in entrepreneurial venture strategies to secure performances and hence earn their commission. However, engaging in the wider business strategies that surround the music venture integrates the artist with the external and internal processes that will ultimately unlock greater value and a greater sense of entrepreneurial perspective in the music venture, for all parties involved.

REFERENCES AND FURTHER READING
Books

Baron, R. and Shane, S., *Entrepreneurship – A Process Perspective* (Independence, KY: Thomson South Western, 2008).

Baskerville, D. and Baskerville, T., *Music Business Handbook and Career Guide: Ninth Edition* (London: Sage, 2010), pp. 303–321 and 453–472.

Bolton, B. and Thompson, J., *Entrepreneurs – Talent, Temperament, Technique* (Oxford: Butterworth, 2000).

Booms, B.H. and Bitner, M.J., 'Marketing Strategies and Organization Structures for Service Firms', in J.H. Donnelly and W.R. George (eds), *Marketing of Services* (Chicago: American Marketing Association, 1981), pp. 47–51.

Borden, N.H., 'The Concept of the Marketing Mix', in G. Schwartz (ed.), *Science in Marketing* (New York: John Wiley & Sons, 1965), pp. 386–397.

Fifield, P. and Gilligan, C., *Strategic Marketing Management* (Oxford: Butterworth-Heinemann, 1996).

Fill, C., *Marketing Communications: Engagements Strategies and Practice* (Harlow: Pearson, 2006).

Gelfand, M., *Strategies for Success: Self Promotion Secrets for Musicians* (New York: Schirmer, 2005).

Halloran, J., *Why Entrepreneurs Fail* (New York: Liberty Hall, 1991).

Hisrich, R. and Peters, M., *Entrepreneurship – Starting, Developing and Managing a New Enterprise* (London: Irwin, 1995).

Hutchison, T., Macy, A. and Allen, P., *Record Label Marketing: Second Edition* (Oxford: Elsevier, 2010).

Leibert, J., *Smart Business* (Oxford: Capstone, 2004).

Lindstrom, M., *Brand Sense: How to Build Powerful Brands Through Touch, Taste, Smell, Sight and Sound* (New York: Simon & Schuster, 2005).

Lindstrom, M., *Brand Sense: Sensory Secrets Behind the Stuff We Buy* (New York: Simon & Schuster, 2007), p. 102.

Mc Luhan, M. and McLuhan, E., *Laws of Media* (Toronto: University of Toronto Press, 1988).

Mintzberg, H., *The Rise & Fall of Strategic Planning* (London: Pearson Education, 2000).

Palmer, A., *Introduction to Marketing: Theory and Practice* (Oxford: Oxford University Press, 2004).

Rae, D., *The Entrepreneurial Spirit* (Blackrock, Co. Dublin: Blackhall, 1999).

Rae, D., *Entrepreneurship: From Opportunity to Action* (Basingstoke: Palgrave Macmillan, 2007).

Schwartz, D.D., *I Don't Need a Record Deal: Your Survival Guide for the Indie Music Revolution* (New York: Billboard, 2005), pp. 122–172.

Schwartz, D.D., *Start and Run Your Own Record Label* (New York: Billboard, 2009), pp. 185–269.

Southon, M. and West C., *The Beermat Entrepreneur* (Harlow: Pearson, 2005).

Spellman, P., *The Self-promoting Musician: Strategies for Independent Music Success* (New York: Berklee Press, 2000).

Walker, Jr., L.J., *This Business of Urban Music: A Practical Guide to Achieving Success in the Industry, from Gospel to Funk to R&B and Hip-Hop* (New York: Billboard, 2008).

Online resources

Brand Sense Agency. Available at: www.brandsenseagency.com (accessed 25 August 2010).

The Brand Union. Available at: www.thebrandunion.com (accessed 25 August 2010).

Jones, P., 'Entrepreneurialism: The New Rock 'n' Roll', BBC news online (19 December 2005). Available at: http://news.bbc.co.uk/1/hi/business/4542280.stm (accessed 25 August 2010).

Music market research reports. Available at: www.marketresearch.com/browse.asp?categoryid=782 (accessed 25 August 2010).

National Endowment for Science, Technology and the Arts (NESTA). Available at: www.nesta.org.uk (accessed 30 August 2010).

Porter, M.E., 'The Five Competitive Forces That Shape Strategy', Harvard Business Publishing. Available at: www.youtube.com/watch?v=mYF2_FBCvXw (accessed 12 March 2011).

Published music industry market research. Available at: www.bpi.co.uk (accessed 25 August 2010).

Published music industry market research. Available at: www.ifpi.org (accessed 25 August 2010).

Sobel, S.R., 'Entrepreneurship', Library of Econonics and Liberty. Available at: www.econlib.org/library/Enc/Entrepreneurship.html (accessed 12 March 2011).

CHAPTER 12

Trading in the music industry

Paul Rutter

SETTING UP A MUSIC BUSINESS VENTURE TO TRADE LEGALLY

This chapter primarily discusses how to set up in business and function as a freelance music business entity, trading under a professional legal framework. If the intended venture is to become a professional organisation, understanding the logistics of trading practice is essential, alongside recognising the official regulatory bodies in government that define the regulations. The business venture may start as a hobby, but can gradually turn into a money-making 'going concern'. The inspiration to get the business moving is provided by creative strategies, market and business planning, and a passion for the venture (as outlined in the previous chapter). Supplying music products, performances or services can be highly rewarding, but in addition to this, taking care of essential trading matters on a daily basis is required so that the business can function legally. These additional duties are borne out of stringent tax legislation, existing in virtually all developed countries. Wherever music is monetised, there is an income and expenditure account generated; government needs to know this information and will want to see this in a formal annual declaration to calculate any tax payable, or refundable. In the UK, musicians often question whether or not they should pay tax on income generated from local performances (often low sums, paid in cash). For many musicians operating at grassroots level, performance income is usually in addition to earnings from other jobs. Due consideration must also be given to the venue paying the band; the venue must declare the band payment as an expense to their business. All venue *expenses* must be balanced and declared in the running of the venue, including its payments to entertainers. The business *income*, such as bar takings and ticket sales must be declared also. For the band, each individual should declare their individual performance income to the Inland Revenue, alongside their list of expenses (e.g. buying instruments and PA equipment) in order to facilitate the performance. New semi-professionals coming into the music industry often overlook tax regulations in fear of losing their valued income to government. In many cases new businesses operate at a loss, due to the considerable amount of investment required to set up the business. Declaring a bona fide loss in the business may mean the music venture actually earns a tax rebate back from the Inland Revenue as a result of negative end-of-year trading figures. All income and expenditure must be taken into account in the new business; figures can only be agreed where accurate accounting takes place, which can actually be easier than it may first appear, particularly for a small business. For many, keeping simple business records can actually be rewarding, as it provides a financial measurement and provides greater value to the business in gauging its financial strength and sustainability.

CASH FLOW, FINANCIAL ASPECTS AND ACCOUNTS

Keeping accurate business records is the key to successful accounting in any venture. Not all music venturists may want to do this, but it is nonetheless essential; others may not want to calculate their own tax return for the Inland Revenue office, as this can be an arduous task, and so they may appoint an accountant. An accountant can assume much of the recordkeeping, which is essential when businesses become larger and more profitable. Self assessment in the UK *is* an option for the small venture, whereby the business owner themselves can complete their own tax return forms annually and declare income and expenditure to the Inland Revenue. However, some small businesses may find that it is easy to maintain their own profit and loss figures; an appropriate accountant can then be sourced to simply finalise the calculations, complete the tax return and deal directly with the tax office. The advantage for the small business is that the accountant is familiar with constant updates and changes in tax legislation and can therefore field any queries that may result from the Inland Revenue. If accounts submitted to the Inland Revenue appear unrealistic, they may issue further demands for tax payment and investigate the business; an accountant can broker agreements to ensure tax payments are accurate. Certain ongoing recordkeeping duties are essential and must be addressed by the business owner or partners in the venture – this can simply be thought of as money out, money in. A profit and loss account can then be calculated for the business.

Cash flow: Money out

All monetary expenses that pertain directly to the business should be recorded for purposes of accounting annually to Inland Revenue. In freelance building professions, such as a carpenter, a workman can claim against tax, within reason, for their tools. Just as a carpenter needs drills, saws, chisels, nails and a van to get to the job in the first place – the musician's tools are their instruments. DJs need decks, music managers need good technology to communicate and without these tools the job cannot be done, which is why these items are a claimable expense against taxation. However, if the carpenter purchased a large luxury car to get to the job, rather than a commercial vehicle, the Inland Revenue is unlikely to allow this expense offset against taxation. As the Inland Revenue has been in the business of collecting tax for many years, they are acutely aware of the different types of freelance venture and how they run. If business claims are excessive, unproven, arouse suspicion or are unrealistic, the expenses will not be allowed against the business profit. Honest and realistic accounts are far more likely to be passed by the Inland Revenue and generate realistic taxation calculations. For a small music business venture, there are a list of suggested example items below that could be claimed for in whole or in part, as listed, thus making up the expense or 'money out':

- Musical instruments: Essential tools of the trade may include guitars, drum kits, microphones, PA equipment and DJ equipment.

- Studio equipment: Audio recording equipment, software and effects – also studio construction materials if being built (where recording equipment is essential in recording demos or forms a part of the business and generates income).

- Furnishings, fixtures and fittings: Office furnishings, chairs, desks, filing cabinets and essential office equipment (regardless of home or rented office space).

- Communications hardware: Computer, mobile phone, office telephone or other communication devices.

- Transport: Car or van required to get to performance destinations.

The above items could be thought of as fixed assets, as they retain a 'pool' value year on year and could be sold if the business were to close in the future. Capital items in the pool have codes allotted to them by the Inland Revenue and have varying depreciation values applied to them, over a given time. Certain items above, such as cars and mobile phones may be used for purposes other than in direct relation to the business, so only a percentage of their value may be claimed against the business. 'Revenue items' are those expenses that retain no long-term fixed asset value in the business and in the music venture, and could constitute the following:

- Communications services: Phone network connection and computer connectivity, such as broadband.

- Advertising: If the business is a service or product, advertising in key media may incur significant cost.

- Transport: Travelling to meet with music industry personnel, using transport other than own car, or getting to business meetings by train or other transport means. Fuel used in connection with business travel only is included.

- Subsistence: Food and drink costs incurred in connection with business activity.

- Accommodation: If away from home, reasonable overnight accommodation costs may be incurred.

- Recording studios: Where artists do not have their own home recording facilities, external studios may be required for recording mixing and mastering demos and making music products.

- Music product: When tangible media products are made available for sale, product costs such as CD pressings, artwork, inlay sleeves, artist merchandise, packaging or any expense linked to the manufacture and production of the item.

- Promotion: Promotional campaigns may require the appointment of other specialists in the field and PR personnel to launch associated products.

- Stage clothing or business attire: Specific clothing required for performance or attire in which to conduct business, such as a suit.

- Rehearsal rooms: Rehearsal space fees may be payable by the artists themselves or the band manager.

- Repairs and renewals: When a capital item is repaired, renewed or serviced; such as car or general maintenance such as a guitar string change, new drumsticks or repairing a slow computer.

- Stationery and postage: Letterhead, notepaper, pens, pencils, postage for business mailings, such as a mail shot to promote the service or product.

- Subscriptions and books: *Music Week* or *Billboard* (used to increase industry knowledge and research) or other appropriate magazines. Also, online subscriptions and physical entertainment media industry contact books, such as *The Knowledge*, *Showcase International Directory* and the *White Book*.

- Commissions and fees: When an agent or manager takes commissions and fees from an artist in respect of performances or advances, these are deductable expenses from the gross fees earned. Accountant or solicitor legal fees are also a deductable expense.

- Bank charges and loan interest: Usually banks charge commercial rates to businesses, unless the business is run from a personal account. Any loans taken out to fund the business will incur interest and will generate further claimable expenses, as will any dividends paid out to investors in the business.

- Insurances: Public liability insurance may be required for performers for those staging events, covering the possibility of public injury.

- Rent, rates, heat, light: If the business is run from a home premises, a portion of each utility bill may be claimed in respect of the essential business base. If the business profit grows and can support a move to a separate rented office or studio location, this would fall into the claim category.

In some items above, such as advertising, the whole expense may be claimed against profit made by the business as some ventures could not function without it. However, some expenses above are incurred through personal and business use, such as private phone and computer use in the communications items. The Inland Revenue apportions allowances against profit on items that have any shared use, private and business, so a business run from home is allowed to claim percentage of its broadband expense, for example. Proportioned allowances are also apparent in home expenses (if the business is run from home), transport and anything that shares private and business use. If trading occurs from home, such as a recording studio with a steady stream of paying musician clients, local council authorities may wish to know about the trading, in order to levy a business rate charge on the premises. Although paying necessary state National Insurance fees will contribute to UK state retirement pension, some business traders or businesses also start a private pension fund. Often young business owners do not prioritise private pensions as a necessary expense, but sometimes NI contributions will increase as the business becomes more successful. However, paying into a private pension fund is not an allowable expense against taxation.

FIGURE 12.1
Renting office space and trading with an appropriate legal structure, courtesy the author

National Insurance

An essential expense to consider in self-employment is National Insurance (NI) contributions. In other world territories there are similar public and private health insurance schemes in operation. In the UK, a benefit system exists that is funded by National Insurance contributions, which are paid for by working citizens in any employment role; currently NI contributions occur from the age of sixteen. The National Health Service, Pensions, Job Seeker's Allowance and many other benefit types are funded from HM Revenue and Custom's (HMRC) collection of NI. Whether in part- or full-time employment, or self-employment, NI contributions are taken as a percentage of earnings; this is attributed to a unique employee NI number, which is issued at the age of sixteen. NI is taken at source from most regular employment contracts, but for self-employed individuals, agreement must be reached on the classification of NI to be paid with HMRC. The NI class (numbered one to four) will be dependent on the individual person status and business profit; small earnings exemption is also possible if HMRC agree this. If the business earns healthy profits, more NI will be payable, if the business operates on a low profit margin a lower classification of NI payment will be due, paid regularly by a monthly direct debit payment. When trading as a self-employed person, it is important that HMRC knows about the business and establishes that correct NI classification payments are being made, as certain benefits will not be payable if conditions are not being met. If tax credits or benefits are being claimed back at any stage by the individual, the NI number is required and checked, in order to verify the person and that NI payments are current. When setting up in business, addressing the NI contribution requirement is as necessary as registering the business with HMRC. NI contributions cannot be deducted as a running cost of the business and cannot be offset against profit in the tax return. Contribution levels in each classification will change annually; NI contribution and personal classification information can be determined with the Citizens Advice Bureau (www. adviceguide.org.uk) and HMRC (www.hmrc.gov.uk).

Cash flow: Money in

All gross income that is attributed to the business must be recorded so that profit can be calculated accurately; this would include all payments for musical services or products whether paid in cash, or other banking method. Examples of potential income streams are listed below, which would be offset against the expenses incurred. If a music artist works independently and operates their own label (or sub-licenses music to a larger label), they would need to be aware of these key revenue streams:

- Performance income: Live performance income paid to the artist from the venue owners or generated through ticket sales.
- Advances: If a music company, investor or publisher pays any advance to the artist, any commission due from the manager, agent or publisher

(if represented) should be deducted, revealing actual receipt. Both gross and net figures should be listed in the accounts.

- Sales: Gross profit returned for the sale of recorded music products or merchandise, if operating own independent label.

- Publishing royalties: Where the artist's songs, compositions or musical works are exploited, publishing royalties will be returned from performing rights societies (in the UK, PRS for Music). Mechanical royalties from organisations such as MCPS are also due. Additional synchronisation royalties and sheet music sales returns may also be due.

- Record and performer royalties: If a member of PPL in the UK and a recording receives exploitation, royalties are due for phonographic performance (public performance of the recording) to the owner in the recording and performers taking part in the recorded work. The same applies to video exploitation in media; royalty fees are collected by VPL. In each global territory collection societies can generate royalties for exploited recordings and videos.

- Interest: If a surplus of profit is generated and invested in a savings account, any bank interest earned forms part of the income.

INCOME TAX ON PROFIT

When yearly accounts have been completed (or agreed by an accountant if appointed), a tax return is submitted to HMRC at the trading year end. When HMRC reviews the tax return, taxes payable (or to be credited back) are notified to the business owner. Tax paid by the business occurs at the trading year end, in one lump sum, unlike regular tax payments made in Pay-As-You-Earn schemes, diluting any tax burdens. Through business planning, many profitable businesses save regular amounts monthly, leading up to the year end, anticipating the tax sum, and therefore being prepared and able to pay HMRC on time. Any tax paid to HMRC cannot be claimed as an expense, unlike claiming for bank interest charges. For example, if the business paid £2,000 in tax to HMRC, this is not a deductable expense that can be offset against the next tax demand. Taxation levels and thresholds change constantly in most world territories due to fluctuating economies, political policies and the social climate. In the UK, official changes in taxation thresholds occur as a result of government budget decisions and annual taxation reviews. The amount of tax any individual business will pay is dependent on individual profit status and earnings, which is ascertained largely through accounts calculations and submission of the annual 'tax return'. Changes that take place concerning the success of the business and its trading framework will also affect taxation, so it is important to determine which type of business structure to embark upon. Taxation is complex, but is made easier to understand as the business trades and subsequent discussion with accountants and HMRC occurs. In the UK, the HMRC provide regular updates on the latest criteria governing the rules and thresholds for UK taxation (www.hmrc.gov.uk).

PAY-AS-YOU-EARN

When intending to start a new music business venture, it is probable that the start-up owner(s) are already in full-time employment receiving a regular wage, using this foundation to fund and build the new business. Even if in full- or part-time employment, registering the new business venture with HMRC is necessary: in effect, the music business venture forms an additional 'self-employed' status for the business owner. As the business owner may continue in full-time employment to fund the venture, tax, National Insurance and pension contributions are being deducted at source through Pay-As-You-Earn (PAYE). In the UK, this wage-withholding system can ensure that the business owner maintains government contributions in each essential area. If the new business only has a low turnover, additional NI and tax payments may not be necessary, but this would be established by completion of the self-assessment tax return. Conversely, if the music venture becomes successful and the business owner needs to employ new persons to work for the business (such as a part-time secretary), the business will need to address PAYE and tax code concerns, as the business then deducts PAYE from the employee's wages. Accountants are usually employed to assist with wage payments; the rules governing PAYE systems for both employee and employer can be investigated further at the UK Citizens Advice Bureau (www.adviceguide.org.uk). Other countries outside the UK operate similar taxation systems, but territorial government rules on self-employment, additional income and taxation systems would need further investigation.

BALANCING THE BOOKS

Many new businesses are expected to show a loss in their first year or two of trading. Injecting cash into a business to make it run and sustain profitability can take time, but making a continued loss year on year is not sustainable, and if losses cannot be recouped the business may go into liquidation. However, some businesses that try to offset huge expenditure against profit year on year will arouse suspicion from taxation authorities. If expenses outweigh profit each year, the business income to pay the expenses must come from somewhere – sometimes businesses use undeclared cash income to pay for capital items such as instruments, cars or other equipment. If a claim is made on the items against tax, accountants and HMRC can assess that there is unaccounted income, resulting in investigations, audits and estimated demands for unpaid tax on undeclared profits. Businesses that run honest accounting procedures do not usually arouse the suspicion of the HMRC, but fraudulent activity practiced by businesses can and does result in prosecution and confiscation of assets. In any business, balancing the books is an important measure, which experienced accountants are well versed in and therefore they should be appointed where the business can afford it. In the UK, HMRC can legally investigate any business's previous financial records for up to six years, should it need to; all businesses are advised by HMRC to keep all old financial records for six years. The most important issue in respect of any expenses incurred is that they can actually be proven to an accountant or Inland Revenue official. This can only be done if original receipts are available in evidence of expense. Businesses that cannot prove their expenses may not be allowed to offset certain costs against their profit account; the Inland Revenue can issue an estimated tax demand to businesses without accounts, which is non-negotiable and may be a considerable financial sum – far beyond the figure that would have been due if profits were accurately declared. Keeping actual receipts for everything is the safest measure, receipts that are not regarded as claimable expenses can then be simply disregarded when the accounts are collated. Keeping all bank statements, bank books, credit card statements and receipts in the relevant items listed above, in dated order, will provide a legitimate basis on which to create proven, believable accounts.

DETERMINING VENTURE VIABILITY AND OCCUPATION FLEXIBILITY

Thinking simply in terms of 'money in – money out' permits an understanding of essential cash flow in business and the balance sheet, thus predicting if there is enough money in the venture to make it viable over a period of time. As many small music ventures may take time to build a sustainable income, music may become a long-term, part-time occupation for many. Such ventures may form a significant part of the personal income and therefore should have a business record and accounts system. Understanding music ownership, copyright and the exploitation of music (as outlined in previous chapters) increases knowledge in tracing the potential income that can be generated in relation to music – essential in producing a business plan. If providing a service in the music industry, such as publishing or an agency or management venture, income would be derived from some of the items listed above on a commission basis. If offering promotions, public relations mediation or plugging services, a set fee is usually charged to the artist, manager or label concerned. These fees are set in respect of the market conditions and the 'going rate', but more crucially, higher profile music services will command higher fees and generate higher incomes. Being able to produce a simple 'money in – money out' spreadsheet will permit easy assessment of the feasibility and viability of the business venture, understanding the concept of profit and loss. Having an accurate estimate of what it will cost to launch the venture and build a sustainable business is possible through this type of simple financial modelling, in order to anticipate possible financial problems in cash flow.

WHICH LEGAL TRADING STRUCTURE, TYPE OR CLASSIFICATION IS BEST SUITED TO THE VENTURE?

Initially it may be difficult to decide which type of business you may wish to be a part of. Once the business idea, plan and brand have been laid out, setting up as a legal trading entity is advisable when the business looks set to make money and trading expenses are formally logged. In the UK anyone can set up a small business with a suitably chosen trading name; if the business is starting out in a small way (without large loans and investments), many ventures simply get on with the business of trading in order to begin to build the venture gradually, testing viability as it progresses. In naming the business, it is best to search for original identities, names and brands where possible to avoid confusion or possible litigation if trading under the name of another registered business. There may be no need to register the trading name formally, especially if trading under one's own personal name, for example, Joe Smith, musician. If Joe Smith releases music on his own recording label imprint named 'Superstar Music', it may be cheaper and easier in banking terms to set up as 'Joe Smith trading as Superstar Music'. This move would keep Joe Smith's personal account and associated name under one umbrella. If this was not done, two bank accounts would be needed, one for Joe Smith and one for 'Superstar Music', a more costly option, especially if the label does not make money in its development phase. Given this example, it is better to get a business started, keep accurate accounts and monitor how the business is building and decide whether it is a viable entity, over time. Where more people are involved in the business or higher investment and loans are put into the new music venture, the appropriate official trading classification must be chosen before registration of the business with the Inland Revenue. Common legal business trading models follow, which could be applied to any music venture, depending on its status.

Sole trader

This is the simplest form of trading classification, requiring no registration fees. The benefits of being a sole trader are realised when accounting to the Inland Revenue, as requirements are simplified when the business has a low turnover under a certain threshold. With lower earnings in the business, a 'short' tax return can be submitted. If registering using this model, all profits in the business go to the independent self-employed sole trader. They are, however, personally responsible for any debts run up by the business and have 'unlimited liability'; if the sole trader borrows heavily and gets into difficulty, personal assets can be seized, such as house, car and capital items of value. In respect of a musician who earns a living playing collaboratively with others, individual accounts must be compiled. If playing in a band, each member can register as a self-employed sole trader (musician) and complete and submit their own tax returns. Bands would not usually register the business model as a 'partnership', even though the work is shared with others.

Partnership

Where two or more persons form a business together, a partnership could be formed. Each partner can contribute to the business, pooling experience, sharing investment and responsibilities. Each person in the partnership must register as 'self-employed' and accounting is more complex, as both the partnership side of the business and each individual must make annual returns to HMRC. Disagreements between partners can cause issues, and any losses made will be shared by the partners, as will any costs and potential profit returned. Partnerships are unlimited liability concerns and further complexities can arise; if a partner leaves and the business owes money, creditors can claim from the remaining partners, even though they may not be responsible for the debt.

Limited liability companies

Registering the company in this way allows the company to function within its own financial structure, separating it from the personal finances of the company owners. Depending on the company status, it may become a Private Limited Company or Public Limited Company, but it must be formally registered with Companies House in the UK. A limited company will need to have a director, who can make decisions in association with an appointed board of directors. Finance for the company may be raised through loans, shareholders or company profits accrued. Profit distribution is more complex than other business structures, as 'dividends' may be paid to the shareholders when accrued. Accounts are dealt with by Companies House and audited annually. A Limited Liability Partnership is a variation on this type of company classification, affording the flexibility of a partnership but with the benefit of limited liability. Although the limited liability company model provides safeguards in protecting personal assets, it is often an inappropriate and costly structure to engage in for the small music entity.

Social enterprises

Where a business is set up to trade for a social purpose only, any profits generated from the business are reinvested directly into the community or its own social objectives as a company. For instance, a local youth music community enterprise scheme may adopt this form of legal business structure, whereby no profits will be paid to the shareholders or owners. The legal business structure of a social enterprise may take many forms, such as a trust, a charity, limited company, association or community interest company. Government regulation and scrutiny in these structures can, however, be stringent, in order to guarantee that any company profits go to the benefit of the social aspect as declared by the business owners.

Franchise

It is possible in some cases to buy into a franchise agreement, where a business or brand is already established and a contract is signed to permit trading using the brand name. The business may be run under any business framework above, which can be decided by the franchisee, who may purchase a licence to use the name of the franchisor company. Established brands in dance music have become franchisable across geographical regions, as have music television show formats.

LEGAL ADVICE ON TRADING

It is worth seeking advice from a solicitor to engage in the correct legal business structure, especially when going into business with others; in the music industry, ventures are often short-lived. In any form of partnership, contracts should be drawn up to set out clear terms by which each partner should abide by. A realistic investigation carried out using business planning strategies will also assist in choosing the right business model at the outset. After the business has been trading for a while and is established, it is prudent to review the business structure and decide whether to change the business classification. Many companies that start as small sole-trading entities can re-classify themselves when cash flow, turnover and borrowing increases, as a result of growing success.

VALUE ADDED TAX

It is beneficial to know about being a value added tax (VAT) registered business when a company is particularly successful and generates a larger cash flow. Most member states in the EU operate a common VAT system, whereby VAT sales tax is commonly payable on many goods or services. At the time of writing, if a business has a turnover of over £70,000 within twelve months or less in its trading cycle, the business should register with HMRC for VAT. Company turnover does not constitute pure profit earned, but the actual amount of money flowing through the business. HMRC raises the threshold figure for VAT by around £1,000 each year, in line with rising costs. Being VAT registered means that VAT can be charged to customers, on top of the goods or services provided. In addition, where VAT is paid out by the business for goods or services that pertain to the venture, this VAT can be claimed back from HMRC. For instance, a particularly successful record label could then charge VAT for any services it provides to a third party and could claim back VAT on its business costs (such as VAT paid out on promotional costs). However, the main issue with VAT registration is that the high turnover VAT business is more closely audited than smaller businesses; VAT payments and claims are issued by HMRC on a quarterly basis, which means increased auditing and quarterly agreements made with accountants, naturally increasing the operating fees of the business. If a new venture does become particularly successful, advice from HMRC and business advisers will suggest if it is necessary to be VAT registered. Other world territories have their own taxation mechanisms for high turnover enterprises, which can be researched and legal advice taken, if setting up or working abroad.

TOURING AND EARNING OVERSEAS

Profitability in many music ventures occurs by expanding audiences internationally. Musicians and the touring infrastructure that supports them often find overseas work attractive, provoking further questions on taxation and where and how it should be paid. Music venturists working overseas, however, may find themselves paying tax twice. This can happen when the taxation is taken 'at source' by the overseas employer in that territory, *after* the work was carried out. Further issues may occur if bringing the payment home in the form of cash payments; some territories need declarations made on the sums of currency being brought into the country. If money is transferred into a UK bank account from overseas, even though it has already been taxed in its foreign territory, money coming into the business account will need to be declared. Touring expenses could be declared as a business expense, but money coming into the business on the UK side will be classed as earnings and will have to be declared; once again this may incur taxation. Fortunately for some, the UK has 'double taxation' agreements with some countries to ensure taxation may only occur once, either in the UK or country of payment. Taxation on overseas earnings depends on individual status and how long individuals work overseas and their conditions of residence. Visas or work permits will be required in many territories; before undertaking work overseas, checking taxation abroad is advisable, ensuring that the tour will be profitable. However, many artists tour internationally to break new territories and do not expect to make a profit initially, but seek to sell music products and build a fan base over time as part of the long-term business plan. Updated advice and eligibility for double-taxation agreements can be researched on the government website (www.direct.gov.uk).

SUCCESS OR FAILURE?

Often new businesses fail; a failure rate of 50 per cent within the first four years is common for conventional small businesses, with youth entrepreneurship and inexperience a contributing factor to these statistics. The chances for successful entrepreneurship are improved when the business is started for the right reasons at the outset. Common failures in 'motivational business thinking' include poor management and insufficient capital in setting the business up and getting things moving as they should. Good planning and not expanding the business too quickly or being overly ambitious will stand the business on firmer foundations. In the case of an expanding music label, only enough CDs should be pressed as can be sold realistically. Customer reaction to initial product runs should be measured cautiously to safeguard against 'overstocking' and unnecessary product manufacture before there is enough demand. Making the business work and realising its aims through determination, patience, positive attitude and learning from mistakes are character attributes that must be married to the realisation of the socioeconomic factors governing the venture. Further research into the demographic – age, gender, profession – buying patterns, income and customer location must be considered. The business location should also not be overlooked; although the internet age permits electronic flexibility in communications, being sited close to the customer is often the only way many businesses can function. Music plugging and promotion services often have to be situated where their targets are, for example, large cities or in a capital music hub such as London. If placing the customer at the centre of the business, geographical imperatives may once again apply. Where one person alone cannot run the venture, it is worth considering partnerships and alliances. Businesses can only really move forward where there is a clear customer demand and the music business owner can identify that demand. Setting up a music company to trade legally and professionally can prove to be a very rewarding experience for the venturist, regardless of the venture's size. Understanding the monetisation of music and how trading structures wrap around the venture will assist greatly in ensuring legal obligations are being met in the business plan.

REFERENCES AND FURTHER READING

Books

Baskerville, D. and Baskerville, T., *Music Business Handbook and Career Guide: Ninth Edition* (London: Sage, 2010), pp. 407–472.
Beattie, W., *The Rock and Roll Times Guide to the Music Industry* (Oxford: Spring Hill, 2007), pp. 221–234.
Davis, S. and Laing, D., *The Guerrilla Guide to the Music Business* (New York: Continuum, 2006), pp. 370–373.
Deeks, D., *Understanding Tax for Small Businesses, Second Revised Edition* (London: TY Computing, 2009).
Lloyd, D., *Small Business Accounting: Teach Yourself* (London: CPI, 2010).
O'Berry, D., *Small Business Cash Flow: Strategies for Making Your Business a Financial Success* (Hoboken, NJ: John Wiley and Sons, 2007).
Parks, S., *Small Business Handbook* (Harlow: Pearson, 2006).
Schwartz, D.D., *Start and Run Your Own Record Label* (New York: Billboard, 2009), pp. 56–89.
Walker, Jr., L.J., *This Business of Urban Music: A Practical Guide to Achieving Success in the Industry, from Gospel to Funk to R&B and Hip-Hop* (New York: Billboard, 2008), pp. 97–148.
Williams, S. and Lowe, J., *JFT Guide to Personal Tax 2009–2010* (Financial Times Series), (Harlow: Pearson, 2009).

Online resources

Businesslink: Practical Advice for Businesses (official UK site). Available at: www.businesslink.gov.uk/bdotg/action/home (accessed 25 August 2010).
Citizens Advice Bureau, UK. Available at: www.adviceguide.org.uk (accessed 25 August 2010).
Companies House. Available at: www.companieshouse.gov.uk (accessed 25 August 2010).

HM Revenue and Customs (HMRC). Available at: www.hmrc.gov.uk/index.htm (accessed 28 August 2010).

National Insurance Contributions. Available at: www.direct.gov.uk/en/MoneyTaxAndBenefits/Taxes/BeginnersGuideToTax/DG_4015904 (accessed 28 August 2010).

Official UK Government website. Available at: www.direct.gov.uk/en/index.htm (accessed 25 August 2010).

PAYE (Pay-As-You-Earn). Available at: www.hmrc.gov.uk/paye/payroll/year-end/annual-return.htm (accessed 25 August 2010).

Trading Standards Office. Available at: www.tradingstandards.gov.uk (accessed 25 August 2010).

Value Added Tax (VAT). Available at: www.hmrc.gov.uk/vat (accessed 25 August 2010).

CHAPTER 13

Into the future

Paul Rutter

NEW MEDIA AND MUSIC INDUSTRY VALUES

By compartmentalising the two key music industry sectors of 'live' and 'recorded', it is easier to understand the functionality in each and, more importantly, be able to look at the current health of each sector. Other than improved technology and hardware used in connection with live and concert music performances, little has changed in the live music industry sector in its principle operations since the 1960s. A steady increase in ticket sales demonstrates that the business of live music has endured well, largely due to the value that concert and gig-goers ascribe to the 'live' experience. However, the recorded music industry sector has experienced turbulence through the advent of new media technologies and has had to consider new strategies by which it can survive into the future. The concept of owning one's music is now brought into question as consumers strive to find mobile technologies with enough capacity to hold their whole music collection; infinitely, there will always be more music to download, store, own and keep. The notion that it would be better to keep all the music one needs on a remote server and download or simply stream it at will has increasingly gained ground. The International Federation of the Phonographic Industry entitles its 2010 report, taking the futurists perspective, *Music How, When and Where You Want It* (IFPI, 2010) and cites the significance of mobile media technologies as the driving force behind new consumer demand. Media futurist Gerd Leonhard describes 'music like water', a concept comparable to the way in which metered water is piped into the home, for a fixed monthly fee (2005:2). Music 'subscription services' such as Napster offer unlimited music downloads for a fixed monthly fee, and Leonhard predicts that this model could be widely expanded. Swedish digital music industry writer Patrik Wikström opens up the arguments concerning the lack of ability for music firms to control the flow of information via hosting through the concept of 'music in the cloud' and the cloud's resultant financial implications, with lower sums returned as a result of streaming (2009:6). Yet if consumers were to subscribe to music streaming on a vast, global scale, it is thought that a more stable, profitable recorded music industry would evolve to the benefit of all those releasing commercial products. It is regarded that mass global 'streaming' would outmode current 'a-la-carte' music distribution models such as Apple iTunes and the notion of the individual or multiple song purchase. New 'advertisement-based' services offer free music to listeners, whereby adverts actively fund their existence – for example, YouTube videos. This idea simply mirrors that of commercial radio and its advertising method, as this music is not owned but simply streamed. However, YouTube MP3 extraction and conversion programs can devalue the recorded work when downloaders strip away audio from the video to take ownership of the MP3 soundtrack (without paying for it).

A question presides over whether the shape of the music industry inherited today is the industry that global audiences really want collectively? It could be argued that popular culture en masse has contributed greatly to the shape of the music industry that we now have. It has responded to the major music industry and its output very favourably since its growth, from the turn of the nineteenth century onwards. Record companies, publishers, artists, producers and songwriters have responded to popular culture's needs by feeding it; where popular culture rejects music, the industry looks for another commodity that will satisfy the appetite. As music is subjective, the subjective argument will endure; mass purchased music is bought by many but not everybody; solvent contemporary societies and cultures have embraced new technologies and the media that accompany it.

In the major versus indie label argument, indies can no longer argue that they do not have a global platform (due to limited finance) in order to make audiences and fans aware of their products in the online age. If major music labels cannot invest in new artists due to squeezed revenues, they may align more with independent label structures in the future. The promise of a level playing field has emerged with social media platforms and product digital aggregation; for very little investment, any label or artist can make their music available to the world. It is how popular culture en masse responds to the new media music industry that will shape the future of the current music industry. Popular culture still responds well to old passive consumption media forms in TV, radio and press, and then further interacts with new media – the public at large are happy to be guided in their music purchasing choice through this whole process. It is likely that this 'guiding' trend will continue and consumers will continue to look for recommendation before they buy music or go to a concert; purchasers need to know that they have 'heard of the artist' before they will part with their hard-earned wages. Far fewer music purchasers are investigative, active consumers, who search out new music using their global internet tools. Should active consumption become a greater trend in music discovery via further improved technologies, it is expected that major music investors would try to harness this in guiding the active consumption towards home products.

In order to change today's passive music consumption landscape, could consumers actually effect new changes by adopting a more proactive approach towards mainstream media and the way they use it – becoming more active in voicing what they would like from it? Keith Negus examined corporate cultures and industrialised music production, arguing that 'musical sounds and meanings are not only dependent upon the way an industry is producing culture, but also shaped by the way in which culture is producing an industry' (1999:13). The way culture responds passively to commercial music perpetuation shapes the industry, as it is unlikely that the general public would lobby Ofcom (radio's licensing body in the UK) to make their views heard on the type of music they want to experience. When a commercial radio station applies for its licence, it sets out the type of music it will play and its intended demographic, so largely the tone is set before the station goes on air (see www.ofcom.org.uk). Although radio is criticised for homogenised output, in order to survive, commercial radio is market and survey led, so it would not be there if it only catered for a 'vocal' minority.

GLOBAL PERSPECTIVES

It is worth considering the music industry in other world territories and how their music industry structures have evolved, as many differ from the developed music industry models in territories such as Europe, North America and Japan. In countries where economic instability and a lack of disposable income are apparent, there is a very different type of music industry in operation. Music remains a luxury commodity in many of these territories, so piracy involving the duplication of millions of counterfeit music products is commonplace. In regions such as Central and South America (Argentina, Peru, Brazil, Columbia and Mexico, etc.) there is less or no government recognition of popular music arts. Without vital official recognition, copyright law is often unenforced, giving rise to piracy of recorded music products from developed countries. In this regard there is still a music industry, but musicians must rely on fees from live performance rather than royalties generated from the recorded work. Asia lacks the more highly developed music industry infrastructure that the UK, US and Europe possesses; in India and other parts of Asia, the cassette still reigns supreme due to the unsustainable cost of CDs and technology for the consumer. Naoki Sekine highlights that over 70 per cent of India's popular music artists are home-grown film stars as opposed to other types of music product; there are huge piracy problems with the illegal duplication of cassettes of Indian music stars, yet this form of piracy, ethical or not, promotes and popularises them with audiences new and old. The pirated cassette is therefore regarded as a calling card for the artist, fuelling interest and swelling attendance at concerts of the pirated artist's performances. As a result of this, artists have done little to take legal action against the pirates. Sekine also notes that Payola systems are also in operation in many Asian territories in order to ensure airplay in mainstream media (Bernstein *et al.*, 2007:226). The less developed music industry model in Asia demonstrates that despite the difficulties of piracy, a music industry still exists with its own stars and music companies. There are comparisons being drawn with the Asian model and how the notion of free recorded products are used in the digital age to promote artists to fans, with less reliance on recorded music income and more from live performance. In this regard, artists or songwriters that could not tour or play live would be financially disadvantaged by a free or very low priced recorded music model as demonstrated in India. The growth in the Chinese economy has filled many music venturists with optimism, seeing China as a sizeable business opportunity for those that can penetrate its huge potential music market. China's population does not yet have enough disposable wealth for entertainment products or a mobile business to rival those in Japan or Korea, but it is a rising economy. When technology and high speed internet connection eventually catches up with that of Europe and North America, it is expected that these populations will join purchasing populations of music. Sekine highlights this argument: 'As computers spread to the poorest nations . . .' the trend of music access will only accelerate and create further opportunities (Bernstein et al., 2007:266). Experts predict that technological empowerment through expansion of economies in poorer regions of Central and South America and Asia is likely to see the world domination of US music steadily reduce as a result. And in the US, the predicted growth of the Spanish-speaking population is expected to give rise to further cultural crossover in music due to cultural integration and the changing demographic.

CULTURAL VALUE AND THE MUSIC INDUSTRY

World government approaches can steer the music industry by their approach to their own home-grown music cultures by supporting 'home content' laws, whereby a set percentage of local or national music (often 30 per cent or more) should be supported through mainstream media exposure. Countries such as Canada, Australia and South Africa (Figure 13.1) have approved content laws to enhance and encourage their own territorial music cultures, therefore assisting in the protection of incomes for their own artists and national music industry. This move has been reflected in South Africa's music stores too, as fewer multinational label brands are stocked in favour of their own artists' CDs; in this regard government has stepped in to protect the cultural value held in its own music and regional exposure, changing its music landscape in favour of its own region. Blocking foreign content in mainstream media prevents the cultural invasion of music that is largely imported from the US, as established US product exists in virtually all world territories. With this, many may argue that 'government arts control' is counterproductive in censoring what can be broadcast and limiting consumer choice, yet it could be argued that US product is overexposed on a worldwide level and always has been, since recordings were invented. Roy Shuker comments on a 'one way media flow' in favour of products from the US creating cultural imperialism in its wake (2005:65–66). Other communications theorists such as Marshall McLuhan (1992) have highlighted the 'cultural capital' issue evidencing itself in the resultant imposition of western culture through music in electronic media across world territories, creating a 'global village'. As records originated from the US at the turn of the twentieth century, the blossoming effect of the US music industry and its products across the world is perhaps no surprise. Music from the UK has also enjoyed market penetration across the world from the 1960s onwards due to the success of its pop and rock bands primarily. The UK is only situated twenty-two miles from France, but it has yet to experience any large-scale modern cultural invasion of French popular music, either in live performance or recorded work. Much UK and US popular music, however, has been exported to Europe and still features heavily in European playlists and charts. The multinationals defend their products by arguing that consumers do have a choice and the reason western music products feature heavily in other territories is simply because they are of high quality and appeal to consumers. It has been proven that good quality major music artists with the right promotion can penetrate markets that are accepting of English lyrics in the music.

If world governments and music collection societies re-invested in their own music, their local, cultural music scene could be enhanced further, but this requires

FIGURE 13.1
Local music content laws in South Africa ensure promotion of home-grown products in their music stores, courtesy the author

governments to place higher value on music and the arts. Naturally, governments will support their national industries in order of preference, for example, is the music industry more important than the car manufacturing industry? What can global governments do to provide continuing equal protective legislation to safeguard economies in each? With increased government priority, the music industries could prosper and return wealth to their own national economies. The internet, however, facilitates cultural enlightenment and dismantles cultural boundaries by overriding the exclusivity of any government home content law in national mainstream media. For the active consumer, instant access to all cultures is possible, for instance, streaming a radio station from Cuba can be facilitated in seconds on most computers with broadband access.

SELLING MUSIC CULTURE

There is an additional argument concerning how record companies support their own music cultures; are acts signed because they are culturally significant in their own territories or are they signed because they have instant global appeal, or both? Selling music culture abroad has been commonplace for many years; in many music stores a 'World Music' section is often given rack space, offering a variety of global music product. Issues have always surrounded the multinational music conglomerate labels and whether they have concern for the cultural value of music. These labels have regional offices in many world territories and sign and work with local artists, but this must be tempered with the significant amount of imported international artists that are released through the 'regionals', many of which are big name US imports. In this regard it could be argued that US music culture (e.g. rap) is providing cultural enrichment for new territories that otherwise would not have heard the music. Music landscapes abroad have been shaped by multinationals who can boast the international success of many products, but as global territories become more technologically advanced, they also generate their own music products and scenes.

Online world music can easily be searched and generally includes folk and popular music from territories outside the US, UK and Europe. When music artists sing in their regional accents, this is often a cultural selling point abroad. For instance, UK alt-pop act Arctic Monkeys have succeeded in global territories in the mid-2000s, singing lyrics in their native Sheffield regional accent. Particularly in the UK, British singer and entertainer George Formby, Jr., succeeded with this concept from the 1930s to the 1960s, singing in a regional Wigan dialect using a similar popular 'folk' technique. A strong selling point for music is its cultural identity, novelty through geographic origins and local storytelling in music. A world in which independent labels focusing on producing music that has regional cultural musical identity and the multinationals with their sophisticated pop productions co-exist is a reality in some shared markets on a global level. Arthur Bernstein's optimistic view highlights that in the future exploitation of music, there is limitless opportunity to experiment with the integration of music from different cultures, further cultivating profitable cross-genres that will fuel the music industry as: 'The emergence of musical hybrids is a never ending process' (2007:4).

THE CHANGING FACE OF THE MUSIC INDUSTRY

Consumer fascination with a plethora of new media commodities has compromised the purchase of recorded music in favour of items such as computer games. There are, however, musical benefits to be found in things such as computer games, especially for composers. Having a song synchronised in a computer game today exposes music to a 'gamer' and often promotes an awareness of the artist resulting in subsequent music sales. Trends in media consumption have shown that, as with clothes fashion, media often has a shelf-life before audiences move to the next 'must have' item. Consumers that re-purchased music collections on CD, having tired of their vinyl records, are now compiling music collections in music media file formats MP3, MP4 and others. Historically, when new music formats arrive, sales increase as a result and there is no reason to suspect that this will not happen repeatedly, with new improved technologies, increased audio quality, digital protections and enhanced visual aesthetics in music players and products. If the music industry can increase the entertainment experience for the consumer, there is a high probability that consumers will buy repeatedly. New initiatives and amalgamations through integration between live performance and recorded music products could revitalise music markets, as consumers are prepared to pay higher ticket prices to see music live at concerts. The recorded music industry sector could not have predicted the changes brought about by the internet, seeing a computer manufacturer, Apple, as the world's largest single digital distributor. Sekine predicts that in foreign territories such as Japan, there have been indications that new IT labels will become apparent, developing and distributing their own original artists (Bernstein et al., 2007:259).

LABEL FUTURES

Generally independent music venturists would be in favour of change in the developed music industry model, whereby a fairer system would exist in a world that would see even greater chances for independent product exposure. This argument has always fuelled the major versus indie debate, but greater national recognition for local artists has always been problematic when large multinationals retain the greater market share of any national exposure opportunities. A new range of global TV talent shows does facilitate national exposure for some solo singers, but support for independent labels in mainstream media remains difficult to achieve.

Many independent products face criticisms from a quality perspective, but as music making becomes increasingly 'laptop' orientated there is always scope for well produced home-grown products to be 'up-streamed', if licensed by a multinational. There is always scope for independents to grow business operations starting in small way, from live to recorded works. Many independents have proven their ability to discover talent but often lack the business acumen to be commercially viable, so up-streaming would provide this progressive step. It is common for multinationals to diversify their business interests by acquiring their independent competitors; in the 1970s and 1980s this was a very common occurrence. As multinationals invest less in music due to financial restraint, up-streaming is likely to become more common, allowing the independent to sign and build new acts before the major steps in to distribute and capitalise on buzz.

Music retailers have diversified, not just selling music product but clothing ranges, merchandise and a host of other entertainment products in order to survive. The closure of Virgin Megastore in Times Square in central New York in 2009 created marked discussion surrounding the demise of such large music retailers, yet news reports declared that the store was actually a profitable venture to the tune of $9 million per year (Christman, 2009). Although Virgin has now continued to sell off its Megastore brand and close stores in the US, UK and Ireland, over seventy profitable Megastores remain open for business in many other world territories. Other entertainment retailers such as Zavvi (in the UK), have bought Megastore sites and continue to sell a range of diverse entertainment products, including music. The significance of this is that music retail is still alive and well, contrary to media speculation on the failing health of music retail.

DIGITAL FUTURES

The small independent music venturist can look forward to the future with optimism and a positive outlook, regardless of financial limitation or the complexities of the digital age. Changes in the post-modern commodified music age will not stop music enthusiasts making, discovering and promoting exciting new music for self and consumer, executing impassioned performances to grassroots audiences, festivals and music gatherings. Although the internet is forcing changes in the thinking that surrounds copyright duration and how composers, artists and music publishers should be paid in the future, currently little has changed, if at all. Music futurists predict that a new worldwide organisation could be employed to collect royalties for publishers and songwriters, in place of regional collection societies currently in place. Organisations such as UNESCO and the World Intellectual Property Office seek to unite and promote common arts law globally, streamlining copyright procedures for all creatives.

In the 2000s speculative media reports cast doubts into the minds of the public arguing whether there would be a music industry in the future, due to weakening economic status of the multinational music companies and the decline in revenues gathered from recorded products. Yet when media report on the sector, using the umbrella term 'music industry', they refer to the industry in relation to recorded products only even though the term is not (nor ever really was) restricted to music products alone; playing music live to an audience large or small for money was the beginning of the music industry, long before emerging technologies afforded the recorded work. Monetised live music performance remains a constant and looks unlikely to change as the foundation of the music industry on a simplified global scale. The rise of media technologies has changed the way in which we receive and perceive music industry. When internet searching becomes as simple and quick as turning on a TV or radio, the internet is likely to increase in popularity and therefore become the mainstream media source for listening to and consuming music. The 'active' consumer has been growing in number in countries where mobile media exist and are serviced, especially in the younger age demographic; they fully embrace mobile media technologies, capitalise on the benefits of mobile entertainment and are contributing to the erosion of older consumption methods in radio and TV. At the time of writing the current world population is estimated at 6.8 billion and steadily rising, with Asia contributing 3 billion alone to this figure from India through to China. When and if mobile technology becomes commonplace in these territories, it could be argued that there will be increased opportunities for the music venturist who can examine the market requirements of these populations and capitalise on it with their music products. Although globalisation and the multinationals have changed the way in which music is monetised, in the evolutionary mechanism of music exploitation, the music industry is nonetheless built on the shifting sands of consumer subjectivity. The values consumers ascribe to music are built on hearing, seeing and owning music products that reside with those that take ownership in these music outputs. For the music industry to survive into the future, it needs a consumer audience that is prepared to value it and be prepared to pay a fair price for its outputs. Music value has become the topic of discussion through the 2000s, fostering the idea that consumers were prepared to pay more for a cup of coffee than they would for a single music download. This emergent disparity does not reflect the markets of the 1980s for instance. Devaluation has occurred on three counts – 'a-la-carte' buying of single track downloads through the unbundling of albums, the lower price of CDs driven largely by supermarket chains and, lastly, the practice of file sharing. In 2010, John Kennedy, Chairman and CEO of the IFPI voiced the concerns of industry:

> Governments from France to South Korea have recognised that online piracy cannot go unchecked without causing immense damage to investment in culture.

Protecting industry is an ongoing endeavour whereby governments have intro-duced legislation to migrate illegal downloaders to hundreds of legal services offering music.

Looking at the positive side of recorded music income streams, existing catalogues of well known music still produce sizeable revenues for label owners and songwriters, and although much of it is 'old' music, it gets airplay on a constant daily basis until it loses relevance and awaits perhaps some future revival. The future of the music industry does not lie purely in the hands of music creators, performers, producers, promoters and investors in musical talent, as the industry relies heavily on entrepreneurial music venturists, technologists and strategists to make music a sustainable profitable entity. Greater consideration should be given to the live music industry sector in its proven ability to succeed, capitalising on the interest of its audience, amalgamating with the recorded work. Technology provided the mechanism by which music could eventually be brought to a mass global audience; technology and music are married forms that cannot now seem to exist without one another. German-born musicologist, sociologist and philosopher Theodor Adorno, famously argued in 1936 that populations were manipulated by mass produced cultural commodities; that commercial music products (largely focused on jazz) pacified consumers through their standardised approach (Adorno, 2002). Popular music sits in a mass market and a vast majority of artists design music with mass consumption in mind, creating music for public consumption in order to sustain a career. Creating music for the 'self' only suggests a hobbyist approach without the need to monetise music for any commercial purpose unless purely 'sharing' with others. Yet music venturists also seek to excite audiences with their shared music products and performances and do not seek to not pacify them (unless the music has been specifically designed to pacify). Music creation often sits 'ill at ease' with business, providing a source of conflict and tension that has been evident throughout the history of the music business. The way that the music industry *is* should not deter an artist from creating or performing music, a label from signing and promoting music, or a commentator from writing about it. Moreover, the way the music industry *is* provides the very reason for being a part of it.

REFERENCES AND FURTHER READING

Books

Adorno, T. (in Leppert, R., ed.), *Essays on Music* (California: University of California Press, 2002).

Bernstein, A., Sekine, N. and Weissman, D., *The Global Music Industry* (Oxford: Routledge, 2007).

Blake, A., *The Music Business* (London: Batsford, 1992), pp. 108–122.

Hutchison, T., Macy, A. and Allen, P., *Record Label Marketing: Second Edition* (Oxford: Elsevier, 2010), pp. 403–414.

Kusek, D. and Leonhard, G., *The Future of Music: Manifesto for the Digital Music Revolution* (Boston: Berklee Press, 2005), p. 2.

Longhurst, B., *Popular Music & Society* (Cambridge: Polity Press, 1995), pp. 55–90.

McLuhan, M. and Powers, R.B., *The Global Village: Transformations in World Life and Media in the 21st Century* (New York: OUP, 1992).

Negus, K., *Popular Music in Theory: An Introduction (Geographies)* (Cambridge: Polity Press, 1996), pp. 164–189.

Negus, K., *Music Genres and Corporate Cultures* (London: Routledge, 1999), p. 13.

Robinson, D.C., Buck, E. and Cuthbert, M., *Music at the Margins: Popular Music and Global Cultural Diversity* (Communication and Human Values series) (London: Sage, 1991).

Schwartz, D.D., *I Don't Need a Record Deal: Your Survival Guide for the Indie Music Revolution* (New York: Billboard, 2005), pp. 264–268.

Schwartz, D.D., *Start and Run Your Own Record Label* (New York: Billboard, 2009), pp. 286–327.

Shuker, R., *Popular Music: The Key Concepts: Second Edition* (Oxford: Routledge, 2005), pp. 65–67.

Toynbee, J., *The Popular Music Studies Reader* (The Industrialisation Of Music) (Routledge: Abingdon, 2006), pp. 228–238.

Wikström, P., *The Music Industry: Digital Media and Society Series* (Cambridge: Polity Press, 2009).

Online resources

Arctic Monkeys. Available at: www.last.fm/search?q=the+arctic+monkeys&from=ac (accessed 20 August 2010).

Christman, E., 'Times Square Virgin Megastore to Close', *Billboard* (13 January 2009). Available at: www.billboard.com/news/times-square-virgin-megastore-to-close-1003929817.story#/news/times-square-virgin-megastore-to-close-1003929817.story (accessed 20 August 2010).

George Formby, Jr. Available at: www.last.fm/music/George+Formby (accessed 20 August 2010).

International Federation of the Phonographic Industry (IFPI). Available at: www.ifpi.org (accessed 20 August 2010).

Ofcom (Independent regulator and competition authority for the UK communications industries). Available at: www.ofcom.org.uk (accessed 20 August 2010).

United Nations Educational, Scientific and Cultural Organization (UNESCO). Available at: www.unesco.org/new/en/unesco (accessed 20 August 2010).

Virgin Megastore. Available at: www.virgin.com/company/virgin-megastore (accessed 20 August 2010).

World Intellectual Property Office (WIPO). Available at: www.wipo.int (accessed 20 August 2010).

Zavvi. Available at: www.zavvi.com/home.dept (accessed 20 August 2010).

Glossary

360-degree deal: Where a music company is contracted to take care of the collective business interests of the artist's income. In music this would constitute recorded music sales, publishing, concert revenues, sponsorship and product endorsement income.

A&R: Artists and repertoire is a concept originating in music publishing and recording companies that involves the reviewing of artist demonstration recordings, considered for possible signing with a music company. A&R departments also co-ordinate production developments such as selecting others to work with artists and artist development processes.

A&R theory: The reasons behind A&R signing processes, the theories that govern its wider operation and the way in which artists respond to it.

advance: Monetary sum given to an artist or songwriter by a music company – in exchange for the supply of music works or products usually set under legal contractual obligation.

AES: Founded in the US in 1948, the Audio Engineering Society has offices in many international territories. It represents the collective global interests of audio engineers and promotes worldwide knowledge and research in new audio advancements.

aggregator (digital): Company that acts as a conduit to distribute recorded digital music products out to many larger digital retailers such as iTunes.

AIF: The Association of Independent Festivals is a trade organisation existing in the UK to represent music festivals and campaign on behalf of its membership.

AIM: The Association of Independent Music was formed as a trade organisation in 1999 to provide a collective voice for the UK's independent music label industry. The association represents small grassroots labels and larger independents alike, offering advice on how to set and run an independent recorded music label.

airplay: Time granted to music played in mainstream media in order to showcase and exploit the musical recording or video.

album: A collection of recorded musical works, usually released on CD consisting of 30 minutes or more of music.

alternative: A term usually associated with radio or genre whereby the music style is 'alternative' to music that appeals to a mainstream mass market, often termed alt-rock or alt-pop.

ancillary income: Income derived from additional revenues; in relation to concert promotion, this may constitute catering sales or income not commissionable by the artist, manager or promoter.

ASCAP: In the US, the American Society of Composers, Authors and Publishers licenses music performance rights for song composers, authors and music publishers. The UK equivalent is PRS for Music.

assignment of copyright: When permission is granted by a copyright owner in assigning their copyrights to others in order that the musical work may then be exploited by them. When a songwriter signs to a music publisher they assign their 'right to copy' over to the publisher. Copyright can be assigned in many ways to permit exploitation of the musical work, this could also occur in assigning rights in the recorded work to others to provide a licence to permit replication of the recorded work in other products, such as sound compilation recordings.

audio engineer: In the reproduction, recording and facilitation of sound, the audio engineer is a key figure. The role is not confined to the recording studio and is pivotal in live sound re-enforcement through front-of-house sound and monitor engineering. Sound recordings made in the home are engineered by the demo-makers themselves, usually learning their craft on a regional music technology course, or by being self-taught.

audio engineer (FOH): Front-of-house sound personnel that will engineer the sound in a live concert situation facing the front of the stage, mixing and balancing the sound.

audio engineer (monitor): Sound personnel that will provide a personal monitor mix for onstage performers in order to hear their own sound rather than the projected sound into front-of-house.

audit clause: In a contract, this clause permits examination of accounting practices. Where an artist is signed to a record label or publisher, the artist's manager may wish to financially 'audit' the accounts of the music company to verify that business accounting practices are legitimate and transparent.

author: Songwriter, composer or lyricist who is declared as the author of the musical work in whole or in part.

background music: Music composed for synchronisation purposes that is not a main feature of the finished produced article but merely lies behind other elements which feature in the foreground, for example, background music used in a radio commercial with an actor's voice-over on top.

bar code: A series of vertical black lines found on products to denote their country, company and producers origin. The Universal Product Code (UPC) is carried in the information derived from the bar code, which is usually read at point-of-sale (POS) when it passes through a bar code reader at the till or checkout.

bar codes acquisition: When manufacturing professional products intended for sale to the general public, a bar code can be obtained from a bar code supplier online. In the UK, GS1UK is a primary supplier of machine readable bar code product information.

BASCA: UK association that represents the interests of British song composers and authors, lobbying government and industry bodies, also acknowledging the achievements of its members.

blanket licence: Music licence issued by a performing rights society (or other rights society) that permits the blanket usage of all music for a negotiated fee to the user; for example, businesses that use music to enhance their spaces such as high-street shops.

blanket licence revenue: Royalty payment due to composers and songwriters as a result of blanket licence monies collected from rights organisations such as PRS for Music in the UK.

BMI: In the US, Broadcast Music Incorporated is a broadcaster-owned performing rights organisation. In the UK, PRS for Music fulfils a similar function. BMI licenses TV, radio and businesses to publicly perform songs and composed works in the US.

bootleg: An illegal copy of a recorded musical work.

BPI: The British Phonograph Industry represents the collective interests of the recording industry in the UK.

break: The point at which a music company succeeds in bringing the work of a new music artist product to a wider consumer audience through mainstream media.

breakeven point: A term used in concert promotion whereby gross revenues from the concert run are equal to that of the total cost to stage the tour. Neither profit nor loss is demonstrated at the breakeven point.

business manager: Person employed in addition to the 'personal manager' to look after the financial affairs of successful music artists.

buyout: Whereby a music user pays the copyright owner (or composer of the music) a 'one-off' payment for exclusive use of their music. The buyout will often allow the music user (such as an advertising agency making a TV commercial) to synchronise the music with a certain product or advert for an indefinite period. The buyout may be preferred by the music copyright owner in order to avoid royalty accounting delays.

buzz: The point at which viral marketing of a music product performance or entity has taken effect and a group of persons are discussing it. Unforced word-of-mouth, blogging and a vibrant social network can facilitate buzz for promising acts, which then generates subsequent increased industry and audience interest in the artist.

catalogue: Reference made to the sum total of song compositions or recorded works residing in the publisher, songwriter or music company catalogue.

CHR: Contemporary hit radio is a playlisting format that concentrates on playing 'hits' in regular rotation. Popular chart-orientated music is prioritised for recurrent airplay.

CIS: A common information system used in a global database for the tracking and distribution of royalties.

CISAC: Headquartered in Paris, the International Confederation of Societies of Authors and Composers has international offices and co-ordinates the work of authors societies around the world. CISAC facilitates a global network to enable composer and publisher society representation.

clearance: When permission has been granted by a third party to use a musical work; clearance can be effected to permit further exploitation, such as registering the work with a performing rights organisation.

commercial acceptance: Terminology used by music companies in assessing the level of commercial audience appeal in an artist's work or recordings.

commission: The percentage sum taken from income of the artist by the personal manager or agent. The average commission taken by the personal artist manager is around 20 per cent of net earnings.

commissioned work: Where a bespoke musical work or composition is requested by a company or person. Music created for synchronisation purposes with moving video images are often commissioned works that have been requested by a film company.

composer: Person that, through musical creation, uses songwriting skills, composition (and sometimes lyric writing) with melody combined. Musical composition is represented across all music genres and includes synchronisation usage in respect of video and film.

compulsory licence: Licence granted by the copyright act to permit use of a musical composition or recorded work. The licence becomes compulsory where the user conforms to terms set out by the statute of copyright law in respect of royalty payments.

conceptualisation: Application of a theme to a product or music venture or event. Conceptualising music events and products can provide individuality and boost presence in an overcrowded market.

conglomerate: Large business corporation that is formed by association with wider business interests and company divisions. Multinational music companies such as UMG have interests in publishing, video and other entertainment products.

controlled composition: Compositions owned in whole or in part by song composers and artists that retain a controlling share in their musical works.

co-publishing: When a song or musical composition is administered by more than one publisher in regional or overseas territories.

copyright: Intangible personal property right that exists in a creative musical or authored work. Owning copyright in a work permits the owner the right to 'do' – granting the owner the right to copy, distribute or assign the work to a third party.

copyright (in recordings): The automatic right that exists when a record producer creates a recorded work (known as the first copyright owner). Where a company or person funds the studio time to enable recording of the work (usually a music label or company) – copyright ownership in the recording defaults to the music label, unless other contractual agreements specify other ownership parties in the recorded work.

copyright (in songs): The automatic right granted when song composers or authors create musical works. Although copyright ownership defaults to the original composers, this copyright may be assigned to others by contract (such as music publishers) to enable promotion and exploitation of the musical work.

copyright control: Where the copyright owner in the song or musical work declares that they are administering their own copyright. Often, an independent songwriter will print or declare the words 'copyright control' on the recorded work to signal that they own copyright and self-publish the work. They may then wish to assign the copyright to a publisher or other music company in the future.

corporate: Descriptive term used to categorise music often released by a multi-national as in 'corporate rock', created with a mainstream appeal market intentions.

counterfeit product: Product cloned from an original and sold as an illegal, unlicensed pirate copy in the marketplace.

cover: A rendition of an original musical work executed by performers or artists other than the those that originally played or performed it.

cross-collateralisation: Terminology used to describe the recoupment of investment and advance monies paid out by a music label. These investments could be offset against future products, mechandising or new music releases to recoup expenditure in a cross-collaterilasation move.

cue sheet: Log of musical works used in connection with synchronisation to video or film. The cue sheet accurately specifies the scene and timed music usage and is supplied to the broadcasting TV network and performing right society such as PRS for Music. The cue sheet is important in ensuring the correct performance royalties are paid to the composers and publishers of the synchronised musical work.

DCMS: The Department for Culture Media and Sport exists in the UK to champion the creative and leisure industries alongside its commitment to sport and tourism. DCMS is responsible for a wide range of government policies in the arts and is active in digital economy policy making.

demo: Reference made in respect of a demonstration recording, which is differentiated from a 'master recording', which has a higher sonic quality and production value. Demonstration recordings are often made in home studios or smaller local studios.

demo-maker: Person(s) that makes demonstration recordings in a self-contained way, usually working from home using a workstation, music technology, or limited tools. The resultant recorded work is often of a lower perceived production quality than a professionally produced master recording of broadcast standard.

derivative work: A musical work that is based on an already existing musical work, essentially creating a new copyrightable work. This could include edits, remixes and sampled musical compositions.

development deal: Contract granted to an artist or performer that provides financial backing in order to allow the artist, songwriter or performer enough time to develop their craft before marketing to the wider public.

digital aggregation: Recorded works that are digitally distributed through an aggregator, to key digital point-of-sale music retailers online, such as iTunes.

digital sampling: Sounds that are recorded with digital equipment that effectively 'map' the original analogue sound or signal to produce a digital representation of the sound in 0s and 1s, which can be read and replayed by a computer. A digital sample can be edited, manipulated and replayed in a variety of ways.

disc jockey: Person or announcer that plays records in radio stations and broadcast media. The term DJ also includes those that play and remix music in nightclubs and in dance music scenes.

download: Single or multiple songs can be 'downloaded' from an online server in an audio file format. Popular audio download file types include MP3, MP4, WAV or AIFF.

dubbing: Term usually used in post-production circles whereby audio is dubbed onto a film track in synchronisation with visual images. 'Overdubbing' in a studio setting means adding further instruments or voices to pre-existing recorded audio tracks.

EPK: The electronic press kit is a digital information package usually containing essential information on an artist or music entity. EPKs often contain edited items such as full artist biographies, news releases, music samplers, video files, artist video interviews and online links to other relevant material.

ERA: The trade body for all retailers in entertainment in the UK is the Entertainment Retailers Association. Formed in 1988, ERA acts as a forum for both wholesale and retail sectors of the music, DVD, video and multimedia products industry.

established artist: Recording artist who is usually signed to a larger music label and has had around four album releases widely publicised through mainstream media.

evergreen song: Published musical work having recurring success due to being 'covered', recorded and released many times by a variety of artists.

exclusive contract: An agreement made whereby an artist may only make recordings for one label in particular.

exclusive licence: Exclusive permission granted to only one user to exploit a musical work or recording, ensuring that no other competing user has similar permissions to exploit the same work.

exclusive rights: The right of the copyright owner in the musical work or recording, to assign rights in their work exclusively to others for exploitation purposes (such as music publishers or recording companies).

exclusive songwriter agreement: Contractual arrangement that ensures the songwriter produces musical works for one publisher or music company only.

flown: Suspension and hanging of sound cabinets and lighting rigs in live sound re-enforcement and concert venues.

four Ps: Business tool used to establish marketing strategies: Product, Price, Place, Promotion.

freelancer: Individual that works on a freelance basis being 'self-employed' in the given sector. A freelancer is usually paid on an ad-hoc basis and does not receive a regular monthly salary as in full-time employment.

gatekeeper: Person that permits or facilitates opportunity in the music industries. Getting heard by the gatekeepers in the industry is a challenge for artists, managers, PR persons and pluggers. Gatekeepers are key decision makers from A&R to mainstream media, deciding on who is granted opportunity and who is not.

grand rights: Rights associated with dramatic performance, usually associated with musical theatre or opera.

grassroots level: A small-scale music entity usually operating at 'local amateur' level or regarded as semi-professional status.

hype: Shortened term for 'hyperbole'; the term denotes exaggerated worth of a particular event or product using a range of media conduits.

IFPI: The International Federation of Phonographic Industries represents the worldwide interests of the recording industry lobbying government on issues such as piracy and the importance of world music economies. IFPI is represented in many global territories and produces global music market research on a regular basis to assist in predicting world trends in music consumption.

IMMF: The International Music Managers Forum (see MMF).

independent distributor: A music wholesaler that distributes products supplied by independent music labels to retail outlets.

independent label: A music label not owned by a multinational music label conglomerate. Often referred to as 'indies', they may operate on a grassroots level, owned by artists creating their own 'imprint' label. Indies may be self-distributed or by other music companies to include majors.

indie: Shortened form of the term independent label, which could include indie artists, distributors and music entities.

infringement: Legal term used to describe the violation of copyright in a recorded work or composition. Infringement could also constitute a breach of agreement made by a contracted person or party in a music assignment.

IPO: Intellectual Property Office; in the UK this government organisation offers advice on copyright and protecting original works via advice on intellectual property rights (see WIPO also).

ISP: An internet service provider provides individuals and customers with access to the worldwide web via computer technology hardware and devices.

ISRC: The system known as the International System for the Identification of Sound Recordings is used to create a unique digital identifier in sound recordings. The code is embedded into the recorded work, prior to manufacture or distribution.

lead sheet: A handwritten score specifying the essential elements of a popular music song. The melody, lyrics and harmony define the popular song in legal terms contained in a lead sheet.

library music: Collection of recorded musical works licensed specifically for use in synchronisation with media, for example, background or theme music in TV, film or radio programmes.

licence: Grants a music user permission to exploit copyright in a musical work or sound recording in a variety of ways.

licensee: A music user who applies for a licence in order to use music for a purpose – such as synchronising music to a TV programme or video.

litigation: Civil process for resolving public and private legal disputes in a court of law. 'Litigious' activity is used to describe actions that favour the resolution of matters in a judicial way, in order to seek agreement.

logging: Radio and TV stations log music usage in order to provide accurate returns to performing rights organisations such as PRS for Music in the UK. Accurate logging ensures correct payments are made to song composers and authors.

LP: Acronym originating from the vinyl long playing record, an LP would usually constitute a series of recorded musical works totaling 30 minutes or more. The digital LP exists on CD or download format.

mainstream media: Major media disseminated through terrestrial broadcast conduits including TV, radio and popular print media, which appeals to the majority of consumers.

major label: Music company with multinational status having offices in many world territories and a large company investment infrastructure. In the UK four major recording labels are in existence, Universal Music Group, Warner Music Group, Sony Music and EMI.

majors: Music companies that have a greater presence in the industry, such as UMG, Live Nation or other larger music conglomerate.

master: Music recording that has a greater sonic production value than that of a 'demo'. A 'mastered' recording has usually undergone an advanced 'finishing' process in a mastering phase, preparing it for broadcast or sales exploitation. Original studio multi-track recordings are also often referred to as 'master recordings' or 'master tapes'.

mechanical licence: In the UK the MCPS grants a mechanical licence to allow songs and music compositions to be reproduced mechanically on a recorded format such as CD or DVD. Bulk replication or duplication of commercial music products is illegal in the UK without the appropriate MCPS licence being applied for and in place.

mechanical royalties: A mechanical royalty is generated via the MCPS when a song title or music composition (registered with the MCPS) is reproduced and duplicated in a tangible medium such as CD or DVD. The royalty is returned to the publisher or copyright owner in the exploited, replicated work (calculated as a percentage) for each copy sold.

micropreneur: Small-scale venturist who exercises business acumen and who may also be classified as a solo-preneur.

MIDEM: The Marché International du Disque et de l'Edition Musicale is an international music industry trade fair held each year in Cannes each January. Historically MIDEM has attracted thousands of industry delegates each year and provides a platform for global music companies to showcase their products.

MIDI: Music Instrument Digital Interface was developed to allow conversation between electronic instruments. This communications protocol extends to lighting and other types of electronic equipment in music and live events.

MMF: Also part of the International Music Managers Forum, in the UK. The Music Managers Forum represents the professional interests of music managers and this forum lobbies government on IP value and copyright legislation, among many other representations.

mom-and-pop-store: Grassroots family-run retailer selling music and other goods. The term is often applied to family run shops in the Far East and the US but can be applied to similar trading styles in other world territories.

MOR: Middle-of-the-road is the term given to a music style that generally appeals to an older audience demographic.

MPA: Music Publishers Association, a body that represents the collective interests of its own music publisher members in the UK.

multinational: Major music company or label that has offices in many world territories.

music technology: Terminology used to describe music making and recording using electronic sound equipment to produce music. The term is often used in connection with courses and modules of study in the music learning environment.

music venturist: Entrepreneurial action taken by a musician, artist, songwriter, producer, manager, promoter, commentator or other person involved in the pursuit of a monetised music business venture – particularly where there is an element of financial risk involved.

Musicians Union: In the UK the Musicians Union is funded by its members and represents the interests of musicians working in all sectors of the industry. The MU advises its members on issues regarding copyright protection and musician contracts.

niche market: Smaller consumer group that responds to music products rather than a mass market. Niche markets such as country music and jazz often provide steady revenues over long periods for respected artists working in the genre.

non-music brand: A brand that is not an artist name or band moniker. Music artists are often associated with brands that are not music orientated, yet through brand association and sponsorship, the artist's career is enhanced.

OCC: The Official Charts Company compiles music sales data for the UK. The OCC is a joint venture created by the BPI (British Phonograph Industry) and ERA (Entertainment Retailers Association) and is concerned with the creation of official music and video charts.

Ofcom: The independent communications regulator that licenses the UK TV and radio sectors to permit public terrestrial broadcast.

oligopoly: A market dominated by a small number of music product producers.

one-stop: A music distributor (dealing in digital or tangible product) that sells all labels' products to all retail outlets.

payola: Payment made (usually to radio stations) in order to secure airplay for new sound recordings. Although this practice is deemed illegal in licensed terrestrial transmissions, no prosecutions have been brought against payments made for online airplay.

pay-to-play: To gain wider exposure on tour, some artists, labels and managers pay-to-play on the concert bill of established artists. This practice extends to other venues in key locations and can grow the fanbase of a new artist.

peer-to-peer: Computer users share and exchange files with each other over P2P networks. Illegal music downloads have become increasingly widespread as a result of unauthorised P2P software programmes.

performance right: The right granted to perform a musical work to the public through conduits such as live concert performance, radio and TV airplay. The performance right extends into music played in public and business spaces.

performance royalty: The royalty generated when a musical composition is performed or played in public. This royalty is returned to the copyright owner in the work through a performing right society (PRS for Music) back to the publisher and song composer/author of the work.

personal manager: The personal manager is appointed by the artist to look after business affairs. Negotiating live performance fees with promoters, securing tours, record label deals, sponsorship and dealing with publishers all fall to the personal manager. The personal manager takes payment via commission, usually set at 20 per cent of net income.

phonogram: Historic international term used for sound recordings.

piracy: Illegal duplication of a sound recording (without licence or permission from the original owner in the product), then offering the product for sale to the public. Recordings made of artists unofficially at live performances then offered for sale en masse are also regarded as pirate copies.

pitch: A promotional music venture approach made by a plugger, artist, manager or public relations person to a music company or media entity.

plugger: Person who primarily circulates and 'plugs' music product to radio (producers of music shows) and other mainstream media (producers of TV shows and press).

POS: Point-of-sale is the moment at which music product is sold over the counter. Items with a UPC bar code are scanned at POS whereby sales data can be recorded in order to compile a music chart.

PPL: In the UK the Phonographic Performance Limited collects royalties on behalf of its record company members and performer registrants. A PPL royalty is generated when a sound recording is used in a TV, radio broadcast or other public usage. A share of PPL royalties is also distributed to performers taking part in the exploited recordings, if they are registered with PPL.

PRO: Performing rights organisation, the first of which was formed in France in 1851. These organisations act as an interface between rights holders (publishers and song writers) and song composition users, such as radio, TV or other businesses that use music publicly. In the UK, PRS for Music collects royalties on behalf of its copyright holder members.

producer: The overseeing person in charge of a finished sound recording made in the studio environment. Often A&R or record company personnel can act as 'executive producers', calling for changes to be made in recorded products and approving the final work of the producer.

professional manager: In the music publishing sector the professional manager works as a song-plugger, using their extensive contacts in order to secure covers for the musical works that the publisher administers. They also seek to develop the song catalogue of the publisher with new song acquisitions.

project studio: Small-scale recording studio usually situated in the home and self-financed on a low budget to facilitate the production of demonstration recordings.

promotions person: Classification applied to a music label plugger or independent contracted communications person to secure airplay via mainstream media conduits.

PRS for Music: A UK performing right organisation that collects royalties on behalf of its publisher and composer members for use of song compositions performed in public, by playing a recorded work or performing a song or composition 'live'.

public domain: Term used for a musical work that has no copyright due to expiration of copyright or is not subject to copyright protection. Older works that fall into the PD category do not need licences or clearances and can be recorded by anyone.

racking: Term associated with the display and stocking of tangible products such as CDs and DVDs in music retail outlets.

RAJAR: Established in 1992, the Radio Joint Audience Research Limited is the primary research company for audience figure, listenership and measurement in the UK radio industry.

recording engineer: Person associated with the sonic management of a sound recording by using a combination of audio skills in the studio environment. Microphone placement, knowledge of mixing console operation, signal routing and processing are all practiced by the recording engineer.

recoupable: When an advance is paid to an artist or songwriter, subsequent royalties earned (due to exploitation of the works) pay back the advance in 'recoupment'. If an artist or songwriter fails to recoup, compulsory payback of the advance is not usually enforced in contract.

returns: Where tangible music products fail to sell in retail outlets, any overstocked product is returned to the distributer or music supplier. If the music retailer has paid the distributor for product that has not sold, the retailer can invoice the distributor for the unsold 'returned' product.

RIAA: The Recording Industry Association of America is a trade organisation for US music labels. The RIAA produces consumer, technical and industry research in connection with music sales and trends.

rider: Additional supplement to a music contract that details specific requirements. Riders are common in live concert artist agreements whereby special technical, stage and food requirements may be requested.

roadie: Umbrella term that describes the road crew that travel with a touring band or music entertainment show. Roadies provide technical support and show logistics in sound, production of the show and transport duties. Larger music tours requiring security, tour managing and catering roles would also be included in this 'on-the-road' term.

royalties: The terminology used for the payment made to an artist, publisher or music company when their works are exploited and monies are returned as a result.

sampling: Different from 'digital sampling', when a performing rights organisation monitors radio or TV airplay, a sample is taken of broadcast music usage. The PRO then checks the sample against cue sheets or radio logs to ensure the correct royalties are being paid by the broadcaster in respect of the music works used.

score: Classification of music when music is traditionally notated in a readable format or terminology, also used when music is composed in synchronisation with an audiovisual work.

SESAC: In the US, the smallest of the three performing rights organisations, the Society of European Stage Authors and Composers formed in 1930, today simply known as SESAC.

seven Ps: Regarded as the 'extended marketing mix', this business tool is used to establish marketing strategies (used as an extension of the four Ps): Product, Price, Place, Promotion, People, Process and Physical environment.

single: A single song release was derived from a typical two-track record consisting of an A and B side. The single song release was often deemed the song with the most popular appeal. Download singles today only consist of one song, but may still form part of a collection of songs on an album.

single song assignment: Publishers often issue a contract to sign and promote only one song from a songwriters repertoire. Because the single song assignment facilitates promotion of one specific song, the songwriter is free to assign other songs from their catalogue to other publishers.

SOLAADS: Formula used in the construction of a press release: Subject, Organisation, Location, Advantages, Applications, Details and Source. The SOLAADS rules can guide a press release towards inclusion of the most relevant and concise facts.

song-plugger: The person usually employed by a publisher to secure as many covers of songs as possible by promoting their catalogue of song works to artists, managers, A&R and creative departments.

SOR: When a music retailer agrees to place product 'on the racks' on a sale-or-return basis, no monies are paid up front for the stock. If any stock sells, the retailer will pay the music supplier for the stock and return any unsold product back to the supplier. Often small independent music producers, suppliers and grassroots artists sell music using the SOR method via local music retailers.

sound recording: The first copyright owner in the recorded work (or sound recording) is the music producer that made the recording. Yet whoever pays for the recording to be made in the first instance (such as the music recording company) ultimately becomes the final copyright owner in the work.

sound re-enforcement: Electronic sound equipment used to enhance and amplify audio signals in a live environment. Public address systems that includes microphones, mixers, speakers, amplifiers and signal processors augment and re-enforce sound for use in a concert situation.

source licence: When a producer, person or company has been granted a source licence to record or distribute a musical work, for example, in a radio programme in perpetuity. No further permissions or licences are required when the source licence is in place, unless otherwise specified.

split publishing: If a song is co-published by more than one publisher, split publishing would dictate that the rights in the song are administered on a shared basis.

staff songwriter: Songwriters that are exclusively signed to one particular publisher are regarded as staff writers. For the reservation of such exclusivity on the songwriters part, an advance is payable from the major publisher.

stiff: After a music recording has been released to media and it fails to achieve airplay or does not sell convincingly in retail sectors, the industry regard the product as having 'stiffed'.

sub-publishing: Where songs and musical works are represented or released in foreign territories, the home publisher will appoint a sub-publisher overseas. The sub-publisher can promote the musical work to their foreign contacts and utilise royalty collection societies and agencies to maximise overseas income.

SWOT: Strategic team action planning tool originally designed to assist groups of business executives to manage change. Analysis of Strengths, Weaknesses, Opportunities and Threats provides a situation analysis tool that can assist in pinpointing areas for research and development actions.

synchronisation: Using the recorded work or song composition in tandem with an audio/visual medium, for example, synchronising music in TV programmes with moving images.

synchronisation right: The exclusive right held by the copyright owner in a musical work to permit synchronisation of the work with moving images.

TALK: Strategic business development tool used to identify key components and actions required in the construction of a music brand: Target, Appeal, Legend and Kudos.

UNESCO: United Nations Educational Scientific and Cultural Organisation based in Geneva, Switzerland. The organisation promotes cultural diversity, global communication and dialogue.

UPC: A unique product code can be affixed to tangible music product by use of a printed bar code, which is read at point-of-sale (see bar code).

USP: The unique selling point of a recorded product or music artist is usually outlined in a specially designed press release. The USP will communicate to press, media and consumers how the product differs from others in the same field or genre.

VPL: The Video Performance Limited resides under the wing of the PPL in the UK and collects royalties (on behalf of its music company members) for music videos that have been used in connection with TV broadcast or public performance use.

webcasting: The online streamed transmission of a musical performance or work.

WIPO: The World Intellectual Property Organisation. Established in 1967 and based in Geneva, Switzerland – its world member-states promote the protection of intellectual property (IP) in global territories.

WTO: The World Trade Organisation exists as an international body dealing with the rules of trade between nations, supplying statistical research and trading profile information concerning its members. It is active in the promotion of the 'Berne' convention and global IP policies.

Index

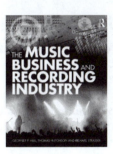